The Elements of Law

The

Elements of Law

THOMAS E. DAVITT, S.J.

Associate Professor of Jurisprudence
School of Law
Marquette University

LITTLE, BROWN AND COMPANY

Boston · Toronto

1959

Published simultaneously in Canada
by Little, Brown & Company (Canada) Limited

PRINTED IN THE UNITED STATES OF AMERICA

To the Men of the Law

Preface

This is an introductory book on jurisprudence. Jurisprudence is here taken as the philosophy of law. It is concerned with the structure of law, that is, with the elements that make law what it is, that run throughout its problems and that integrate their solutions. A comprehensive ethical evaluation of a part of that structure — law's content — pertains to a separate study, by whatever name it may be designated.[1]

Cases are used to show what judicial thinking is on many points, to note acceptance of controlling definitions, to exemplify thinking consonant with the positions taken in this book, and to point out instances of thinking that is not in such agreement — all of which tends to show the extent to which the questions considered arise in the everyday work of courts, legislators, and lawyers. Dicta are not distinguished from holdings, because the philosophy of law relied on by courts is revealed in the one as well as in the other.

Discussion of fact situations is limited. This is done both because of the possibility of too much overlapping with the sectional courses and more especially because the validity of the principles used in cases derives not so much from the fact situation of each case as from other sources.[2]

Experience in teaching test editions of this book has shown that under some conditions it may be advisable to cover Parts

[1] "I believe that the task of jurisprudence is to abstract and systematize the essential principles of law 'without reference to their goodness or badness.' I cannot by any means see why any intelligent person, when he has discharged that task to the best of his ability, should not proceed to criticize the goodness and badness of laws. But that criticism I should hardly call jurisprudence. . . . Jurisprudence, then, would seem to be the scientific synthesis of the essential principles of law." Allen, Legal Duties 18, 19 (1931). See Chapters 3 and 19 on the distinction between law as prudence and the science of jurisprudence. If jurisprudence is defined, as some have done, in terms of "legal science" as opposed to "legal philosophy," it should be kept in mind that according to the root meaning of science, philosophy is a science.

[2] Cases on various aspects of jurisprudence may be found in Wu, Cases on Jurisprudence (1958).

One and Two fairly rapidly and reach Part Three as soon as practicable, in order that the student may see in good time the relation between principles and solutions to problems with which he is familiar. Pertinent sections of Parts One and Two may be reviewed when needed. In this manner, the student, afforded with examples of the application of principles to problems, is in a better position to grasp the value of the principles themselves. Part Four may be taken as the need for a more complete understanding of the background of law is felt.

My grateful thanks are due to those many colleagues who, by their interest and suggestions, have been of invaluable help. They are conscious, I am sure, of my deep appreciation.

THOMAS E. DAVITT, S.J.

Introduction

Every lawman — legislator, judge, practitioner, teacher and student — has some kind of a philosophy of law as well as a philosophy of life. In order that his thinking be integrated, there should be a consistency between the two. In this book an attempt is made to trace the outlines of such a coherence between a means-end philosophy of life and the philosophy of law. For those whose philosophy of life is none too definite, the direction which the law takes may be of little concern. But for those of some conviction, this path cannot but be a matter of commanding importance.

The aim of this book, then, is not primarily to acquaint the student with the law as it is. That is the work of the sectional course treatment. Its purpose is rather to make the student aware of the relation between problems in law and their non-legal assumptions. Men in legislative halls and on court benches work for better law when they are dissatisfied with the law as it is. Such discontent stems from critical appraisal of situations examined in the light of held principles. An awareness to some degree of the kind of principles he holds and their impact on his evaluations of law should be acquired by the student before he leaves the law school.

Although a knowledge of the development of both man-made law and the different philosophies of law is necessary for a comprehensive understanding of law, any attempt at either type of survey has been omitted here. A number of such surveys are available.[1] Besides, a systematic survey of the varying schools of jurisprudence leaves the accent on the variety of opinions held and not on the meaning and significance of the problems to be solved and the inner consistency of their solutions. Such a survey can be more profitably undertaken, if a partial grasp is had of the problems the various authors are trying to solve and their non-

[1] For instance, the various schools of jurisprudence are presented in Patterson, Jurisprudence: Men and Ideas of the Law (1953). On the development of law, there are many historical treatises.

legal assumptions. This can be got best by examining, even provisionally, some definite position.

Our method in general will be first to isolate the essence of law by examining man-made law. This done, an expression of this core meaning of law will be sought in men's basic drives, which quest will be seen to disclose a man-discovered law. Finally the resulting principles and patterns will be applied to problems that are controlling in practical areas of man-made law.

Summary of Contents

PART IV

Background of Law

Table of Contents

Part I. MAN-MADE LAW

CHAPTER 1

THE NATURE OF LAW

CHAPTER 2

END OF MAN-MADE LAW

CHAPTER 3

CONTENT OF MAN-MADE LAW

CHAPTER 4

SOURCE OF MAN-MADE LAW

CHAPTER 5

SANCTION OF MAN-MADE LAW

CHAPTER 6

OBLIGATION OF MAN-MADE LAW

Part II. MAN-DISCOVERED LAW

CHAPTER 7

REFERENCES TO A LAW NOT MAN-MADE

NATURE OF MAN-DISCOVERED LAW

CONTENT, SOURCE AND END OF
MAN-DISCOVERED LAW

CHAPTER 10

SANCTION AND OBLIGATION OF MAN-DISCOVERED LAW

CHAPTER 11

RELATION OF MAN-DISCOVERED TO MAN-MADE LAW

Part III. INTEGRATION OF MAN-MADE LAW

CHAPTER 12

PRINCIPLES AND PATTERNS OF INTEGRATION

CHAPTER 13

CONSTITUTIONS

CHAPTER 14

CRIMES

CHAPTER 15

TORTS

CHAPTER 16

PROPERTY

CHAPTER 17

CONTRACTS

CHAPTER 18

EQUITY

Part IV. BACKGROUND OF LAW

CHAPTER 19

LAW — INSTRUMENT OF GOVERNMENT

CHAPTER 20

POLITICAL UNION AND THE COMMON GOOD

The Elements of Law

PART I

Man-made Law

CHAPTER 1

The Nature of Law

The first problem that confronts us is to determine what precisely is the act or event that is known as "law." The importance of this problem lies in the fact that only after this act or event is located can the other aspects of law be examined — its purpose, its content, its source, its sanction and obligation.

I. How "Law" Is Used

Any attempt to understand the nature of law on the practical level may well start with a cursory glance at the way "law" is used in legal contexts. After this orientation, the essence of "law" may be more discerningly sought.

What is recognized as "law" is multifold.[1] The broadest use of "law" regards constitutions,[2] for they are the fundamental and paramount law of the land.[3] Most commonly "law" means statutes,[4] and it is to statutes that such phrases as "required by law" usually refer.[5] Decisions of courts may be law,[6] even though higher courts have not passed on them,[7] as may the body of prin-

[1] State ex rel. Conway v. Superior Court of Greenlee County, 60 Ariz. 69, 131 P.2d 983, 986 (1942).

[2] Van Horne's Lessee v. Dorrance, 2 Dall. 304, 310, 1 L. Ed. 391 (1795).

[3] Marbury v. Madison, 1 Cranch 137, 177, 2 L. Ed. 60, 73 (1803).

[4] Board of Education v. Town of Greenburgh, 277 N.Y. 193, 13 N.E.2d 768, 770 (1933).

[5] Shute v. Frohmiller, 53 Ariz. 483, 90 P.2d 998, 1001 (1939).

[6] Miller v. Huntington & Ohio Bridge, 123 W. Va. 320, 15 S.E.2d 687, 692 (1941).

[7] West v. American T. & T. Co., 311 U.S. 223, 236, 61 Sup. Ct. 179, 183 (1940).

ciples, standards and rules which the courts apply in deciding controversies brought before them.[8] A proclamation by a Chief Executive may have the status of law.[9] "Law" in the United States can also include by adoption the common law of England and all statutes and acts of parliament made prior to 1607.[10]

More particularly, rulings such as those of administrative agencies may be law.[11] The order of a railroad commission in fixing rates has been considered to be a legislative act.[12] Regulations regarding the working conditions of employees in mines have been held to have the force of law.[13] Municipal ordinances may be law.[14] An ordinance of a city council establishing and fixing a street grade[15] or requiring the work of dressing stone used in municipal contracts was held to be law.[16] The action of a city council in removing civil service commissioners was also found to be law.[17] Injunctions can also be considered as having the force of law.[18] Joint resolutions may or may not be law,[19] depending principally on whether there is a constitutional requirement that all laws should be enacted by bill only.[20]

On the other hand, not all decisions of bodies with lawmaking authority are law inasmuch as they do not directly affect the public good. The fixing of the salary of a clerk by a town board of park commissioners[21] and the consenting by a legislature to purchase land have been held not to be law.[22]

II. ESSENCE OF LAW

These examples of what is taken to be law give us merely an introductory notion of what law is. They do not tell us anything

[8] State ex rel. Conway v. Superior Court of Greenlee County, 60 Ariz. 69, 131 P.2d 983, 986 (1942).

[9] Williams v. State, 146 Tex. Cr. R. 430, 176 S.W.2d 177, 184 (1943).

[10] State ex rel. McKittrick v. Missouri Public Service Commission, 252 Mo. 29, 175 S.W.2d 857, 861 (1943).

[11] Inman v. Sandvig, 170 Wash. 112, 15 P.2d 696, 698 (1932).

[12] Louisville & Nashville R. Co. v. Garrett, 231 U.S. 299, 34 Sup. Ct. 48 (1913).

[13] Rich Hill Coal Co. v. Bashore, 334 Pa. 449, 7 A.2d 302, 312 (1939).

[14] Forbes v. Savannah, 160 Ga. 701, 128 S.E. 806, 807 (1925).

[15] U.S. Fidelity and Guaranty Co. v. Guenther, 281 U.S. 34, 38, 50 Sup. Ct. 165, 166 (1930).

[16] Taylor v. City of Philadelphia, 261 Pa. 458, 104 Atl. 766, 768 (1918).

[17] McAllister v. McAllister, 200 Ark. 171, 138 S.W.2d 1040 (1940).

[18] United States v. Pendergast, 35 F. Supp. 593, 599 (W.D. Mo. 1940).

[19] Ward v. State, 176 Okla. 368, 56 P.2d 136, 137 (1936).

[20] Scudder v. Smith, 331 Pa. 165, 200 Atl. 601, 604 (1938).

[21] McCarthy v. City of Malden, 303 Mass. 563, 566, 22 N.E.2d 104, 107 (1939).

[22] Koenig v. Flynn, 238 N.Y. 292, 179 N.E. 705, 707 (1932).

concerning the nature of law itself. There still remains to be determined what it is about constitutions, statutes, decisions, ordinances and the like, that makes them law.

A. *Descriptive Approaches*

There have been attempts to describe further what law is and they bespeak different approaches to the subject. Predilections determine emphasis.

1. *Official Acts.* If there is a preoccupation with the *official* aspect of lawmaking, law will be so described. "Acts are legal or illegal if certain officials adjudge them to be so, these officials being primarily people designated as judges, or justices, or magistrates, and include, in a less degree, a vast army of administrative or executive officials, so far as they are called upon to make such judgments in the course of their activities." [23] "This doing of something about disputes, this doing of it reasonably, is the business of law. And the people who have the doing in charge, whether they be judges or sheriffs or clerks or jailers or lawyers, are officials of the law. *What these officials do about disputes is, to my mind, the law itself.*" [24]

2. *Rule of conduct.* Or, if the *guidance* of the people is the main consideration, law will be described as a rule. Such was Blackstone's definition which has found its way into the opinion of many courts. "Law is defined by Blackstone . . . as 'a rule of civil conduct prescribed by the supreme power in a state, commanding what is right and prohibiting what is wrong.'" [25] "Blackstone in his Commentaries, defining law as 'A rule of civil conduct prescribed by the supreme power in a state, commanding what is right and prohibiting what is wrong,' proceeds to say: 'And, first, it is a rule; not a transient sudden order from a superior to or concerning a particular person; but something permanent, uniform and universal.'" [26]

[23] Radin, My Philosophy of Law 287 (1941).
[24] Llewellyn, The Bramble Bush 12 (1951). In all fairness it should be noted that the author, in the Foreword of the 1951 reprint, says regarding this statement, "They are, however, unhappy words when not more fully developed, and they are plainly at best a very partial statement of the whole truth. . . . '[R]ealism' (which was and still is an effort at more effective legal technology) was mistaken for a philosophy . . . A single sentence, if it made a good brick-bat for a current fight, was enough to characterize a whole man and his whole position." Id. at 9-10.
[25] Rich Hill Coal Co. v. Bashore, 334 Pa. 449, 7 A.2d 302, 312 (1939). The reference is to 1 Blackstone, Commentaries 44.
[26] City of Bangor v. Inhabitants of Etna, 140 Me. 85, 34 A.2d 205, 208 (1943). Law has also been defined as "A body of rules prescribing external

3. *Remedy.* Or, if law be looked at as an instrument for relieving injustices, it can be called a *remedy.* "Every person ought to find a certain remedy in the laws for all injuries or wrongs which he may receive in his person, property or reputation." [27] Such is the implication in the definition of contracts when it is stated that a contract is "A promise or set of promises for breach of which the law gives a remedy." [28]

4. *Rules established by courts.* Emphasis on the part *appellate courts* play in the legal process has resulted in law being described in terms of rules established by judicial decision. "The law of the State or of any organized body of men is composed of the rules which the courts, that is, the judicial organs of that body, lay down for the determination of legal rights and duties." [29] ". . . [L]egislation has to be interpreted by the courts before it becomes a part of Law." [30]

5. *Prediction.* Or if one takes the viewpoint of the advocate, who is interested in the results of adjudication, or if one expects a predictability in law as one would in the physical sciences, law will be described in terms of *prediction.* "A principle or rule of conduct so established as to justify a prediction with reasonable certainty that it will be enforced by the courts if its authority is challenged is, then, for the purpose of our study, a principle or rule of law." [31]

Prediction may also refer to a statement regarding legal relations. "A law is a rule concerning human conduct, established by those agents of an organized society who have legislative power. When a rule of law has been reduced to words it is a statement . . . that certain facts will normally be followed by certain immediate or remote consequences in the form of action or nonaction by the judicial and executive agents of society. Whenever any such operative facts exist the persons who will be affected by the stated consequences are said to have a legal relation each to the other. . . . A statement that a legal relation exists between A

---

conduct and considered justiciable." Kantorowicz, The Definition of Law 21 (1958).

[27] Ill. Const., art. 2, §19 (1870).

[28] 1 Williston, Contracts 1 (3d ed. 1957). This definition is adopted by 1 Restatement of Contracts §1 (1932).

[29] Gray, The Nature and Sources of the Law 84 (2d ed. 1921).

[30] Id. at 268. It has also been stated that ". . . law may be taken for every purpose, save that of strictly philosophical inquiry, to be the sum of the rules administered by courts of justice." 1 Pollock and Maitland, The History of English Law xxv (2d ed. 1899).

[31] Cardozo, The Growth of the Law 52 (1924).

and B is a prediction as to what society, acting through its courts or executive agents, will do or not do for one and against the other. If A invades B's house, we are able to predict that the police will eject A, that a court will give judgment for damages, and that the sheriff will levy execution." [32]

The predictive aspect of law will also receive the emphasis if the outlook of the "bad man" is adopted. "You will find some text writers telling you that it [law] is . . . a system of reason, that it is a deduction from principles of ethics or admitted axioms or what not, which may or may not coincide with the decisions. But if we take the view of our friend the bad man we shall find that he does not care two straws for the axioms or deductions, but that he does want to know what the . . . courts are likely to do in fact. I am much of this mind. The prophecies of what the courts will do in fact, and nothing more pretentious, are what I mean by the law." [33]

6. *Institution for social control.* Focus on what law is supposed to *accomplish* — the general and social welfare of the community — will result in law being described as a regime of social control. Law will be thought of ". . . as a social institution to statisfy social wants — the claims and demands involved in the existence of civilized society — by giving effect to as much as we may with the least sacrifice, so far as such wants may be satisfied or such claims given effect by an ordering of human conduct through politically organized society. . . . [I]n legal history [there is] the record of a continually wider recognizing and satisfying of human wants or claims or desires through social control; a more embracing and more effective securing of social interests; a continually more complete and effective elimination of waste and precluding of friction in human enjoyment of the goods of existence — in short, a continually more efficacious social engineering." [34]

". . . [Law] is a regime of control. . . . We may think of a regime which is a highly specialized form of social control, carried on in accordance with a body of authoritative precepts, applied in a judicial and in an administrative process." [35]

7. *Coercive order.* A predisposition to see law as *force,* and to keep it free from moral elements, results in the statement that ". . . law is a coercive order." Law is a legal norm only because

[32] Corbin, Legal Analysis and Terminology, 29 Yale L.J. 163, 164 (1919).
[33] Holmes, The Path of the Law, 10 Harv. L. Rev. 457, 460, 461 (1897).
[34] Pound, An Introduction to the Philosophy of Law 47 (1954). By permission of the Yale University Press.
[35] Pound, Justice According to Law 48-49 (1951). By permission of the Yale University Press.

". . . it regulates human behavior by providing an act of coercion as sanction." [36]

8. *Guide to economico-political revolt.* Finally, preconceptions regarding the primacy of *economics* as based on dialectical materialism produce a view that sees law as an instrument for bringing about a new communistic society. "Law is nothing but an aggregate of coercive norms serving to express a typical instance of the accomplishment of economic phenomena." [37] It is ". . . a system of rules of conduct (norms) established in a legislative procedure by the power of the toilers and expressing the will of the whole of the soviet people, which is guided by the working class with the Communist Party at its head for the purpose of the protection, strengthening, and development of socialist relations and the building up of a communist society." [38]

Law is to be used ". . . to defend, to secure, and to develop relationships and arrangements advantageous and agreeable to the toilers, and completely and finally to annihilate capitalism and its remnants in the economic system, the way of life, and human consciousness — in order to build a communist society." [39] In this view ". . . the necessities of using law as one of the means of the struggle for socialism — of recasting human society on a socialist basis" [40] are clear. Admittedly this position ". . . characterizes law by its service to the ruling class." [41]

B.   *Opinions Regarding Essence*

These descriptions of what law is, however, are much like the endeavors of the six blind men of Hindustan, in the well-known fable, who went to touch the elephant to find out what he was like. Upon returning home, they reported respectively that an elephant was like a wall, a spear, a snake, a tree, a fan, and a rope. A somewhat similar situation seems present here.

Granting that most of the above descriptions are true in some sense, the problem still remains: what is the elephant in itself? What is law in itself? What is it that is done officially, that is a rule of conduct, that gives a remedy, that constitutes the ruling of

[36] Kelsen, General Theory of Law and State 19, 123 (Wedberg trans. 1945). By permission of the author.

[37] 2 Ziber, Collected Works 134, quoted by Pashukanis, The General Theory of Law and Marxism, in Soviet Legal Philosophy 118, n. 11 (Babb trans. 1951).

[38] 11 Lenin, Collected Works 418 (2d Russian ed. 1926-1932), quoted in 1 Gsovski, Soviet Civil Law 180 (1948).

[39] Vyshinsky, The Law of the Soviet State 50 (Babb trans. 1948).

[40] Ibid.

[41] 1 Gsovski, Soviet Civil Law 178 (1948).

the court, that furnishes the basis for predicting, and that is an instrument of social control, or that is — if you will — a guide to revolt? It is one thing to know, for instance, that a mechanism like a watch is a rule or measure of time, but it is entirely another thing to know what a watch is in itself. The problem still remains of determining what the essence of law is. A more penetrating analysis of our subject is indicated.

1. *Words — Proposition — Command.* Attempts to probe deeper than these superficial descriptions show the need of using the cutting edge of philosophy as an instrument sharp enough to lay open the essence of law. Some have said that law in its essence is simply the *words* used by lawmakers. "A law may be defined as an assemblage of signs declarative of a volition conceived or adopted by the sovereign in a state, concerning the conduct to be observed in a certain case by a certain person or class of persons, who in the case in question are or are supposed to be subject to his power." [42] Or "A law is a discourse — conceived mostly in general, and always in determinate, words — expressive of the will of some person or persons, to whom, on the occasion, and in relation to the subject in question, whether by habit or express engagement, the members of the community to which it is addressed are disposed to pay obedience." [43]

Others have said that law is a *proposition* stating a categorical command of the will of the lawmaker. "A law is a proposition announcing a categorical imperative. He who commands by law is a lawgiver, and is the author of juridical obligation." [44] Law is ". . . a categorical command [that] . . . proceeds from the will." [45] "An imperative is then no more than a formula, expressing the relation betwixt objective laws of volition and the subjective imperfection of particular wills (e.g. the human)." [46]

Following this same emphasis on the will, others have also stressed law as the *command* of the sovereign which is the expresson of his will. "Every law or rule (taken with the largest signification which can be given to the term properly) is a command. Or rather, laws or rules properly so-called, are a species of command." [47] "If you express or intimate a wish that

[42] Bentham (1748-1832), The Limits of Jurisprudence Defined 88 (Everett ed. 1945).

[43] Bentham, Chrestomathia, App. IV, §viii, div. 19n (1816).

[44] Kant (1724-1804), The Metaphysic of Ethics 190 (Semple trans. 1936).

[45] Id. at 189.

[46] Id. at 27.

[47] Austin (1790-1859), Lectures on Jurisprudence or the Philosophy of Positive Law 3, 12 (Campbell ed. 1874).

I shall do or forebear from some act, and if you will visit me with
an evil in case I comply not with your wish, the expression or
intimation of your wish is a command." [48] "Every positive law
or every law simply and strictly so called, is set by a sovereign
person, or a sovereign body of persons." [49]

2. *Act of will.* Others have located law in the *will* of the
lawmaker saying that law ". . . is the act of a just and right will
by which the superior wills to oblige the inferior to do this or
that." [50] The command is an act of the will of the ruler.[51]

3. *Act of intellect.* Still others locate the essence of law in an
act of the lawmaker's *intellect.* Law is ". . . an ordering of
reason for the common good, by him who has charge of the community, and promulgated." [52] "It pertains to law to command.
Command is of the reason. Law is, therefore, of the reason." [53]
"Command is an act of the reason, presupposing an act of the will,
in virtue of which the reason, by its command, moves to the execution of the act." [54]

C. *Essence: Directive Judgment of Means to End*

Which of these explanations most accurately locates the essence
of law? Where can a clue be found that will give us a lead as to
where we should look?

1. *Directive.* A clue indicating where the essence of law can
be found is furnished by the one characteristic that is presupposed
by all the explanations given, that law is a *directive.* ". . . [T]he
word 'law' has a fixed and definite meaning. In its general sense
it imports 'a rule of action.' . . . [T]he word 'rule' [is] 'A prescribed guide for conduct or action: government direction.' " [55]

The idea of direction is paramount in all legislation. "The
legislative act [was] a direction to the people of the state demanding certain things to be done, fixing a time, a place, and a man-

---

[48] Id. at 12-13.

[49] Id. at 116-117. For the logical consequences regarding obligation, see
Chapter 6.

[50] Suárez (1548-1617), 1 De Legibus 5, 13 (Coletus ed. 1740). The translations of Suárez are mine.

[51] Id. at 4, 8.

[52] Aquinas (1225-1274), 1-2 Sum. Theol. 90, 4. The translations of Aquinas
are mine.

[53] Id. at 90, 1.

[54] Id. at 17, 2.

[55] Baldwin Township's Annexation, 305 Pa. 490, 158 Atl. 272, 273 (1931).

ner which had to be followed. From the legislature [came] a mandate, the disobedience of which would result in penalties or legal consequences. Naturally, this would be effected in the same way as all other like mandates. The action of the legislature would, therefore, be in the form of a law. . . . That which must be obeyed and followed by citizens subject to sanctions or legal consequences is a law. Such a direction must take the form of law." [56]

Direction implies a relation or order of one thing to another. ". . . [To] 'direct' is defined thus: 'to determine the direction of; especially to cause to point or to go straight toward a thing' . . . 'to instruct or guide with authority; order; command' . . . 'to point or aim in a straight line toward a place or an object' . . . 'to control the course of; regulate; guide or lead; govern; cause to proceed in a particular manner' . . . 'to order; instruct; point out to, as a course of proceeding, with authority; prescribe to.' " [57]

Hence if law directs, it is itself a directive. It indicates the direction people should take in matters legal. A speed law prescribing a limit of 40 miles per hour is a directive to drivers regarding what is necessary for the safety of themselves and others.

2. *Judgment regarding means to end.* This directive is a judgment formed in the mind of those with lawmaking authority. Its content, the factual relation of means to end, can be perceived only by the mind, not the will. Only the intellect can comprehend the ordering of 40 miles per hour to safety. The purpose and end of all law is the common welfare of the people. Hence only the mind or intellect can embody this ordering in a directive judgment that directs actions accordingly. Unity of directive judgment among many lawmakers is achieved through agreement reached according to the majority-minority principle of government. [58]

3. *Promulgation.* The directive judgment that is law must be made known to the people in order that it may serve as a rule for them. It must be promulgated. To promulgate means: " 'To make known or announce officially and formally to be public' . . . The law does not provide in what manner . . . decisions . . . shall be promulgated. The purpose of promulgation is to give notice." [59] "Laws are nothing more than rules promulgated

---

[56] Koenig v. Flynn, 258 N.Y. 292, 179 N.E. 705, 707 (1932).

[57] In re Durkee's Estate, 183 Misc. 382, 47 N.Y.S.2d 721, 725 (1944).

[58] See Chapter 19.

[59] Brown v. Democratic Committee of St. Bernard Parish, 183 La. 967, 165 So. 167, 168, 169 (1935).

by government as a means to an ordered society." [60] Hence, accompanying their directive judgment is the intention of the lawmakers to promulgate the directive to the people.

Although promulgation is necessary if the law is to serve as a guide to the people, it is not part of the law itself. What is made known must be already constituted what it is before it can be made known. The law must exist before it can be promulgated. The only way that promulgation may be said to be part of law is therefore from the standpoint of the people for whom there is no law unless it is made known to them.

Promulgation of a law, therefore, should not be mistaken for the law itself. The printed page of the Revised Statutes or the Supreme Court Reporter, while taken as law in the legal sense, is not law in the philosophical sense. It is but the printed expression of the law which in itself is the directive judgment already formed in the minds of the lawmakers.

4. *Definition of law.* Law is defined therefore as a *directive judgment,* in the mind of those with *lawmaking authority,* ordering *means necessary* for the *common good.* Or law is ". . . an ordering of reason for the common good, by him who has charge of the community, and promulgated." [61] Thus a statute restricting the sale of narcotics is in reality a directive judgment, in the minds of the majority of the legislators, that such a limitation is necessary for the welfare of the people. The people in turn are obliged to observe the statute because what it demands is necessary for their own good.

Only when the essence of law is seen as the directive judgment of the lawmaker does the relation between law and the demands of everyday fact situations become clear. For these demands are recognized by the lawmaker as necessary means-end relations and as such become the content of his directive judgment. Further implications of thus locating the nature of law in this directive judgment will become evident as our examination of the elements of law proceeds.

5. *Directive judgment and command.* Is this directive judgment the same as "command"? Certainly it is not the same if "command" is taken as an expression of the will of the sovereign and the subject is obliged to obey simply because the sovereign wills it.

[60] Miami Laundry Co. v. Florida Dry Cleaning and Laundry Board, 134 Fla. 1, 183 So. 759, 764 (1938); see also People v. Garcia, 37 Cal. 2d 763, 98 P.2d 265, 271 (1939).

[61] Aquinas, 1-2 Sum. Theol. 90, 4.

The directive judgment can be the same as "command" if what it prescribes is factually necessary for the common good and for this reason ought to be done. ". . . [I]t is of the essence of the command that it imply a relation to an end, inasmuch as that which is commanded is necessary or expedient for an end." [62] It is this objective necessity of means conducive to the public good, expressed in the directive judgment, that demands or commands the observance of all the people. The directive judgment may therefore be taken as a command.

Some may prefer to call such a command — one not based on the will of the sovereign but on the necessity of means to end — a precept. If such is the case, the directive judgment may also be looked upon as a precept.[63]

6. *Directive is mandatory.* In law "mandatory" refers to what is required for validity as distinguished from "directory" which concerns something that is not so required. A statute providing that absent voters' ballots be placed in ballot boxes was held to be directory and not mandatory.[64] Or "mandatory" may relate to a statutory provision which must be observed, while "directory" concerns a provision which leaves it optional with those to whom it is addressed to obey it or not. A statute providing that a court may appoint an official shorthand reporter when in its opinion the business requires it was declared to be directory and not mandatory.[65] But the limitation of the word "directory" or "directive" to what is merely discretionary and the failure to extend it to include what is of command and mandatory, would seem to be a vestige of the theory that only the command was mandatory because it expressed the will of the sovereign. Anything else was "merely a directive."

Courts commonly speak this way. "The law . . . clearly constitutes a direct mandate to the people of duty, or a direct prohibition of some act or thing. In its very essence it must be a requirement and demand, a mandatory order or rule, in order to be of the nature of a law. The law, civil or criminal, creates liability, and liability cannot be predicated upon those things

[62] Id. at 99, 1.

[63] Kantorowicz, The Definition of Law 30 (Campbell ed. 1958).

In view of the fact that law is a directive judgment in the mind of the lawmaker, the emphasis placed by American "Realists" on the lawmaker himself, while lacking a sharp focus, was not entirely misplaced. On the "Realists" see Reuschlein, Jurisprudence — Its American Prophets 183-275 (1951).

[64] Siedschlag v. May, 363 Ill. 538, 2 N.E.2d 836, 838 (1936).

[65] State ex rel. Dworken v. Court of Common Pleas of Cuyahoga County, 131 Ohio St. 23, 1 N.E.2d 138, 139 (1936).

that are merely advisory, merely directory — only upon those things that are obligatory and mandatory. . . . It may be that in some cases, gathered from the entire context of the law, some provision may be clearly directory or discretionary, and when so it should be so interpreted and so applied; but this directory character, this optional character, must be clear and convincing." [66]

However, from the viewpoint of a means-end philosophy of law, since an authoritative directive implies the necessity of means for the common welfare and for this reason it obliges, a directive is mandatory and, in this sense, a command. Anything else is advisory or discretionary.

D.   *Comment*

From the above opinions regarding what law is and from our own findings as to its essence, it is evident that the interpretation lawmen put on law is controlled by the philosophical presuppositions with which they approach the problem. Divergencies on one level stem from those of another. The parting of the ways lies far back of these practical differences.

The first parting comes at the point of decision regarding the nature of men. Are they mere units of matter only, or are they composites of matter and mind? If they are of matter alone, the meaning given to law by followers of Lenin and Marx is logical.

Granted that man is a composite of matter and mind with powers of knowing and deciding,[67] another parting must be faced. Can men actually know enough of the objective world to form ideas of ends and means and their interrelation? If they cannot do so and are not in such knowing contact with objective things, these concepts must come from within a man and Kant's founding of law and obligation on the will's inner necessity makes sense. So also does Bentham's and his pupil Austin's similar emphasis on the will.

But even though men can know enough of the external world to recognize means-end relations, still another parting of the ways presents itself. Which is men's prime power, the intellect or the will? If the preoccupation is with keeping the will supreme and free from any determination by the intellect, then law and obligation again will be centered in the will, and the position taken by Suárez and others is consistent.

[66] Devine v. State ex rel. Tucker, 105 Ohio St. 288, 136 N.E. 922, 923 (1922).

[67] This is the only datum on which the basic equality of all men, regardless of their individual differences, can be grounded. For a further treatment of the powers of men, see Chapter 14.

However, if men's intellect is the prime power, then law is the intellect's directive judgment of means objectively necessary for an end and obligation is based on this relation. This is the position held by Aquinas and others. And because it squares better with facts and experience to hold that men are composites of both matter and mind, that they can know enough of the objective world to perceive the relation of means to end, that men are primarily knowing rather than willing beings since the will is a "rational" will, this position is also maintained here.

The factors that influence our philosophical thinking and cause us to take one parting of the ways rather than another are sometimes simple and obvious, at other times complex, mysterious and obscure. No attempt will be made here to analyze and evaluate these various schools of thought. This is the province of the pre-legal study of philosophy and its history. For somewhat as chemistry is a prerequisite to medicine, so also is philosophy presupposed by law. Suffice it here merely to suggest, as we have, the relation between positions in law and their roots in philosophy and to take a stand for a means-end philosophy anchored in the rational nature of men. This relation between law and philosophy will become more evident especially when we examine the content of law, the sanction and obligation of law, the nature of a law not man-made, and the connection between this law and man-made law.[68]

E. *Summary*

Law, then, described *in its function* as a guide for the people, is the sum of rules promulgated. From this viewpoint "a law" may be said to refer to a particular statute, rule or decision; "the law" embraces the sum total of these; and "law" relates to the whole area of legal activities that have to do with directing the people for their common good.

Defined, however, as it is *in itself,* law is a directive judgment of those with authority ordering means necessary for the common good. In a word, law in its essence is not something nebulous and empyrean. It is as definite and factual as is the particular directive judgment in the mind of men with lawmaking authority. This directive judgment is the "agate point" on which turn the balances of law.

[68] On the ultimate consequences of Thomistic, Suárezian and Kantian principles, see the excellent treatment in Ibranyi, Ethica secundum S. Thomam et Kant (1931).

CHAPTER 2

End of Man-made Law

The problem here is to ascertain as accurately as possible the purpose of law. For whose good does law operate and to what extent? This is important because the end of law sets the limit to which law may go in touching the lives of the people.

I. THE COMMON GOOD

The end of law has always been said to be the common good of the people. It is their common good that is the ultimate purpose of all legislation and adjudication. "All free governments are established by the people for their benefit, and the powers delegated are to be exercised for their common good. . . . All the departments of government are instituted to exercise the functions of government for the common good." [1] But what is the common good?

The common good embraces all those goods that are communicable to all the citizens. These goods are also spoken of, though less technically, as public good or general good. They are also referred to more loosely and with accent on the condition of the people as public welfare, common welfare and general welfare.[2]

A. *Peace and Security*

Foremost among these goods are the overall conditions of peace and security. These conditions are the prerequisite climate for the development and improvement of the individual members of the community and their pursuit of happiness. For it is in the exercise of free decisions that men develop themselves.

[1] Mott v. Pennsylvania R. Co., 30 Pa. 9, 27, 35 (1858). See also State ex rel. Wyatt v. Ashbrook, 154 Mo. 375, 394, 55 S.W. 627, 632 (1900); Jacobson v. Massachusetts, 197 U.S. 11, 25, 25 Sup. Ct. 358, 363 (1904).

[2] "Public interests," "social interests" and "social values" may mean the same thing providing "interests" and "values" convey a meaning related to the actual needs of men and therefore signify a good truly perfective of men and not some content arbitrarily decided upon.

War and revolution have been considered a temporary common good, because they can be a necessary means of arriving at a just peace. If war were an evil in itself, however necessary, no one could rightly engage in it and all laws of mobilization, conscription, and the like would be morally unjust. But it is in relation to peace that war and revolution find their justification. And although men may perfect themselves during the chaos of strife by bearing its hardship and suffering well (providing these are not too intense and prolonged), nevertheless this is possible only because of the moral strength acquired during times of peace. As a way of life men need a stable degree of peace and security if they are to advance themselves, their civilization and their culture. Accordingly, men involved in war and revolution naturally long for peace.

If the techniques of "total" war have developed to the point where destruction is so widespread that more harm will result from it than any possible good, such war cannot be justified.

B. *Maintenance of Order*

Peace and security are achieved by the maintenance of order. Order is preserved chiefly by the protection of just claims and by certain institutions which promote such protection.

There is need of protecting just claims regarding life, bodily members, health, safety, family relations, property, a good name, truthfulness in dealings with others, freedom of activity especially concerning education, work and worship.

Likewise in the protection of these claims there are needed institutions and organized methods of solving disputes such as courts (national and international), of entering upon agreements like contracts and treaties, of uniting politically and being governed by laws, of having the members of the community educated to the necessity of cooperative effort in community living.

This, in general, has been the legal understanding of the public good and the public welfare. "The public welfare embraces a variety of interests calling for public care and control. These are: 'The primary social interest of safety; order; and morals; economic interests; and nonmaterial and political interests.' " [3] "In its inception the police power was closely concerned with the preservation of the public peace, safety, morals, and health. . . . As our civic life has developed so has the definition of 'public welfare' until it has been held to embrace regulations 'to promote

[3] State v. Hutchinson Ice Cream Co., 168 Iowa 1, 147 N.W. 195, 199 (1914).

the economic welfare, the public convenience, and general prosperity of the community.' " [4]

II. COMMON AND PROPER GOOD

The common good must be carefully distinguished from what is a proper good. The common good is communicable to all, while the proper good is communicable to only one.

A. *Distinguishing Mark: Communicability*

The primary characteristic of common good as distinguished from proper goods, then, is that it is *communicable* to all the members of the community and may be participated in by all. Proper goods are not thus communicable. Conditions of peace and security, of settling disputes, and the like are such goods. On the other hand, the land I own, the food I eat, the clothes I wear are proper goods because by their nature they are not communicable to all.

It may seem at first glance that common goods are actually proper goods because they are eventually enjoyed by individual persons. Are not conditions of health and safety ultimately a proper good to me when I participate in them? The communicability of the good itself is what constitutes the difference. Although my enjoyment of a common good is inevitably proper to me, the good itself — say conditions of health — is of its nature something in which all may participate. Not all the members of the community have to participate actively in it, but of its nature this good is capable of being communicated to all.

B. *Need of United Effort*

There is a secondary aspect of a great part of the political common good, besides the primary characteristic of communicability to all. This is the necessity of *united effort* of all to produce it. The combined efforts of all are needed if peace, security and the other common goods are to be realized. This is the reason for political union.[5] True, not every single member may cooperate in promoting the common good. But this only means that

[4] Miller v. Board of Public Works of City of Los Angeles, 195 Cal. 477, 234 Pac. 381, 383 (1925).
[5] See Chapter 20.

factually the political common good is never perfectly accomplished. More or less close approximations are the reality.

The common good in general, then, is a good that is communicable to all. The political common good is that *complexus of goods* that is *communicable to all* and in large part is brought about by the *united effort of all* the members of the community.

C. *Not Sum Total or Collective Good*

The common good, then, is not the sum total of proper goods. The common good of a country is not the total arrived at by adding together all the proper goods of the citizens. It is a good of an entirely different and unique nature.

Nor is the common good a collective good. A collective good, such as the meal in which a family is about to participate, must be divided and become the proper good of individuals if they are to participate in it. As the number of participants increases, the good decreases and each one has less. Similarly, the amount of productive and consumer goods in a country is, strictly speaking, a collective good. In contrast, the common good of peace, security, and the like is not decreased by the number of participants nor does this number cause each one to have less.

D. *"Public" — "Private"*

The terms "public" and "private" as used in law may or may not have the same meaning as common and proper. It depends on the context in which courts use them.

1. *Same as common and proper.* Sometimes "public," in contradistinction to "private," refers to a good in which all may participate such as just mentioned. In this use it is synonymous with common. " 'Private' is defined . . . as 'belonging to, or concerning, an individual person, company, or interest.' 'Public' is defined as 'of or pertaining to the people; relating to, belonging to, or affecting, a nation, state, or community at large; — opposed to private.' " [6]

2. *Referring to relative number.* At other times "public" may refer to the relative number of persons involved in a particular situation. "What is a public use, and how many of the people must be interested in the establishment of a road before it can be said to be laid out for the 'public welfare'? Is not a use public,

[6] People v. Powell, 280 Mich. 696, 274 N.W. 372, 373 (1937). See also State ex rel. Freeling v. Lyon, 63 Okla. 285, 165 Pac. 419, 420 (1917).

when every person in the state has a right to it? If so, why is not
the use of a township road a public use? . . . [T]here must be a
public necessity for the use . . . to justify taking private property
for it. . . . [B]ut what is a public necessity or the public welfare?
Must every citizen in the state have a particular interest in the
establishment of a state road, every citizen of a county a like interest in respect to a county road; and every citizen of a township
such an interest in a township road, before it can be said that
they are required for the public welfare? I think this will hardly
be pretended, and if not, then it must be admitted that the welfare . . . of a less number of the people may suffice. And applying the familiar maxim, that a law is to be construed with reference to its subject matter . . . it will not be found difficult to say
that the persons interested in the establishment of a mere township
road need not be so numerous as would be required to create a
public necessity for a state or county road. A necessity for the
convenience of the applicants and other neighbors, is what the
statute requires." [7]

3. *Different from common and proper.* There are still other
uses of "public" and "private" that are not directly related to
common and proper. For instance, in the matter of natural
resources such as gas, oil, coal and uranium, or utilities like water
and electricity, or carriers such as railroads, steamships, buses and
airplanes, or communications like mail, telegraph and radio,
ownership may be either public or private. Either type of ownership may make available to all a sufficiency of these products and
facilities at reasonable prices. This availability contributes to the
common good. But whether it should be brought about by public
or private ownership and so supported by law depends on which
best accomplishes this availability.

Similarly, regarding the control of prices, say of food or rent,
this also can be private or public. Under normal conditions
when it is easier for people to be honest and just, private enterprisers can make accessible a sufficiency of food and housing at
just prices. During these times public control would not be
necessary and hence would not be fit content for a law. Under
different conditions, such as emergencies when it is more difficult for individuals to exercise self-control, ceilings on food
prices imposed and enforced by the government may be called for.
But again whether controls should be exercised by public authority or not depends on whether it is necessary in order to make

[7] Shaver v. Starrett, 4 Ohio St. 495, 499 (1855). See also Chicago, B. &
Q.R.R. Co. v. Krayenbuhl, 65 Neb. 889, 91 N.W. 880, 882 (1902).

available a sufficiency of food and housing at reasonable prices. In these instances "public" is not necessarily related to the common good.[8]

III. LIMITS CONTENT OF LAW

The end of law fixes the limit of the content of law. It determines in general how far law should go in directing the lives of citizens. Law is supposed to work directly for the common good of the people and not their proper good. This they should do for themselves. Law should be concerned with the proper goods of citizens only when they indirectly relate to peace and security, for instance as happens in torts.

Hence, "public policy" must be defined in relation to the common or public good. Public policy is ". . . that principle of law which holds that no subject can lawfully do that which has a tendency to be injurious to the public, or against the public good."[9] Unless public policy is thus anchored to the common good of the people, it becomes arbitrary and whimsical.

It follows that, since law's end is the common good of all the people, it should not be used as an instrument for furthering the proper goods of favored individuals, whether these be cliques or a dictator himself. Nor should law be used as a weapon of discrimination and suppression of those who happen to be in disfavor and are a minority.[10]

Law, then, if its end is the common good of the people, is not a barrier to the people's freedom and progress. It is something like the rails that guide a locomotive. These restrict its movement from side to side but only in order that it may go forward to its destination. Similarly, law curbs the activities of citizens but only that they may more readily attain what is necessary and good for them.

[8] See Chapter 16 on ownership.
[9] Egerton v. Brownlow, 4 H.L. Cas. 1, 196, 10 Eng. Rep. 359, 437 (1853).
[10] For further discussion of common and proper goods see Chapters 9 and 20.

Content of Man-made Law

The problem that concerns us next is how to determine what should be the content of law, that is, how to tell whether it is just or unjust. This problem in turn presupposes another, that of fixing the meaning of "just" and "right." The solution of these problems is of key importance because on it depends the meaning of "right," the place of morals in law, and the viewing of law as prudence, not science.

I. CONTENT: WHAT IS JUST

The content of the directive judgment which is law includes whatever is necessary for the public good. It embraces all the things that must be done or not done in order to accomplish this objective. Such are the provisions, stipulations and requirements of all statutes and decisions. That these be just is admittedly the aspiration of all law. ". . . [T]he object of all law, common or statutory, is the establishment and enforcement of 'justice.' " [1] "Every person is entitled to a certain remedy in the laws for all injuries, or wrongs which he may receive in his person, property, or character; he ought to obtain justice freely, and without being obliged to purchase it, completely and without denial, promptly and without delay, conformably to the laws." [2] "It should be unnecessary to remind ourselves that constitutions and laws are designed 'to establish justice.' The Constitution was never intended to be a cloak for strategy or other device employed to defeat the plainest principles of justice." [3]

The content of law, seen in this perspective, is a means to the end of law. Justice is a means of bringing about peace and security and the other common goods. It is a prerequisite for the common welfare.

---

[1] State v. Williams, 14 Del. 508, 18 Atl. 949, 950 (1890).

[2] Wis. Const., art. 1, §9 (1848). See also State ex rel. Department of Agriculture v. McCarthy, 238 Wis. 258, 299 N.W. 58, 64 (1941).

[3] State v. Wells, 134 Ohio St. 404, 17 N.E.2d 658, 661 (1938).

II. The Anatomy of What Is Just

But what is "just"? "Just" ordinarily takes its meaning from what is "due." What is "due" must, in turn, be related to some "title."

A. *My Title to Things*

Title implies a relation between a thing, tangible or intangible, and a person. "Title is the means whereby the owner of lands has the just possession of his property." [4] Since title is controlling regarding what is just, an examination of the process by which it originates is indicated as a prerequisite to a further understanding of justice.

1. *Relation of title.* Let us suppose, to use a primitive example, that I am walking with a party of men across an island uninhabited and unclaimed by any country. Each of us finds a sea shell. I could rightly say the shell I found is "mine." The others should say regarding me that it is "thine." What is the basis of this natural judgment of "mine" and "thine"?

A man instinctively recognizes that whatever has a unique relation to him and to no one else is "his." Starting with my own body, I recognize that this hand is uniquely related to me as a part of me and to no one else, and is therefore "mine." I judge instinctively "it is my hand"; "it is my own hand"; "I possess it"; "it is proper to me." I may further judge, "I own it"; "it is my property"; "I shall use it as I see fit." This natural judgment is extended to whatever becomes uniquely related to me even though it is not physically a part of me. The sea shell became uniquely related to me and to no one else when I found it and occupied it. That is why I judge it to be "mine."

The foundation for what is "mine," therefore, is the way a thing stands uniquely in relation to me and to no other person. This is the relation of title. A title is, then, basically a sign that a unique relation exists between some thing and myself. This relation of title between a thing and myself, as will be seen later,[5] constitutes property in the strict sense. It may be created by the processes of occupancy, labor, contract, gift inter vivos, wills and intestate succession, accession, and adverse possession.

[4] Horney v. Price, 189 N.C. 820, 128 S.E. 321, 323 (1925).
[5] For a discussion of title and the justification of private property, see Chapter 16.

It is vital to note that this relation of title may come into existence independently of any man-made law. Such was the case of occupancy just analyzed. Here the relation arose consequent upon the elementary demands of my nature only, that whatever is uniquely related to me and to no one else be titled "mine." Although it may be difficult to determine in many cases what is "mine," nevertheless "mine" is not limited to such tangible things as "hand" and "sea shell." It certainly includes intangibles such as "my" ideas. Courts have recognized this as will be seen later.

2. *Natural and legal titles.* This relation of title between things and persons is natural if it follows the rudimentary demands of a man's nature. It is legal if these demands are recognized and worked out in detail by legislative or judicial thinking in answer to immediate needs and made enforceable in law.

Since titles may be created independently of man-made law as well as dependently on it, just actions and claims, which are based on titles, may also be either natural or legal as will be noted shortly.

B. *Others' Duty to Respect this Title*

Although the sea shell I found is "mine" something more is required if I am to "own" it. In order that mere occupancy become ownership the unique relation of title must be made *exclusive.* Others must be excluded from usurping the object that is "mine."

1. *Exclusiveness presupposed.* Exclusiveness is a recognized aspect of possession, ownership and property. "Occupancy or possession, by one, implies the exclusion of every other individual from the occupancy and possession." [6]

Ownership supposes this exclusiveness inasmuch as ownership implies that the owner is entitled to control and dispose of a thing. "One who has no right to control, handle, or dispose of a thing cannot be considered its owner, for the essential attributes of ownership of property, real and personal, are the rights in the owner to control, handle, and dispose of the thing owned." [7]

This exclusiveness underlies the concept of property itself. It

---

[6] Starits v. Avery, 204 Iowa 401, 213 N.W. 769, 771 (1927). See also Redfield v. Utica & Syracuse R.R. Co., 25 Barb. 54, 58 (N.Y. 1851).

[7] Hardinge v. Empire Zinc Co., 17 Ariz. 75, 148 Pac. 306, 312 (1915). See also Trustees of Phillips Exeter Academy v. Exeter, 92 N.H. 473, 33 A.2d 665, 673 (1943).

is taken for granted that ". . . property implies exclusive owner-ship." [8]

2. *Exclusiveness from others' respect.* But how is my occupa-tion, possession and use of this sea shell actually made exclusive? A unique relation exists, as a matter of fact, between a dog and the bone he holds in his mouth. No other dog "possesses" the bone. But does the dog "own" the bone as I own the sea shell? It is his own until a stronger dog takes it away from him. Power and might are the determining factors.

My ownership of the sea shell rests on an entirely different basis. The unique relation between myself and the shell becomes exclusive by *others* making it so.

Others must respect this relation. Otherwise, ownership would depend solely on possession by power and force. This would reduce human living to an animal level. For, inasmuch as men acted in complete disregard of relations of title, and promiscu-ously attempted to take for themselves whatever others have, the existence of men would become one of struggle, strife, insecurity and fear. Men, however, are so endowed with intelligence that they are destined for higher development and happiness. They develop and perfect themselves by their free decisions. This de-mands conditions of peace and security. These conditions are impossible unless others make the possession of what is "mine" exclusive by their non-interference and respect for it, rather than by my making it exclusive as animals do by force.

It is only in cases when others fail to respect what is "mine" that physical force may be resorted to. This force will be ex-ercised by me personally or by someone acting in my behalf. It will depend on the conditions under which the interference takes place.

In a word, the exclusiveness that must accompany the unique relation of title between me and a thing and which makes the thing my "own" derives from the disposition and actions of *others.*

3. *The essence of being "just."* The action of others by which they *respect my relation of title* and thereby make my possession and use exclusive is the essence of being "just." For, to be "just" implies giving what is due. To me are due recognition and respect regarding my relation of title to a thing, and the action by which others do this is the "just" action itself. This just action is not a vague gesture but is proportioned to what is

[8] State v. Cowen, 231 Iowa 1117, 3 N.W.2d 176, 180 (1942).

due to me. And since the obligation of others to act justly in my regard is necessary as a means of avoiding a life of animal struggle, to be just is a distinctly human quality. Only persons can be just to one another. A person cannot be just to an animal or a thing.

In ordinary parlance "justice" and what is "just" are taken as synonymous and perhaps rightly so. However, strictly speaking there is a difference between them. One is the habit of which the other is the act. Justice is an interior habit of will disposing a man to do exteriorly what is just. ". . . [T]he meaning of the term 'justice' . . . is indicated and might be very well and truly expressed in the definition which Justinian has given us of that word, viz., 'The constant and perpetual disposition to render everyone his due.' " [9]

The tendency to take "justice" and "just" as synonymous derives, it would seem, from a good historical reason. Plato's concept of justice, while taking account of the ordering of a man's inner life, stressed the harmony caused by each part of the city-state doing its task. This notion of justice puts the accent on the exterior condition of just order. Aristotle and Aquinas considered justice to be a habit of will. They emphasized the interior disposition of a man that causes the exterior just order.[10]

Hence, as a man must assure control of himself by developing other necessary habits, he must also form the habit of justice. By way of completing and perfecting themselves, men must choose what is right and good. To do this regarding food, drink and sex requires the habit of *moderation;* regarding extraordinary difficulties and dangers requires the habit of *courage.* So also as regards giving others their due, the habit of *justice* is necessary.

4. *Jural relations.* The just action by which others respect my relation of title, then, constitutes the relation of justness between others and me. This is the elemental *jural relation* to which I can lay claim and for which, if others do not in duty manifest it toward me, I can seek enforcement and remedy in law. It is this jural relation, founded on my relation of title, that is strictly speaking the object of their *habit* of justice.[11]

5. *Naturally and legally just.* Inasmuch as a man's relation of title to something may come into being with or without recognition by law, so accordingly the just actions of others regarding it

[9] Collier v. Lindley, 203 Cal. 641, 266 Pac. 526, 530 (1928).
[10] Plato, 4 Republic 434, 444 (Shorey trans. 1953); Aristotle, 5 Nicomachean Ethics 1, 1129a3 (Ross trans. 1941); Aquinas, 2-2 Sum. Theol. 58, 1.
[11] Lachance, Le Concept de Droit selon Aristote et S. Thomas 213 (1948).

have a natural or legal basis.[12] The distinction between the naturally and the legally just has always been recognized by man-made law. ". . . [T]he word 'just' may apply in nearly all of its senses to either ethics or law, denoting something which is morally right and fair and sometimes that which is right and fair according to positive law." [13]

6. *Kinds of justice.* Since the goods that are the basis of justice may be either proper or common, justice has different facets.

a. *Commutative justice.* When it is a question of an individual person respecting the proper good of other persons as individuals, the disposition or habit of his will to do so is exchange or commutative justice. ". . . [J]ustice in its common acceptance means the rendering to every man his due, so that neither party may gain by the other's loss." [14]

b. *Contributive justice.* When it is a matter of a member of the community having concern for the common good of other members as members, his disposition of will to do so is contributive justice. Each member of the community owes it to every other member to work for their mutual common good. Without such cooperate effort it cannot be obtained. "The right and power of society to demand that each of its members shall contribute his share to the common necessities is a natural and alienable right, for without it there can be no organized society." [15] If this duty in contributive justice is made enforceable by legislation and adjudication, the disposition of will to promote it by obeying the law is known as legal justice.

c. *Distributive justice.* When, finally, it is a question of those in government being mindful of the common good of the members as distributable to them, their disposition of will to do so equitably is distributive justice. Societies and unions are formed to procure the common good of their members. Those who govern them should be disposed to distribute the common goods proportionate to just norms. Hence, the governmental head of

[12] The John E. Mulford, 18 Fed. 455, 458 (S.D.N.Y. 1883). See also Monongahela Bridge Co. v. United States, 216 U.S. 177, 195, 30 Sup. Ct. 356, 361 (1910); Hebert v. Louisiana, 272 U.S. 312, 316, 317, 47 Sup. Ct. 103, 104 (1926); Snyder v. Massachusetts, 291 U.S. 97, 105, 54 Sup. Ct. 330, 332 (1934); Brown v. Mississippi, 297 U.S. 278, 286, 56 Sup. Ct. 461, 465 (1936); National Surety Corp. v. Mullins, 262 Ky. 465, 90 S.W.2d 707, 708 (1936); State ex rel. Department of Agriculture v. McCarthy, 238 Wis. 258, 299 N.W. 58, 64 (1941).
[13] Lake Hancock & C.R. Co. v. Stinson, 77 Fla. 333, 81 So. 512 (1919).
[14] Livingston Oil Corp. v. Henson, 90 Okla. 76, 215 Pac. 1057, 1059 (1923). See also Wisdom v. Board of Supervisors of Polk County, 236 Iowa 669, 19 N.W.2d 602, 606 (1945).
[15] Mott v. Pennsylvania R.R. Co., 30 Pa. 9, 35 (1858).

any type of society — domestic, labor, business and especially political — should have this habit developed of justly distributing the goods that are common to its members. Thus taxes, which are a public good although they may be a private burden, should be levied in proportion to the resources and income of various classes of citizens. It would be unjust to tax every citizen the same amount. Such things as the punishment of criminals — also a public good but a private evil — should be proportional to the crime and the criminal.

Benefits likewise, as well as burdens, should be justly distributed. Educational opportunities, police protection, the use of courts, and the like become a matter of discrimination and favoritism if not made available in proportion to the need of each individual.

d. *"Social justice."* A much used phrase is "social justice." Its exact meaning is hard to determine. Used in the context of "social engineering," it can mean one thing; employed within the framework of dialectical materialism, it connotes another; used in a papal encyclical, it can imply still another.

Even when justice is taken as a habit of the will to give others their due, the phrase "social justice" is indefinite in meaning. If it refers to the justice that should obtain between "institutions," say employers as a group and employees as a group, it should be borne in mind that there is no such thing as an "institutional will" or "group will" in which this habit may be formed — unless a philosophy of "artificial person" be adopted as some have done regarding corporations and the state.[16] There is factually only the will of individual employers and employees to be disposed to render each other what is due commutatively, contributively or distributively. The goods said to be the object of "social justice" seem to be, upon closer inspection, included among management's and labor's proper and common goods, which are already the object of commutative, contributive and distributive justice.

If "social justice" is used to denote the objective condition brought about by the exercise of the above-mentioned aspects of justice, it would seem to be simply what has always been known as a "just order."

C. *My Claim on Others' Duty*

In view of the fact that others have the duty to be just toward me and respect my title to a thing, say the sea shell, I can make

16 See Chapters 17 and 19.

demands on them to fulfill their obligation. I can call on them to do this. I can lay claim to this. In other words I "have a claim" on them.

1. *Claim is a demand.* A claim is essentially a demand on another. "A claim is a demand of some matter, as of right, made by one person upon another, to do or forebear to do some act or thing, as a matter of duty." [17] "The word [claim] is derived from the Latin *clamor,* meaning a call, a demand. In its ordinary sense the term imports the assertion, demand or challenge of something as a right." [18]

This claim or demand has commonly been expressed in terms of "right," as in the phrase "I have a right" to the sea shell. ". . . [A] right is a claim for the enforcement, redress, or protection of which the jurisdiction of a court may be properly invoked." [19]

2. *Natural claims.* Natural claims or rights are distinguished from legal ones in man-made law on the same basis as natural titles are distinguished from legal titles. As a matter of fact when we speak of a natural claim on others we are implying that it is natural because founded on a demand of nature and a natural title.

a. *Natural claim to life, liberty, and property.* Emphasis thus far has been on natural claims or rights pertaining to property. This has been done because an analysis of property seems to afford the best introductory view of "just" or "justice." This same meaning of claims in justice also extends to life and liberty, as is commonly recognized. There is, however, a difference to be noted concerning the basis of claims and obligation in these areas.

The ground for others' obligation to respect my property is my title to something that is "mine," as we have seen. But concerning life, the basis for others' obligation to show regard for my life is that they do not have authority over it because they did not create it. This dominion or title belongs to the Creator of life and life may be taken by men only as a means of self-preservation. Again, concerning the free use of my powers of knowing and deciding, the reason others are obliged not to interfere in their exercise is that I am entitled to this mode of action which is necessary for me if I am to fulfill a basic demand of my nature — that I so use these powers that I progress in my own develop-

[17] Ingram v. Colgan, 106 Cal. 113, 38 Pac. 315, 317 (1894). See also Tanner v. Best's Estate, 40 Cal. App. 2d 442, 104 P.2d 1084, 1087 (1940).

[18] Uintah State Bank v. Ajax, 77 Utah 455, 297 Pac. 434, 438 (1931). See Mellinger v. City of Houston, 68 Tex. 37, 3 S.W. 249, 253 (1887).

[19] State v. Grosnickle, 189 Wis. 17, 206 N.W. 895, 896 (1926).

ment and the attainment of my end. Not to allow me this free exercise of my powers, as far as is compatible with social living, is to thwart the very purpose of human existence.[20]

The natural claims to life, liberty and property are the triune underpinnings of law. "The right of life, liberty and property, was not conferred by society. The highest obligation of government is to defend and protect persons in their enjoyment." [21] "That there are inherent rights existing in the people proper to the making of any of our Constitutions is a fact recognized and declared by the Declaration of Independence, and by substantially every state Constitution . . . 'among these are life, liberty and the pursuit of happiness.' " [22]

These natural claims are clearly recognized by law. But whether this recognition rests on a solid or shaky foundation remains to be examined.[23]

b. *Bulwark against despotism.* When the "inalienable" aspect of natural claims is violated the result is tyranny and slavery. "It must be conceded that there are such rights in every free government beyond the control of the State. A government which recognized no such rights, which held the lives, the liberty, and the property of its citizens subject at all times to the absolute disposition and unlimited control of even the most democratic depository of power, is after all but a despotism. It is true it is a despotism of the many, of the majority, if you choose to call it so, but it is nonetheless a despotism." [24]

It is only to be expected that, if the natural claims arising from men's nature for their own good be disregarded and trampled, the result will be a condition of tyranny. *"Hoc volo, sic iubeo, sit pro ratione voluntas"* is the despot's substitution of his own will for natural claims.[25]

[20] For a further development of these points see Chapters 9 and 16.

[21] Brown v. Board of Levee Commissioners, 50 Miss. 468, 487 (1874).

[22] Nunnemacher v. State, 129 Wis. 190, 200, 108 N.W. 627, 629 (1906).

[23] See Chapters 8 and 13.

[24] Loan Assn. v. Topeka, 87 U.S. 655, 663, 22 L. Ed. 455, 461 (1874). See also Van Horne's Lessee v. Dorrance, 2 Dall. 304, 310, 1 L. Ed. 391 (1795); United States v. Perkins, 163 U.S. 625, 628, 16 Sup. Ct. 1073, 1074 (1895); Surocco v. Geary, 3 Cal. 69, 73 (1853); Henry v. Dubuque & Pacific R.R. Co., 10 Iowa 540, 543 (1860).

[25] "This I will, thus I command, let my will be the reason." Juvenal, Satires 6, 223 (A.D. 116) (my trans.). "A government according to law and not according to men" is a phrase sometimes used in contrasting a democratic regime with a dictatorial one. What this phrase actually implies, if law is a directive judgment as explained above, is that in a democracy the directive judgment of lawmakers is guided by those legal and non-legal norms that bespeak the common good of the people; in a dictatorship this judgment may simply represent the will of the dictator himself.

3. *Legal claims.* A *legal* claim is a natural claim recognized and made enforceable by positive law. A man has a natural claim on others to respect his property. When the law recognizes this claim, when it is embodied in statutes and decisions which guarantee its enforcement, he also has a legal claim.

When the word "claim" is used in law, it ordinarily refers to a legal claim. "The term 'claim' . . . means of course a valid claim under the statute and this only." [26] "A right has been well defined to be a well-founded claim, and a well-founded claim means nothing more or less than a claim recognized or secured by law." [27]

a. *Legal claims related to natural claims.* Underlying a legal claim is a natural claim that may be more or less evident. Even in the case of legal claims that arise from contract this is true. For, a valid agreement rests on some sort of reasonable grounds which are related to the nature of the facts in the case.

For instance, is a workman's claim to priority over those whose tenure is not as long as his a natural claim? Certainly it is not as obviously a natural claim as the basic claims regarding life, property and liberty. "To be the subject of adjudication by the courts, it is necessary that such rights, if they exist, be legal rights. Legal rights, existing in a government of laws, may be roughly classified as natural rights, rights existing as the result of contracts, and rights created, or recognized, by law. Seniority rights as applicable to train men have been defined to mean 'that a man shall be entitled to preference in matter of choice of and right to work in his occupation in accordance with length of time he has been employed.' . . . Under the above classification of rights in which class, if any, is the right of seniority herein asserted? It could hardly be contended, we think, that it is a *natural right* (called in the Declaration of Independence an *unalienable right*). It is not a right of that classification, a violation of which constitutes a tort. We entertain no doubt that such right, if a legal right, exists only as a creature of contract." [28]

But because this claim is not as plainly a natural claim as some others, it does not follow that it is in no way a natural claim. Is it "natural" for a man who has worked with a company for a longer period of time than others to be given preference over them providing he can do the work as well as they? Is seniority

[26] Tennessee Consolidated Coal Co. v. Commissioner of Internal Revenue, 117 F.2d 452, 454 (6th Cir. 1941).
[27] Mellinger v. City of Houston, 68 Tex. 37, 3 S.W. 249, 253 (1887).
[28] Fine v. Pratt, 150 S.W.2d 308, 311, 312 (Tex. Civ. App. 1941).

a natural thing and its recognition natural? Even though a court will say no natural claims exist in a case, eventually it will discuss natural grounds and reasons in support of its decision. In this particular case, the natural grounds turn out to be property and employment. ". . . [N]o good reason is apparent why . . . such rights may not be enforced in the courts by application of remedies usually employed in the enforcement of other legal rights. It may be true that such rights are not property rights in the usual sense of the term; but there would appear to be no such difference in principle as to require a different classification. . . . A right such as that under consideration which quite evidently may effect so materially the ability of one to make a livelihood, or which may involve the difference between gainful employment and unemployment, would certainly, it seems to us, be entitled to protection by the courts." [29]

The pitfall to be avoided in legal thinking in such matters is to declare there is no natural claim in a case simply because the evidence of it is not immediately recognizable. For ordinarily, soon after making such a declaration, the court will assess the natural facts themselves which are evidence of a natural claim and the reasons for it.

b. *Object of legal and natural claims: Jural relations.* Since my claim is a demand and expectation that others fulfill their duty of being just in their relations toward me, it is these just or jural relations on their part that are in fact the object of my claim as mentioned. The object of my natural claim is the jural relations that others should maintain toward me because of my natural titles to things. The object of my legal claim is the jural relations others are obliged to keep in existence regarding me because of my legal titles to things. Hence, a right can be said to be "A legal relation between two persons" implying "an enforceable claim to performance (action or forebearance) by another." [30]

The dependence of legal relations on natural relations is already manifest from the reasons adduced for statutes or judicial decisions that "create" new legal relations. The ultimate ground for any law is the common good of the people. This implies not only the fulfillment of needs by goods that are communicable to all but also the citizens' duty to cooperate in this effort. This duty carried out results in natural jural relations. When these

[29] Ibid. See also Hitchman Coal and Coke Co. v. Mitchell, 245 U.S. 229, 252, 268, 38 Sup. Ct. 65, 72 (1917).

[30] Corbin, Legal Analysis and Terminology, 29 Yale L.J. 163, 167 (1919).

natural jural relations are made enforceable by law, they become legal jural relations.[31]

III. The Ambiguity of "Right"

The word "right" is one of the most equivocal and, at the same time, one of the most important words in law. A lawman should be fully aware of its variant meanings.

A. *Right as Just*

In its root meaning, the word "right" designates something that is straight or true, something that goes directly to an end. Actions that lead to a man's completion and perfection are, therefore, *recta,* right actions. The opposite is "wrong" or "wrung," that is, a thing that is bent away from the true and does not go straight to the end. We say "This is the right road" or "This is the wrong road," "This is the right thing to do" or "This is the wrong thing to do." In this sense right and wrong are synonymous with good and bad.

Hence, "right" in this primary sense may refer to actions regarding myself inasmuch as it is right to be moderate in eating, drinking and sex relations, or to be courageous in enduring hardships or essaying great ventures. Or it may refer to actions regarding others insofar as it is right to respect what is theirs. Such right actions regarding others are also *justa,* just actions.

B. *Right as Claim*

The word "right" is also used with another meaning in the phrase "I have a right." In this context right means a claim. Frequently it implies a legal right. ". . . [A] right is a claim for the enforcement, redress, or protection of which the jurisdiction of a court may be properly invoked." [32]

1. *As reasonable expectation.* It is in this sense that right has been described as a reasonable expectation. "By further develop-

[31] Legal relations have been called the units of legal reasoning. They have been said to be to the lawyer what atoms are to the chemist. "In many, and perhaps most legal problems that arise in practical life, the legal relations to be dealt with are already so obvious that the intellectual operation is concerned chiefly with an application of legal rules rather than the interplay of legal relations. . . . Many legal problems cannot be conveniently, and at the same time accurately, treated without a clear recognition of the juristic elements that enter into them." Kocourek, Jural Relations 77 (1927).

[32] State v. Grosnickle, 189 Wis. 17, 206 N.W. 895, 896 (1926).

ment [from the idea of justice] we get the idea of the maintenance or administration of that which is just, and hence, the regime of rendering to everyone his due or his rights, or as I prefer
to say, his reasonable expectations." [33] Such an interpretation of
right keeps it, so to speak, facing in the proper direction. My
claim should look toward *others* who are expected to do what is
just. I have a claim on them to do so.

2. *As title or interest.* Right has been used as synonymous
with title. "The ordinary significance of claim, is that of right or
title." [34] In this same sense right has also been defined as an
interest. "A right is an interest recognized and protected by a
rule of right. It is any interest, respect for which is a duty, and
the disregard of which is a wrong." [35] Emphasis here is obviously on the relation of title between a thing and me. This view
of right makes my claim as claim point toward the thing to which
I have a title, and not toward others who should respect my title.

3. *Right in rem and in personam.* Another equivocal use of
the word "right" is in the phrases "right in rem" and "right in
personam." A "right in rem" is explained as a "real" right
"availing against the whole world." A owns a farm and therefore
has a right against B, C, D, etc., that they shall not trespass. But
in spite of its description in terms of the object (in rem), it is
actually a claim on persons. For it is a claim on *all* other persons
that they should not trespass on this farm. Such was my claim
based on occupancy of the sea shell described above.

A "right in personam" is usually described as a "personal"
right "availing against a definite individual." A holds B's promissory note for $1,000 and therefore has a right to the money. In
truth, this right is a claim that A has on B to perform his duty regarding the title A originally had to the money loaned. Such a
right is a claim on a *certain* person or persons, regarding some
object, based on contract.

In law, then, "right" usually has the meaning of an enforceable
claim based on title to life, liberty and property. The correlative
of my claim is others' duty to respect it.

4. *Privilege.* Still more confusion is experienced when the
word "right" is examined in some of its other uses. The lumping
together of the words rights, property, privileges, immunities,
and powers is common. Courts speak of ". . . the sole and abso-

[33] Pound, Justice According to Law 3 (1951). By permission of the Yale
University Press.

[34] Lawrence v. Miller, 2 N.Y. 245, 254 (1849).

[35] Salmond, Jurisprudence 229 (10th ed. 1947).

lute possession and enjoyment of all . . . rights, privileges, franchises, powers, immunities, improvements and property" [36] and of ". . . property, franchises, immunities, rights, powers and privileges connected therewith or in respect thereto." [37] Upon examination it becomes evident that privilege is reducible to claim, immunity to power, and property to the relation of title.

Privilege, however, has the character of a special claim. "The term 'privilege' is defined . . . as 'a peculiar benefit, favor or advantage.' 'A right not enjoyed by all; a special right or power conferred or possessed by one or more individuals.'" [38] It is in terms of privilege that franchises are described. The granting of a franchise to operate a water system in public streets,[39] or to exist and engage in the business of operating a street railway within a city,[40] results in a privilege. Since this "conferred title" is factually the basis for a peculiar claim on others to be allowed to engage in certain activities, a privilege is best defined as a special claim.

An easement is a privilege. "An easement is a liberty, privilege, or advantage in land without profit, existing distinct from the ownership of the soil." [41] Privilege is a matter of claim-duty relationship, for among the essential qualities of easements is that ". . . there must be two distinct tenements, the dominant, to which the right belongs, and the servient, upon which the obligation rests." [42] The notion of a special claim is also present in easement inasmuch as the use of the land of another is ". . . for a special purpose not inconsistent with the general property of the owner." [43]

The special claim which is privilege is not a property claim. "A license to operate an automobile upon the highways of the

[36] Joy v. St. Louis, 138 U.S. 1, 9, 11 Sup. Ct. 243, 245 (1890).
[37] Indiana Harbor Belt R. Co. v. Green, 289 Ill. 81, 124 N.E. 298, 300 (1919).
[38] Coke v. Flanery, 70 Cal. App. 738, 234 Pac. 845, 849 (1925).
[39] Waterloo Water Co. v. Village of Waterloo, 200 App. Div. 718, 193 N.Y. Supp. 360, 362 (1922).
[40] Lord v. Equitable Life Assur. Soc. of U.S., 194 N.Y. 212, 87 N.E. 443, 447 (1909).
[41] Harrison v. Boring, 44 Tex. 255, 267 (1875).
[42] Id. at 267.
[43] Holloman v. Board of Education of Stewart County, 168 Ga. 359, 147 S.E. 882, 884 (1929). See also Frye v. Sebitt, 145 Neb. 600, 17 N.W.2d 617, 621 (1945). Frequently self-defense and voting are referred to as "privileges." Self-defense refers rather to the ordinary claim that a man has to life and the means of preserving it. Voting would seem to pertain to the citizen's natural authority or claim to direct himself — part of which he delegates to those he chooses to direct him. For further development of this point, see Chapter 19.

commonwealth is a privilege and not a property right, and the power of the Secretary of Revenue to suspend or revoke such operating privileges is an administrative and not a judicial function." [44]

A privilege, then, is a special claim I have on others to be allowed to engage in some definite activity and is usually based on a title acquired or granted. The privilege of driving a car or maintaining a water system in public streets derives from a contract between government and certain citizens by which the government obliges itself to honor its agreement to allow these citizens to carry on these pursuits subject to specified conditions. To have a "right" to drive my car implies, then, that because of this concession I can lay claim on others' duty, including those in government, to allow me to drive. These others have a duty toward me that they do not have toward all other citizens. I am privileged. The correlative of my privilege is others' duty to respect it.

5. *Immunity.* Immunity is frequently spoken of as a "right" which is synonymous with privilege. "The word 'privilege' in common acceptation, means some immunity or advantage . . . The words 'privilege' and 'immunities' are synonymous or nearly so." [45]

But even though immunity may appear at first glance the same as privilege, nevertheless it is not the same. Privilege, as we have seen, is reducible to a special claim. Immunity, on the other hand, relates to a particular exemption from a duty — which is the correlative of claim. Immunity is the exempt condition of A who cannot be put under duty by B, as can C, D, E, etc., because B does not have the basis or title for doing so. I, who am a citizen of New York, have no land, goods or business in California. I am immune from being taxed by the State of California. The State of California, having no grounds or title on which to base a claim on me, as it has on its citizens, cannot change jural relations between me and itself. Consequently, I am not liable and am exempt. For this reason, ". . . the term 'immunity' is an apt one to describe an exemption from taxation." [46] A more particu-

[44] Commonwealth v. Cronin, 336 Pa. 469, 9 A.2d 408, 410 (1939).

[45] Sacramento Orphanage and Childrens' Home v. Chambers, 25 Cal. App. 536, 144 Pac. 317, 319 (1914). See also State v. Griffin, 226 Ind. 279, 79 N.E.2d 537 (1948).

[46] Buchanan v. Knoxville & O.R. Co., 71 Fed. 324, 334 (6th Cir. 1895). It is especially in regard to the nature of privilege and immunity that differences of opinion show themselves. Kocourek correctly criticizes Hohfeld

lar type of tax immunity is enjoyed by certain organizations —
such as schools, churches or hospitals — that render public service
and are therefore exempt from taxes.

The status of citizens regarding self-incrimination is frequently
said to be one of privilege. "Originally, all persons might be required to appear in court and there compelled to answer under
their oaths in the manner and form provided by law as to any
matter about which the court sought to inquire. This was a duty
which the citizen owed to the state, and one which he might by
appropriate legal process be compelled to perform. With the
development of the doctrine that one should not be compelled to
incriminate himself, a witness was released from the performance
of this duty to that extent. This situation is described as privilege from self-incrimination." [47]

But if the matter of self-incrimination pertains to exemption
from the duty to testify, instead of speaking of it as a privilege it
seems more accurate to describe it as an immunity from self-
incrimination. The same would also seem to be true of the so-
called "privileged" statements or communications of witnesses in
court. They are rather exemptions from the general duty to
testify.

To have a "right" then, say not to be drafted, is to be in a
condition of immunity from military service. Immunity is exemption from being under an obligation or being put under it by
a change in jural relations. The correlative of my immunity is
sometimes said to be others' disability to put me under obligation.
But, strictly speaking, my immunity connotes the absence of an
actual correlative — others' ability to put me under obligation according to existing or changed jural relations.

---

for reducing privilege to freedom, saying that freedom has no correlative.
This is correct because freedom itself is not the term of a jural relation. If it
were, it would have a correlative. But, "ex nihilo, nihil fit." Freedom, in
the legal sense, is the general condition of anyone who is under no obligation.

Kocourek himself holds that privilege is a "capacity to refuse" and that its
correlative is inability. But a man has a capacity to refuse to act (as in the
matter of self-incrimination) only because he is not under an obligation to
act. Hence, what Kocourek refers to as a privilege — that is, the capacity
to refuse — is rather an immunity from obligation. In our analysis privilege has been identified as a special claim. This recognition of privilege as
a granted or acquired claim is closer to Terry's "permissive right" ("easement is a permissive right"). See Terry, Leading Principles of Anglo-American Law, *passim* (1884). See also on this matter Hohfeld, Fundamental Legal
Conceptions, *passim* (1913); Kocourek, Jural Relations, *passim* (1927); and
the materials reprinted in Hall, Readings in Jurisprudence 457-531 (1938).

[47] State v. Grosnickle, 189 Wis. 17, 206 N.W. 895, 896 (1926).

C. *Right as Power*

Right is also spoken of as a power. Power can be understood as either physical power or as moral power.

1. *Physical power.* Physical power is the same as might. It is synonymous with strength and force. The use of the word "right" in this sense of force is one of the most disastrous equivocations that has ever entered law and government. For if right is force, then the larger and stronger have "rights," while the weaker minorities have no "right." This is the opposite pole from the democratic ideal that all men should be free because they have certain "inalienable rights."

2. *Moral power.* Moral power, on the other hand, refers to the powers of intellect and will and the ability to make free decisions. Used in this connotation, to "have a right," say to accept or reject your offer of contractual terms, means I have the faculty of freely deciding to enter into promissory agreement with you and thereby changing jural relations between us. My decision to pick up the unpossessed sea shell mentioned above was an exercise of this moral power. It created new jural relations between myself and the other men on the island regarding what was to become "my" sea shell, which entitled me to use it as I saw fit.

In a word, right as power means the moral faculty I have of deciding to change jural relations. The correlative of my power has been said to be others' liability to be put under obligation by me. More precisely, there is no factual correlative of my power. There is only the possibility of a claim-duty jural relationship being created by my exercise of it.

This meaning of right is sometimes used in reference to authority. Thus a judge has the right, that is, the power, of deciding one way or another according to his convictions based on law. He has the power of creating new legal relations between citizens. This in turn is based on still another right, the claim to direct others.[48] It is because of this claim that he may exercise his power of decision. Still different is the question of whether his use of this power is right in the sense of correct, good or just. These differences have a practical value in legal thinking. ". . . [T]he 'power' to render a particular judgment means that the judgment must be in accordance with law. . . . Power is synonymous with authority or right; and it may be argued that the 'right' to give a particular judgment depends upon the law,

[48] See Chapter 19.

and that, if it is not in accordance with law, it is necessarily unlawful, and, being unlawful, it is void." [49]

3. *Relation to "will" theories.* The reasons why right or *ius* became confused with moral power are undoubtedly related to the influence of "will" theories on legal thinking. For those who saw in man's will the prime power, the tendency was logically to view the entire legal order in relation to this faculty. Law was defined as an act of the legislator's will by which he intended to oblige subjects.[50] Obligation was the necessity of doing what the lawmaker wished.[51] And right was defined as the power of the will of doing or possessing something.[52]

Impetus was undoubtedly given to restatements of this position by voluntarists faced with positivism's theory of right. The advocates of materialism proclaimed that right consisted merely in material fact, that is, in physical force or might. As a counteraction to this, the proponents of "will" theories insisted that right was a moral force, a spiritual power of the will.[53]

Regardless of the reasons why right came to be understood as a moral power, the result of such an interpretation has been to give to right an orientation toward objects rather than toward the duty of others regarding my relation to an object. "Right [ius] is accustomed to be called properly a certain moral faculty which each one has regarding what is his or what is due to him." [54] This idea has been predominant in certain currents of the so-called "scholastic" tradition. "To this moral power we give the name of right, which, therefore, we define as the 'moral power (facultas) of doing or possessing something.' " [55] As a result right becomes directly related to objects. Right [ius] is said to be correctly defined as "potestas moralis in rem suam," that is, a person's moral power over what is his.[56]

4. *Comment.* Various attempts have been made to assess the different meanings of right and to determine which of them represent true jural relations. Tables of jural "correlatives" and "opposites" are common.[57] But — suffice it here to say — according to the analysis of right and just made above and presupposing

---

[49] State v. District Court of Eighth Judicial District in and for Natrona County, 33 Wyo. 281, 238 Pac. 545, 548 (1925).

[50] See Chapter 1.

[51] See Chapter 6.

[52] 2 Cronin, The Science of Ethics 661 (1939).

[53] Lachance, Le Concept de Droit selon Aristote et S. Thomas 295 (1948).

[54] Suárez, 1 De Legibus 2, 4 (Coletus ed. 1740).

[55] 2 Cronin, The Science of Ethics 661 (1939).

[56] Cathrein, Philosophia Moralis 208 (1915) (my trans.).

[57] See Hall, Readings in Jurisprudence 527 (1938).

title of some kind in the claimant, claim-duty is the only basic
jural relation. Privilege is a special aspect of this relation. Immunity is the condition of a person who is not or cannot be made
a party to this relation regarding a certain matter. Power of
decision is a prerequisite condition for the creation of this jural
relation. In a word, regarding the claim-duty relation: privilege
is a special kind, immunity implies its absence and power connotes its possibility.

D.   *Right as Law*

Another use of the word "right" is to denote law itself. This is
not prevalent in England and the United States as it is in other
countries. In many languages the word for "right" also means
law in general. In Latin there is *ius* and *lex;* in French *droit*
and *loi;* in German *Recht* and *Gesetz;* in Italian *diritto* and
legge; and in Spanish *derecho* and *ley.*

The reason for this confusion seems to lie in the word "ius."
For, *ius* can be taken in the objective sense of law and the subjective sense of claim which is based on law. "The different
meanings of the word *ius* had of course long been familiar to the
lawyers who had been brought up in the study of the Roman law.
They had carefully distinguished between 'objective' and 'subjective right,' between the *norma agendi* (the rule of action)
and the *facultas agendi* (the right to act) which can both be indicated by the same name of *ius,* and which are indicated in English
by the different names of law and of right. But they had never
overlooked the fact, which [some seem] either to ignore or implicitly to deny, that the two meanings of *ius* are not antithetic,
but correlative. In the language of the law-schools, *ius* could be
used in an 'objective' as well as in a 'subjective' sense; but the
latter always presupposes the former. There is a *facultas agendi*
inasmuch as there is a *norma agendi.* There is a 'right' inasmuch
as there is a law." [58]

Perhaps it has been the struggle for liberty over the past several
hundred years that is in part accountable for the failure to give
equal emphasis to both *ius* and *lex.* For this effort was preoccupied with winning freedom for the exercise of the "rights of
men." There was not as much concern for the "obligations of
men" which bespoke law and authority. Declarations of Human

[58] D'Entrèves, Natural Law 59-60 (1951). By permission of the Hutchinson
University Library Press.

Rights are now a commonplace. Eventually these will have to be counterbalanced by Declarations of Human Obligations.

E. *Need of Functional Terms*

In view of the ambiguity of the word "right," the employment of more functional terms is indicated and has long since been recognized. While it would be unrealistic to expect the use of the word "right" to be discontinued altogether, nevertheless the discerning use as much as possible of more accurate words in its place will be helpful.

In its root meaning of direct, correct or good, the meaning of right is well stated in legal matters by *"just,"* "what is just," or "justice." The full implication of the phrase "to have a right" is better conveyed by *claim*. It more obviously connotes a correlation with others' duty to be just. Privilege and immunity are better expressed in terms of special claim and exemption from duty respectively. Rather than use "right" at all to denote any type of power, it is better to call a power what it actually is, a *power*. Factually it is either material *force* or the spiritual capacity for *free decision*.

The misuse of the word "right" can be carried to ridiculous lengths. "Blackstone actually opposes 'rights' in the sense of capacities, to 'wrongs' in the sense of 'unrighteous acts.' . . . The absurdity is carried a step further by people who write to the newspapers about 'copy-rights and copy-wrongs.' " [59]

The cause of clarity would be better served if the claim aspect of right was kept prominent in contradistinction but in correlation to the duty side of law. For I have a claim on others to act justly toward me and respect my relation of title to some particular thing, because they are already obliged by law to do what is just and should be disposed by the habit of justice to act so.

IV. Determining What Is Just

A constant problem confronting lawmakers is how to determine what is just in particular statutes or decisions. Any solution of this problem must take into account the necessity of non-legal directives and the fact that the directive judgment which is law is one of prudence and not one of science.

[59] Holland, Elements of Jurisprudence 83 (11th ed. 1910).

A. *Necessity of Non-legal Directives*

Into the content of law go many knowledges or sciences that serve as background helps. History and especially the history of law is such. A cursory examination of the content of law discloses many others.

1. *Sciences.* Prominent among these helps are anthropology, economics, engineering, sociology, social psychology, and the physical sciences. Some of these are more exact and reliable than others. A statute based on the evidence of hematology regarding the value of blood tests in paternity cases is likely to be on a more solid basis than one based on the predictions of social psychology regarding integration.

2. *Morals.* But more prominent among these background helps are the extralegal knowledges of right and wrong that precede lawmaking and are presupposed or reasoned to by lawmakers. Legislators and judges themselves must be guided by valid non-legal directives that are for the people's good regardless of their source. The directives that are either known connaturally from the experienced demands of a man's basic drives or are the result of reasoning therefrom are the content of ethics or moral philosophy. Ethics or morals is the science of the goodness and badness, rightness or wrongness of human actions. These actions regard either moderation, courage or justice in human actions. The broad principles of justice are part of the background of law as well as the principles of other sciences. Lawmakers, however, have to proceed further than general principles and decide about specific details and the imposition of penalties. Morals and law are at odds only if law prescribes or allows something that morals from its point of view considers wrong and unjust.

Ethics concludes that the corruption of the morals of children is wrong and unjust. No statute is needed to establish the truth of this proposition. The problem confronting any given group of lawmakers is, taking this premise as valid, to decide when such a situation is on hand at a definite time and place, and to adopt whatever measures are necessary to curb it. A defendant who invited minors to his home, served them liquor and then invited them to have sex relations with him was found to have contributed to the corruption of the morals of children. This as well as all other principles of morality must have a place in law.

As the court said, "It should be remembered that we are not here dealing with a moral concept about which our people widely differ; corrupting the morals of children is condemned through-out our land. According to common understanding, the term 'morals' must be taken to refer to the moral standards of the com-munity, the 'norm or standard of behavior which struggles to make itself articulate in law.' . . . 'Sound morals as taught by the wise men of antiquity, as confirmed by the precepts of the gospel . . . are unchangeable. They are the same yesterday and today.' We see no reason to retreat from those ideas. 'We are a religious people whose institutions presuppose a Supreme Being.' . . . Our Federal and State Constitutions assume that the moral code which is part of God's order in this world, exists as the substance of society. The people of this State have acted through their legislature on that assumption. We have not so cast ourselves adrift from that code nor are we so far gone in cynicism that the word 'immoral' has no meaning for us. Our duty, as a court, is to uphold and enforce the laws, not seek reasons for destroying them." [60]

There are also directives that are either known through faith in a higher source or are the result of reasoning from them. These are revelation and moral theology. Long since have law-makers recognized in them a certain and sure groundwork for any legal structure. ". . . [I]t is said that the illustrious King Alfred adopted the Ten Commandments as the foundation of the early laws of England, contained in his Doom Book. These command-ments, which like a collection of diamonds, bear testimony to their own intrinsic worth, in themselves appeal to us as coming from a superhuman or divine source, and no conscientious or rea-sonable man has yet been able to find a flaw in them. Absolutely flawless, negative in terms, and positive in meaning, they easily stand at the head of our whole moral system, and no nation or people can long continue a happy existence in open violation of them." [61] Sometimes certainty on some matters can be had only from higher directives.

It is in the content of law that the unavoidability of morals is experienced. What should be the content of statutes and deci-sions regarding flag saluting, blood transfusions, medication, sur-

[60] Commonwealth v. Randall, 183 Pa. Super. 603, 133 A.2d 276, 279 (1957), *cert. denied sub nom.* Randall v. Commonwealth, 355 U.S. 954, 78 Sup. Ct. 539 (1958).
[61] Moore v. Strickling, 46 W. Va. 515, 33 S.E. 274, 277 (1899). Upon those who reject the necessity for law of non-legal directives is the inevitable bur-den of supplying other norms. For such an attempt see Cahn, The Moral Decision (1955), and the critical review of it by Witherspoon, 1 Natural Law Forum 146-164 (1956).

gery, adultery, divorce, artificial insemination, contraception, abortion, euthanasia, Sunday closing of stores, obscenity, censorship, and the like? What is "just" in these cases? Deliberations on these questions by lawmakers are certain to manifest the necessity of facing up to the moral convictions of citizens, reasoned or believed, which must be taken into account by lawmakers when they are considering the content of law.

Anything like a complete understanding of the content of law can come only from an examination of its relation to non-legal presuppositions and directives. These are the benchmarks in relation to which the content of law must be surveyed. This is a field that lies beyond the scope of an introductory book such as this. For, to be satisfactory, such an examination would have to range at least over the principal areas of human activities controlled by law and uncover in pertinent parts of the content the incidence of morals. Whatever attempts are made in this regard, however, cannot but show the necessary relation of the content of law to these non-legal directives.

3. *Disturbing alternative.* The alternative to a content of law which reflects moral directives is one that recognizes no moral standards at all. This would be a ghastly situation directly in conflict with the common good of all the people. But at this juncture a question demands to be raised: is not the legal system of the United States of America which officially recognizes no particular code of morals, philosophical or theological, committed to such an amoral content of law? Why, among other numerous examples, should the law enforce store closing on Sundays if it acknowledges no particular religious belief? The law of some other countries recognizes the moral codes of certain religious persuasions: in Great Britain, the Anglican Church; in Italy, the Catholic Church; in Sweden, the Lutheran Church.

The dilemma which must ultimately be faced seems to be this: if non-legal moral directives are necessary in law and the legal system of the United States does not recognize any, then either this legal system is fated in the future to work great harm against morals by its inability to take a needed legal stand on key subjects, or moral principles will have to be brought into law as they have been in this country during the past two centuries, that is, by individual legislators and judges incorporating them into the content of law as their own personal convictions. In effect, this means that the moral principles which the majority of legislators and judges hold will be the principles that will be the active ferment in the content of law.

4. *Comment.* Anxiety over the incursion of morals into law seems to be one of the main inspirations of "legal positivism." In this theory there is only one law: positive, man-made law. It takes guidance from no other "law." Separation of law and morals is its chief concern. "What is" in positive law is not subject to any rectification by "what ought to be" according to any other norm. "What is" and "what ought to be" are coincidental in this theory. This is the position of Bentham, Austin, Gray, Holmes, Kelsen, Hart and many others.[62] Its preoccupation with the ambiguity of words in relation to facts has much in common with logical positivism.[63] Logical positivism maintains that "metaphysical problems" arise solely from the inadequacies or misuse of language. Hence such problems are to be solved either by the formulation of an ideally perfect language or by the elucidation of the uses of ordinary language.

Legal positivism is open to the objection that law necessarily assumes points of departure that relate to morals. The inevitable incidence of the relation of means to end is one of these. On this score, therefore, much of legal positivism's energy (though by no means all of it) seems to be misspent on quixotic tilting at semantic windmills. But, although it is bootless to struggle against the presence in law of morals in general, there is a vital and meaningful stand that can be taken regarding the presence of this or that code of morals in particular. It is on this terrain, rocky though it be, that an actual adversary can be met and perhaps profitably engaged. For it is here that the guiding principles of citizens' individual lives are encountered, regarding which law cannot be oblivious if it is to fulfill its purpose of working for the common good of these same citizens.[64]

[62] For a discussion of legal positivism, see H. L. A. Hart, Positivism and the Separation of Law and Morals, 71 Harv. L. Rev. 593-629 (1958); Fuller, Positivism and Fidelity to Law, id. at 630-672. Regarding the relation of is and ought, fact and value, required reading as a point of departure for any discussion is Aquinas' analysis in terms of complete and incomplete being. 1-2 Sum. Theol. 18, 1.

[63] See Auerbach, On Professor H. L. A. Hart's Definition and Theory in Jurisprudence, 9 J. Legal Ed. 39-51; Ayer and others, The Revolution in Philosophy (1956); and Joad, A Critique of Logical Positivism (1950).

[64] For an analysis of the possibility that analytical positivism, as well as legal realism have reached an impass inasmuch as they have failed to recognize the non-positive sources of law, see Bodenheimer, Analytical Positivism, Legal Realism, and the Future of Legal Method, 44 Va. L. Rev. 365-378 (1958).

B. *Prudential Judgments*

The problem of deciding what is just in man-made law arises when universal judgments are applied in particular instances. It is exact and certain that murder and robbery are unjust. But whether what occurred in this individual case is actually murder or robbery and, if it is, how it should be punished, is not so readily decided. In the particular instance, it is the contingent and variable facts of everyday living that have to be considered, not necessary and immutable principles. Hence, in the determination of what is just, scientific exactness cannot always be looked for. At times only an approximation to complete justice can be expected.[65]

1. *Variables in human living.* The judgment of what is just in every detail, then, cannot always be an exact science such as mathematics is. "Moral matter is such that perfect certitude is not consonant with it. . . . For there cannot be such certitude in variable and contingent matter as in necessary matter which is always the same. . . . Mathematics is about matter in which is found complete certitude. . . . [Morals] is occupied with civil matter in which multiple variation takes place." [66]

Only those who naïvely think that all things, even human activities, can be reduced to scientific formulas will crusade for a scientific determination of what is just to the last detail in all possible instances. "Our discussion will be adequate if it has as much clearness as the subject-matter admits of, for precision is not to be sought for alike in all discussions, any more than in all the products of the crafts. Now fine and just actions, which political science investigates, admit of much variety and fluctuation of opinion, so that they may be thought to exist only by convention, and not by nature. And goods also give rise to a similar fluctua-

---

[65] Science is here taken as a habit of the mind according to which conclusions are drawn from premises by demonstration. Involved are the mental operations of conception, judgment and reasoning. "Science, mathematics and philosophy, in their strictest sense, are habitual ways or types of rational procedure, for it is only the perfection of acting correctly that brings ease and speed, accuracy and consistency into reasoning and investigation. In its fullest or widest sense, 'science,' in addition to its direct denotation (demonstrative habit), primarily implies an organized and interrelated body of conclusions . . . and secondarily, under our present conditions, implies the symbolic representations of the principles, reasonings, and conclusions in printed or otherwise recorded forms." Klubertanz, The Philosophy of Human Nature 283 (1953). See also id. at 173 regarding conception, judgment and reasoning.

[66] Aquinas, 1 In Ethicorum Aristotelis 3 (Pirotta ed. 1934).

tion because they bring harm to many people; for before now men have been undone by reason of their wealth, and others by reason of their courage. We must be content, then, in speaking of such subjects and with such premises to indicate the truth roughly and in outline, and in speaking about things which are only for the most part true and with premises of the same kind to reach conclusions that are no better. In the same spirit, therefore, should each type of statement be received; for it is the mark of an educated man to look for precision in each class of things just so far as the nature of the subject admits; it is evidently equally foolish to accept probable reasoning from a mathematician and to demand from a rhetorician scientific proofs.

"Now each man judges well the things he knows, and of these he is a good judge. And so the man who has been educated in a subject is a good judge of that subject, and the man who has received an all-round education is a good judge in general." [67]

2. *Approximations of what is just.* In many cases only a determination of what is just within a margin, a range or a band can be expected. Whether second degree murder should be punished by imprisonment for exactly 5 years, 12 years or 7.4 years, whether the percentage of tax on certain incomes should be 10 per cent, 20 per cent or 14.7 per cent, whether the amount of time a couple should be made to wait after applying for a marriage license before they are allowed to marry should be 3 days, 3 months, or 3 weeks, cannot be scientifically determined.

Besides, no one has been given divine insight into the precise solution of these problems. All that lawmakers can do in many instances is use their power of reasoning deductively, supplement this by the inductive reasoning of research, experiment and testing, and make as close an approximation to what is just as is within their capacities. Five years is too little for second degree murder, 20 years too much; 7 per cent tax is insufficient, 25 per cent unnecessary; to require no waiting time before marriage has proved unwise, to require a wait of months is impractical. Striking the just mean between these extremes will at best be an approximation. The content of man-made law, therefore, will represent justice with a greater or lesser degree of exactness, as is true of some of law's ancillary sciences.

3. *Law is prudence — Not science.* Regardless of the status of these background sciences, lawmaking itself is not a science. It is prudence. Prudence is the habit of mind according to which a

[67] Aristotle, 1 Nicomachean Ethics 3, 1094b12-1095a2 (Ross trans. 1941).

man directs himself to act rightly regarding means to end.   Its three steps of deliberation, evaluation and decision to act entail the application of knowledge to action.   A judge has before him the facts of the case.   Many of them are perhaps of a scientific nature.   Others are not necessarily the actual facts at all, they are what counsel for the plaintiff thought could be proved or defense counsel thought it necessary to admit.   Many times the fact that there is only one defendant does not mean that he acted only by himself.   It only means he was the only person who could be proved to have acted.   The court, however, must judge which facts are material and which are immaterial.   On this, will rest his ratio decidendi.   This judgment is not one of science.   It is one of prudence.   It is the judgment by which theoretical knowledge is applied to practical action.   Such is the directive judgment that is law.[68]

There can, however, be a science about what law is.   There can be a factual study of the elements of law, its operations, and its underlying principles.   These can be subjected to philosophical examination.   Such is the attempt made in this book and such is jurisprudence in the sense of the philosophy of law.   In other words, there can be a science about prudence and a scientific treatise can be written on the subject, although prudence itself is not science.

The best assurance, then, that justice will pervade the content of law lies not only in lawmen knowing the law but in their being convinced of the value of non-legal directives and in being trained in the processes of deliberation, evaluation and decision.   The problem of determining what is just in law is not to be solved by the use of scientific formulas.   It is to be solved only by using the directives available — scientific and non-scientific, legal and non-legal — and making the best possible prudential judgment.   The variables of human living will not be reduced to the constants of nature.[69]

V. Justice and Love

One of the most important aspects of the political common good is peace.   But peace cannot be brought about by the content of law and justice alone.   Something more than justice is needed.

[68] "The discernment [of the materiality or immateriality of facts] must be left to the prudence of the judge."   Aquinas, 2-2 Sum. Theol. 70, 2, 2.   For a further discussion of law as prudence see Chapter 19.

[69] For further discussion of this problem, see Chapter 19.

This is love. Justice removes the main obstacle to peace: in-justice. Only when this barrier is eliminated can love bring about that union of persons which results in peace. "Peace is the work of justice indirectly inasfar as justice removes the obstacles to peace. But peace is the work of love directly because love of its very nature causes peace. For love is a 'unitive force' . . . [and] peace is the union of appetitive inclinations." [70]

Justice causes actions toward other persons because of a *duty* to respect what is due them; love causes actions toward others sim-ply because of the *persons* themselves. "Love has no why." The content of law is necessarily limited to the realm of justice. Hence, when the content of law is described as "all things neces-sary for the public welfare," this must be understood as pertain-ing to all things within the area of justice which have a bearing on the public good. The rest is beyond human justice and the laws of men.

[70] Aquinas, 2-2 Sum. Theol. 29, 3, 3.

CHAPTER 4

Source of Man-made Law

The problem now is to determine whence comes the authority to make the decisions or directive judgments that are law, who has this authority, and whether the directive judgments of one group of lawmakers are primary in relation to those of another. Upon the solution of this problem depends the position to be taken concerning legislation's control of adjudication, adjudication's role in proceedings without legislation or even against it, and custom's effect on both legislation and adjudication.

I. THE MEN WHO MAKE THE LAW

The source of man-made law is the men who make the law. It is the men who, having lawmaking authority, issue directives for the common good. Hence, the source of law is either the representatives of the people or the people themselves. This is looking at law for what it is in itself, a directive judgment. Looked at as reflecting various factors that influence its content, there may be said to be other "sources." These will be seen later.

A. *Lawmaking Authority*

Since laws are directives and lawmaking implies the claim to issue these directives, this claim to direct is presupposed in lawmaking. It is termed authority, sovereignty, or "police power."

1. *Claim to govern from the people.* It is necessary, of course, that those in government be endowed with the authority to direct the people to their common good. This is why they are in government. "From the very design that induces a number of men to form a society which has its common interests, and which is to act in concert, it is necessary that there should be established a public authority to order and direct what is to be done by each in relation to the end of the association. This political authority is the sovereignty, and he and they who are invested with it are the sovereign. Sovereignty in government may then be defined to be that public authority which directs or orders what is to be done

by each member associated, in relation to the end of the association." [1]

The ultimate claim to govern, however, which is authority or sovereignty, remains with the people. "Sovereignty itself is, of course, not subject to law, for it is the author and source of law; but in our system, while sovereign powers are delegated to the agencies of government, sovereignty itself remains with the people, by whom and for whom all government exists and acts." [2]

"Police power" is but another name for the exercise of authority delegated to the government. It is ". . . the power vested in the legislature by the constitution, to make, ordain and establish all manner of wholesome and reasonable laws, statutes and ordinances, either with penalties or without, not repugnant to the constitution, as they shall judge to be for the good and welfare of the commonwealth, and of the subjects of the same." [3]

The phrase "police power" is not a happy one if law is primarily direction and not enforcement. For the phrase implies an idea of law that makes power-sanctions its essence. The directive, means-end aspect of "police power" must be kept in mind if the phrase is to be understood in an acceptable democratic sense.[4]

2. *Divisions of governmental authority.* Governmental authority is divided into the three well-known divisions of legislative, judicial and executive. "Free government consists of three departments, each with distinct and independent powers, designed to operate as a check upon those of the other two co-ordinate branches. The legislative department makes the laws, while the executive executes, and the judiciary construes and applies them. Each department is confined to its own functions, and can neither encroach upon nor be made subordinate to those of another without violating the fundamental principle of a republican form of government." [5]

[1] Cherokee Nation v. Southern Kansas R. Co., 33 Fed. 900, 906 (C.C.W.D. Ark. 1888).

[2] Yick Wo v. Hopkins, 118 U.S. 356, 370, 6 Sup. Ct. 1064, 1071 (1886). When the people are spoken of as being the source of authority, it should be noted that they are such relatively, that is, in relation to the political government to which they delegate authority. On the ultimate source of all authority, see Chapter 19.

[3] Commonwealth v. Alger, 7 Cush. 53, 85 (Mass. 1851). See also Parkes v. Bartlett, 236 Mich. 460, 210 N.W. 492, 494 (1926); Smith v. Higenbothom, 187 Md. 115, 48 A.2d 754, 761 (1946); Wheeler v. Board of Trustees, 200 Ga. 323, 37 S.E.2d 322, 329 (1946).

[4] The test of constitutionality of the "police power" is precisely in terms of the means-end relationship. See Nebbia v. New York, 291 U.S. 502, 532, 54 Sup. Ct. 505, 514 (1933).

[5] In re Davies, 168 N.Y. 89, 61 N.E. 118, 121 (1901). See also State ex rel. Jameson v. Denny, 118 Ind. 382, 21 N.E. 252, 254 (1889).

The legislative, judicial and executive branches of government all have a part in the exercise of governmental authority which derives ultimately from the people. And although these branches are distinguished in terms of the origin, construction and execution of laws, nevertheless they all in their own way participate in making law. Legislators, judges, executives and the people themselves are all to be considered as the source of law.

3. *Historical development.* As for the way law actually grew, the process was from custom to judicial decision to statutes. Custom was the manner in which the members of a society first made law — the unwritten law. The members themselves, guided by the elementary directives of their own nature, judged the best ways of acting. This continued way of acting was a source of law.

Adjudication or the settling of disputes by an adjudicator also was a source of law. Conflicts among members of a society needed settling. Their leaders were the logical men to sit in judgment and determine what was just. Hence, adjudicators guided by custom and their own sense of justice were a source of directives that were law.

Finally legislation was a source of law. Only after societies had developed somewhat politically did legislation assume prominence. The presence of legislative enactments of whatever kind in a society is a sign of some political maturity. The content of early statutes consisted to a great extent of what had already been established by custom.[6]

It should be noted that there is no reason why the office of legislator and of judge could not be centered in one and the same man — the chief, the headman, the ruler, the king. As societies grew politically, however, it became evident that legislators, judges and executives should be different men. If the president of a political union is considered the "head" today, it is only in the capacity of executive and not of legislator or judge. Considered in the order of their importance today, the sources of law are legislators, judges and the people's customs and in exceptional instances the executive.

B. *Legislators*

The persons in lawmaking bodies such as municipal councils, state legislatures, the United States Congress, the English Parlia-

6 On the historical development of law, see Allen, Law in the Making (1951).

ment or the Diet of Japan are the source of legislation. Their enactments are law.

1. *Extent of legislation.* The lawmaking authority of legislators is necessarily broad. "This power covers a very wide scope. Indeed, except where it is limited by the provisions of the State and Federal Constitutions, that power is practically and essentially unlimited. In the legislature rests the power to apply the police power of the State, and every other power which confers governmental authority not directly, or by necessary constitutional implication, vested in the executive or judicial departments of the State." [7]

The extent of legislation is limited only by the range of the common good. What the content of law will be is determined by the overall principle of the common good as already mentioned. There are, however, certain general aspects of the extent of legislation that deserve to be noted here.

a. *Not every good or evil.* Legislation is limited to what is necessary for the common good, but it cannot concern itself with every possible need and every possible good. It will have to limit itself to the promotion of those goods that are necessary for the public welfare. The fulfillment of private needs must be left to the initiative and dispositions of individual citizens. For instance, for all citizens to have a college education may be a good, but it is hardly necessary for the public well-being at the present time. Hence, it is not now proper matter for legislation.

Similarly, legislation should not attempt to inhibit every possible evil. It must restrict itself to those evils whose restraint is necessary for the public good and from which it is possible for citizens by and large to abstain. To forbid citizens to overeat would not be content for a statute.[8]

b. *All citizens.* Another aspect of the extent of legislation regards the citizens themselves. Does legislation extend to all citizens or are some excepted? Are those in government obliged by their own laws?

It is the purpose, the spirit, of legislation to bring about conditions helpful to all. Hence, all should contribute to this effort — including those in government. Those only are excepted whose adherence to the *letter* of the statute or ordinance would work against the public welfare. Thus, firemen, policemen, ambulance

[7] State v. Huber, 129 W. Va. 198, 40 S.E.2d 11, 18 (1946).
[8] But see the "fat boy case," United States v. Shepherd, 9 U.S.C.M.A. 90, 25 C.M.R. 352 (1958).

drivers, and the like are exempted by legislation itself from observing traffic regulations in the performance of duty. In like manner some are exempted from paying taxes, from being drafted, and so forth.

In all such instances it is the spirit of the statute, to promote the public welfare, that must prevail even if it is against the letter. This finds recognition in the foreseeing and embodying of such exemptions in the legislation itself.

c. *Emergencies.* There is another area of activity in which citizens are exempt from observing the letter of legislation. These are emergency situations concerning which it is impossible for legislators to take full cognizance in legislation. An emergency situation is one that is of sudden, unexpected occurrence that demands immediate action.

Suppose a child is seriously burned in a fire at 2 A.M. and her father starts immediately to rush her to the hospital. The letter of the law demands that he drive no more than, say, 25 miles an hour. If he does not drive faster there is a great possibility that the child will die. The spirit of the ordinance is to promote the public good which is sharable by each individual citizen. But it is not intended to work against the citizen's own private good. In such an instance, the spirit of the law would permit him to go as fast as is prudent in view of his own need and the safety of himself and others, even though the letter forbids driving faster than 25 miles an hour.

Such an on the spot interpretation of legislation in emergency situations is an aspect of epikeia which in turn is related to equity. Its justification lies in the nature of legislation. Legislation has to be general and universal rather than specific and particular. If legislation attempted to cover all the possible details of its own interpretation and application, it would be too cumbersome ever to be written. These are ordinarily left for the more deliberate process of the courts. But in situations suddenly occurring, where delay would be injurious to the private good of the individual, immediate interpretation is necessary and justified.

Epikeia's kinship to equity is evidenced by the fact that both are judgments formed beyond the letter of the law but according to its *spirit* which is the promotion of the public welfare. But the judgments of equity are matter for a special court. Epikeia is not to be confused with "private interpretation" of law. Epikeia is a justifiable process made necessary by a sudden occurrence. "Private interpretation" is a usurpation of a function that belongs to the courts. A man may believe that a law is unjust. However, unless it is patently unjust according to generally recognized moral principles (as would be, for instance, genocide), his private interpretation as to its validity is an arrogation to himself of authority he does not possess as an individual citizen. He must await a declaration of its invalidity by some authoritative agency.

2. *Changes in legislation.* Changes in legislation may be brought about by legislators through the repeal of a statute previously enacted, the amendment of an existing statute, or the enactment of an entirely new one. Or changes may be made by the people themselves through referendum or plebiscite.

a. *Periodic changes.* Revision of legislation is necessary. As needs change, so also should legislation change which is designed to fulfill these needs. Instances are plentiful of outmoded statutes and ordinances. These range from regulations governing the erection of hitching posts to compulsory service in the community fire department. Today's needs for legislation run from the restriction of television sets in automobiles to controlling the sale of alcoholic beverages on airplanes.

Changes in legislation are also especially needed at regular intervals regarding punishment. This is shown by the outmoded example of "$30 fine or 30 days in jail." The alternative punishment in this sentence at one time expressed an equality. A day's labor was then valued at one dollar. But as the value of money decreased and the worth of a day's labor increased, the equality was lost. The result is injustice of varying degrees. This simple example only symbolizes the need of revised statutes regarding the imposition of fines.

Need for change in legislation is also present when newer methods and kinds of punishments have been recognized and made available. Statutes that stipulate punishments which are mainly retributive, when they should be imposing punishments which are also corrective, can only be classed as obsolete.

b. *Caution — Courage.* Care, however, must be exercised in changing legislation even though it be periodically necessary. Change should not take place precipitously and rashly, but carefully and only after due consideration. The reason for this is that the citizens form habits of observing laws as now constituted. These habits are desirable and good inasmuch as they promote the common welfare. But when new laws are enacted, old habits will have to be broken and new ones formed. This can result in serious confusion and, if the matter warrants it, danger to life.

Thus, if a statute forbidding automobiles to make a left turn on a green traffic light is repealed and they are allowed to make a left turn on such an indication, there is a great possibility of confusion on the part of drivers and pedestrians and consequent danger to both. Drivers and pedestrians had formed the habit of driving or walking with a green light without having to be on their guard against cars making a left turn. Now all will have to form a new habit and take into account this added threat to life and limb. In the meantime, between the breaking of the old habit and the forming of the new one there is sure to be confusion and perhaps disaster.

Legislators, then, who are contemplating changes should take all such possibilities into account and act with caution. On the other hand, if obvious injustice is being perpetrated, legislatures and courts must act with courage to stop it. Such would be the situation today regarding some invasions of privacy.[9]

Although the theory and fiction is that legislative authority — particularly that of Congress — cannot be delegated, nevertheless in practice and in reality it is delegated. This takes place inasmuch as administrative agencies of necessity fill in the gaps of preexisting legislation.[10] In this sense legislative authority is delegated.

Delegation of legislative authority may be necessary when conditions arise which make it a practical impossibility for legislative bodies themselves to deliberate on and enact directives in the detail required by the circumstances. Where it would be necessary, let us say, to pass laws regulating food prices, the working out of detailed provision could best be left to departments established for this purpose. An Office of Price Stabilization would be such a department.

The regulations and directives of such departments are law. They have this status because of the legislative authority delegated by the legislature when the departments are constituted. The same is true of the many "boards" now necessary in the complex economic and social conditions of modern living. While the personnel of departments and boards may be determined by executive appointment, the legislative authority they possess is delegated to them by the legislators themselves.

The question is sometimes raised whether an increasing number of statutes and agencies with delegated authority is good or bad. The answer depends on the reason for the increase. If it is neces-

[9] See Yoeckel v. Samonig, 272 Wis. 430, 75 N.W.2d 925 (1956); Recent Decisions, 41 Marq. L. Rev. 85 (1957); and Pollock, Judicial Caution and Valour, in Jurisprudence in Action 367-388 (1953).

[10] See Panama Refining Company v. Ryan, 293 U.S. 388, 421, 55 Sup. Ct. 241, 248 (1934).

sary on account of the manifold nature of society, it is good. On the other hand, if more laws are necessary because the citizens have lost the inspiration and ability to govern themselves as far as possible in all things not directly related to the public good, while it may be good immediately, it is ultimately bad. For it is a symptom that the body politic is becoming debilitated and that men are no longer strong enough to govern themselves in those areas wherein they must do so if their individual liberties are to be preserved.

Legislation, then, is the most importance source of law. It is, especially so as embodied in constitutions, the prime act of political prudence.

C. *Judges*

Another source of law is the men who constitute the courts of a nation. The manner in which they make law differs, however, from that of legislators and not every decision they reach is law.

1. *Meaning of adjudication.* Adjudication is described in many ways. "Legislation consists of formulating a rule for the future. A judgment applies the law to past or present facts." [11] Adjudication ". . . is the power which a regularly constituted court exercises in matters which are brought before it, in the manner prescribed by statute, or established rules of practice of courts, and which matters do not come within the powers granted to the executive, or vested in the legislative department of the government. The legislature may impose duties, judicial in character, upon the courts, but having once imposed these powers it has no right to control the exercise thereof; and that, we think, constitutes judicial power." [12] Adjudication, all in all, is concerned with determining what is just according to some already established rules or norms of law. [13]

a. *Interpretation.* Such a determination entails the interpretation or construction of pertinent legislation and also of precedent where it has the status of law. The meaning of words used and the intention of the writers has to be ascertained as far as possible.

[11] Eastern Oil Refining Co. v. Court of Burgesses of Wallingford, 130 Conn. 606, 36 A.2d 586, 589 (1944). See also People ex rel. Graves v. Sohmer, 207 N.Y. 455, 101 N.E. 164, 167 (1913); People ex rel. Argus Co. v. Hugo, 101 Misc. 481, 168 N.Y. Supp. 25, 27 (1917); Miller v. Scobie, 152 Fla. 328, 11 So.2d 892, 894 (1943); Samuel Goldwyn, Inc. v. United Artists Corp., 113 F.2d 703, 706 (3d Cir. 1940).

[12] State v. Huber, 129 W. Va. 198, 40 S.E.2d 11, 18 (1946).

[13] The Latin word for "judge" is *judex,* which signifies *jus dicere,* that is, to declare what is just.

Not only the letter is important but also the spirit. "With respect to statutes, construction is strict or liberal. Strict construction refuses to extend the import of words used in a statute so as to embrace cases or acts which the words do not clearly describe; liberal construction is that by which the letter of the statute is enlarged or restrained so as more effectually to accomplish the purpose intended." [14]

A knowledge of grammar, custom and usage may be aids in ascertaining the meaning of words, and familiarity with the records of committee deliberations, statements by the legislators themselves or their clerks may also be a help in finding the underlying intention. Once interpreted, the law is *applied* to the case at hand.

b. *Complex process.* But to imply that the interpretation and application of law by adjudication is an efficient, methodical, cut and dried procedure would be to oversimplify a process that is not only complex but at times ambiguous and uncertain.

In the interpretation of legislation, the intention of legislators is often vague. Conflicting statements by the legislators themselves as to the purpose of a law sometimes furnish evidence of this. Confirmation of this fact is had in the various interpretations to which some pieces of legislation have lent themselves. For instance, the vagaries of construction that the Mann Act has had put upon it during its history is an example in point.[15]

Anent interpretation, perhaps there is much to the idea that the meaning of words in legal usage is to be sought as well in those to whom the words are addressed as in their authors. For such words can be said to be ". . . delegations of the right to interpret them, in the first instance by the person addressed, in the second and ultimate instance by the courts who determine whether the person addressed has interpreted them within their authority. . . . Language . . . in legal documents, does not fix meaning. It circumscribes meaning." [16]

Difficulties of interpreting and applying case law are no less formidable. Theoretically a judge looks for a similar case, takes the rule of law found in it and applies it. But the ratio decidendi of a prior case is based directly on the facts that the previous court has decided to admit as material. These may be found to be irrelevant by the present judge. Ultimately it will not only be

[14] Causey v. Guilford County, 192 N.C. 298, 135 S.E. 40, 46 (1926). See also Read v. Dinges, 60 Fed. 21, 29 (4th Cir. 1894).

[15] See Levi, An Introduction to Legal Reasoning 24-38 (1950).

[16] Curtis, A Better Theory of Legal Interpretation, in Jurisprudence in Action 155, 158 (1953).

the intention of the previous court as expressed in the ratio decidendi that will have to be determined, but more importantly the
basis for deciding that certain facts are material and others are
immaterial.[17]

2. *Legislation primary to adjudication.* Adjudication is, as
noted, the determination of what is just. If this judgment is not
to be arbitrary and capricious, it must be formed according to
some rule.

a. *Previous rule.* This norm must be either man-made legislation or legislation of a more fundamental kind that precedes
the judicial decision.[18] This is evident in cases of "first impression." In such cases the court is confronted with a new question
of law and cannot find a guide in any existing statute or precedent.
Whatever the decision may be, it must be based on some previous
idea of justice.

This being so, adjudication of its very nature must be concerned with the interpretation and application of some kind of
legislation that existed before it. Hence, legislation is *primary* to
adjudication.

b. *Universality.* Legislation also regards the universal. It is
concerned with general directives and the future. It cannot de-
scend, as noted, to all the details that might possibly be implied.
Adjudication, on the other hand, regards the singular. It is concerned with a particular aspect of the rule and with facts past and
present. Again legislation considered in this perspective is primary to adjudication.

But even though legislation is prime, it does not follow that adjudication is not an absolutely *essential* source of law. It is as
essential as is the singularization of the universal and the particularization of the general. It is in adjudication that the particularized details of a piece of legislation have their source. The
precise manner of interpreting and applying a statute or precedent originates with adjudication. "The opinion of a judge is
somewhat like a particular law concerning some particular fact.
Hence, just as a general law should have coactive force, . . . so
also the opinion of the judge ought to have coactive force by which
each party is constrained to heed the opinion of the judge." [19]
In so far as judicial decisions are the law of the land, adjudication is an essential source of law.[20]

[17] Frank, Courts on Trial 14-102 (1949).
[18] On this more fundamental kind of legislation, see Part II.
[19] Aquinas, 2-2 Sum. Theol. 67, 1.
[20] On the position that adjudication is absolutely primary, see Gray, The
Nature and Sources of Law 170-178, 267-268 (1948).

c. *Judicial review.* There is, however, a way in which adjudication is sometimes said to be prime. In the United States, although judicial review is not necessary for constitutionality, the Supreme Court may declare legislation enacted by Congress unconstitutional. This is done by its power of judicial review. Regarding this power, two things are to be noted. First, such an ultimate subjection of legislation to adjudication is not necessarily demanded by the nature of law or the interrelation of legislation and adjudication. There are other countries where legislation is not subject to judicial review. In England, for instance, the Acts of Parliament are supreme. Second, even when the United States Supreme Court adjudicates the "constitutionality" of an enactment, the Court is guided by legislation. It is guided by the provisions of the Constitution itself, and by the demands of fundamental justice which are basic to the Constitution and directive of the Court's own thinking.[21] ". . . [T]he particular phraseology of the constitution of the United States confirms and strengthens the principle, supposed to be essential to all written constitutions, that a law repugnant to the constitution is void, and that the courts, as well as other departments, are bound by that instrument." [22]

Adjudication is essential, then, inasmuch as only through it does legislation receive necessary particularization. But legislation, furnishing the general directives without which there could be no particularization by judges, is of its very nature primary. For the only way that the singular can, upon repetition, avoid being unrelated, disorganized, and chaotic is by some universal principle that will unify and order it. This principle in regard to adjudication is legislation — man-made or otherwise — as is evidenced in the growth of common law.

d. *Codes vs. cases.* Preference for the singular (as represented in cases) over the universal (as embodied in codes) seems to account to some extent for the difference in stress placed on cases in England and especially in the United States and on codes on the Continent. Continental law men have always considered legisla-

[21] "Judicial review was fundamentally an outgrowth of colonial and Revolutionary political philosophy. Its basic postulates were the supremacy of the constitution, the limited power of the legislature, and the independence of the judiciary, achieved through the separation of powers." Kelly and Harbison, The American Constitution 98 (rev. ed. 1955). See also Corwin, The Natural Law and Constitutional Law, 3 University of Notre Dame Natural Law Institute Proceedings 54-71 (1950).

[22] Marbury v. Madison, 1 Cranch 137, 180, 2 L. Ed. 60, 74 (1803). See also Eakin v. Raub, 12 S. & R. 330, 346 (Pa. 1825).

tion to be the primary source of law. Precedent is instructive, but not authoritative. "Res judicatae" are not a source of law, but only evidence of legal rules. In England and the United States, on the other hand, the tendency is to consider judicial precedent as a primary and independent source of law. A case is cited, not as instructive in discerning the law, but as authoritative in declaring the law.

Who is guilty, in this situation, of the fallacy of misplaced emphasis — Continental lawyers or English and American lawyers? Should not the fundamental aspects of law be the same everywhere? To answer this question fairly and completely would necessitate a careful evaluation of the historical context in which each way of legal thinking arose and developed. To do so is obviously beyond the scope of a book such as this. However, it does seem that the inevitable tendency of lawmen to systematize and classify individual cases and ultimately reduce them to some sort of code is evidence of the human mind's natural tendency to unify the singular by the universal. "Case law is gold in the mine — a few grains of the precious metal to the ton of useless matter — while statute law is coin of the realm ready for immediate use." [23]

3. *"Good law till reversed."* A statute is considered valid until it is repealed or declared unconstitutional by a court having the power of judicial review. Reversal of prior decisions that were based on a statute later held unconstitutional does not affect the validity of the statute. It is valid till repealed or declared unconstitutional. "The consequence of the overruling of these cases was, that the statutes which, according to the rulings therein, would have been held unconstitutional, were valid, not from the time of overruling these cases, but from the time of their enactment until they were repealed. It was not the overruling of those cases which gave validity to the statutes; but the cases having been overruled, the statutes must be regarded as having all the time been the law of the State. This court has no power to repeal or 'abolish' statutes. If it should hold an act of the legislature unconstitutional, while its decision remains, the act must be regarded as invalid. But if it shall afterward come to the conclusion that its former ruling was erroneous, and overrule it, the statute must be regarded for all purposes as having been constitutional and in force from the beginning." [24]

But what of a decision later reversed by a higher court? Was it good law till it was reversed? Or was it not good law at all but

[23] Salmond, Jurisprudence 179 (8th ed. 1930).
[24] Pierce v. Pierce, 46 Ind. 86, 95 (1867).

only a mistake according to which people acted at their own risk? It has been said that such an overruled decision was not law at the time it was made. "In strict sense the decisions of courts are not the law of the land, but the evidence of it. Courts cannot make laws. They determine only what the law is; and while their decisions may operate as laws upon the property and rights of parties, they are only declaratory, and not creative like legislative acts and treaties; but the language must be taken in its practical sense. The counsel for the appellant is quite correct in saying that a decision of a court overruling a prior decision is a legal adjudication that the prior decision was not the law at the time it was made, although there may be rights of contract acquired under the first which the last decision will not affect." [25]

However, it would seem that the opposite opinion is the better one: decisions are good law until they are reversed. The reasons for this are two. First, a judge's decision is, like all law, a directive judgment of political prudence. In contradistinction to a judgment of science, it is true if it results from the intention of arriving at the best possible conclusion based on facts available and pertinent at the time.[26] This represents the closest approximation to rightness and justness of which the judge is capable. More cannot be expected. Until a closer approximation be made by others with more data and perhaps clearer insight, his judgment must stand as good law. Second, from the practical viewpoint it seems that decisions must be accepted as good law until they are overruled. Otherwise there never could be a decision that was known with certainty to be law. For who could predict with any degree of assurance that there never would be a future decision that would not reverse a prior one? Besides, if decisions were not considered good law till reversed, ". . . every reversal would give rise to hundreds of actions for recovery, which condition would produce legal chaos." [27]

4. *Judges' election v. appointment.* Judges are makers of law in a particularized sense, as we have seen. In the United States of America judges are either appointed by executives and legislators or elected by the people.

According to democratic principles of government, all political authority must come ultimately from the citizens.[28] So also must the political authority of judges come somehow from this same

[25] Woodruff v. Woodruff, 52 N.Y. Rep. 53, 58 (1873).
[26] See Chapters 3 and 19.
[27] Henderson v. Folkestone Waterworks Co., 1 T.L.R. 329 (1885).
[28] On the source of political authority, see Chapter 19.

source. Should it come directly by election or indirectly by appointment?

If the people are to maintain control over the three branches of government as completely separate, the direct delegation of authority to judges by the people through election appears to be the surest way of accomplishing it. Elected in this manner, the judiciary would be to a large degree independent of executive and legislative influence.

There seems, however, to be a distrust of the citizens' ability to elect judges intelligently, somewhat as there was among the founding fathers regarding direct popular election of the executive. "This idea received little favor with most of the delegates, in part because of the anti-democratic views of many delegates, in part because the idea of a popularly elected executive was as yet largely foreign to American experience." [29] The electoral college was the result. But if citizens are considered capable of electing the legislators who enact statutes, it would seem that by the same token they are fitted to elect the judges who interpret them and also make laws in their own right.

A compromise in the problem of election vs. appointment of judges is the nonpartisan court plan. As proposed by the American Bar Association, a judge would be appointed by the executive, ". . . but from a list named by another agency composed in part of high judicial officers and in part of other citizens, selected for the purpose, who hold no other public office." [30] After the judge has served for a period of time he should ". . . go before the people upon his record, with no opposing candidate, the people voting upon the question 'Shall Judge Blank be retained in office.' " [31] In some places the members of the local bar evaluate the record of the incumbents before the election. The results of this appraisal are published as an aid to the voters.

It is true that no plan yet devised is foolproof against selfish political influence. However, the nonpartisan court plan, in its main attempt to transcend party lines and offer qualified men to the citizens for approval or rejection, is in keeping with the best aspirations of government for the common good.[32]

[29] Kelly and Harbison, The American Constitution 133 (1948). By permission of the W. W. Norton Company.

[30] Summary of Proceedings, 62 A.B.A. Rep. 1033 (1937).

[31] Ibid.

[32] On the nonpartisan court plan see Hyde, Judges: Their Selection and Tenure, 30 Am. Jud. Soc. 152 (1947); Bundschu, The Missouri Non-Partisan Court Plan — Selection and Tenure of Judges, 16 U. Kan. City L. Rev. 55 (1948); Tighe, The Pennsylvania Court Plan, 22 Temp. L.Q. 316-321 (1949); Erskine, The Selection of Judges in England, 39 A.B.A.J. 348 (1953).

D. *Executives*

Executives also participate in governmental authority. Although their chief activity is not lawmaking but the execution of laws, they do at times make law.

1. *Executing law.* The main function of the executive is to carry legislation into effect. "The executive power . . . extends to the detail of carrying into effect the laws enacted by the Legislature, as they may be interpreted by the courts. Except where limited by the Constitution itself, the Legislature may stipulate what action the executive officers shall or shall not perform." [33]

2. *Lawmaking decrees.* The executive, however, can be a source of law through his decrees. Just as one and the same man who is head or leader could also be the judge of disputes that might arise, so also he could decree what is to be done and not done. In such a case his decree would oblige as an enacted statute and he would be a source of law. Such could be the situation of an absolute monarch or dictator.

In more advanced forms of government wherein the functions of legislation, adjudication and execution are centered in different men, the decree of the executive is also said at times to have the status of law. "The generally accepted rule . . . now appears to be that a legislative body may, after declaring a policy and fixing a primary standard, confer upon executive or administrative officers the power to fill up the details, by prescribing rules and regulations to promote the purpose and spirit of the legislation and to carry it into effect." [34]

However such proclamations, decrees or orders are law only inasmuch as they represent lawmaking authority delegated by the legislature. In a time, therefore, when many commissions, boards, departments and offices are necessary to lighten the executive load and when their orders in many instances have the standing of law, it behooves the legislature to maintain constant vigilance over their activities and to spell out carefully the limits of their delegated powers.

The executive branch of government should be looked upon for what it actually is, a *part* of the government. The executive is not the government itself. There are many others engaged in

---

[33] State v. Huber, 129 W. Va. 198, 40 S.E.2d 11, 18 (1946). See also In re Railroad Commissioners, 15 Neb. 679, 50 N.W. 276, 277 (1884); Tucker v. State, 218 Ind. 614, 35 N.E.2d 270, 290 (1941); Gray v. State ex rel. Coghlen, 72 Ind. 567, 578 (1880).

[34] Williams v. State, 146 Tex. Cr. R. 430, 176 S.W.2d 177, 184 (1943).

legislative and judicial capacities. The executive or "head" is not the government any more than he is the "state."

E. *The People*

Besides legislators making law through statutes and judges through decisions, the people also make law by establishing custom — the "living law" as it has been called. This is consonant with their position as the immediate source of delegated political authority.

1. *Custom as originating law.* Custom, as mentioned, historically preceded judicial decisions and statutes. For it is essentially the determination by the people themselves of ways of acting that are necessary for the common welfare. It is the result of men applying the demands of their nature to the needs of a particular time and place. Thus rules regarding the possession and exchange of property, the use of waterways, and the like were established by the people long before there were legislative bodies.

a. *Law of nations.* In this manner the "law of nations" arose. This *ius gentium,* or "common law of civilization" [35] was the unwritten law accepted as the guiding rule of intercourse among nations. " 'The law of nations is a system of rules, which reason, morality, and custom have established among civilized nations as their public law.' . . . The obligation of the ordinary *ius gentium* depends upon the persuasion that other nations will observe the same rules in their intercourse with us, which we observe towards them; or if they fail to observe these rules, that they will incur the general hostility of nations. But this persuasion cannot exist, as to those races of men who do not recognize one law of nations." [36]

b. *Not "international law."* There is a tendency to speak of international law as being the same as the law of nations. "International law, as understood among civilized nations, may be defined as consisting of those rules of conduct which reason adduces as consonant to justice, from the nature of the society, existing among independent nations; with such definitions and modifications as may be established by general consent." [37] However, the law of nations or *ius gentium* is not the same as "international law." The law of nations is the result of the same common response of men in all nations to the rudimentary needs that are

[35] Maritain, Man and the State 98-101 (1951).
[36] Herin v. Bridault, 37 Miss. 82, 91 (1859).
[37] Ibid.

common to all.   International law, on the other hand, is the consequence of treaties and agreement among certain nations regarding certain specific needs.   It is further questionable whether the
phrase "international law" has any valid legal meaning beyond
that of contractual agreement.   If law presupposes governmental
authority, international law must be enacted by an international
government.   Failing this, what is known as "international law"
is not law, except in the sense that the parties to a treaty agree
that its provision will be "law" among themselves.

Consideration of the "law" aspect of "international law" cannot
but lead to a realization of the necessity of a government that is
international in scope as its source.   " 'International law' is a term
which has not, as yet, perhaps been fully and accurately defined,
or rather the specific matters to which it may extend, and its scope,
may not be fully settled. . . . The closer the world comes to a
realization of the poet's dream of 'the parliament of man, the
federation of the world,' the wider will be the scope of international law." [38]

c. *Embodied in statutes.*   These accepted ways of acting by
peoples, reflected in the law of nations, were eventually recognized
as guiding norms by the courts and upon the advent of legislation
were embodied to a great extent in statutes.   Customs were assumed into the common law of England.   Early customs later became statutory law in the United States of America.   In California, for instance, during the gold rush of 1849 civil authority was
weak and the miners established their own rules regarding contract, property and possession.   These customs were later incorporated into the Civil Practice Act of California of 1851.[39]   The
importance of custom as a source of law, in this originating sense,
has lessened since legislation became more widespread.

2. *Custom as law through interpretation.*   Custom is ordinarily a source of law in another more particular way.   It is a source
of law inasmuch as it determines the *construction* to be put on
certain parts of common and statute law.   Mercantile law is an
example.   " 'Consuetudo,' said Sir Edward Coke, 'is one of the
main triangles of the laws of England; those laws being divided
into common law, statute law and particular customs, for if it be
the general custom of the realm, it is part of the common law . . .
the custom of merchants is part of the common law of this kingdom of which the judges ought to take notice, and if any doubt
arise to them about the custom they may send for the merchants

---

[38] United States v. White, 27 Fed. 200, 201 (C.C.E.D. Mo. 1886).
[39] See Gray, Nature and Sources of Law 296 (2d ed. 1921).

to know their custom.' That a custom so general and notorious may exist as to authorize the captain of a steamboat to effect an insurance on it for the benefit of the owners without their express directions, we think well settled by authority. It would not be in conflict with any statute, nor would it be unreasonable or contrary to public policy. . . . [I]t was held that evidence was properly received to prove that a custom and usage existed in the city of Washington which authorized a tenant to remove any building erected by him. . . . [I]t is held, a usage or custom varying the liability of common carriers by water from that of the common law may be proved, even to give construction to the words 'inevitable dangers of the rivers.' . . . A custom so long persisted in as to be known and practiced by a community is the law of the particular business in which it exists." [40]

a. *Custom as "reasonable."* Custom also many times determined the meaning of fair, reasonable, usual, and the like. For, "Fair, reasonable, equitable, proper, due, they are all familiar enough, and they are so nearly empty of any but emotional meaning that they express little more than an attitude. They are receptacles to be filled from some future context of circumstance. They are bournes to be achieved as well as believed." [41]

b. *Custom as "usual."* Custom may mean what is ordinary and usual. A hotel clerk, for example, introduced guests who were real estate agents to prospective purchasers of land. He was entitled to the compensation ordinarily and usually paid to subagents, which was one fourth to one third of the commission received by the principal agents. ". . . [I]t is very clear in this case that the petition in asking compensation for the plaintiff such as is 'customary among real estate agents in the city of Des Moines' makes use of these words in their more popular, if less technical, sense as meaning such compensation as is ordinarily and usually paid for services of the kind he claims to have rendered. In the absence of other testimony bearing on the question, proof of what is usually and ordinarily paid for a given service is sufficient evidence on which the jury may find its reasonable value." [42]

Taken in the sense of "usual," custom may not mean "fixed and binding." "The evidence shows without dispute that store fronts were usually changed to suit new tenants, especially those going into a new line of business; and the word 'customary' was plainly

[40] Adams v. Pittsburgh Insurance Co., 95 Pa. 348, 355, 40 Am. Rep. 662 (1880).

[41] Curtis, A Better Theory of Legal Interpretation, in Jurisprudence in Action 169 (1953).

[42] Montgomery v. O'Donnell, 178 Iowa 588, 159 N.W. 1025, 1026 (1916).

used as a synonym for 'usual,' and not in the sense of a fixed custom by which any one was to be bound." [43]

c. *Custom as "practice."* Custom may be the same as practice but it is not the same as usage. "The word 'practice' is a synonym for 'usage' and 'custom,' and it is so treated generally in the law books, though there is a distinction between a usage and a custom. A lawful custom is a part of the common law, while a lawful usage, 'proved and shown to affect both parties, may be described as the law of their case.' " [44]

d. *Custom is not abuse.* Since custom is a source of law, it must contribute to the common welfare. Hence a long practice that is not contributing to the public good but is detracting from it, regardless of its other aspects, is not a custom. It is an abuse. If its injurious effect on the common good is serious, it should be prohibited. If this effect is not serious, it may be tolerated for proportionate reasons.[45]

3. *Evidence of custom.* The existence of a custom is to be established as any other fact, that is, by evidence. "In former days it was held by a few courts that 'one witness was not enough to establish the existence' of a custom, but it is now well settled that a custom may be proved as any other fact." [46]

Evidence of a custom is that it be certain, uniform, well-known, of long duration and without dispute. "Before a custom or usage can acquire the force of law, it must appear that it is general and uniform in the business to be affected by it, and that it has been peaceably acquiesced in without dispute for a long period of time. . . . It must be certain, or the measurements by this standard will be unequal or unjust. It must be uniform; for, if it vary, it furnishes no rule by which to mete. It must be known, or must be so uniform and notorious that no person of ordinary intelligence who has to do with the subject to which it relates, and who exercises reasonable care, would be ignorant of it; for no man may be justly condemned for the violation of a law or a custom which he neither knows nor ought to know." [47]

---

[43] Woods v. Postal Telegraph Cable Co., 205 Ala. 236, 87 So. 681, 686 (1920).

[44] United States Shipping Board Emergency Fleet Corp. v. Levensaler, 290 Fed. 297, 300 (D.C. Cir. 1923).

[45] It may be well to note, too, that custom is distinct from prescription. Custom is a long practice that results in a source of law, while prescription is a long practice that results in a source of claims or "rights." Prescription is a way that a title may be transferred. Custom is a way that a law may originate or be changed. On prescription, see Chapter 16.

[46] Goslin v. Kurn, 351 Mo. 395, 173 S.W.2d 79, 86 (1943).

[47] United States Shipping Board Emergency Fleet Corp. v. Levensaler, 290 Fed. 297, 300, 301 (D.C. Cir. 1923). On evidence of custom see Allen, Law in the Making 127-134 (1951).

It is not always easy to determine whether what is alleged to be a custom may actually be so. The inability, for instance, of a trainman ". . . to give the per cent of trains that did not dim the headlight moving in the yards [does not destroy] his evidence that there was such a custom." [48] However, his ability to speak only in terms of "quite a few" did affect the value of his evidence.[49]

F. *Each Source a Directive Judgment*

Legislation, adjudication, executive decree, and custom are all directive judgments by those with authority ordering means necessary for the public good. The directive judgment in the mind of legislators which is law is characterized by the generality of its provisions for the common good, judicial decisions by the particularization of these general rules, executive decree by the legislative origin of its delegated lawmaking authority, and custom by the continued action of the people themselves in ways they judge are necessary for the common welfare. These directive judgments representing the exercise of various aspects of lawmaking authority are all true law.

A question can be raised regarding the manner in which custom, as law, is promulgated. The explanation lies in the very nature of custom. Because exterior words and actions manifest interior judgments and decisions, the people's directive judgment by which they govern themselves in customary ways of acting is made known or promulgated by their *repeated actions*.

". . . [J]ust as the reason and will of a man are manifested in practical matters by speech, so also they are made known by deeds. . . . Hence by oft repeated actions which make a custom, a law can be changed and interpreted. . . . Something can be established which has the force of law, inasmuch as by repeated external actions the interior movement of the will and concepts of the reason are most effectively declared. Accordingly, custom has the force of law, abolishes law, and is the interpreter of law." [50] Custom is promulgated, therefore, by the repeated actions of the people themselves.

Custom may be abolished by statute. If it conflicts with a statute and is not abolished, it can be considered to be accepted by legislators as amending the letter of existing statutes. The legislators have adopted as their own the directive judgment that orig-

[48] Goslin v. Kurn, 351 Mo. 395, 173 S.W.2d 79, 86 (1943).
[49] Ibid.
[50] Aquinas, 1-2 Sum. Theol. 97, 3.

inated with the people. The indication of this is the fact that they permit the custom to continue which is tacit approval of it.[51]

G. *How Law Continues in Existence*

If law is a directive judgment in the mind of legislators and judges, how can it be said to continue in existence? Obviously the lawmaker cannot keep this judgment constantly in mind once he has formed it. Does the law cease to exist as soon as this judgment is no longer consciously present in his mind?

A law is like any other directive judgment made by one in a position of authority. The father of a family directs that the only time liquor may be served in the house is with the evening meal. A commander in the field gives an order to advance at dawn on a day one week away. The directive judgments of both these men, which are manifested in their pronouncements, cease to be actually in the forefront of their minds. But even though this mental act of judging has ceased, what does remain is the fact that the judgment was made and the directive given. The father did "lay down the law" regarding the use of liquor, and the commander did issue an order to advance.

The directive judgment which is law in like manner continues to be effective. It perdures, not as the mental act of judging itself, but as the fact that a lawmaker reached a decision, formed this directive judgment, and made it known as a rule to be followed. That he *did so direct* is the fact that is constant.

Similarly, the lawmaking judgments of legislators and judges out of office or long since dead continue as law. Their actions established rules to be followed. This fact is controlling until superseded by other lawmaking actions. New legislators and judges may be assumed to have made the directive judgments of their predecessors their own unless they show the opposite by attempting amendment or repeal.

[51] "The people among whom a custom is introduced may be of two conditions. If they are a free people who can make their own laws, the consent of the whole people to observe something which is of custom is more important than the authority of the sovereign who does not have the power of enacting law except inasmuch as he represents the people. Hence, although individual persons cannot enact law, nevertheless the custom that prevails among such a people has the force of law insofar as it is tolerated by those to whom it pertains to make laws for that people. By this very fact, they are seen to approve what custom has introduced." Aquinas, 1-2 Sum. Theol. 97, 3, 3.

II. OTHER "SOURCES" OF LAW

"Source" of law can have other meanings besides the men who make law. It can refer to those knowledges or sciences that legislators and judges should have in determining the content of law as noted.

A. Background Knowledges

Besides those knowledges and sciences already mentioned, others are helpful. A knowledge of political science is requisite if law is to be seen in its perspective as an instrument of government. For grasping the full implication of the common good as fulfilling the needs of human beings, a knowledge of the nature of men and the reason for their existence is indispensable.

B. Records

"Source" of law may also refer to records of the law. These are the recordings and promulgations of statutes and decisions that have been preserved from early to recent times.

Such would be the Institutes of Gaius written about A.D. 161 and the Institutes of Ulpian about A.D. 200; or the Corpus Juris Civilis completed in 534 by a group of lawyers commissioned by the Emperor Justinian and comprising Institutes, Digest and Code. Other "sources" would be the Decrees of Gratian which were written about 1140 and embodied in canon law; or the Year Books of England which were reports on cases from the reign of Edward I (1272) to Henry VIII (1509). The "sources" of law best known in the United States are, of course, constitutions, statutes and reports of decisions that are the working tools with which every lawman is familiar.[52]

C. Group Influences

"Source" of law can also be used in yet another sense. It can refer to the various groups that affect lawmakers and lawmaking. These may be writers on legal subjects, strong and active bar associations, jurisconsults, public opinion of the people, political ma-

[52] On these sources of law see Morgan and Dwyer, Introduction to the Study of Law 166-283 (1948); Price and Bitner, Effective Legal Research *passim* (1953).

chines, and lobbies. The interests represented may be social, economic, political, religious or underworld.

Such pressures on lawmakers are an inevitable part of the democratic process. They should, however, be seen for what they are. Strictly speaking they are not so much "sources" of law as they are *influences* on the men who are the source of law. This clarification is important in terms of responsibility. The ultimate responsibility for a statute or judicial decision whether good or bad rests with the men who make them. They are the ones who have been chosen for this purpose. It is they who allow themselves to be affected by these influences for better or for worse, against great or small odds. And it is they and they alone who betray or are loyal to the responsibility entrusted to them.

The word "source," then, regarding law can be used with several different meanings. But only when it is used to refer to the men who make law does it have a meaning directly related to the act of lawmaking.

Sanction of Man-made Law

The problem to be solved here is what is the evil or the good that follows violation or observance of a law. Sanction refers to the consequences of breaking or keeping a law. For, if laws are designed to accomplish some good, their infraction cannot but entail some evil.

I. MEANING OF SANCTION

In its root meaning sanction means to make something inviolable,[1] even under pain of punishment. This is the underlying idea of the oath, namely, that falsehood will be punished by the Supreme Being. As rewards or punishments that result from doing or not doing what is prescribed, sanctions are inducements for observing the law.

A. *Extrinsic Sanction*

In view of the fact that sanction is necessary for law enforcement, rewards or punishments are *affixed* to most statutory directives. For this reason they are called extrinsic sanctions.

Rewards offered by laws include sums offered for the arrest and conviction of criminals,[2] remuneration for enlistment in military service,[3] pensions to encourage working in public services,[4] and bounty for animals,[5] and the like.

[1] From the Latin *sancire*, to render sacred. Another meaning of sanction, "to confirm," is not as directly related to law and punishment. "The verb 'sanction' has very definitely in the language a distinct and different shade of meaning from 'authorize.' Repeatedly in the arena of lawmaking, acts of the President, particularly on occasions of national emergency, have, upon the reconvening of Congress, been by it sanctioned. 'Sanction' means to assent, to concur, to confirm, or ratify." United States v. Tillinghast, 55 F.2d 279, 283 (D.R.I. 1932).

[2] Kinn v. First National Bank of Mineral Point, 118 Wis. 537, 95 N.W. 969 (1903).

[3] Abbe v. Allen, 39 How. Pr. 481, 488 (N.Y. 1869); see also Iowa v. Mc-Farland, 110 U.S. 471, 480, 4 Sup. Ct. 210 (1883).

[4] In re Hoag, 227 Fed. 478, 479 (S.D.N.Y. 1915).

[5] Ingram v. Colgan, 106 Cal. 113, 38 Pac. 315, 316 (1894).

Punishment is more ordinarily the meaning carried by sanction. The essence of punishment is *deprivation*. "It is plain that to be a punishment there must be a deprivation of property, or of some right, such as the enjoyment of liberty; and the same may be said of a penalty." [6]

The deprivation in which punishment consists takes several forms. It may entail the loss of property by fine or forfeiture,[7] of freedom by imprisonment, of physical well-being by flogging, of claims and privileges,[8] or of life itself by execution. As a deprivation, therefore, punishment is primarily retributive. Fear of having to undergo some of these deprivations further serves to deter from future violations of the law and thereby to correct thinking in regard to keeping the law.

B. *Intrinsic Sanction*

Even though no added rewards and punishments were affixed to statutes by their makers, nonetheless there are rewards and punishments that follow the very obeying or disobeying itself of a law independently of such additions. Besides the extrinsic sanction of law, there is its intrinsic sanction.

1. *From end of directives.* A man who disobeys a speed law immediately incurs the penalty of being deprived of safe driving conditions. This dangerous situation may lead to further deprivations of his physical well-being and of even his life. On the other hand, if he obeys the law, he automatically enjoys the reward of safety and the preservation of his life and members.

In a word, the common good that a law is intended to accomplish or the common evil it is designed to avoid are the intrinsic sanction of law. The end of a law is its truest sanction.

2. *Differs from motive.* Intrinsic sanctions should be distinguished from motives. Motives are the reasons why a man obeys a law; sanctions are the good or evil that accrues to him as a result of his obedience or disobedience. True, a man's motives should for the most part coincide with and be based on the good that comes from obeying laws. If he is prudent and civic-minded, they probably will.

This, however, is not necessarily so. A man's motives may be "a sense of guilt or shame" [9] or "habit or imitation or social

[6] State v. Cowen, 231 Iowa 1117, 3 N.W.2d 176, 179, 182 (1942).

[7] The restitution of what has been wrongfully taken is not punishment. It is justice. See State v. Hondros, 100 S.C. 242, 84 S.E. 781, 783 (1915).

[8] Jenkens v. State, 14 Ga. 276, 80 S.E. 688, 690 (1914).

[9] Patterson, Jurisprudence: Men and Ideas of the Law 161 (1953).

pressures." [10]   Or it may be most men are "honorable men." [11]
These, however, are not "intrinsic" sanctions.   They are individual motives.[12]   The word "intrinsic" refers here not to something intrinsic to the citizen in question, but to the law itself.

Failure to make this distinction can only result in the one controlling fact being left out of legal analysis: what the law is intended to accomplish.   A man's motive for obeying an ordinance
forbidding the use of explosives on the Fourth of July could be,
if he were superficial enough, "a sense of shame" — since no other
family in the neighborhood is using them.   The extrinsic sanction
or punishment for violating the ordinance would be the fine imposed, say $500.   The intrinsic sanction or punishment for dis-
obeying, and the basis for what his motive should be, is the possible blowing off of the hands of the man and his children.[13]

The sanction of law, then, includes all the evils or goods that
result from its violation or observance — whether these follow
from the intrinsic content of the law itself or from the fact that
they have been extrinsically affixed.

3. *Unreal exclusion of intrinsic sanction.*   Since these goods
or evils have social implications, it is an unreal exclusion of fact
to say that the term sanction should be "limited to the harmful
consequences imposed by officials," [14] or to "evils inflicted by government force for non-compliance." [15]   Unquestionably such imposed evils are sanctions and this is what the term usually signifies.
But this use of the word should not be allowed to obscure the fact
that there are other actual evils consequent upon non-observance
besides the ones that are extrinsically imposed.

II.   Necessity of Sanction

It would seem that men, being endowed with intelligence,
would always follow the directives that are framed for their own
good.   The whole burden of historical evidence, however, is to
the contrary.

[10] Id. at 169.

[11] Snyder, Preface to Jurisprudence 224 (1954).

[12] Patterson, Jurisprudence: Men and Ideas of the Law 161 (1953).

[13] What has caused such considerations to be ruled out as "moral," and
therefore not pertinent to law, is examined in Chapter 6.

[14] Patterson, Jurisprudence: Men and Ideas of the Law 162 (1953).

[15] Snyder, Preface to Jurisprudence 223 (1954).

A. *Threat of Punishment Needed*

Video meliora proboque, deteriora sequor [16] is the testimony of the ages. There is a tendency in men not to do what they know they should do. There seems to be a radical perverseness at work in all of us. The threat of loss of the good which observance of the law is designed to bring to us is oftimes not enough. The added threat of punishment by fine, imprisonment and the like is needed.

In some instances the opposite may be true. The sight of hands and faces burned by the explosion of fireworks may do more to deter a man from using them on the Fourth of July in violation of an ordinance than the threatened penalty of fine or imprisonment. So also may this be the case in many other dangerous activities. By and large, however, it is the threat of punishment imposed by law that assures its observance. Men being what they are, sanctions extrinsically added to laws are necessary.

B. *Perfect and Imperfect Sanction*

The sanctions that are affixed to laws are either sufficient to bring about observance or they are not. If they are adequate, they are "perfect sanctions." If they are not, they are "imperfect sanctions." If no sanction is imposed, the law is simply "unsanctioned."

C. *Punishment and Valid Law*

Is a law valid if no sanction is added? Does a crime have to be defined in terms of imposed fine and imprisonment? The distinction between a law's intrinsic and extrinsic sanction points the way to a solution.

If law is essentially a directive with its own intrinsic sanction, it is already constituted a law before other sanctions are added. A valid law is possible without any penalty being affixed. "While the term 'law' is generally understood, and is quite generally defined, as 'a rule of civil action prescribed by the supreme power in a state commanding what is right and prohibiting what is wrong,' there has been a good deal of discussion as to whether such rule is of any force or effect unless there be a penalty, or

[16] "I see the better and I approve, but I follow the worse." Ovid. Metamorphoses 7, 2 (A.D. 1-7) (my trans.).

sanction, affixed. But we regard much of this discussion as academic, and are persuaded that either the congress or the legislature may make a perfectly valid statute a rule of action, without providing any penalty or sanction." [17]

Though there is some opinion to the contrary regarding criminal statutes, there seems to be no reason why they as well as civil statutes cannot be valid without imposed penalties. Validity should not be confused with enforceability. ". . . [U]nder the Code definition of a crime, neither the imposition of a fine nor sentence of imprisonment is essential to make the act a crime. Penalty is no part of the crime but is simply a consequence flowing from its commission." [18]

Sanction, then, although it refers to the punishments that are consequent upon the violation of a law, includes also the rewards or goods that result from its observance. These may follow from the intrinsic content of the law itself or from extrinsic imposition.

[17] State v. U.S. Express Co., 164 Iowa 112, 145 N.W. 451, 455 (1914).

[18] Jenkens v. State, 14 Ga. 276, 80 S.E. 688, 690 (1914). Legal positivism considers that ". . . coercion is an essential element of law . . . because a careful examination of the social orders termed 'law' in the history of mankind shows that these social orders, in spite of their great differences, present one common element, an element of great importance in social life: they all prescribe coercive acts as sanctions." Kelsen, What is Justice 289 (1957). It must be commented that this is like saying that, because the education of boys has always been found to be accompanied by a birch rod standing in the corner (if it has), birch rods are an essential element and education should be so defined. This is mistaking the accidental, simply because it appears frequently, for the essential.

CHAPTER 6

Obligation of Man-made Law

The problem confronting us in this chapter is why do laws oblige, that is, what is meant by obligation and on what is it based? This is of major importance because it concerns the reason why men ought to obey laws and, for that matter, why they ought to do anything that is right and just rather than what is wrong and unjust. The obligation of law regards the reason why I "ought to," "must," "should," "have to" observe the law rather than violate it. It is concerned with my "duty" to keep the law rather than break it.

I. MEANING OF OBLIGATION

Obligation differs from sanction. Whereas sanction refers to the consequences of obeying or disobeying, obligation regards the basis of why I ought to choose to obey. Sanction concerns rewards and punishments, obligation relates to the moral necessity of choosing.

Obligation and duty are often used as synonymous. However obligation is broader than duty. Obligation covers why I ought to do what is right regarding both myself and others. Duty is usually limited to why I ought to do what is right regarding others only. It pertains, not to moderation and courage, but to justice.[1]

A. *Obligation from Means-End Relation*

The basis of obligation is the touchstone that tests the practical value of law. It stands at the point of incidence between the directives of law and the fact situations law is designed to control.

1. *Basis of obligation: Factual relation of means to end.* The end of a law limiting speed to 65 miles per hour is to preserve human life. It is not to collect fines. The reason why a person should obey this law is that limited speed is necessary for safety. The relation between the two is a factual one. It can be demon-

---

[1] See Helvering v. British-American Tobacco Co., 69 F.2d 528, 530 (2d Cir. 1934); Bankers Deposit Guaranty and Surety Co. v. Barnes, 81 Kan. 422, 105 Pac. 697, 698 (1909).

strated by tests. Traffic engineers can show that, the make of cars being what it is and the curvature of roads being what it is, there is a speed beyond which cars cannot negotiate curves. Hence, the basis of obligation, the means-end relation, is factual. The law ought to be obeyed because what it directs and demands is a means necessary for the preservation of human life.

2. *Necessity of choosing means on account of end desired.* Because of this means-end relation, I am under the moral necessity of choosing to drive below 65 miles per hour and to so direct myself — if I desire to preserve my life. This unique type of necessity which refers to the necessity of making a free decision derives *from the end desired.* "From the will to cross the sea comes the necessity in the will of choosing a ship." [2]

This means-end relation is the heart of law's obligation. "Every law is ordered to the common welfare of men and in this it has the force and essence of law; but insofar as it fails in this, it does not have the power of obliging." [3] "The command of law, since it is obligatory, regards something that ought to be done. That a thing ought to be done arises from the necessity of some end. Hence, it is evident that it is of the essence of a command that it imply a relation to an end inasmuch as what it commands is necessary . . . for an end." [4] Hence, "To 'direct' is to assume the role of a director, one whose directions are binding." [5] The promptness with which the means to an end are chosen is a gauge of how efficaciously the end is desired. It indicates the difference between velleity and volition.

Obligation, then, is defined as: the *moral necessity* of *freely choosing means* that are *necessary for a desired end.* Although I am physically free to violate the speed law if I so choose, I am morally necessitated not to do so. Obligation is related to intrinsic sanction, although it is different from it. It is completely unrelated to extrinsic sanction. On this choice of means is based the directive judgment of prudence.

The difference between this type of necessity and other types are examined later, as also the fact that obligation, although seemingly hypothetical and relative (*if* I desire an end), is ultimately categorical and absolute.

3. *Means: Necessary and useful.* The means that are necessary for the common good are not necessary in exactly the same degree.

[2] Aquinas, 1 Sum. Theol. 82, 1.
[3] Id. at 96, 6.
[4] Id. at 99, 1.
[5] Gentle v. Frederick, 234 Ala. 184, 174 So. 606, 607 (1937).

They may be necessary absolutely or relatively, or they may be merely useful and therefore not matter for the content of law.

a. *Absolutely necessary.* A thing is absolutely necessary for the common good when without it not even the more elemental common needs would be fulfilled. Thus police surveillance, men being what they are, is absolutely necessary for the protection of citizens' basic claims to life and property, thereby insuring conditions of order and peace.

b. *Relatively necessary.* A thing is relatively necessary for the common welfare when without it other important needs would not be fulfilled, although the more elemental claims to life and property may be fulfilled. The necessity for surveillance of pure foods and drugs is not so great or absolute as the necessity for constant protection against robbery and murder. Nevertheless it is necessary, to some degree at least, that the purity of foods and drugs be assured lest the citizens become poisoned or preoccupied with a fear that would exclude a sense of security and safety. Hence the assurance of pure foods and drugs is relatively necessary. It goes without saying that what would be only relatively necessary for the public welfare under some conditions of time and place might under other conditions become absolutely necessary and vice versa. Thus, if the contamination of foods or the adulteration of drugs became widespread for whatever reason, the necessity of assuring their purity would be absolute.[6]

c. *Useful or convenient.* Those things that are absolutely and relatively necessary for the public good should be distinguished from those things that are simply useful for the common good. The useful is that without which both elemental and all other important common needs can still be fulfilled but not with as much ease. The useful in regard to the common good is what would help bring about the fulfillment of the absolutely or relatively necessary with greater facility. It was merely useful at one time to have directional turning lights on the front and rear of automobiles. Since such lights are an easier and more certain way of indicating the direction in which a turn is about to be made, they contribute to conditions of safety. Formerly, they were neither absolutely or relatively necessary for safe driving. The use of hand signals was all that was needed to indicate the direction of a turn, although the use of a mechanical signaling device would have been useful. Now, however, because of the increased number of cars and changed traffic conditions, it is no longer debatable

[6] On the various ways things may be necessary, see Aquinas, 2-2 Sum. Theol. 80, 1.

whether or not such devices are necessary — if not absolutely, at least relatively. Hence what is simply useful in one set of circumstances may become necessary in another set of circumstances and therefore matter of law.

Because the content of law is limited to what is necessary for the public good, only what is absolutely or relatively necessary should be included, not what is merely useful. It is the burden of legislators and judges in their deliberations and evaluations to determine which is which in everyday situations. What is designated as matter for law must somehow be necessary for the common good.

Courts have always recognized the need for proper construction of the concept of "necessary" in the means-end relationship of law. "Does it [the word "necessary"] always import an absolute physical necessity, so strong, that one thing, to which another may be termed necessary, cannot exist without that other? We think it does not. If reference be had to its use, in the common affairs of the world, or in approved authors, we find that it frequently imports no more than that one thing is convenient, or useful, or essential to another. To employ the means necessary to an end, is generally understood as employing any means calculated to produce the end, and not as being confined to those single means, without which the end would be entirely unattainable. The word 'necessary' . . . has not a fixed character peculiar to itself. It admits of all degrees of comparison; and is often connected with other words, which increase or diminish the impression the mind receives of the urgency it imports. A thing may be necessary, very necessary, absolutely or indispensably necessary. To no mind would the same idea be conveyed, by these several phrases. . . . It is, we think, impossible to compare the sentence which prohibits a State from laying 'imposts, or duties on imports or exports, except what may be absolutely necessary for executing its inspection laws,' with that which authorizes congress 'to make all laws which shall be necessary and proper for carrying into execution' the powers of the general government, without feeling a conviction that the convention understood itself to change materially the meaning of the word 'necessary,' by prefixing the word 'absolutely.' This word, then, like others, is used in various senses; and, in its construction, the subject, the context, the intention of the person using them, are all to be taken into view." [7]

[7] McCulloch v. Maryland, 4 Wheat. 316, 414, 4 L.Ed. 314, 412 (U.S. 1819). For a practical application of the relative nature of necessity, see Chapter 14 "Purely Penal Law."

B. *Requisites for a Just Law*

Implicit in obligation is the norm of a just law. "Just" implies
something due to others. A law then is just when it brings about
the common good of the citizens. "Laws enacted by men are
either just or unjust. If they are just, they have the power of
obliging in conscience . . . laws are said to be just both from
their end (when they are directed to the common good), from
their author (when the law enacted does not exceed the authority
of the lawmaker), and from their form (when burdens related to
the common good are imposed on subjects according to a proportional equality) . . . such laws, imposing burdens proportionately, are just and oblige in conscience and are legal enactments." [8]

1. *Necessary and possible.* The first requisite of a just law,
then, is that its content be something *necessary* for the common
good — keeping in mind that only persons with political authority can make laws. The second requisite is that the law be *possible* of fulfillment. The economic, social and moral conditions of
the citizens must be taken into account when the provisions of the
law are being considered. There must be a proper proportion between the demands of the law and the citizens' ability to fulfill
these demands. A tax law that would require 90 per cent of the
income of *all* citizens indiscriminately would lack such a proportion.[9]

2. *"Unjust law is no law."* Expressions such as "an unjust law
is no law at all," have been the cause of much misunderstanding.
From the strictly legal point of view, such statements seem meaningless. To the average lawman, if a statute or a judicial decision
has not been repealed or overruled, it is still the rule that will
govern all legal actions regardless of any other consideration.
Hence to say that a law is no law, when it is still obviously the law,
is to a lawman so much nonsense.

The statement, however, that "an unjust law is no law" bespeaks a philosophical and moral, rather than a legal, approach to
the problem. Such an expression refers to a quality that a law
must have if it is to fulfill the prerequisites of a law: that it be just
and conducive to the good of the people. Hence from this point

[8] Aquinas, 1-2 Sum. Theol. 96, 4.

[9] The citizens' ability to fulfill what is demanded by a law should be distinguished from the government's ability to enforce the law. The government's inability to enforce liquor laws would not make them unjust laws.
Perhaps this inability is due to an inadequate police force. If the citizens in
general so needed and used spirits that they were unable to observe such
laws, for this reason the laws would be unjust.

of view, a statute or judicial decision that does not fulfill these requirements of a just law is not a just law. And because "justness" is an essential quality of law, it is not law but "violence." [10] Such would be a "law" that decreed the gassing of millions of "political enemies" of a dictator. This would be to the philosopher of law the same as saying that, insofar as the statute was not just, it was no true law. In other words, the actual situation is: what may be considered morally bad law by philosophers is taken to be legally valid law by lawmen until it is repealed or overruled.

The misunderstanding that has arisen regarding the meaning of this phrase is a good example of the failure of two groups of men, who approach the same subject from a different angle, to appreciate each other's point of view.

II. NATURAL AND LEGAL OBLIGATION

Obligation, like title and claim, may be natural or legal. The manner in which they are related is of capital importance.

A. *Interrelation*

Legal obligation is related to moral obligation as what is specifically and in detail necessary for the common good is related to what is generally and in the large necessary. Although natural obligation does not include legal obligation, legal includes natural obligation. It does not exclude it. "It would not be correct to say that every moral obligation involves a legal duty; but every legal duty is founded on a moral obligation. A legal common law duty is nothing else than the enforcing by law of that which is a moral obligation without legal enforcement." [11]

1. *Specific determinations.* Men should not go around promiscuously killing each other. Every member of the community recognizes the general necessity of this for the common good. Each member is, therefore, naturally obliged to refrain from such action. But will there be such unity of recognition regarding the specific necessity of not carrying firearms for the security of the community? One man may judge he should not carry firearms because they are too dangerous to handle and he may shoot himself. Another may judge that he should carry arms to defend himself. These men can not be expected to be concerned first and

---

[10] Aquinas, 1-2 Sum. Theol. 96, 4.
[11] Queen v. Instan, 17 Cox Cr. Ca. 602, 1 Q.B. 450, 453 (1893). For comment on this point, see Allen, Legal Duties 207-208 (1931).

foremost with the common good. Their chief preoccupation is with their own proper good and rightly so.

If any unified action regarding the carrying of firearms is to be had, it must come from a governmental directive. This is the purpose of government, whose guiding interest is the public good. Hence, legislators and judges determine that, although carrying firearms may be permitted in exceptional cases, for the general run of men carrying them would constitute a threat to the peace and security of the community. Consequently, statutes and ordinances are passed forbidding the carrying of firearms. In view of the fact that these laws designate means that are specifically necessary for the security of the community, each one is obliged to observe them. And since this determination was made by lawmakers, this is a legal obligation.

Such is the case regarding other areas of public activities, for instance, taxes. Most men would recognize the necessity of government and that it must somehow be supported by the people. But, left to their own judgment, would the members of the community judge alike as to how this should be accomplished? Some could judge that they should make voluntary contributions to this good cause. Others could reason that their individual contributions would mean little, and so forth. Again, a unifying directive is necessary. This can come only from lawmakers. Since tax laws demand what is specifically necessary for the support of the government, all are obliged to obey. The decision was reached by lawmakers and so it is a matter of legal obligation.

2. *Same ultimate basis.* But regardless of whether the means necessary for the common good is something general, as "no promiscuous killing," or something specific, as "no carrying of firearms," the ultimate ground for natural and legal obligation is the same. This is the necessity of means to end. Promiscuous killing and carrying firearms are threats to the common security. This is determined by the nature of their overt acts. Difference in degree of threat does not change the fact that they are threats. Both must be curbed. The obligation to do so — natural in the one case and legal in the other — rests on the same basis: such a curbing is a means necessary for the common good.

Hence, if the necessity of means for an end is recognized by the natural, non-legal prudence which every man exercises, the obligation to perform these means is natural. If it is recognized with its cluster of specific details by legal prudence and embodied in a statute or judicial decision, the obligation is legal. The fact that penalties would be imposed by this ordinance for violations does not constitute the essential difference between legal and natural obligation, as will be adverted to shortly.

3. *Other meanings of obligation.* In law the word "obligation" has, of course, other less comprehensive meanings. It can refer to debts,[12] to the binding effect of contracts,[13] or to liability arising from tortious conduct.[14]

B. *Obligation In Conscience*

Regarding obligation, the question can be raised as to what "obligation in conscience" means. Is all obligation, obligation in conscience? According to the means-end basis of obligation, men have the overall obligation to avoid those things that are evil for them and keep them from attaining their end, and to pursue those things that are good and necessary and which lead to their end. For only in this way can they attain their perfection.

1. *Conscience.* Conscience is the judgment a man makes regarding what is good or bad, right or wrong for him — and therefore what he ought or ought not to do. Conscience derives from ". . . the application of our knowledge or science to what we do. . . . [I]t is applied insofar as we judge by our conscience that something should be done or not done." [15] Implied in conscience is accountability and sanction of some kind when these judgments are not followed.

These judgments of conscience necessarily enter into lawmaking as part of the background knowledges mentioned above. "What is conscience? . . . Every man of ordinary intelligence understands, in whatever other words we may express it, that conscience is that moral sense which dictates to him right and wrong. True, this sense differs in degree in individual members of society; but no reasonable being, whether controlled by it or not in his conduct, is wholly destitute of it. Greatly enlightened it is in some by reason of superior education, quickened in others because of settled religious belief in future accountability, dulled in others by vicious habits, but never altogether absent in any. Every statute enacted by a legislature, every decision pronounced by a court, every verdict of a jury, is professedly based on a moral

[12] Schwartz v. California Claim Service, 52 Cal. App. 2d 47, 125 P.2d 883, 887 (1942); McDonald v. Teft-Weller Co., 128 Fed. 381, 385, 386 (5th Cir. 1904).

[13] Sturges v. Crowninshield, 4 Wheat. 122, 197, 4 L. Ed. 529, 549 (1819); State v. Citrus County, 116 Fla. 676, 157 So. 4, 6 (1934).

[14] Enyeart v. City of Lincoln, 136 Neb. 146, 285 N.W. 314, 318 (1939).

[15] Aquinas, 1 Sum. Theol. 79, 13.

sense, prescribing what is right and prohibiting what is wrong.
. . . [Some one may say] 'It is simply a difference in judgment,
and no question of conscience whatever in the case.' But judgment is only the result or conclusion of conscience, after the latter
has performed its office in the different steps leading up to the
conclusion; and this conclusion, then, is the very truth to him who
has arrived at it by conscientious perception and reasoning." [16]

The directives of law indicate to a man what is good for him in
a particular instance and consequently what he ought to do.
Hence, law is formative of a man's conscience and helps him
judge what is good for him and what he ought to do. In a word,
to say that laws oblige in conscience means that laws direct a man
to do something that is good and necessary for him — an end to
which he is already obliged by his very nature.

Therefore, in view of the fact that every statute or court decision presents to the citizen a means-end relation that embodies a
good that is necessary for him, he is obliged "in conscience" to
follow it.[17] Otherwise he would not be doing what he knows
from his conscience is right, and this is the heart of not being
"true to one's self."

2. *Natural and legal obligation in conscience.* Both natural
and legal obligation bind in conscience. It is certainly true that
purely natural obligations are no concern of law. "With purely
moral obligations the law does not deal." [18] Unless such actions
have entered the realm of law through the portals of legislation
and adjudication they are beyond the legal ken.

But this fact should not be mistaken for another, namely that
both natural and legal obligation bind in conscience. Such has
not always been the insight of some courts. Legal obligation has
been spoken of as if it did not bind in conscience. ". . . [We]
are bound to the performance of a contract, or to make compensation for the failure to perform it, not only by its legal obligation,
but by the obligation of conscience . . . [T]he obligation depending upon conscience alone, is obviously beyond the reach of human legislation . . . From its very nature, therefore, the obligation depending upon conscience, can not be the subject of human
laws. Let these laws declare to the contrary, as they may, the
perception of right and wrong, and the state of feeling consequent upon that perception, will still remain the same in the

[16] Miller v. Miller, 187 Pa. 572, 41 Atl. 277, 280 (1898).

[17] From the theological viewpoint to be obliged in conscience means to be
obliged under the sanction of sin, grave or slight as the case may be.

[18] Buch v. Amory Manufacturing Co., 69 N.H. 257, 260, 44 Atl. 809, 810
(1898).

breast of the enlightened and virtuous. In vain would the legislature of any country declare that conscience should be no more, or that its obligation should cease. Conscience could not be thereby extinguished, and the virtuous citizen, who perceived his duties, would still feel the unabated force of his obligation to perform those duties." [19]

More accurate would it have been if this judge had opposed natural to legal obligation with the implication that, although natural obligation is no concern of law, nevertheless both natural and legal obligation oblige in conscience.

A practical example of the recognition of natural obligation in conscience is had in quasi-contracts. A contract may be unenforceable, though not void, because it does not meet the requirements of the Statute of Frauds. The plaintiff, who has repudiated this unenforceable contract, now sues to recover benefits which he has already conferred upon the defendant. Courts, recognizing that he is under a natural obligation to fulfill his contract, will refuse to allow recovery in quasi-contract.[20]

In sum, if a judge were really convinced that obligation in conscience is beyond the reach of law, to be consistent he should never take it upon himself, as a judge, to rebuke a law violator as being "conscienceless" and acting contrary to what he knew "he ought to do." For this would be overstepping the legal limits of his office. Only a reprimand to the wrongdoer would be in place for having brought upon himself the penalties imposed by law.

C. *Obligation and Motive*

Obligation is sometimes confused with motive, as we also saw sanction is. But they are different. Obligation is the moral necessity of choosing to perform an action because it is necessary for an end; motive is the reason why a man chooses to perform this action. Again it is true that the end and the motive may and should coincide, but this is not always so. A man ought to obey laws because he is motivated by a desire of promoting the public good which includes his own good. He may, however, obey for a different motive. He may want to avoid the punishment inflicted for disobedience. He may want to avoid the censure of friends. These are motives, but they are not the source of his obligation to obey the law. This source is a means-end fact situation.

Obligation is wrongly cut off from law and relegated to the

---

[19] Blair v. Williams, 4 Litt. 34, 41 (Ky. 1823).
[20] For further development of this point, see Chapter 18.

province of morals when it is confused with motive or sanction. When this occurs, the ability to see obligation as deriving from the necessity of means for an end in legal fact situations is precluded. The *end* and *purpose* itself of enacted law — the public good — becomes inoperative in legal thinking regarding law, sanction and obligation. Law in such thinking is said to be concerned only with enforcement; and if obligation is to be given any meaning at all in law, it is that of added sanction.

III. OBLIGATION IS NOT FORCE

When obligation is not seen clearly as resting on a factual means-end relation but is confused with sanction, it inevitably takes on the meaning of force. Legal obligation is then said to be what can be enforced, natural obligation is what can not. "A 'moral obligation' in law is defined as one 'which cannot be enforced by action but which is binding on the party who incurs it, in conscience and according to natural justice.' " [21]

Unquestionably a vital mark of difference between legal obligation and natural obligation is that one can be enforced and the other can not. "The vital distinction between a legal obligation and a moral obligation is that it is practicable to enforce the former and impracticable to enforce the latter." [22]

But this does not mean that force constitutes obligation. It is not its essence. For there can be valid laws, as we saw, even though no penalty is attached. Enforceability is simply a *sign* that a natural obligation has been made a legal one and that legal means have been provided which make enforceability possible. The added penalty does not form either law or obligation.

A. *Right and Remedy*

When obligation is made synonymous with force, a lack of force is said to imply a deficiency of obligation. This invites the unsupportable distinction between "perfect" and "imperfect" obligation. "The doing of justice, then, in a judicial sense, is the performance towards another of whatever is due to him in virtue of a perfect and rigorous right, the execution of which he may demand by forcible means unless we satisfy him freely and with good will. While, on the other hand, the performance of duties due to another only in virtue of an imperfect or non-rigorous obli-

[21] Backhaus v. Lee, 49 N.D. 821, 194 N.W. 887, 890 (1923); see also Bailey v. City of Philadelphia, 167 Pa. 596, 31 Atl. 925, 926 (1895).
[22] Westerman v. Mims, 111 Tex. 29, 227 S.W. 178, 183 (1921).

gation which can not be insisted on by violent methods, but the fulfilling of which is left to each man's honor and conscience, are comprehended under humanity, charity, or benevolence, in opposition to justice." [23]

The moral necessity of obligation becomes, in this theory, "real" or physical necessity. For ". . . the obligation arising from conscience is but an imperfect obligation. It is called an obligation . . . in an improper sense; for it rather influences than obliges, and even its influence operates with various degrees upon different individuals; whereas the legal obligation is a perfect obligation; it is the chain of the law, which binds equally all men, and compels them, by a real necessity, to perform their duties; and it is that necessity which constitutes the true character of an obligation." [24]

Inevitably, in this view, right becomes coextensive with remedy. "The obligation of a contract includes everything within its obligatory scope. Among these elements nothing is more important than the means of enforcement. This is the breath of its vital existence. Without it, the contract, as such, in view of the law, ceases to be, and falls into the class of those 'imperfect obligations,' as they are termed, which depend for their fulfillment upon the will and conscience of those upon whom they rest. The ideas of right and remedy are inseparable. 'Want of right and want of remedy are the same thing.' " [25]

To say that the "ideas of right and remedy are inseparable" may be admissible if the statement means that rights are of little practical legal value if no legal remedy is available. But if it means anything else, it is wholly unacceptable. For then it would mean that a man has a right only when he has a remedy — which is to reduce right to might. Those men and those countries only would have rights who have power. Those who have no such remedial power have no rights. True, where there is no power there is no enforcing of a right. But this does not mean that there still may be no right — as is the case of all minorities. To say otherwise is to redefine justice.

B. *Comment*

Ideas about obligation, like law and most other important concepts, do not spring full-blown and original from the heads of the

[23] Borden v. State, 11 Ark. 519, 528, 54 Am. Dec. 217, 220, 221 (1851).
[24] Blair v. Williams, 4 Litt. 34, 41 (Ky. 1823).
[25] Blakemoor v. Cooper, 15 N.D. 5, 106 N.W. 566 (1906). See also Harrison v. Bush, 5 El. & Bl. 344, 349, 119 Eng. Rep. 509, 512 (1855).

men who have them. We are all the intellectual heirs of the thinking of men who have preceded us. Our thinking usually has its roots in theirs.

The notion that obligation is the same as force or that it derives from the will of the lawmaker or sovereign suggests the influence of certain older philsophers of law.

1. *Nineteenth century.* A hundred years ago the idea was prevalent that the command obliged because the sovereign or superior had the power to inflict pain. "Laws and other commands are said to proceed from superiors, and to bind or oblige inferiors." [26] ". . . [T]he term superiority signifies might: the power of affecting others with evil or pain, and of forcing them, through fear of that evil, to fashion their conduct to one's wishes." [27] "Being liable to evil from you if I comply not with a wish which you signify, I am bound or obliged by your command, or I lie under a duty to obey it." [28] "If you express or intimate a wish that I shall do or forebear from some act, and if you will visit me with an evil in case I comply not with your wish, the expression or intimation of your wish is a command. A command is distinguished from other significations of desire, not by the style in which the desire is signified, but by the power and the purpose of the party commanding to inflict an evil or pain in case the desire be disregarded." [29]

At this time the obligation of law was explained as liability to force with the consequent distinction between so-called perfect and imperfect obligation. "The difference between Sanction and Obligation is simply this. Sanction is evil, incurred, or to be incurred by disobedience to command. Obligation is liability to that evil, in the event of disobedience." [30] "An imperfect law . . . or law of imperfect obligation . . . (with the sense wherein the term is used by the Roman jurists) is a law which wants a sanction, and which, therefore, is not binding. A law declaring that certain acts are crimes, but annexing no punishment to the commission of acts of the class, is the simplest and most obvious example. An imperfect law is not so properly a law, as counsel or exhortation addressed by a superior to inferiors." [31]

In this opinion there was law only when it obliged perfectly, that is, with a sanction. "Many of the writers on morals, and on

[26] Austin, Lectures on Jurisprudence 19 (Campbell ed. 1875).
[27] Id. at 20-21.
[28] Id. at 13.
[29] Id. at 12-13.
[30] Id. at 311.
[31] Id. at 22.

the so-called laws of nature, have annexed a different meaning to the term imperfect. Speaking of imperfect obligations, they commonly mean duties which are not legal; duties imposed by commands of God, or duties imposed by positive morality, as contradistinguished to duties imposed by positive law. An imperfect obligation, in the sense of the Roman jurists, is exactly equivalent to no obligation at all. For the term imperfect denotes simply that the law wants the sanction appropriate to laws of the kind. And imperfect obligation in the other meaning of the expression is a religious or a moral obligation." [32]

2. *Eighteenth century.* In the century preceding this, famous thinkers in law were holding that "even where rewards are proposed as well as punishments threatened, the obligation of the law seems chiefly to consist in the penalty; for rewards, in their nature, can only *persuade* and *allure;* nothing is *compulsory* but punishment." [33]

At the same time a philosophy of law was being evolved which, because of its basic assumptions, could not help but make the obligation of law synonymous with coaction. "For since law respects that only which is external and phenomenal in an action, strict law, i.e. law in which no ethical consideration is introduced, can require no internal, but merely external, determinators of choice, even although coaction be required to do so. All law whatever rests, it is true, on the consciousness of obligation under the moral law itself; but pure or strict law, in the sense now taken, does not expect that this consciousness should be the spring of conduct; but supports itself as a legislation for external actions, on its principle of coaction." [34] ". . . Law, strictly so called, always implies the power to co-act." [35]

Consequently in this theory morals or ethics is walled off from law. "All obligations incumbent on man to fulfill, are either juridical, for which outward laws are admissible to co-act their observance, or ethical, where no such legislation is conceivable; and these ethical offices cannot fall under any outward co-active legislation, because such offices depend on certain ends and de-

---

[32] Ibid. Another use of the distinction between "perfect" and "imperfect" obligation is made by some Scholastic writers whose position may be called "voluntaristic." For these, who do not consider the order manifested in natural drives as an expression of a directive judgment of the Creator of this order, "imperfect" obligation arises from the necessity perceived in the order of one thing to another. It is "perfect" obligation only if it is known to be a manifestation of the will of God. See Nivard, Ethica 114, 117 (1928).

[33] 1 Blackstone (1723-1780), Commentaries 57.

[34] Kant, The Metaphysics of Ethics 195 (Semple trans. 1936).

[35] Id. at 197.

signs which it is the imperative duty of man to propose to himself. But no outward compulsion can give any person certain intentions, for these depend on himself alone; for even though outward actions can be extorted, tending to that end, still the subject himself may be disinclined to it." [36]

The logical conclusion of these premises was that law and obligation are something for their own sake and not for the sake of an end to be attained. "This separation [between morals and law] is grounded on this, that the idea freedom, common to both these, renders necessary a distinction of duties into the offices of outward, and those of inward liberty, whereof the latter are alone moral." [37] "Duty is the necessity to act out of reverence for the law. For an object as the effect of my proposed action I can have an inclination, but never reverence, precisely because it is merely the effect, and not the activity, of a will. Only something which is conjoined with my will solely as a ground and never as an effect . . . and therefore only bare law for its own sake, can be an object of reverence and therewith a command." [38]

3. *Seventeenth century.* Another century and a half before this a philosophy of obligation based on the efficacious will of the lawmaker was widespread. The substance of law was said to be ". . . the command proceeding from the efficacious will to oblige, of him who has the authority. And an efficacious will produces its effect." [39] Hence there were said to be two kinds of laws, "One indicative and the other preceptive. . . . The first is entirely in the intellect and does not depend on the will. For it consists in a judgment indicating the thing itself as it is. But the second depends on the will inasmuch as it wishes to impose this or that obligation." [40]

As mentioned, positions regarding the meaning of law, its obligation and sanction, are directly related to certain non-legal assumptions from philosophy. For those, such as Marx and Lenin, who hold that men and life are coextensive only with matter, force is obviously the only meaning that could be given to the obligation of law.

Likewise for those who hold a "will" theory of the type of Blackstone, Kant, Bentham or Austin which precludes an objective, factual means-end basis of obligation by conceiving obligation as deriving solely from the inner necessity of the will itself,

[36] Id. at 203-204.
[37] Id. at 242.
[38] Kant, Groundwork of the Metaphysics of Morals 68 (Paton ed. 1947).
[39] Suárez, 1 De Legibus 14, 4.
[40] Suárez, 7 De Bonitate et Malitia 1, 5.

force is also the only meaning that can be given to the "external" obligation of law.

For others like Suárez who hold a "will" theory of law but one which is completely different from that of Kant and the others, force is not the core of obligation. Respect for the will of the lawmaker obviates such a dire conclusion, and sanction is seen for what it is, sanction, and not obligation. But although obligation in this theory was never confused with force, nevertheless its preoccupation with the will of the lawmaker as the source of obligation again precludes the factual relation of means to end being given consideration as the foundation of obligation. This same position was held by many philosophers of law going back to the thirteenth century.[41]

Hence, as already stated,[42] because either the great tradition of mankind or the preponderance of evidence or a more discerning analysis of reality points to the fact that man is not matter alone but also mind, that he can know enough of the nature of things to form ideas of means-end relations, and that he can make free decisions whose root is in knowledge, the above positions are untenable. Force is not obligation but extrinsic sanction and obligation is the moral necessity of making a free decision regarding a means-end fact situation.

C. *Attitudes*

There is more at stake in this examination of obligation than the mere uncovering of theoretical presuppositions and academic philosophies of law and obligation. These two divergent views of obligation, once they have worked their way into the mentality of the citizens, result in two entirely different attitudes toward law and the common good.

In one attitude, law and obligation are considered principally a matter of enforcement. The preoccupation is with avoiding the penalties of violation. The viewpoint here is that of the "bad man" and leads to the "bad man" theory of law. The "bad man . . . cares nothing for the ethical rule which is believed and practiced by his neighbors" but only wishes ". . . to avoid an encounter with the public force." [43] And since in this view ethics or morals is limited to ". . . the actual internal state of the individual's mind, what he actually intends," [44] it cannot concern itself

[41] Davitt, The Nature of Law 9-108 (1951).
[42] See Chapter 1.
[43] Holmes, The Path of the Law, 10 Harv. L. Rev. 457, 459 (1897).
[44] Id. at 463.

with external things such as enforcement. This is said to be the province of law only.

In the other attitude, law and obligation are first and foremost a matter of obtaining the common good. The main concern is with doing those things that will contribute to the general welfare. The viewpoint here is that of a means-end philosophy of life and law. In this view it is not a question of separating morals from law, but of obtaining the public good. And since in this view morals includes the same means-end relations as law, the attainment of the public good through statutes and decisions is a matter of morals as well as law.

In the "bad man" theory the dynamic of law is exclusively the fear of the superior's use of might. In the means-end analysis it is primarily the inferior's desire of doing what is right and secondarily the fear of punishment. In the "bad man" theory the fact that many will not fulfill their obligations and obey the law unless threatened by punishment is taken as an indication of what the nature of law and obligation is in itself. In the means-end analysis this fact has nothing to do with the true nature of law and obligation. It is indicative only of the necessity of punishment to assure the fulfillment of obligation and the observance of law.

Obligation in one explanation takes its meaning from the evil that is extrinsically imposed if the law is violated. It is germane with penalty and punishment, force and might. Obligation in the other analysis is based on an objective means-end relation. It is congenial with the common good to be attained rather than with punishment to be suffered, with claim and right rather than with force and might.

It is not difficult to see which of these two attitudes results in public-mindedness and a developed sense of common responsibility — whether on the national or international level. Only when the end of law — the common good — is the leitmotiv of law and obligation and sanction, can such an attitude grow and flourish.

The consequence of making enforceableness the essence of obligation and right is ultimately the reduction of these to power. This raised to the political level spells power politics, *Realpolitik* — of which the world has seen, and undoubtedly will continue to see, more than its share.

PART II

Man-discovered Law

CHAPTER 7

References to a Law Not Man-made

In judicial decisions and legislative enactments a phenomenon is observable which demands explanation. Occurring from time to time are references to a law that is presupposed by man-made law. They take for granted that another kind of law exists.

I. VARIOUSLY EXPRESSED

This presupposed law is referred to in various ways. It may be in terms of "fundamental principles," "a higher law," "common right and reason," "natural immutable and inherent principles of justice," "inalienable rights by nature," "law of nature," or "humanity."

A. *Fundamental Principles*

Speaking of whether a retrial in a murder case, after appeal by the prosecution, would constitute double jeopardy and therefore violate due process, a court asks: "Does it violate those 'fundamental principles of liberty and justice which lie at the base of all our civil and political institutions?' " [1]

This court was only voicing previous judicial recognition of these same basic principles. In discussing the statutes of a State regarding imprisonment and their relation to the due process clause of the Fourteenth Amendment, it was said ". . . that state action, whether through one agency or another, shall be consistent with the fundamental principles of liberty and justice which lie at

[1] Palko v. Connecticut, 302 U.S. 319, 328, 58 Sup. Ct. 149, 153 (1939).

the base of all our civil and political institutions and not infrequently are designated as 'law of the land.' Those principles are applicable alike in all the states and do not depend upon or vary with local legislation." [2]

B. *Higher Law*

In holding that the failure of railroad employees to aid an injured trespasser was not a violation of a legal duty, the court said, "With the humane side of the question courts are not concerned. . . . For withholding relief from the suffering . . . penalties are found not in the laws of men, but in that higher law, the violation of which is condemned by the voice of conscience, whose sentence of punishment for the recreant act is swift and sure." [3]

C. *Common Right and Reason*

In holding that a college of physicians was not entitled, under statute, to punish a physician for practicing medicine in the city without its license, the court said, "And it appears in our books, that in many cases, the common law will controll Acts of Parliament, and sometimes adjudge them to be utterly void; for when an Act of Parliament, is against common right and reason, or repugnant, or impossible to be performed, the common law will controll it, and adjudge such Act to be void; and therefore . . . some statutes are made against law and right which those who made them perceiving, would not put them in execution." [4]

D. *Natural and Inherent Principle of Justice*

In discussing the constitutionality of an act regulating the working hours in mines, mills and smelters, the court said, "This court

[2] Hebert v. Louisiana, 272 U.S. 312, 316, 317, 47 Sup. Ct. 103, 104 (1926). See also Monongahela Bridge Co. v. United States, 216 U.S. 177, 195, 30 Sup. Ct. 356, 361 (1910).

[3] Union Pacific Ry. Co. v. Cappier, 66 Kan. 649, 72 Pac. 281, 282 (1903). Sometimes the phrase "higher law" is used by courts in reference, not to a law that is not man-made, but to a more fundamental aspect of the laws of men. For instance, the individual rights of property must give way, in times of disaster, to "the higher laws of impending necessity." See Surocco v. Geary, 3 Cal. 69, 73 (1853).

[4] Dr. Bonham's Case, 8 Co. Rep. 107a, 118a, 77 Eng. Rep. 638, 652 (1609). The opinion expressed in this case was not adopted as the law of England. Acts of parliament are not subject to judicial review. See Plucknett, Bonham's Case and Judicial Review, 40 Harv. L. Rev. 30 (1926).

has never attempted to define with precision the words 'due process of law,' nor is it necessary to do so in this case. It is sufficient to say that there are certain immutable principles of justice which inhere in the very idea of free government which no member of the Union may disregard, as that no man shall be condemned in his person or property without due notice and an opportunity of being heard in his defence. . . . Recognizing the difficulty in defining with exactness the phrase 'due process of law,' it is certain that these words imply a conformity with natural and inherent principles of justice, and forbid that one man's property, right to property, shall be taken for the benefit of another, for the benefit of the State, without compensation." [5]

E. *Inalienable Rights by Nature*

The publication in moving picture of incidents in the past life of a former prostitute was declared to be an invasion of her inalienable right to pursue and obtain happiness. The court said ". . . the Constitution [of California] provides as follows: 'All men are by nature free and independent, and have certain inalienable rights, among which are those of enjoying and defending life and liberty; acquiring, possessing, and protecting property; and pursuing and obtaining safety and happiness.' The right to pursue and obtain happiness is guaranteed to all by the fundamental law of our state. This right by its very nature includes the right to live free from the unwarranted attack of others upon one's liberty, property, and reputation. Any person living a life of rectitude has that right to happiness which includes a freedom from unnecessary attacks on his character, social standing, or reputation." [6]

The denial of a passport was said to be a deprivation of the natural right to travel. "The right to travel, to go from place to place as the means of transportation permit, is a natural right, subject to the rights of others and to reasonable regulation under the law. A restraint imposed by the Government of the United States upon this liberty, therefore, must conform with the provision of the Fifth Amendment that 'No person shall be . . . deprived of . . . liberty . . . without due process of law.' " [7]

[5] Holden v. Hardy, 169 U.S. 366, 390, 18 Sup. Ct. 383, 387 (1898). See also State ex rel. Henshall v. Ludington, 33 Wis. 107, 116 (1873); Calder v. Bull, 3 Dall. 386, 388, 1 L.Ed. 385, 387 (1798).

[6] Melvin v. Reid, 112 Cal. App. 285, 297 Pac. 91, 93 (1931).

[7] Shachtman v. Dulles, 225 F.2d 938, 941 (D.C. Cir. 1955).

F.   *Law of Nature*

A marriage in which one of the persons was insane at the time of marriage was declared null.   The court, in support of its judgment, said: "That such a marriage is criminal and void by the law of nature, is a point universally conceded." [8]

G.   *Humanity*

Courts have also spoken of crimes that are "inhumane" and "against humanity."   "Crimes against humanity are . . . defined as 'Atrocities and offences, including but not limited to murder, extermination, enslavement, deportation, imprisonment, torture, rape, or other human acts committed against any civilian population, or persecutions on political, racial or religious grounds whether or not in violation of the domestic laws of the country where perpetrated.' " [9]

II.   NOTE OF CAUTION

Undoubtedly to assign to this presupposed law a position so basic to man-made law is to make of it something of first-rate legal importance.   What is implied in the above citations is that there is some kind of rule or norm or law that precedes the man-made law of legislation and adjudication and which is the basis for presupposing legally that there is any difference at all between right and wrong actions, between justice and injustice.   On this law rests the legal assumption that claims have a factual, primordial meaning and value, that there is an actual difference between a claim that is called just and one that is termed unjust.

It is further implied in such statements that a man is "obliged" to observe this basic law and that he "ought" to recognize and respect the just claims of others.   In a word, courts and legislators find the justifying base for elementary non-legal presuppositions in a law that is "higher," "more fundamental" and "natural."

But high-sounding though these phrases may be that are used in referring to this basic law, we should be immediately on our guard against reading into them any preconceived meanings that we may have in mind.   Maybe the courts have the meaning in

[8] Wightman v. Wightman, 4 Johns. Ch. 343, 349 (N.Y. 1820).
[9] 1 Trials of War Criminals Before the Nuernberg Military Tribunals 913 (1949).

mind we think they do; maybe they do not. What assurance is there that these phrases are anything more than aureate expressions of vague ideals? Do they refer to anything factual? Does there actually exist a law that is "fundamental" and "of nature"? In order to find and lay hold of such a law if possible, we must go beyond euphonious language and noble contexts.

Nature of Man-discovered Law

The general expressions quoted in Chapter 7 clearly refer to some kind of fundamental law but when attempts are made to describe it in detail a great variety of opinion shows itself. The very difficult problem to be solved at this point is to determine what this more fundamental law is. Depending on how this problem is solved rests the possibility of any "law of nature" as well as any valid meaning that can be given to it in legal references.

I. OPINIONS REGARDING "NATURAL LAW"

The prevalent opinions regarding the meaning of "natural law" vary. Some conceive it to be some sort of body of ideal precepts known by reasoning that will furnish mathematically certain conclusions. Others consider it to include also what is known from divine revelation. Still others interpret it as expressive of the economic pressures that are predominant at any particular time.

A. *Body of Ideal Precepts*

This law is commonly said to be ". . . a body of ideal precepts of universal validity for all peoples, all times, and all places, derived from ideas of what an ideal man would do and not do, would claim and would concede as the claims of others, and arrived at by pure reason." [1] Or it has been considered to be "The deduction of legal rules from certain *a priori* principles of right and wrong," [2] the origin of which principles is quite uncertain.

1. *Gives no specific solution.* This notion of natural law supposes that it will give specific solutions for everyday problems of torts and crimes. "Suppose a professional forger draws a check on the account of a well-known businessman so skillfully that what

[1] Pound, Social Control Through Law 3 (1942). By permission of the Yale University Press.
[2] Keeton, The Elementary Principles of Jurisprudence 8 (1949).

appears to be his commonly known signature is recognized by everyone. He takes it to a department store, makes some purchases, and tenders the check with his endorsement in payment. The cashier and credit man recognize the signature and know the bank to be that in which the apparent drawer has his account. The forger is given the balance in cash and disappears with the goods and the cash. The check is endorsed by the store company and deposited in its bank which gives credit therefor. It is sent to the clearinghouse the next day which gives credit therefor to the first bank and sends it for collection to the second bank, the one on which it was drawn. That bank, seeing the well-known signature of a regular depositor with a good balance, pays the amount to the clearinghouse. At the end of the month, when the canceled checks are sent to the supposed drawer, the forgery is discovered. Who is to bear the loss? It can hardly be divided by four. Some one of the four equally innocent persons must bear the loss. But is any one at fault beyond the forger who is out of reach? What moral precept will decide such a case? . . . It is because there is no 'natural' guide to solution of so many of these conflicts and overlappings of competing claims and expectations that we must have positive law or go back to private war." [3]

Or, to take another example of how this law is conceived, it is said, "In the field of traffic law it had long been thought by lawmakers that twenty miles an hour was a proper speed for city traffic and that stop lights on all dangerous corners could prevent accidents. During the last two or three decades traffic engineers with delegated powers of lawmaking have begun to investigate these 'obvious natural law theories' with startling results. A single example will suffice. It was observed that at a certain crossroad an unusual number of accidents were occurring. The city fathers immediately concluded that the obvious thing to do was to put in stop lights; but when these were installed, to their consternation, accidents increased. They then called in a traffic engineer. After studying the situation with radar speed recorders, automatic counting machines, statistical correlations and other devices of modern science, and relying on previous experiments, they changed the rule of law from a traffic signal to two phychologically tested stop signs on one of the intersecting roads. The town fathers were certain that the traffic engineer was obviously wrong; but a further study revealed that the new device reduced accidents over a similar period of time in a ratio of from

[3] Pound, Justice According to Law 8, 15 (1951). By permission of the Yale University Press.

fourteen to one, while at the same time speeding up the traffic." [4]

2. *Is not practically concise.* It is this same notion of natural law that looks for deductions that are scientifically exact and accurate. ". . . [N]one of the numerous natural law theories has so far succeeded in defining the content of this just order in a way even approaching the exactness and objectivity with which natural science can determine the content of the laws of nature, or legal science the content of a positive legal order." [5] "For, in the process, its content has to be increasingly assimilated to positive law or reduced to empty formulas, such as 'Equal things shall receive equal treatment'; 'Suum cuique'; 'Injure no one without a just cause'; 'Do good and avoid evil,' etc. Without presupposing the existence of a positive legal order all these formulas are devoid of sense; but if related to any positive legal order they can justify it. Furthermore, the natural-law teachers contend, in a version which has remained a stereotype from the church fathers down to Kant, that positive law derives its entire validity from natural law; it is essentially a mere emanation of natural law; the making of statutes or of decisions does not freely create, it merely reproduces the true law which is already somehow in existence, and positive law (the copy), whenever it contradicts natural law (the model or archetype), cannot have any validity." [6]

In this conception, natural law is thought of as a master blueprint of which positive law is merely a faithful tracing. "This is the typical picture which natural-law doctrine draws of the legal world — its legal-world picture so to speak: In the foreground is positive law, essentially in uncontested validity; behind positive law, duplicating it in a peculiar manner, is a natural law, representing a higher order, the source of all validity and social value, whose function in the main is the justification of positive law." [7] "Natural law doctrine is characterized by a fundamental dualism between positive and natural law. Above the imperfect positive law, a perfect — because absolutely just — natural law exists; and positive law is justified only insofar as it corresponds to the natural law." [8]

[4] Beutel, The Relationship of Natural Law to Experimental Jurisprudence, 13 Ohio St. L.J. 167, 174 (1952).

[5] Kelsen, General Theory of Law and State 9-10 (Wedberg trans. 1945). By permission of the author.

[6] Id. at 416.

[7] Id. at 417.

[8] Id. at 12.

B. *Known Partly from Revelation*

Another way natural law is conceived by some is as including norms that are known, not only from reason, but also from divine revelation — oral or written. "It is not consonant with twentieth-century American justice to say that property may be destroyed by any one, much less the State (the very symbol of correctness in organized society), with legal immunity. The law of nature, *compounded* of the dictates of the Supreme Lawmaker and reason emanating from untrammeled intellect, rebels against this antiquated doctrine of irresponsibility, no matter by whom or by what exercised." [9]

Courts have said, "Not less wonderous than the revelations of the starry heavens, and much more important, and to no class of men more so than lawyers is the moral law which Kant found within himself, and which is likewise found within, and is consciously recognized by, every man. This moral law holds its dominion by divine ordination over us all, from which escape or evasion is impossible. This moral law is the eternal and indestructible sense of justice and of right written by God on the living tablets of the human heart and revealed in his Holy Word." [10]

1. *Deductions from revelation.* Some think of this law as norms that are deduced not only from reason but also from revelation. "At the present there is a revival of natural law . . . which would give us a theory of the end of law by logical deduction from what is given us by revelation and by intelligence." [11]

2. *Includes revelation.* Others look upon this law as including revelation. "The natural law theories of the past and present seem to offer two ways of discovering this higher or perfect law. One is reason; the other divine guidance or revelation. . . . Among those who purport to have been in contact with the Source of all wisdom are Christ, Buddha, Mohammed, Confucius, to name only a few." [12]

---

[9] Boorse v. Springfield Township, 377 Pa. 109, 103 A.2d 708, 713 (1954). (Emphasis added.)

[10] Moore v. Strickling, 46 W. Va. 515, 33 S.E. 274, 277 (1899).

[11] Pound, Justice According to Law 28 (1951). By permission of the Yale University Press. The word "revelation" could be used to connote the "revealing" of a law through a man's basic inclinations. However, the word is usually taken in the technical sense of sacred sayings or writings. References to the Bible, Talmud, Koran, and the like, in these discussions of natural law, would seem to indicate that the word is intended in this latter sense.

[12] Beutel, The Relationship of Natural Law to Experimental Jurisprudence, 13 Ohio St. L.J. 167, 170 (1952).

This same notion is to be found in court thinking. ". . . [B]y the law of nature [is understood] those fit and just rules of conduct which the Creator has prescribed to man, as a dependent and social being; and which are to be ascertained from the deductions of right reason, though they may be more precisely known, and more explicitly declared by divine revelation." [13]

Still others take natural law as synonymous with the Golden Rule and look upon it as incorporated in the Decalogue. "It [the natural law as the Golden Rule] is universal, unchangeable, eternal. It is reasonable and full of logic. From it there can be no plausible deviation. It is complete. But its universality is what is so amazing. We speak of races as savage, wild, uneducated, uncivilized. Yet, they discovered this rule of life, even as they discovered mother-love and the stars and the periodicity of life. As man began to think and believe, this rule of life came to him and with it, gradually, other rules which were finally incorporated in what my ancestors called the Ten Commandments. This is the essence of revealed truth." [14]

C. *Expression of Socio-Economic Conditions*

Another way the phrase "natural law" is understood is as denoting the normative pressure of prevailing conditions, especially economic. In this view natural law is a ". . . body of rules governing legal development in accordance with prevailing economic, social and political conditions." [15] Such a view has received much impetus from legal thinkers whose inspiration is dialectical materialism.

II. BACKGROUND OF OPINIONS

Whose theories of natural law are reflected in the above opinions? It is of capital importance at this point to indicate what positions of natural law are being discussed in these statements.

A. *State of Nature — Mathematical Certainty*

The notion that natural law is a body of ideal precepts derives from the hypothesis, which was current in the seventeenth and

[13] Wightman v. Wightman, 4 Johns. Ch. 343, 349 (N.Y. 1820).
[14] Sokolsky, The Source of Human Rights, 4 University of Notre Dame Natural Law Institute Proceedings 7, 16 (1951).
[15] Haines, The Law of Nature in State and Federal Judicial Decisions, 25 Yale L.J. 617 (1916).

eighteenth centuries, that men lived in a state of "nature" before uniting into political society and that conclusions in morals could be deduced with the certainty of mathematics.

1. *Pre-social state of nature.* It was the contention of Hobbes that men lived in a warlike condition of mere nature, before entering society in order that they might have peace. That there was actually a historical time when men lived in such a "state" seems to have been what Hobbes had in mind. For the life of man, he says, was then not only "nasty" and "brutish," but also "solitary." ". . . [I]t is manifest that during the time men live without a common power to keep them all in awe, they are in that condition which is called war; and such a war as is of every man against every man." [16] "For the laws of nature, which consist in equity, justice, gratitude, and other moral virtues on these depending, in the condition of mere nature . . . are not properly laws, but qualities that dispose men to peace and obedience." [17] ". . . [A]nd the life of man, solitary, poor, nasty, brutish, and short." [18]

It was also held by Locke that the "law of nature" was related immediately to the "state of nature." "The state of nature has a law of nature to govern it which obliges everyone; and reason, which is that law, teaches all mankind who will but consult it that, being all equal and independent, no one ought to harm another in his life, health, liberty, or possessions." [19]

The idea of a historical state of nature was solidified by Montesquieu who said clearly that it existed "before" the organization of society. "Antecedent to all these laws [political and civil laws] are those of nature, so called because they derive uniquely from the constitution of our being. In order to understand these well, it is necessary to consider man before the establishment of societies. The laws of nature will be those that he received in such a state." [20]

Further impetus to the idea of a "state of nature" as an "original" state was given by Rousseau. "Let us assume that men have reached the point where the obstacles to their self-preservation in the state of nature are too great to be overcome by the forces each individual is capable of exerting to maintain himself

[16] Hobbes (1588-1679), Leviathan, Pt. I, c. 13 (Molesworth ed. 1839).

[17] Id., Pt. II, c. 26, n.4.

[18] Id., Pt. I, c. 13.

[19] Locke (1632-1704), Two Treatises on Government, Second Treatise, c. 2, 6 (Cook ed. 1947).

[20] Montesquieu (1689-1755), 1 De l'Esprit des Lois, Bk. 1, p. 2 (my trans.).

in that state. This original state can then no longer continue; and the human race would perish if it did not change its mode of existence." [21] . . . "This passage from the natural to the civil state produces a very remarkable change in man, substituting justice for instinct as the guide to his conduct, and giving his actions the morality they previously lacked. Then only is it that the voice of duty takes the place of physical impulse, and law the place of appetite." [22] "Instead of destroying natural equality, the fundamental compact, on the contrary, substitutes moral and legal equality for such physical inequalities as nature may have created among men; and different as they may be in physical or intellectual powers, they all become equal by convention and in the eyes of the law."[23]

This concept of the natural law as based on a "state of nature" was adopted by Blackstone and through him found its way into the thinking of many courts. "A right of privacy in matters purely private is therefore derived from natural law. . . . It is one of those rights referred to by some law writers as 'absolute' — 'such as would belong to their persons merely in a state of nature, and which every man is entitled to enjoy, whether out of society or in it.' 1 Bl. Comm. 123. . . . The individual surrenders to society many rights and privileges which he would be free to exercise in a state of nature, in exchange for the benefits which he receives as a member of society. But he is not presumed to surrender all those rights, and the public has no more right, without his consent, to invade the domain of those rights which it is necessarily to be presumed he has reserved, than he has to violate the valid regulations of the organized government under which he lives. The right of privacy has its foundation in the instincts of nature." [24]

Courts have also shown "state-of-nature" thinking regarding property. "But what is the law in regard to private property? In a historical examination of the question we find that man in the rudest state of nature was not without some notions of exclusive property, and that jurists in every age, as civilization advanced, have maintained that what a man has obtained by the honest exertion of his own mind, or his own hand, is by natural

21 Rousseau (1712-1778), Du Contrat Social, Bk. I, c. 6 (Watkins trans. 1953).
22 Id., c. 8.
23 Id., c. 9.
24 Paveshich v. New England Life Insurance Co., 122 Ga. 190, 50 S.E. 68, 69, 70 (1905).

right his own property. Indeed, it may be said that the protection of this right is the main security to the enjoyment of life." [25]

2. *Mathematical certainty.* The notion that a body of precepts could be deduced from the principles known in the "state of nature," even as in mathematics, is also traceable to authors of this period. This was the position held by Grotius. It is necessary ". . . that we diligently distinguish between general principles, such as one must live virtuously, that is, according to reason, and certain principles proximate to these, but so manifest that they do not admit of doubt, such as one should not take what belongs to another; and between inferences some of which are easily known, as in marriage there should be no adultery, others that are known with greater difficulty, such as revenge which is satisfied in the pain of another is vicious. This is almost the same as in mathematics, where certain principles are known first then those proximate to these, then certain demonstrations which immediately are understood and assented to, then certain principles which are true but which are not obvious to all." [26]

Perhaps as much as anyone else, Locke promoted the idea that morality and therefore law was a science capable of demonstration like mathematics. "I am bold to think that morality is capable of demonstration, as well as mathematics: since the precise real essence of the things moral words stand for may be perfectly known, and so the congruity and incongruity of the things themselves be certainly discovered; in which consists perfect knowledge." [27] Locke places ". . . *morality* amongst the *sciences capable of demonstration:* wherein I doubt not but from self-evident propositions, by necessary consequences, as incontestible as those in mathematics, the measures of right and wrong might be made out, to any one that will apply himself with the same indifferency and attention to the one as he does to the other of these sciences." [28] "Confident I am, that, if men would in the same method, and with the same indifferency, search after moral as they do mathematical truths, they would find them to have a strong connexion one with another, and a

[25] Atchison & Nebraska R.R. Co. v. Baty, 6 Neb. 40, 29 Am. Rep. 356, 357 (1877).
[26] Grotius (1583-1645), De Jure Belli ac Pacis, Lib. II, cap. XX, XLIII, 1 (Whewell ed. 1853) (my trans.).
[27] Locke, An Essay Concerning Human Understanding, Bk. III, c. 11, n. 16 (Fraser ed. 1894).
[28] Id., Bk. IV, c. 3, n.18.

more necessary consequence from our clear and distinct ideas, and to come nearer perfect demonstration than is commonly imagined." [29]

The "real essences" of human actions, for Locke, were not variables but constants as in mathematics. ". . . [M]orality is capable of demonstration as well as mathematics. For the ideas that ethics are conversant about, being all real essences, and such as I imagine have a discoverable connection and agreement one with another; so far as we can find their habitudes and relations, so far we shall be possessed of certain, real, and general truths; and I doubt not but if a right method were taken a great part of morality might be made out with that clearness, that could leave, to a considering man, no more reason to doubt, than he could have to doubt of the truth of propositions in mathematics, which have been demonstrated to him." [30] ". . . [T]he truth of all these moral rules plainly depends upon some other antecedent to them, and from which they must be deduced: which could not be if either they were innate or so much as self-evident." [31]

B. *Scriptures Part of Law of Nature*

The idea that natural law is partly known from revelation or includes it, seems to have been furthered by men like Blackstone who spoke of the commands of Holy Scripture as part of the law of nature. "The doctrines thus delivered we call the revealed or divine law, and they are to be found only in the holy scriptures. These precepts, when revealed, are found upon comparison to be really a part of the original law of nature, as they tend in all their consequences to man's felicity. . . . [T]he moral precepts of this law are indeed of the same original with those of the law of nature . . ." [32]

This manner of speaking of revealed and natural law was adopted by courts. "Mr. Blackstone in his Commentaries, says: 'If our reason were always, as in our first ancestor before his transgression, clear and perfect, unruffled by passions, unclouded by prejudice, unimpaired by disease or intemperance . . . we should need no other guide. . . . But every man now finds the contrary in his own experience, — that his reason is corrupt and his understanding full of ignorance and error.' This, as the

---

29 Id., n.20.
30 Id., c. 12, n.8.
31 Id., Bk. I, c. 2, n.4.
32 1 Blackstone, Commentaries 42.

author argues, made it necessary for benign Providence to discover and enforce its laws by an immediate and direct revelation. These precepts are contained only in the Holy Scriptures, and on examination and comparison by unclouded reason they are found to be a part of the original law of nature, as 'they tend in all their consequences to man's felicity.' " [33]

C. *Principles Founded on Economic Conditions*

The notion of natural law as expressive of social, economic and political conditions is, of course, an attempt to interpret a traditional idea in terms of Marx's dialectic of matter. The law of nature in this context is the law of economic facts. All ideas derive their significance thereform.

Laski expressed this new foundation of thought with characteristic clarity. "The basis of our principles is to be found in the economic conditions of our times." [34] Consistent with this view, then, ". . . soviet socialist law is the aggregate of rules of conduct (norms) established or approved by the state authority of the socialist state, and expressing the will of the worker class and of all the toilers; the application of these rules of conduct is guaranteed by the coercive force of the socialist state to the end of defending, making secure and developing relationships and arrangements advantageous and agreeable to the worker class and to all the toilers, of destroying completely and finally the survivals of capitalism in the economy, mode of life and consciousness of human beings, and of building communist society." [35]

D. *Comment*

Certain brief comments must be made on the assumed "state of nature" and mathematical certainty of natural law precepts, on the difference between conclusions based on evidence and those resting on authority, and on the basing of all principles — moral as well as legal — on a dialectic of matter.

1. *No "state of nature" or mathematical certainty.* The notion of natural law that is based on a "state of nature" is without foundation. There is not a shred of historical evidence that men

---

[33] Moore v. Strickling, 46 W. Va. 515, 33 S.E. 274, 277 (1899). The reference is to 1 Blackstone, Commentaries 41.

[34] Laski, The Basis of Vicarious Liability, 26 Yale L.J. 111 (1916).

[35] Golunskii and Strogovich, The Theory of the State and Law, in Soviet Legal Philosophy 386 (Babb trans. 1951). By permission of the Harvard University Press.

ever lived in such a state before the organization of society. In fact, all data indicate the contrary, that men have at all times lived in some sort of society. "Political organization comes into being wherever societies are segmented on the basis of kinship, economics, religion, sex, fraternities, or community. Where there are subgroups that are discrete entities within the social entirety, there is political organization — a system of regulation of relations between groups or members of different groups within the society at large." [36]

Hence, the necessary presupposition in any verifiable concept of natural law must be that man is by nature a social animal who has always lived in a state of society. "The social-contract explanation left the tracks at the start when it assumed a 'state of nature' in which men had no social ties, so that they had to come together and agree to set up, under government, a social order. It was necessary to go back to the rejected insight of Aristotle, that man is a social animal." [37] To hold that men have no natural urge to live in society, and that historically they led a pre-social life of status before entering into a life of social contract, is to go contrary to the facts at hand.

The aspiration to mathematical certainty regarding detailed precepts of human actions, as has been mentioned and will be noted again, rests on a false assumption: that human actions are constants as are the data of scientific analysis. This supposition fails to take into account the difference between the necessary and the contingent. One is the judgment of science, the other the judgment of prudence.

2. *Evidence vs. authority.* Nor are the demands of man-discovered law, as such, known from oral or written revelation such as is contained in the Bible. The reason for this confusion could be the fact that what is known through man-discovered law *may also* be known from revealed law. That it is wrong to take for "mine" what is "thine" would be such an example. But the *different manner* in which this is *known* is what separates the one from the other. The elementary demands of man-made law, as we will see, are known without reasoning from the observable data of the basic drives. The commands of revealed law are known by faith and belief in the credibility of the one revealing. The assent of the mind based on evidence is one thing; the assent

[36] Hoebel, Man in the Primitive World 376 (1949). See also Hoebel, Authority in Primitive Societies, in Authority 222-234 (Friedrich ed. 1958); Lowie, Primitive Society 358-396 (1920).

[37] MacIver, The Web of Government 20 (1947). By permission of the Macmillan Company.

of the mind based on authority, though truly an assent, is another. These are separate and distinct ways of knowing.

Another reason for the present confusion of natural law with revelation, seems to have been the manner in which men like Blackstone discussed this subject. His statement that one law is "part" of the other, if not properly understood as referring to their ultimate content, can be completely misleading when taken as relating to the manner in which each is known. Further, the law of nature of which he speaks as guiding our first ancestor "before his transgression," can be easily mistaken by the unwary for Hobbes' and Locke's law of nature which supposedly guided men in a hypothetical "state of nature" which existed before political society.

The actual state of man before his *transgression,* however, must be clearly distinguished from the hypothetical state of man before union in *society.* The one state is a historical fact which is known by faith in revelation. It refers to the first instance of a man violating a law. There is historical evidence of the deleterious effect of this incident in the constant perverseness manifested by the human race. This state "before the fall," to speak technically, is opposed to the subsequent state of "fallen nature." [38] But in this state man was naturally social.

The other supposed state is an assumption for which, as already noted, there is no evidence or reason to believe that it ever existed. This "state of nature" is contrasted with the "state of organized society." In this hypothetical "state of nature" man, so it was said, was naturally antisocial and antipolitical.

The manner of speaking about the law of nature, then, in which Blackstone and others indulged was not conducive to distinguishing accurately between natural law and revelation. While it is true that what is demanded by men's nature and what is demanded by revelation have the same source (the Creator) and have the same general content (although it is clearer in detail in revelation), nevertheless they are known in an entirely different manner. This is their main distinguishing mark.

3. *Matter and mind.* The notion that men are merely economic units of matter and in no way possess a mind has the preponderance of observable evidence against it and runs counter to the conviction of the majority of mankind. To come to grips with this issue in pre-legal thinking, however, has the merit of

[38] For a discussion of this point see Niebuhr, Nature and Destiny of Man 241-264 (1943).

joining forces over the central non-legal assumption of law: the nature of man.

E. *Dilemma*

If any of the meanings outlined above is given to natural law, obvious difficulties immediately arise. First, it is a matter of experience that solutions are not reached in many practical cases simply by applying a logically deduced rule. Induction and research are often required. Secondly, if natural law is known through supernatural revelation how can it be natural? To know something on authority is not the same as knowing it from evidence. Third, if natural law is merely an expression of the coactive pressure of economic phenomena how is it a law in the sense of a directive issued by a lawmaker? For law originates in legislators and judges, that is, persons and not things.

Hence, if there is such a thing as a "more fundamental" and "higher" law for men that is also a natural law, it must somehow be found in the *nature* of men and be related to a directive judgment that is *law*.

III. The Essence of Man-discovered Law

The burden now remains of determining precisely what this law in men's nature is which differs from any of the descriptions given above. The approach to the problem is controlling at this point.

A. *Approach: Locate Expression of Directives*

If this "fundamental law" is actually a law, it must manifest itself as a directive. For, as we have seen, law is essentially a directive. The approach to the problem, then, is by way of searching for something in a man's natural way of acting that can be identified either as a directive or as the expression of a directive. [39] Since a directive implies a relation of means to end, this inquiry is the same as seeking an ordering of means to end in the nature of men.

[39] "Natural" refers to something arising from nature. "Nature" is the intrinsic, essential principle of a thing which makes it be what it is. In a living being it is that which guides its internal structure, growth and functioning, and on account of which a thing has the peculiar characteristics it has. See Wild, Introduction to Realistic Philosophy 279, 481 (1948).

This directive, if it is to be ultimately recognizable as a law, must issue from someone with lawmaking authority and have as its end a common good. Hence these aspects of law must also eventually be located.

B. *Basic Drives Express Directives*

It is in a man's basic drives that the evidence of directives is discoverable. These drives are characterized by the fact that they are concerned with the preservation of existence in one way or another and with giving meaning to this existence.

1. *Order of means to end.* In the basic drives there are observable data of an ordering of means to end which is the essence of a directive. This is observable in the drives for happiness in general, for self-preservation, sexual union, living in community and doing so rationally.

a. *Self-preservation.* The end and purpose of the instinct of self-preservation is obviously the preservation of a man in existence. The means demanded by this drive are all the self-preserving actions that are necessary to keep a man alive. It may be jumping out of the path of an automobile, throwing the hands up in front of oneself, or taking the innumerable measures that are necessary for the preservation of good health. There is a relation between these self-preserving actions demanded by a man's drive for self-preservation and his continued existence which is the end this drive is designed to secure.

b. *Sex, community, rational living.* The same is true of a man's other drives. An order is observable in them. There is a relation between the sex acts that are demanded by the drive to unite sexually and the continuance of the human species. There is an order between just actions as demanded by the drive to live with other men and the fulfillment of proper and common needs. There is a connection between the acts of acquiring knowledge, of exercising free decision as demanded by the drive to use the intellectual-volitional powers, and the attainment of a man's highest development.

c. *Happiness.* More fundamental, however, than the order discernible in the drives concerned with a man's existence in its various phases is the order observable in his master drive for happiness. This drive is for that object or end or good that will assure his highest development and perfection and thereby give meaning and happiness to his existence. There is a relation discernible between the self-developing actions demanded by a man's master drive for happiness and the final attainment of his goal.

In a word, it is in a man's basic drives demanding happiness and the means to be used to reach this end that an order is observable which is the first essential evidence of a directive that can be called law.

2. *Cause of directive: An intelligent being.* A law is a directive judgment formed by someone with lawmaking authority. Can the order and direction observable in a man's basic drives be caused by some person and therefore be an expression of a directive judgment?

a. *Simple order and chance.* Order may be simple or complex, unrepeated or repeated. When the order or relation of one thing to another is simple enough, the human mind admits the possibility of chance. Thus, if a man were walking along a beach and found two pieces of driftwood lying in such a position that they formed the letter T, an explanation satisfactory to his mind would be that the position of the two pieces of driftwood was brought about by chance.

b. *Complex order implies intelligence.* If the man were to continue walking down the beach for a mile, however, and every ten yards found pieces of driftwood lying in the same position, mere chance would appear to his mind as an insufficient explanation. The repetition itself of the simple order of one piece of driftwood to the other would seem to indicate that these might be symbols having some meaning.

All the more would chance appear as an unsatisfactory explanation if several pieces of driftwood were found placed in such a relation to each other that they formed the letters T L T L T. Here the complexity of the order shown would almost certainly rule out chance as an explanation satisfying the mind. The order and relation of the pieces would seem to express a meaning. The formation of the pieces is a means to the end of expressing this meaning. When a meaning is seen in something, it implies that there is something intelligible about it, and to be intelligible denotes that it has been caused by an intelligent being — a person. The conclusion that any normal man would draw if he found the pieces of driftwood forming the above mentioned letters would be: "Someone has been here and done this." It is a normal function of the human mind to account for observable order by attributing to it an intelligent cause — that is, a person.

So also in regard to the order observable in a man's basic drives.

The only satisfactory explanation of these drives, manifesting the invariable order of means to end that they do, is that they are caused by an intelligent being, by some person.[40]

3. *Creative authority*.   The identity of this person and the source of his claim to authority must be determined.   He cannot be a man (much less an animal or any lower living being).   No man knows enough about himself, say, of his own biological functions, to order and direct their operations.   No man can eliminate his own drive for self-preservation.   Hence if an intellectual being is the cause of the order discernible in a man's basic drives, he must be extratemporal, transmundane, suprahuman. In a word, he must be someone with the *power of giving existence* to creatures with such ordered drives.

The counterpart of "authority over" is "subjection to."   A man has no choice over the fact that he is made the way he is with dynamic drives that demand a certain way of acting.   Willy-nilly he is "subject to" their demands.   And if he is "subject to" these directives, the one who established them has "authority over" him.   Hence the one who gives existence to a man whose nature expresses directives that must be followed is in a position of authority over him.   The overall end of these directives will be examined later.

C.   *Promulgation Through Drives*

Those who are to be guided and directed by a law know of it first through its promulgation.   The same is true of man-discovered law which, as is now evident, is creator-made.

Starting with the order and direction of means to end observable in a man's basic drives, we trace the cause of these data. Only the directive judgment in the mind of the creator of these drives that express such an ordering, furnishes a rationale for this phenomenon.   Chance is the only other explanation.   But this

[40] "Wherever we see a well-ordered arrangement of things, we instinctively assume that someone has intentionally placed them in that way."   Polanyi, The Logic of Liberty 154 (1951).

To say that we always think order bespeaks an intellectual cause because of custom (we know from experience that "effects" have "causes") only begs the question: why has this been the custom?   Why in our experience is order always the effect of an intellectual cause — a person?   Why do not brute animals give evidence of producing order in new complexities as men do?

Whether or not a man as presently constituted is — in some regards — the product of evolutionary processes does not change the main problem: how explain the order observable in a man's basic inclinations?   Still to be answered would be the question: How could evolutionary processes produce this order?

flies in the face of our daily experience with ordered patterns, which we know are conceived only by intelligent beings.

In a word, the directive judgment of the creator is made known and is expressed in the demands of the basic drives. Creator-made law is promulgated in a man's dynamic nature and therein it is man-discovered. "It is evident that all things participate somehow in the eternal law, namely, in so far as from its impression they have inclinations to their proper acts and ends. . . . The expression of an active intrinsic principle is to natural things what the promulgation of law is to men; because by the promulgation of law there is impressed on men a directive principle of human actions." [41] This promulgation is a continuous phenomenon. How men know this without a reasoning process will be examined shortly.

D. *Summary*

In brief, the order observable in a man's basic drives is the expression of a law. The cause of this datum is the directive judgment of ordering in the mind of the Prime Orderer. The one ordering is in a position of authority, because men are, by the very way they are made, subject to his directives as expressed in their basic tendencies. The means ordered are goods that fulfill the elemental needs of a man.

Man-discovered law, then, in terms of what it is *in itself,* is the *directive judgment* of the *Creator ordering means necessary* for the *common good* of all men and promulgated through their basic drives.

In terms of its *promulgation,* a man-discovered law is the *elementary demands expressed through a man's basic drives,* which are *known without a reasoning process.*[42] How this occurs is examined in the following chapter.

41 Aquinas, 1-2 Sum. Theol. 91, 2, and 93.
Creator-made *law,* in so far as, strictly speaking, it is a directive judgment in the mind of the Creator who is eternal, is eternal and is sometimes called "eternal law." Its promulgation, which takes place in space-time, is temporal. Its expression through created natures is often called "natural law"; if it be through irrational natures or things, it is termed the "natural physical law," if through rational natures or men it is the "natural moral law." (Its promulgation through oral revelation which is known not on evidence but through faith is divine law. As such it is beyond the purview of this book.) The development of what is thus known by human beings with political authority is called human law, positive law, or, as in this book, man-made law.
42 See Wild's description of the "natural law" as "the universal pattern of action required by human nature in general (not in the concrete) for its completion or perfection" as based on the universal tendency of all living things

IV. MAN-DISCOVERED LAW AND NATURAL LAW

Is man-discovered law the same as natural law?   Are they different or are they the same thing under different names?

A. *Different Meaning*

Man-discovered law is not the same as natural law if the latter refers to any of the opinions discussed in the early part of this chapter. For natural law in these theories is far removed from the man-discovered law that is expressed in a man's basic drives as he here and now exists, and from which he can know its elementary demands without reasoning.

B. *May Have Same Meaning*

If natural law is taken as referring to these elementary demands, man-discovered law can be said to be the same as natural law. For, as we noted, these drives are nothing but the promulgation of the eternal law and as such are a participation in the eternal law. This participation is one of order: of order manifested in men's basic drives — natural law; of order originating in the mind of the Supreme Orderer — eternal law. Natural law taken as synonymous with man-discovered law may, therefore, be said to be the elementary demands expressed by a man's basic drives, as we have analyzed them, which are known without a reasoning process.

C. *"Natural" Refers to Natural Promulgation*

When speaking of natural law as referring to elementary drives, it is imperative to keep in mind that what is called natural law is actually a natural *promulgation* of eternal law.   To confuse

---

toward the completion of their own beings. Introduction to Realistic Philosophy 504, 46-56, 177-180 (1948), and Plato's Modern Enemies and the Theory of Natural Law 64-69, 172-203 (1953). See also Maritain's explanation that "Any kind of thing existing in nature, a plant, a dog, a horse, has its own natural law, that is, the normality of its functioning, the proper way in which, by reason of its specific structure and specific ends, it 'should' achieve fullness of being either in its growth or in its behaviour." Man and the State 87 (1951).

On natural law, see also Carrel, Reflections on Life 40-60 (1953); D'Entrèves, Natural Law 80-94 (1951); Banner, Natural Law and Social Order, in The Return to Reason 218-234 (1953); O'Sullivan, The Inheritance of the Common Law 73-74 (1951).

eternal law with its promulgation and to call the promulgation natural *law* without referring it to the Creator, can only result in a subjection of the intellectual (man) to the non-intellectual (nature). As has been pointed out, ". . . [I]t is necessary . . . to acknowledge that the natural law participates in the eternal law, which is identical with the reason of God. Should we not make this step, the supreme law would appear to be that which exists within nature, and thus the first and most essential element of the definition of law, an *ordinance of reason*, would be finally nullified, the implication being that the rational universe would be ultimately dominated by irrational nature."[43] Hence, any attempt to adopt the demands of the basic drives as merely natural norms or rules of human action without going further and seeing in them the expression of a law that implies an intelligent lawmaker is open to this criticism.

It must be remembered that "The natural law has the force of law from the fact that it emanates from the divine Reason — in no way from the human reason which knows it but does not in anyway establish it — because the only reason from which it comes is the divine Reason itself." [44]

[43] Simon, Nature and Functions of Authority 51 (1940).

[44] Maritain, Neuf Leçons sur les Notions Premières de la Philosophie Morale 161 (1949) (my trans.).

On the difficulties involved in Aquinas' treatment of "natural law" and the need of its being rewritten at least in part, see Leclercq, La Philosophie Morale de Saint Thomas devant la Pensée Contemporaine 377-400 (1955).

Content, Source and End of
Man-discovered Law

In analyzing the nature of man-discovered law, it has been necessary to touch matter that is implicitly the content, source and end of this law.   The problem facing us now is to ascertain explicitly what the demands of this law are and how they are known, what this law's origin is, and what its end is.   Depending on these solutions, it is possible to see this law as true law and to gauge the extent of its help in making positive law.

I.   CONTENT: DEMANDS OF BASIC DRIVES

The content of man-discovered law, as we have noted, is the demands expressed by men's basic drives.   But before these demands are examined further and because of their paramount importance in man-discovered law, they should be seen as part of the phenomenon of fundamental drives in all living beings for their final completion and perfection.

A.   *The Significance of Drives*

The basic drives of a man, like with any living being, are the dynamic expression of his bio-principle that determines his consistent structure and growth.   The most basic and controlling of these is the master drive for the *highest development* of which the being is capable, for that perfection which specifically characterizes it as what it is.   The master drive of a rosebush, to use an example from a lower type of life that does not have the power to decide whether or not it will follow the directives indicated by these drives, is to produce roses — not anything else. When it does so, it is a "good" rosebush.   Likewise when a man attains the highest development of which he is capable, he is a completely "good" man.   Having reached his completion and perfection, he is happy.

Every man also, again like other living beings, has other drives whose object is to further his *existence*. For he cannot develop himself unless he exists. Just as the rosebush strives to stay alive by seeking water through its roots and sunshine through its leaves, in like manner every man has an elementary drive to preserve himself in existence. Since the race of men must continue if there are to be men, every man, like all other animals, has a drive to unite sexually to keep the race in existence. And, since men need other men, each has a drive to live in community with others. Finally, since men are uniquely endowed with the powers of knowing and willing, they have a drive to use these powers in decision-making existence. These drives regarding the various levels of human existence, then, take their meaning from men's master drive for their highest development.[1]

B. *Recognition of Demands*

The manner in which these demands are known is the key factor in identifying the content of man-discovered law in its strict sense. They are known without a reasoning process.

1. *What is known without a reasoning process.* The judgments a man makes regarding the end of his actions and concerning some of the rudimentary means thereto are made without having to reason about them. They are formed independently of a middle term which expresses a "because" or "why." [2]

a. *Master demand.* From the requirement of his master drive for perfection and happiness, a man knows without a reasoning process that he ought to choose whatever conduces to this end rather than what does not do so. He judges that he should choose good rather than bad actions. This is the preamble of Creator-made, man-discovered law: seek the good, seek what is perfective, seek what gives happiness. ". . . [T]his is the first

---

[1] These essential drives are totally different from the accidental tendencies to evil found in men in varying degrees. The drives for what is good are steady and definite in each man. Tendencies to evil vary. The inclination to steal, murder or commit other crimes is not constant as is the drive to preserve one's life or to live in community. Whether man's inclination to evil stems from his nature as do the basic drives or from a historical incident is a matter well worth investigation by any lawman. See Chapter 8, note 38.

[2] This does not mean that a judgment made without a reasoning process — a connatural judgment — entails no mental operation. In fact, such a judgment is itself one of the mind's operations which presupposes another, apprehension or conception. What it does mean, though, is that such a judgment is not the conclusion of a reasoning process, of a syllogism. On the operations of the mind — conception, judgment, and reasoning — see Klubertanz, The Philosophy of Human Nature 173-180 (1953).

precept of law, that good is to be done and sought after, and evil is to be avoided. All the other precepts of the natural law are based on this; so that all those things to be done or avoided which practical reason naturally apprehends to be human goods, pertain to the precepts of the law of nature." [3]

b. *Elementary demands.* From the demands of his other basic drives regarding existence, he recognizes without a process of reasoning that preserving himself in existence is in itself good and not evil and that he ought to choose it rather than its opposite, self-extinction. In like manner, he also judges that sex in itself is good and not evil; that living in society is good in itself and not evil and that in such living "mine" is different from "thine"; and that knowledge and free decision are in themselves good and not evil.

This judgment concerning self-preservation, the use of sex, and the like, is about these things as they are in themselves. Taken as overt acts in a given, factual set of circumstances they may become evil on account of these very circumstances. If they were evil in themselves, no circumstances surrounding the overt acts could make them good.

A man's natural drives, then, are indicative of the demands of man-discovered law. "Since, however, good has the nature of an end and evil the nature of the contrary, all those things for which man has a natural inclination reason naturally apprehends as good and consequently something to be sought after, and their contraries as evil and to be avoided. Therefore, the order of precepts of the law of nature is according to the order of the natural inclinations. For there is in man, first, an inclination to good according to the nature he has in common with all substances, namely, inasmuch as every substance seeks the preservation of its own being according to its nature. And by this inclination those things by which the life of man is conserved and the contrary impeded pertain to the natural law. Second, there is in man an inclination to things more specific, according to the nature he has in common with other animals. By this inclination those things are said to be of the natural law 'which nature teaches all animals,' such as the sexual union of man and woman, the rearing of children and the like. Third, there is in man an inclination to good according to the nature of his reason, which is proper to him. Man thus has a natural inclination to know the truth about God and to live in society. And according

[3] Aquinas, 1-2 Sum. Theol. 94, 2.

to this, whatever pertains to this inclination belongs to the natural law. As for instance, that man should shun ignorance, that he should not offend those with whom he has to live, and other such things that pertain to this inclination." [4]

c. *Pattern demands.* Besides this knowledge, evidence also shows that men perceive without reasoning certain pattern demands that are immediately connected with the more elementary demands. These are concerned with a limitation on the workings of the basic drives which is necessary if the very purpose of the drives themselves is not to be nullified.

The research of anthropology shows that men, wherever they are found, recognize that it is evil to kill other men haphazardly, to have sexual union with complete promiscuity, to claim as "mine" what is "thine" indiscriminately in communal living, to use the mental powers indifferently. On the contrary, it has been found that men always judge that the killing of others must be done with some discrimination, that sexual union must be according to some qualification, that some distinction between "mine" and "thine" is made, and that there is always some use

[4] Aquinas, 1-2 Sum. Theol. 94, 2. To reject the drives as a factual foundation of morals and to refuse to see in them the expression of a law is to turn one's back on the obvious demands of living things for what is "good" for them. To say that this "natural law conception frequently confuses physical and biological generalities with ethics" (Patterson, Jurisprudence: Men and Ideas of the Law 353 (1953)) is to betray a Kantian denial of the relation betwen objective data and our subjective ideas. As already pointed out, because Kant held that many of our ideas (such as the relation and order of means to end) derive not a posteriori from observable facts but a priori from the mind itself, moral law and obligation had to be for him independent of these.

"Do we not think it a matter of the utmost necessity to work out for once a pure moral philosophy completely cleansed of everything that can only be empirical and appropriate to anthropology? . . . Every one must admit that a law has to carry with it absolute necessity if it is to be valid morally — valid, that is, as a ground of obligation; . . . that here consequently the ground of obligation must be looked for, not in the nature of man nor in the circumstances of the world in which he is placed, but solely a priori in the concepts of pure reason; and that every other precept based on principles of mere experience — and even a precept that may in a certain sense be considered universal, so far as it rests in its slightest part, perhaps only in its motive, on empirical grounds — can indeed be called a practical rule, but never a moral law. . . .

. . . "For if any action is to be morally good, it is not enough that it should conform to the moral law — it must also be done for the sake of the moral law. . . . Indeed a philosophy which mixes up these pure principles with empirical ones does not deserve the name of philosophy. . . . Still less does it deserve the name of moral philosophy, since by this very confusion it undermines even the purity of morals themselves and acts against its own proper purpose." Kant, Groundwork of the Metaphysics of Morals 57-58 (Paton ed. 1947).

of the powers of knowing and deciding in the leading of one's life and in seeking the purpose of life.[5]

Legally it is presupposed that all men do make such judgments. There is a ". . . sense of right and wrong inherent in every person by virtue of his existence as a social entity. He knows by intuition that theft and robbery are wrong, and that every act which deprives another of his own by deceit or stealth and without his knowledge or consent partakes of that nature. Should he find something of great value in the public road, conscience would tell him, in the absence of positive law, that its appropriation by concealment would wrong whoever might be the owner and the conscience of his neighbor would be shocked at his attempt to do so. It is this inherent sense of right and wrong to which the law refers in this instance as conscience, and the natural effect of the wrong on those sharing the same instinct is denominated a shock to that conscience. This shock is not the effect of legal advice. It is our intuitive sense of wrong, and when it follows the contemplation of all the available facts relating to an injury we can find no safer guide to its true character." [6]

In brief, from their master drive men can know without reasoning that they are structured for a certain development and perfection — for happiness. From their other elementary drives they can also know without reasoning what some of the rudimentary goods are that will contribute to this end. From the working of his own nature, a man has a vague indication of where he should be going, and slightly less vague guides as to how he may get there.[7] But, be it noted, among his drives is the one to use his power of reasoning about the implication of

[5] At what age a person forms these judgments is another question. In general it would seem to be sometime before adulthood. For anthropological confirmation regarding killing, see 1 Westermarck, The Origin and Development of the Moral Ideas 331 (1906): "We may accept without hesitation [the] statement that 'no known tribe, however low and ferocious, has ever admitted that men may kill one another indiscriminately.' In every society — even where human life is, generally speaking, held in low esteem — custom prohibits homicide within a certain circle of men. But the radius of the circle varies greatly." See also Lowie, Primitive Society 407 (1920). Concerning sex, see Lowie, id. at 15-26; Hoebel, Man in the Primitive World 187 (1949). On primitive notions of a supreme being, see Hoebel, id. at 405. Regarding the concept of "mine-thine," see Lowie, id. at 205-255, and Hoebel, id. at 327-340. On law and anthropology in general, see Cohen and Cohen, Readings in Jurisprudence 786-822 (1951).

[6] Van Graafieland v. Wright, 286 Mo. 414, 228 S.W. 465, 469, 470 (1920).

[7] The demands of the basic drives are vague only in the sense that they are broad and general — such as the indications of a compass. For this very reason more particular and incisive directives are needed.

the demands of the other drives in varying space-time situations.[8]

2. *What is known by a reasoning process.* In view of the fact that man-discovered law demands that evil actions be avoided and only good actions be done, all human living pertains to it. But what is known by men with their natural powers over and above the elementary demands and the pattern demands immediately connected with them has to be reached as a conclusion of a reasoning process.

From the few elementary guides men must reason further, deductively or inductively, to conclusions about how they should act in more particular instances, about what is just or unjust in specific cases. Such use of reasoning results in decisions regarding what is ethically or morally good or bad, right or wrong, just or unjust. Or it may issue in the ius gentium, the law of nations — which embodies agreements between peoples as to what is just or unjust between them, usually in such elemental matters as barter, use of waterways, and the like. Or, if these reasonings are carried on by men in lawmaking positions, the resultant conclusions become the content of statutes and judicial decisions.

These conclusions are all related to man-discovered law inasmuch as it is the source of the premises from which they are drawn. It is only because it is right and good to preserve life that food and drug statutes, for instance, are just and justifiable. For this same reason, all conclusions concerning what is right are related to man-discovered law. Some require less reasoning and are more readily evident than others. It is more evident and requires less reasoning to conclude that a child should respect his parents than that a man should live with only one woman as long as they both live.

3. *"According to natural law."* Regardless of how little reasoning is required to arrive at one of these conclusions, by the very fact that there is some reasoning involved, such a conclusion is distinguished from the basic judgments of man-discovered law which are formed without such reasoning. This is the line of demarcation.

[8] The discussion regarding the cognitivism of intrinsic value judgments of natural law as opposed to the non-cognitivism of extrinsic value judgments seems to be concerned with a Kantian type of judgment. The statement "If natural law norms could be expressed by 'if . . . then' propositions, they would be empirical statements instead of intrinsic value-judgments" indicates that the type of judgment under consideration is not the same as that dealt with here. See Oppenheim, The Natural Law Thesis: Affirmation or Denial? 51 Am. Pol. Sci. Rev. 41-53 (1957).

Hence, when some such phrase as "according to natural law" or "not according to natural law" is used regarding an action, the controlling question is: How is it known to be so? If it is known to be so without reasoning, as in the case of self-preservation, it is "according to natural law" in the strict sense of being immediately evident. If it is known to be so only after reasons have been examined and judged, although it is "according to natural law" it is not so in the same strict sense of being immediately evident — regardless of the term by which it may be designated. All actions that are necessary for the attainment of man's final end are, inasmuch as they are good, demanded by men's nature and therefore "according to natural law." This is one thing. How they are known to be such — whether without reasoning or with it, whether from the use of reason alone or reason aided by revelation — is quite another.[9]

In the cases cited above, the conclusions can be reached only after some reasoning from the elementary and pattern demands — much or little as the case may be. "Reasons" are involved in the process of thinking which concludes that it is a demand of men's nature that an accused be not retried because of double jeopardy, or that a building should be destroyed in order to facilitate extinguishing a fire, or that medicine should or should not be practiced without a license, or that working hours should be limited, or that unsavory incidents in the past life of a prostitute should not be published because of her right to happiness, or that insane persons are not to marry, or that whole segments of a race should not be gassed, or that freedom to go from place to place should not be restricted.[10]

[9] In other words, the central problem of "natural law" is an epistemological one. For this reason, instead of speaking of the primary, secondary and tertiary "precepts" of the "natural law," it is more accurate to refer to the demands of men's nature as known without reasoning and as known with little or much reasoning. On the inutility of continuing this distinction of "precepts" used by Aquinas, see Lottin, Morale Fondamentale 120-125, 183-188 (1954).

"Natural law" is sometimes said to be "right reason." This is a vague phrase which can become clear only if "right" implies that the judgment of the intellect is rectified by conformity with the basic drives and other norms.

[10] An interesting example of the use of "natural law" in varying ways by judges on the same court (regarding the right of children of a minority religious group to attend the school of a majority religious group which is the only school available) is the Canadian case of Chabot v. Les Commissaires d'Ecole de La Morandière, [1957] Q.B. 707. For a discussion of this case, see Case and Comment, 4 McGill L.J. 268-289 (1958).

C. *Status of Demands*

The basic judgments that constitute the content of man-discovered law are not subject to change. The reasoned conclusions
that follow from them are changeable.

1. *Basic judgments unchangeable.* All men who are normal
will instinctively form the basic judgments. It is only if a man
is not normal that the opposite is true. Only in such a case will
he judge that he does not want to be happy and constantly try
to be unhappy, that it is evil to preserve himself in existence
and persist in trying to kill himself, that all sexual union is evil
and for this reason avoid it at all costs, that all dealings with
other men are evil and always live by himself, that all use of his
reason is evil and refuse to learn anything or make decisions.

So to describe a man is to delineate with broad strokes the
outlines of a man who is abnormal and whom psychiatrists
would recognize as showing indications at least of incipient
psychosis. In sum, it is the characteristic mark of a normal
human being to form the rudimentary judgments that relate to
the elementary demands of his basic drives. Hence the content
of man-made law as constitutive of these judgments is not changeable.[11]

2. *Reasoned conclusions changeable.* The conclusions that
are drawn from these unchangeable premises by deductive or
inductive reasoning may change. For, once reasoning enters into
the mental process of reaching a conclusion, by that very fact the
door is left open for other factors to enter. Philosophies and
theologies of life will enter in when evaluations have to be made;
the circumstances of a problem present a varying face; the mind
of the one reasoning undergoes changed outlooks and prejudices.
The changes of reasoned conclusions, then, occur in one of three
ways.

a. *Change demanded by drives themselves.* The drives themselves demand different conclusions when it is a question of judging the superiority of one good over another. A conscientious
objector could think that if self-preservation is good and ought
to be furthered, under no circumstances should he endanger his

---

[11] It has been said that ". . . as long as this natural-law doctrine does not
answer the question how to distinguish, by an unbiased observation of facts,
distorted (and as such evil) from undistorted (and as such good) tendencies, it
does not furnish this 'stable and universal standard.' " Kelsen, What Is Justice 185-186 (1957). The medical norms for psychosis have long since furnished the basis for this distinction.

life even for the good of his country. Hence, he could feel that he should resist conscription laws because they are unconstitutional since the Constitution protects the lives of citizens.

But it is a demand of one of the basic drives itself — to use the power of reason — that he reason about conflicting needs and goods that are part of everyday living, balance and evaluate them, and decide accordingly. The common good of the community is greater than his proper good. The existence of the community outweighs in value the existence of the individual man. For, without the community, individual men could not continue to exist. Hence it is according to the demands of man-discovered law itself that the basic judgment, "It is good to preserve one's life and it ought to be done," give place in this set of circumstances to another judgment, namely, "It is good to endanger and give one's life and it ought to be done." On this basis conscription laws are valid.

Again, even though a man judges it is good to give his life for his country and acts accordingly, the drive to preserve his life still continues to make itself felt. Indeed, it is this persistence and the accompanying conviction that life is sweet that causes fear of losing it. But it is this very fact too that makes the giving of it heroic. Such changes in judgment are also demanded by the drives themselves regarding the areas of sexual union and communal living.[12]

b. *Change demanded by varying external conditions.* Another way that conclusions reached by reasoning may change is when circumstances are altered. What belongs to another should be returned to him. I have borrowed my neighbor's shotgun. He comes to me asking for its return. His wife who accompanies him begs me not to give it to him, for he has threatened to kill her and himself. Should I at this time give him the gun that is rightfully his?

Or to take a problem of the atomic age, should the hydrogen bomb be outlawed as evil? Can the injuries caused by radiation from nuclear reactors be justified and who is to be held liable

[12] It has been said that men's tendencies to preserve themselves in existence at various levels cannot be taken as an indication of what is good for them and what they ought to do, because men also have a tendency to die. Hence, men's basic tendencies are contradictory and self-canceling. See Kelsen, What Is Justice 181 (1957). But this use of the word "tendency" is obviously equivocal. For men do not have a tendency to commit suicide as they do to preserve their life. Besides, such an objection assumes as an established fact that the degree of development of themselves that men accomplish during their lifetime ceases to have any meaning at the termination of their existence on this mundane sphere.

for them in tort law? Whatever conclusions are reached concerning these subjects must certainly be affected by the changing conditions of the use of atomic energy both in war and peace, as well as by the progress made in developing protective techniques.

c. *Change caused by internal dispositions.* Still another way that conclusions may change is when reasoning processes are affected by environment, education and bad habits. A man may decide to join a suicide cult, having been influenced by associations he has made or by dissipation which has reduced him to a state of despair. He is not judging as a normal man would who was not under such influences. His ability to judge has been warped. However, even though he has reached a state in which he judges he should do something contrary to the demands of nature, nevertheless the elemental drive to preserve his own life still persists. He must struggle against his natural tendency to preserve his life before he can bring himself to end it by his own hand.

II. Source: Creator of Drives

The source of man-discovered law is the source of the drives in which evidence of the promulgation of this law is disclosed. As is already evident from the above analysis, the source of a man and his drives is the Creator of them.

A. *Origin of Each Man's Existence*

The Creator is the source of each man's existence, whose nature dynamically expresses an ordering of means to end through his drives. The precise manner and time this occurs is matter for another field of inquiry.[13] It may be added further that, since political authority derives from men's basic drives,[14] it ultimately has its source in the Creator of these drives.

To speak therefore of a "fundamental," or "natural," or "higher" *law* and not to relate it to the Creator-lawmaker would be, as already mentioned, to make of it a blind, irrational force that is in no way a law. Besides, to view the elementary demands as a law without at the same time admitting the existence of the lawmaker would be like accepting the concavity of a circle without at the same time admitting its convexity.

Hence the main problem concerning man-discovered or natu-

13 See Klubertanz, Philosophy of Human Nature 311-312 (1953).
14 See Chapter 19.

ral law is not whether there can be a "natural" law without its being related to a Creator. The problem is whether or not there is a Creator. A refusal to face up to the full implications of *nature* is a refusal to admit the existence of its Creator.

B. *Known from Evidence*

That there is a Creator-lawmaker who is the source of man-discovered law can be known from the evidence of observable data. Recourse to "religious" faith is unnecessary.

1. *Evidence of order.* This conclusion — that a man's nature bespeaks its Creator — can be reached by examining the evidence of order of means to end in a man's basic drives, especially his master drive (as well as in other examples), and by reasoning from these data to the only possible cause of this order as was done above. This is the natural tendency of the mind of men — to seek adequate explanations of things. It is this drive to reason about the causes of things that impels us to ask ever and again about constantly occurring phenomena: "What is their purpose?" "Who made them?"

2. *Not religious faith.* This manner of coming to a knowledge of the existence of a Creator-lawmaker by reasoning from evidence should be clearly distinguished from another way of arriving at the same fact. This is by faith or belief. Faith is an assent of the mind to a proposition, not because of evidence, but because of the trustworthiness of the one speaking. Men accept answers to a hundred questions asked daily of their fellowmen on faith in the reliability of their word. This is human, natural faith. If the one whose word is trustworthily accepted through supernatural revelation is the Creator, it is divine, supernatural faith. This is the foundation of theology.

Man-discovered law, however, is in no way dependent on faith or theology. In fact, man-discovered law is presupposed by faith. The natural is implied by the supernatural. Nor is man-discovered law related in any way to "religion," if by that most ambiguous word is meant something based on faith. For theogical or religious convictions are based on authority and faith therein; philosophical conviction is based on evidence and reasoning thereon.[15]

---

[15] That men can come to a knowledge of the existence of the Creator by their own reasoning after examining the evidence of observable data is a preamble to faith itself. "God, the origin and end of all things, can be known with certainty by the natural light of reason from things created: 'for, since the creation of the world his invisible attributes — especially his ever-

It is natural for a man to have an origin. If this origin is by an act of creation it is natural for a man to be created and have a Creator. It is part of what goes with being a man. The Creator is, therefore, natural to men. Simply because the Creator is "above" men does not mean that, as Creator, he is supernatural to men. "Supernatural" has a technical meaning related to faith that is entirely different.[16]

To speak therefore of ". . . the inseparable connection of natural law and religion" [17] is inaccurate if "religion" implies faith. The phrase can be made meaningful only if every and any consideration or even mention of a first cause or creator — however evidentially pursued — is termed "religion." Such a use, however, is not the one commonly accepted and ordinarily the term "religion" carries overtones of the Sacred Scriptures and ecclesiastical affiliations and rites.[18]

This is not to say that the eternal law as known by faith — for instance, the Ten Commandments — has not properly found its way into law. But what is to be stressed is that the eternal law as explicitly revealed in the Ten Commandments is known by men through faith in the authority of the one revealing. As implicitly manifested in the drives of men's nature, the eternal law is known by reasoning on evidence.

The eternal law as known both naturally and supernaturally has a place in statutes and decisions. But these are two entirely different manners of knowing and they should be recognized as distinct.

C. Foundation of Legal Structure

The idea of a Creator is, nominally at least, basic to the legal structure of the United States of America. "Man, fearfully and

---

lasting power and divinity — are clearly seen, being understood through the things that are made.' (Rom. 1:20) . . . it was nevertheless, the good pleasure of his wisdom and goodness to reveal himself and the eternal decrees of his will to the human race in another and supernatural way, as the Apostle says: 'God, who at various times and in different manners formerly spoke to our ancestors through the prophets, last of all in these days has spoken to us by his Son' (Heb. 1:1-2)." Enchiridion Symbolorum 1785 (Denzinger ed. 1937) (trans. mine).

16 "Supernatural" refers not only to what is "above" the natural but also to what is in no way "due" to it. Thus, for example, the special help given by God to the human mind by which it is capable of believing his revealed word is "above" the natural powers of the human mind and is in no way "due" to men.

17 Patterson, Jurisprudence: Men and Ideas of the Law 348, n.61 (1953).

18 For instance, dictionaries define "religion" as "belief in a divine or superhuman power."

wonderfully made, is the workmanship of his all perfect Creator. A State, useful and valuable as the contrivance is, is the inferior contrivance of man, and from his native dignity derives all its acquired importance." [19] Regardless of what meaning and content is given the word, the Creator has been officially declared to be the source of "certain inalienable rights" among which are "life, liberty and the pursuit of happiness." These concepts have become basic in Constitutional law and due process.[20]

The alternative must be manfully faced that either these words have a well-founded meaning or they don't. A lawman should clearly have in mind the meaning he is going to give these words when he encounters them in legal contexts. "As in our intercourse with our fellow men certain principles of morality are assumed to exist, without which society would be impossible, so certain inherent rights lie at the foundation of all actions, and upon a recognition of them alone can free institutions be maintained. These inherent rights have never been more happily expressed than in the Declaration of Independence, that new evangel of liberty to the people: 'We hold these truths to be self-evident' — that is so plain that their truth is recognized upon their mere statement — 'that all men are endowed' — not by edicts of Emperors, or decrees of Parliament or acts of Congress, but 'by their Creator with certain inalienable rights' — that is, rights which cannot be bartered away, or given away, or taken away except in punishment of crime — 'and that among these are life, liberty, and the pursuit of happiness, and to secure these' — not grant them but secure them — 'governments are instituted among men, deriving their just powers from the consent of the governed.' " [21]

The place of God the Creator in official public life has received explicit recognition by the Supreme Court. "Appeals to the Almighty in the messages of the Chief Executive; the proclamations making Thanksgiving Day a holiday; 'so help me God' in our courtroom oaths — these and . . . other references to the Almighty . . . run through our laws, our public rituals . . . [A] fastidious atheist or agnostic could even object to the supplication

---

[19] Chisholm v. Georgia, 2 Dall. 16, 43, 2 L. Ed. 418, 453 (U.S. 1793).

[20] See Haines, The Revival of Natural Law Concepts (1930) and The Law of Nature in State and Federal Judicial Decisions, 25 Yale L.J. 617 (1916); Strauss, Natural Right and History (1953); Grant, The Higher Law Background of Eminent Domain, 6 Wis. L. Rev. 67 (1931); Wright, American Interpretations of Natural Law (1931).

[21] Butcher's Union Co. v. Crescent City Co., 111 U.S. 746, 756, 757, 4 Sup. Ct. 652, 660 (1884). See also United States v. Cruikshank, 92 U.S. 542, 553, 23 L. Ed. 588, 592 (1875).

with which the Court opens each session: 'God save the United States and this Honorable Court.' " [22]

This condition in public life is an inevitable result of the fact that our institutions presuppose the existence of a Supreme Being. "We are a religious people whose institutions presuppose a Supreme Being. We guarantee the freedom to worship as one chooses. We make room for as wide a variety of beliefs and creeds as the spiritual needs of man deem necessary. We sponsor an attitude on the part of government that shows no partiality to any one group and that lets each flourish according to the zeal of its adherents and the appeal of its dogma. When the state encourages religious instruction or cooperates with religious authorities by adjusting the schedule of public events to sectarian needs it follows the best of our traditions. For it then respects the religious nature of our people and accommodates the public service to their spiritual needs. To hold that it may not would be to find in the Constitution a requirement that the government show a callous indifference to religious groups. That would be preferring those who believe in no religion over those who do believe." [23]

If there is a relation between the Supreme Being and law, between the Creator and certain fundamental claims, it must be based on the fact that he has created men whose natures express demands that are part of a law. Either the phrases "endowed by their Creator" and "created equal" mean *so made by their Creator* or they are meaningless. Either they have this factual meaning or they are deceptive euphemisms and therefore dangerous. This problem is examined below.

III. END: COMMON GOOD OF HUMAN COMMUNITY

The end of man-discovered law, like all law, is a common good. It is a good that is communicable to all men. The basic drives indicate what these common goods are that will be communicable to all if their demands are observed.

A. *Human Community Conditioned by Justice, Security and Peace*

The end brought about by the observance of the demands of men's elementary drives is the human community pervaded by

22 Zorach v. Clauson, 343 U.S. 306, 313, 314, 72 Sup. Ct. 679, 683 (1951).
23 Ibid.

conditions of peace, security and a just order. These conditions are a good that is communicable to all members of the human race. The fact that these conditions are not perfectly realized signalizes men's failure to observe the demands of their nature. It also raises the question of whether men by themselves have the full capability of doing so, in view of the fact that these demands have never been perfectly observed since the dawn of history.

B. *The Creator Himself*

It is the master drive of men, however, that indicates what the ultimate common good of men is. Inasmuch as man has a master drive for happiness, the good that will bring this about must be the perfect good which, permanently possessed, will make him completely happy. This would be his highest development. The ends of the other drives for existence at various levels are, in this perspective, but means to this ultimate end. So also are the provisions of man-made law only indirect means to this final end.

This perfect good must include all good, otherwise a man's potentiality for all good would be left unfulfilled. But all good is to be found only in its source: the Creator. The Creator himself, then, is the end to which man-discovered law directs. Although this supreme good is in one way a proper good, in another way it is a common good. The attainment of this end is primarily the result of each man's own individual free judgments and decisions and its communication to the individual is in a manner singular to the individual. In this sense, a man's ultimate good is essentially a proper good. But because this good is communicable to all, albeit in differing degrees, it also uniquely takes on the aspect of a common good. Hence, as a common good it is the end of man-discovered law.

That the ultimate end of men is this common good which, permanently possessed, causes complete happiness, is a fact knowable from an analysis of men's powers of intellection and volition. The exact manner, however, in which this takes place and the necessity of certain means beyond men's natural reach, cannot be known from evidence alone. This knowledge can be had with certainty only through faith in their divine revelation. But this does not alter the fact that the end of man-discovered law is the Creator himself knowable from evidence. It only means that men by themselves are incapable of completely attaining this end for which they have a constant desire. Men are made with a drive for God — under the aspect of the good — but without special aid from him they cannot reach this end.[24]

1. *Men's ultimate end.* The most important end of any man, then, is that absolutely ultimate object that will permanently satisfy all of his desires and thereby render him continuously happy. This end, as we have seen, is the Creator himself who is the supreme good. To this supreme end all other ends must be subordered.

2. *Men's intermediate ends.* In relation to his ultimate end other ends are intermediate. They are means necessary for the attainment of this ultimate end. These intermediate ends or goods are either proper or common.

There are intermediate proper goods that relate directly to a man's ultimate good such as his beliefs and his manifestation of them in worship. There are also other intermediate proper goods that pertain to it only indirectly such as food, drink, shelter, and the like.

The intermediate common goods of a man are the ones that are the object of man-made law such as peace and security, the protection of claims, and so forth. These conditions also are but means necessary for a man's personal development and progress toward his supreme goal.

3. *Conflicts.* Conflicts between these ends are inevitable and of constant recurrence. Intermediate proper goods (property, liberty and life) which only indirectly bear on a man's ultimate end may have to be subordinated to the intermediate common political good (peace, security). A man may have to give up part of his income as taxes for the maintenance of the police protection on which he depends. He may have to limit the speed of his driving so that conditions of safety may be enjoyed by all. He may even be called on to expose himself to mortal danger so that others may be protected as in the case of war.

But the intermediate proper goods that directly relate to his supreme end cannot be so subordered. Men are sometimes asked to do things that are against their conscience for the "good" of the "state." Physicians may be ordered to sterilize all women of a certain nationality so that "impure strains" may be removed from the "master race." Such a subordination of a man's intermediate proper good directly related to his final end (known by his conscience) to an intermediate political common "good" (the personal designs of a dictator) could never be justified. A man's supreme good and its demands must remain pre-eminent, even

[24] On this matter in general see Bourke, Ethics 3-43, 414-419 (1951).

though the cost to him be the premature termination of his mortal existence.

The maintenance of the proper relation between these various ends of men is the never-ending and noble task of legislators and judges. From their decisions will come an increase or decrease of the tensions that must always exist between freedom and restriction, between private and public good.

Sanction and Obligation of
Man-discovered Law

The problem that concerns us here is what is the consequence of observing or violating man-discovered law and can the foundation of obligation be found in this law? The ultimate significance of the sanction of law and the final intelligibility of its obligation depend on this solution.

I. Sanction: Natural Rewards and Punishments

The sanction of man-discovered law is the good or evil that follows as reward or punishment for obeying or disobeying the elementary demands expressed by a man's nature. This sanction is intrinsic. Man-discovered law has no extrinsic sanctions.

A. *Follows from Act of Violation or Observance*

When a man violates the elementary demand that he take care to preserve his health, he will inevitably incur the penalty of loss of health or of life itself. When men violate the elementary demand that they deal justly with one another, whether as individuals or as members of municipalities or nations, they will unavoidably bring upon themselves the penalties of resentment, distrust, unrest, retaliation, revolt, disorder, suffering and unhappiness. More important than this, they will be making the type of decisions that impede their self-improvement and progress toward their supreme end and good.

On the other hand, when men follow the demands expressed through their basic drives they enjoy the corresponding rewards. When men obey the demand that they deal justly with each other, their reward will be satisfaction, trust, contentment, cooperation, negotiation, peace, well-being and happiness. And more important than these goods, they will be improving themselves and making progress toward the attainment of their supreme good,

B. *Ultimate Significance of Sanction*

The ultimate significance of sanction is found in its relation to a man's knowing decision to follow or not follow directives that are for his own good. From his decisions follow goods or evils that are actually rewards or punishments for these decisions. This is especially evident regarding disobedience and its punishment.

1. *Disobedience: Adoption of one's own ordering.* The decision to obey a law entails adopting as one's own the ordering of means to end embodied in the law. Men are in this way perfected by their free decision. Their liberty is an opportunity for self-discipline and development. To disobey a law involves a rejection of the ordering embodied in the directive of law and a substitution in its place of an ordering that is one's own. The substitute will be an ordering according to the individual's likes and desires. It will be an ordering to a private good and a dis-ordering from the public good.

2. *Reaction in nature to opposition.* It is a common experience in nature that whenever one thing opposes another, it suffers a reaction from that other. When the attacker seeks to violate the order expressed in the structure of the attacked, he is repressed. The result of the impact of one body on another, or the response of self-defense, are instances of this. This reaction or repression means injury and deprivation of a former condition to the violator. This deprivation is punishment. ". . . [B]y going from natural things to human affairs it is seen that whenever one thing rises up against another, it suffers some detriment from it. For we observe in natural things that one contrary acts with greater intensity when the other contrary supervenes. . . . Therefore we find that the natural inclination of man is to repress those who rise up against him. Now it is evident that all things contained in an order are, in a manner, one in relation to the principle of that order. Consequently, whatever rises up against an order is put down by that order or by its principle . . . and this repression is punishment." [1]

3. *Reaction incurred by men.* Similarly when a man by his free decision opposes the order established by law, he necessarily incurs a reaction, a repression. This entails a deprivation — his punishment. When a man decides to violate the ordering expressed in his basic drives to preserve his life and he disregards a

[1] Aquinas, 1-2 Sum. Theol. 87, 1. See also 1-2 Sum. Theol. 87, 6.

speed law, he is subject immediately to dangerous driving conditions and may find himself overturned alongside the road with serious injury to himself and ruin to his car, as already noted.

4. *Retribution.* He has misused his power of free decision and is guilty of a fault. Insofar as he has done this he will suffer deprivations contrary to what he would have willed. For it is of the nature of punishment that it entail deprivations that would not have been chosen. In this way the order of the law which was rejected by his will now reasserts itself against his will. The judgment of public authority, which decreed that violation of its ordering would bring on a loss of safe driving conditions, is now vindicated. For he now endures this deprivation. This is the price to be paid for opposing established order.[2] To this extent, equilibrium is restored to the imbalance caused by his disdain of public authority and the balance of law and justice is reestablished. In this lies sanction's greatest significance.

The first meaning of punishment is, then, deprivation consequent upon the violation of the order demanded by law. In this sense, punishment is primarily retributive.[3]

5. *Deterrent and corrective.* Deprivation in turn may have the effect of bringing about a desire to follow the order of the law. The loss of the driver's own physical well-being and of the good condition of his car may serve to bring his thinking back into line with the ordering demanded by the speed law. Whether this will be motivated by a desire of the good intended by the law or a fear of the evil threatened by its violation will depend upon the overall disposition of the man. Other drivers too, seeing the wreckage, may be disposed to embrace the order demanded by the speed law and remain uninjured rather than violate it and run the risk of deprivation and injury.

Further deprivations added by the law itself such as loss of liberty by imprisonment, loss of property through fines or confiscation, loss of bodily well-being by flogging or loss of life itself

[2] The punishment of some violations is more immediate and obvious than that of others. But it is always present to some degree.

[3] The true nature of punishment is more clearly seen from the theological point of view. For, as it has been aptly remarked, the everlasting fires of hell do not burn simply to encourage sanctity. Punishment came into the lives of men through the act of disobedience of the first man and woman. Before this time there was no place for it. "The very fact that human nature needs penal medicines is due to the corruption of nature, which is itself the punishment of the first sin. For there was no need, in the state of innocence, for penal exercises in order to make progress in virtue; so that whatever is penal in the exercise of virtue is reduced to the first sin as its cause." Aquinas, 1-2 Sum. Theol. 87, 7.

by execution, all serve to dispose citizens to adopt and observe the ordering specified by the law.

The secondary meaning of punishment, then, relates to the effect its threatened deprivations have. On account of these a man may be deterred from future violations or his will may be better disposed to choose as he ought, that is, according to the demands of the law. Hence punishment is also a *deterrent* and a *corrective*. The deterrent effect on others is the justification for punishing certain types of criminals by depriving them of their life, as will be seen below.

Punishment, then, has two facets. One is retrospective which looks back, so to speak, to its cause — deprivation is the price paid for deciding to violate a law and is retribution for doing so. The other facet is prospective which looks forward to its possible effect — the deprivation may deter the wrong-doer and others from future violations of the law. But a capital point is to be made here: the relation between deprivation and violation of a law is an intrinsic one and one inevitably bound up with the maintenance of the equilibrium of law and public authority. The primary justification and meaning of added deprivations or extrinsic sanctions must be related to this necessary balance of justice.

6. *Caused by free decision.* The whole rationale of punishment, then, lies in its relation to intellectual-volitional free decision. This decision is the cause of the action of which deprivation is a consequence, and this deprivation in turn may bear on future decisions. Requisite for any responsible decision is sufficient knowledge and the ability to make such a decision. These, of course, can be affected by ignorance, social pressures and emotional compulsions and the like, as will be seen later.

II. Obligation: Necessity of Choosing to Follow Basic Demands

Obligation is the moral necessity of choosing means necessary for a desired end. How ends are desired will be examined shortly. The obligation of man-discovered law is the necessity of obeying the directives expressed by the basic drives. This is the natural obligation discussed above. What these drives demand are means necessary for reaching the supreme end.

A.   *Recognized in Master Demand*

This moral necessity of choosing to follow the demands of the drives is recognized without a reasoning process in the first judgment a man makes regarding his master drive. His master drive is for what will make him permanently happy. In recognizing this drive within himself for this end, he implicitly judges that he ought to seek what will lead to this end and avoid what will not do so.

1. *Experienced practically.* That all men do naturally make such a judgment is shown by the evidence. Ask a man if he wants to be happy and his immediate and certain answer is "Yes." It is only when you ask him what will make him happy that his response may become hesitant and uncertain. This is another matter and, except for a few elemental goods, not so readily known. But regardless of how confused he may be about what is truly good for him and will make him happy, nevertheless whatever he does will be done because he desires happiness. These may even be actions that in the estimation of most men are evil and non-happiness-producing. But for him they are related to his idea of happiness, however false it may be.

2. *Preamble of all obligation.* This first judgment expresses the primary demand and obligation of man-discovered law and is the preamble of all the demands that follow. The subsequent demands of the other drives and the conclusions reasoned therefrom concerning all aspects of morality and law presuppose that men have the overall obligation to pursue whatever good is necessary to perfect themselves and thereby attain their final good. "The first principle of practical reason is one founded on the nature of good, which is: good is what all things seek after. This, therefore, is the first command of law, that good is to be done and pursued and evil avoided. All the other commands of the law of nature are founded on this, so that all those things which practical reason naturally apprehends as human goods pertain to the commands of the law of nature as things to be done or avoided." [4] Only if a man is obliged to do what is good for himself in general is he obliged to do what is good in the more particular instances of his daily activities. For the full meaning of individual acts comes from their relation to man's final end.

Hence, without reasoning every man first judges from his master drive that he ought to avoid what is evil and do whatever good

[4] Aquinas, 1-2 Sum. Theol. 94, 2.

is necessary for perfecting himself, and second that the objects of his other drives are prime among these goods.

The obligation of man-discovered law is, then, the foundation of all other obligation, natural and legal.   In this fact lies its paramount importance.

B.   *Obligation Ultimately Is Absolute Not Relative*

Since obligation is based on a means-end relation, it would seem to be relative and hypothetical, as noted above.   It would seem to be merely relative to my variable desires — I am obliged to eat *if* I desire to preserve my life.   But why ought I to preserve my life?   Obligation, however, is actually categorical and absolute.

1. *Final end is desired absolutely.*   Every end that I desire, say self-preservation, has a relation to my complete development, my ultimate good and happiness — in a word to my final end.   Everything I knowingly and freely do will either not be according to what I know my nature demands and will therefore be bad and non-perfecting for me, or it will be according to these demands and therefore good and perfecting for me.   It is this inevitable relation to my final end and the resulting quality of badness or goodness of my actions that makes my obligation regarding them absolute.   For if I categorically desire happiness and the good that will make me happy as my final end, my obligation regarding the intermediate ends which are factually related to it is also categorical.

And this is precisely the case.   My master drive is for the good that will make me happy.   I have no choice about it.   My will is fixed on this as my ultimate end.   I cannot help desiring it, since this is the way I am made.   I categorically and absolutely desire my final end.   "Everything naturally desires its ultimate perfection." [5]   "Just as the intellect of necessity adheres to the first principles, so the will of necessity adheres to the final end, which is happiness." [6]

2. *Obligation is absolute.*   In other words, because every action I perform is factually good or evil, it is related to my last end.   Hence, my obligation to do it or not is categorical and absolute.   The obligation to take a ship to cross the ocean seems merely hypothetical when it is considered solely as depending on

[5] Aquinas, 1 Sum. Theol. 62, 1.
[6] Id. at 82, 1.

whether I wish to cross the ocean. The true categorical nature of this obligation appears when the overt act of crossing the ocean is taken in all its factual circumstances. For then it will either be an evil act that I am categorically obliged to avoid or a good act that is necessary for me and which I am therefore categorically obliged to do. Such is the preservation of my life.

In my fixed desire for happiness and the good that will bring it about, then, is anchored my categorical and absolute obligation of choosing those means that are necessary for realizing it. In this complete perspective, the desired ends that form the web of my daily actions are themselves but means to the ultimate end. Which of these intermediate ends are good and which bad, which are necessary for the attainment of this end and which are not, is for other knowledges to determine — such as moral philosophy and moral theology. Known to be such with certainty by all men and with their natural powers are, at least, the basic demands of man-discovered law.

3. *Necessity: Key to obligation.* Central in the idea of obligation is necessity and what is "necessary." The necessity in obligation is moral necessity. It leaves freedom of choice unimpaired. It is the necessity of choosing means that are recognized as necessary for an end desired. Physical necessity, on the contrary, leaves no freedom of choice. It is with physical necessity that men desire their final end. They have no choice about being made the way they are and having the destiny they do.[7] For this reason, the final end of men is the steady constant of all obligation.

[7] On necessity and the manner in which man's end is determined, see Wild, Introduction to Realistic Philosophy 383-384, 479-481 (1948).

Relation of Man-discovered to
Man-made Law

The problem now is to establish how man-discovered law and man-made law are related. Upon the answer to this question depends the recognition of man-made law as an expanding application of the basic directives of man-discovered law and the viewing of both of them as true law.

I. COMPASS AND NAVIGATION

The relation of man-discovered law to man-made law is that of a compass to navigation. A compass indicates only general directions. A navigator taking these directions as a starting point and guide calculates and decides what further directives have to be worked out for the needs of particular situations of time and place if the ship is to reach a certain destination.

A compass will not solve navigational problems nor relieve the navigator of the task of doing so. He must be skilled in his science, that is, he must be skilled in the use of reasoning in this area of endeavor. But without the basic knowledge and direction he receives from the compass, his navigational calculations and directives are uncertain and aimless. Their validity depends on the compass.

A. *Basic Directives — Evolved Applications*

So it is with the relation of man-discovered to man-made law. Man-discovered law indicates certain basic directives. Man-made law presupposes these directives as a guide and determines what further and more specific directives are necessary in a definite set of circumstances if the common good is to be realized. The directives of man-discovered law will not automatically furnish solutions for the legislator or judge. These men must be capable of sound deliberation, evaluation and decision in legislation and adjudication.

Man-discovered law, for instance, will not indicate the amount of fluorine that is helpful or harmful in drinking water. This will have to be determined by careful scientific tests. What is assumed here though is based on a demand of man-discovered law, namely, that life should be preserved and that to do so is good and not evil. This is so obvious that it is hardly adverted to. But that is because it is an elementary judgment known without reasoning.

In other words, the force of man-discovered law becomes apparent when it is questioned whether the preservation of human life is good or evil in itself or whether it is indifferent, or whether its goodness or badness depends merely on the exigencies of economic conditions. Legislation and adjudication, without elementary directives, are either arbitrary or merely expressions of the interplay between supply and demand. Such prime distinctions as human or inhuman, just or unjust, which are presupposed by all statutes and judicial decisions, must rest on the stabilizing directives of man-discovered law if they are to have any solid foundation.

In sum, the compass of man-discovered law will not solve the practical problems of navigation in man-made law. If this should be mistaken for saying that man-discovered law is not of much use for man-made law, it should be remembered that neither is a compass of much help in solving the problems of navigation — except that without a compass navigation is aimless and meaningless, while with it navigation has purpose and significance. Further, if it should appear that the elementary demands of man-made law contain nothing that is not already evident — that there is a difference between good and bad, justice and injustice, that it is good to preserve one's life, be just and the other rudimentary judgments — this is precisely as it should be. If all men form these prime judgments without reasoning, as observed above, it is only to be expected that the content of these judgments should be evident.

The relation of man-discovered to man-made law is one, then, of the general to the particular, of the undetermined to the determined, of primal directives to directives evolved therefrom.

The process by which this evolving takes place is one of reasoning, as already pointed out. It may be deductive, or inductive, or both. In many instances both may enter into the deliberations and evaluations of lawmakers that precede the decision and directive judgment that is law. Conclusions are inferred from premises already known, whether these be from man-discovered law, other sciences, including morals, precedent or statutes; or conclusions are arrived at as the result of testing and experiment.

For instance, from the premise that things taken by conversion should be restored, it can be deduced in a particular case that restitution or the assessment of damages is just. But what the extent of the damages is may not be so simply inferable. It may be possible to reach a conclusion only after a corps of experts has examined and assessed the damage.

Again, that crime should be punished is a premise from which a lawmaker infers that murder should be punished. But whether it should be punished by imprisonment for twenty years, thirty years or for life, or even by death, may be possible to decide only after extensive studies and detailed examination have been made of the deterrent effect of such sentences on criminals of a definite community in the recent past.

In other words, man-made law is evolved from man-discovered law either by way of conclusions deduced from basic premises, or after the manner of particularization by induction from a generality. "Every human law has just so much of the nature of law, as it is derived from the law of nature. . . . But it must be noted that something may be derived from the natural law in two ways: first, as a conclusion from premises, secondly, by way of certain particularizations of generalities. The first way is like to that by which, in sciences, demonstrated conclusions are drawn from principles. The second way is like to that by which, in arts, general forms are particularized to something individual, as the craftsman needs to particularize the general idea of a house to this or that shape of a house. Some things therefore are derived from the general principles of the law of nature by way of conclusions. For instance, that one must not kill may be derived as a conclusion from the principle that one should do harm to no man. Some things are derived by way of particularization. For instance, the law of nature has it that he who is an evil-doer should be punished. But that he be punished with this or that punishment, this is a particularization of the law of nature. . . . The general principles of the law of nature cannot be applied to all men in the same way on account of the great variety of human affairs. From this comes the diversity of human laws among different peoples." [1]

[1] Aquinas, 1-2 Sum. Theol. 95, 2.

B. *Legal Navigation*

Legal reasoning is, then, to a great extent a voyage over un-charted as well as charted areas. The reckoning, however, always depends, albeit most times without advertence, on the directive of man-discovered law. All provisions of statutes and decisions are, so to speak, calculations based on these directives and evolved according to space-time needs. The destination is always the common good of the people.

Accordingly, laws concerned with health and safety have mean-ing only on the condition that to preserve human life is in itself good and not evil. Laws regarding sex and domestic living have value on the condition that sexual union is in itself right and not wrong. Laws dealing with possession and ownership, agreements, a good name, truthful representation and the like, are valid on the presupposition that to live in society is in itself good for men and that there is a difference to be recognized between "mine" and "thine" in such living. Finally, laws having to do with educa-tion in all its forms, with the exercise of free decision and with the establishment and maintenance of government, are mean-ingful only if it is basically right for men to acquire knowledge and to govern themselves and others by rational, free decisions for which they are responsible.

The content of legislation, adjudication and custom, then, is necessarily related to the basic demands of men's nature. It is in the implementation of these demands, that lies the ultimate significance of man-made law.

II. THE PARADOX

Attempts to deny man-discovered law, in the sense explained here, issue in some paradoxical results. What is ejected with a great stir from the front door of the house of jurisprudence is al-lowed to re-enter quietly through the back door disguised as some sort of assumed axiom. Like the man who bought a new boom-erang and then spent the rest of his life trying to throw away his old one, after lawmen have repudiated natural law as useless they will find it reasserting itself in their thinking and speaking. That right should be distinguished from wrong, "mine" from "thine," justice from injustice, that actions promoting safety and security and the like are good and actions like murder and stealing are evil, these judgments all make their appearance now under a new guise. They now appear as "jural postulates," "rules consistent with human nature," or norms created by the "customary behavior" of men.

A. *Jural Postulates*

The idea of "jural postulates" as formulated by some is, in part, that "In civilized society men must be able to assume that others will commit no intentional aggressions upon them . . . that they may control for beneficial purposes what they have discovered and appropriated to their own use, what they have created by their own labor . . . that those with whom they deal in the general intercourse of society will act in good faith . . . that those who are engaged in some course of conduct will act with due care not to cast unreasonable risk of injury upon others." [2]

B. *Rules Consistent with Human Nature*

Others, who professedly repudiated natural law, in the course of their own court opinions found it necessary to say that "Subject to its conception of sovereignty even the common law required a judgment not to be contrary to natural justice." [3] "I think the word liberty in the Fourteenth Amendment is perverted when it is held to prevent the natural outcome of a dominant opinion, unless it can be said that a rational and fair man necessarily would admit that the statute proposed would infringe fundamental principles as they have been understood by the traditions of our people and our law." [4] "The law has grown, and even if historical mistakes have contributed to its growth it has tended in the direction of rules consistent with human nature." [5]

C. *Norms Created by Customary Behavior*

Still others, who vigorously reject natural law, base their whole theory of law on norms that are created by the "customary" way that men act. Taking it for granted that international law is

[2] Pound, Social Control Through Law 113-115 (1942). By permission of the Yale University Press.

[3] Mr. Justice Holmes in McDonald v. Mabee, 243 U.S. 90, 91, 37 Sup. Ct. 343 (1917).

[4] Holmes in Lochner v. New York, 198 U.S. 45, 76, 25 Sup. Ct. 539, 547 (1905).

[5] Holmes in Brown v. United States. 256 U.S. 335, 343, 41 Sup. Ct. 501, 502 (1920).

prime over national law,[6] "If, again, we ask why this treaty is valid, we are led back to the general norm which obligates the States to behave in conformity with the treaties they have concluded, a norm commonly expressed by the phrase *pacta sunt servanda*. This is a norm of general international law, and general international law is created by custom constituted by acts of States. The basic norm of international law, therefore, must be a norm which countenances custom as a norm-creating fact, and might be formulated as follows: 'The States ought to behave as they have customarily behaved.' . . . The validity of these norms is dependent upon the norm *pacta sunt servanda,* which itself is a norm belonging to law created by custom." [7]

What occurs in the thinking of these men is again what should be expected if men instinctively form certain judgments. When a jurisprudent interprets the meaning of man in such a way as to be led to deny that men make such judgments and in fact they do, we should look for these same jurisprudents to make such judgments. And this is exactly what happens.[8]

What is ofttimes rejected as natural law, then, is not man-discovered law as outlined here. It is rather the notion that natural law is some sort of an ideal, master blueprint of what is just and unjust, complete even mathematically in every detail, which man-made law must faithfully reproduce if it is to be just law. For the "postulates," "rules," and "norms" just mentioned are nothing but judgments that stand as evidence of the working of the demands of men's basic drives on the minds of lawmen themselves.[9]

---

[6] Kelsen, General Theory of Law and State 121-122 (1945).

[7] Id. at 369, 370. By permission of the author. See also the "self-assertion" assumptions of Von Ihering, Law as Means to an End 47-70 (Husik trans. 1924).

[8] See Cahn, The Sense of Injustice (1949).

[9] The exigence of law's non-legal assumptions inevitably appears when there is question of basic justice or of crimes "against humanity" that are not covered by the letter of man-made law. The Nürnberg Tribunal is a case in point — leaving aside the moot question of its jurisdiction, justification or consequences and centering on the reasoning intrinsic to the judgments of the court. Regardless of the meaning given to "international law," the court had to go beyond it to find a more fundamental norm according to which those accused of atrocities could be condemned and punished. It was inevitable that ". . . the boundaries of legal positivism were overstepped, and had to be overstepped, the moment it was stated that the trials were a 'question of justice.' . . . The rejection of the defence of superior orders . . . is nothing less than the old doctrine that the validity of laws does not depend on their 'positiveness,' and that it is the duty of the individual to pass judgment on laws before he obeys them." D'Entrèves, Natural Law 110-111 (1951). By permission of the Hutchinson University Library Press.

Thus after persistent efforts of over a century to eliminate from law the

III.   Use of Phrase "Natural Law"

The phrase "natural law" has had a checkered history.   It is open to many diverse, contradictory and misleading interpretations some of which we have seen.[10]   Used even as synonymous with man-discovered law as here explained, it does not express the meaning it is intended to convey: a *naturally promulgated* law discoverable in its promulgation.

True, some words have to be retained in use even though they are inexact and somewhat unsatisfactory.   Their use has become so common that any attempt to root them out of men's minds would be futile.   Such would be the case with the words "right" and "state."

Is "natural law" however such a phrase?   It seems time that the question be seriously raised.   It is not in such widespread use as "right" and "state."   In fact, a great part of the legal world despises it and looks upon it as meaningless.   Even those who do use it must have recourse to other expressions to give it meaning — if they do not merely mouth the phrase as a magic formula.

Would it not therefore be better to expend our efforts trying to find better ways of expressing what man-discovered law is than to retain the phrase "natural law" tenaciously and then squander our time jousting with the shadowy apparitions which have been conjured up by our use of it?   "There is little sense in quarreling about a name, a label.   But the name, Natural Law, does confuse many. . . .   Surely a name can be found that is less confus-

---

difference between what is and what ought to be, the elementary demands of human nature seem ". . . to have taken revenge upon the very champions of the pernicious doctrine that there is no law but positive law, or that might equals right, since for all practical purposes the two propositions are perfectly equivalent."   Official decrees can be contrary to the common welfare of the people.   If such is the case, the ". . . issue can be solved only on the traditional lines of calling the validity of positive law into question, and . . . it is impossible for the individual to do so unless he decides on the justice of the law which he is asked to obey."   Id. at 109-110.

Not a few legal scholars, confronted with the choice of either condoning war atrocities or admitting a norm in men's nature according to which these actions could be judged "inhuman," have swung from legal positivism to "a law in the nature of man."   Men like Radbruch are examples.   For an account of this, see Fuller, American Legal Philosophy at Mid-Century, 6 J. Legal Ed. 475-485 (1954), and Positivism and Fidelity to Law, 71 Harv. L. Rev. 630-672 (1958).

[10] Chapter 8.   As has been pointedly observed, ". . . eight or more new systems of natural law made their appearance at every Leipzig booksellers' fair since 1780.   Thus Jean Paul Richter's ironical remark contained no exaggeration.   Every fair and every war brings forth a new natural law." Rommen, The Natural Law 106 (1947).

ing. . . . At its best Natural Law has symbolized the unquench-
able, human desire for norms or standards of justice by which to
evaluate existing, legal rules, contrasting the 'is' with the 'ought
to be.' We need a symbol for the demand that statutes be repealed, and judge-made rules abandoned or modified, when they
obstruct moral aims, for the demand that human institutions be
altered when they work injustice. . . . The misleading connotations and embarrassing historical associations of the words Natural Law . . . today must be translated to be understood." [11]

The thing discussed is more important than the words used to
discuss it. If an idea recurs in legal thinking as persistently as
does "natural law" and if it is developed in so many diversified
ways and has so many different meanings, only one conclusion can
be drawn: there is some definite datum that men are trying to explain and its explanation is intricate and complex. If this is the
case, we have pointed up for us, not only the importance, but
also the necessity of properly understanding and interpreting this
fact as a prelude to legal thinking.

In line with the definition of man-discovered law given above,
the phrase "demands expressed by a man's nature" seems to be
one way of designating and referring to this law that is naturally
promulgated. Instead of evaluating some action, therefore, as
being according to or against "natural law," it would seem better
to speak of it as being according to or against the "demands expressed by a man's nature."

Such an expression brings out more accurately than "natural
law" what it is that is being referred to: a law naturally promulgated through men's dynamic nature. Emphasis on these demands, understood primarily in terms of rudimentary judgments
formed without reasoning according to the basic drives, cannot
but force a more precise understanding of *whether* and *how* an
action is known to be according to or again elementary directives
of morality and law.

IV. THE ANALOGY OF LAW

When the word "law" is employed regarding man-discovered
law, is it used in as true a sense as it is concerning man-made
law? Is man-discovered law "law" only equivocally and meta-
phorically?

The solution of this problem depends on what the nature of law
is. If the essence of man-made law is the fact that it is "man-

[11] Frank, Courts on Trial 365 (1949).

made," as it is sometimes said to be, all law is man-made by the
very limitation of the definition.   To indulge in such thinking,
however, is to be guilty of mistaking the efficient cause of a thing
for its formal cause.   A table would be a table, according to this
reasoning, not because it had the form of a table but because it was
made by a carpenter.

But the essence of a thing is *what* it is, not who made it.   If
the very form of a law is the directive judgment ordering means
to the common good, the essence of the law is this ordering judgment regardless of who makes it, providing he be in a position of
lawmaking authority.   This being so, when men discover indications of an ordering of means to end, they may have evidence of a
law if the other prerequisites are fulfilled.   The reason why
both man-made law and man-discovered law are law in a true
sense is the fact that each of them is the directive judgment of one
in authority ordering means to the common good.

The word "law," therefore, is not used equivocally here, with
one meaning for man-made law and an essentially different meaning for man-discovered law.   It has the same essential meaning for
both.   Nor is the word "law" used here univocally, that is, in exactly the same sense with no shade of difference.   For man-made
law and man-discovered law do have obvious differences.

"Law" therefore is used regarding man-made and man-discovered law *analogously,* with partly the same and partly different
meanings.   They are partly the same inasmuch as they both are
essentially directive judgments ordering means to a common good.
They are partly different insofar as they differ in the way each is
a directive judgment.   Man-made law is an act of the intellect of
men; man-discovered law is the act of the intellect of the Creator.
In man-made law, political authority derives from the subjection
by consent of those governed; in man-discovered law, the Creator's authority arises from the fact that he has created individual
men in a state of dependence and subject to him through the direction of their basic drives.   The common good of man-made
law is the complexus of goods that are communicable to all, principal among which are peace and security, and for the accomplishment of which all must unite their efforts; the common good of
man-discovered law is not only the peace and security of the human community but ultimately the Creator himself.

This analogous use of the word "law," then, is not at all the
same as the metaphorical use of a term, for instance, as when the
"state" is called a "ship" in a phrase like "the ship of state."
Man-discovered law is law not because we attribute the word

"law" to it in view of some resemblance it may seem to have to man-made law. For, just as man-made law implies a relation between its directive judgment and the minds of men, so also man-discovered law factually implies a relation between its directive judgment and the mind of the Creator. Since there is a proportional similarity between these relations, the analogy of law is one of *proportionality*.

There is, however, a way in which the word "law" may be attributed to what is not actually law but has a relation to it. We attribute the word "law" to the promulgation of man-made and man-discovered law. We attribute "law" to printed statutes and decisions when we say, "Here is the law of the land." We do the same regarding men's basic drives when we indicate, "Here is the law of nature." Neither the printed page nor the basic inclinations are law. They are, to repeat, the promulgation of law. But, by that very fact, they are related to law inasmuch as they are its expression. Hence, the word "law" is with justification attributed to them. Consequently, when "law" is used regarding printed statutes and basic drives it is used analogously but by an analogy of *attribution*.[12]

V. Need of Complement

Man-discovered law needs the complement of man-made law. The directives that men receive through man-discovered law are few in number and they are broad in scope. Men caught in the crosscurrents of daily living, however, need many directives and they need them to be very specific. It is one thing to know that there is a difference between justice and injustice, that justice should be done and injustice avoided. It is an entirely different thing to know what is just or unjust in a particular instance regarding life, sex, learning and freedom, and property.

The essential help that man-discovered law can furnish is the general compass-directive pertaining to one of these areas and the directive to use the power of reason — deductively and inductively — in determining as closely as possible what is right and just in the case at hand. The attempts to determine what is just and unjust in everyday actions pertaining to the common good, when carried on by legislators and judges, results in man-made law.

[12] On analogy of proportion and attribution, see Renard, Philosophy of Being 92-108 (1946).

PART III

Integration of Man-made Law

CHAPTER 12

Principles and Patterns of Integration

The problem to be solved in the next part is the integration of certain vital areas of law according to the principles and patterns outlined thus far. Applied to specific problems in these areas, they point the direction in which integration lies.

I. APPLICATIONS

In this brief chapter let us merely indicate what some of these pattern applications will be. Regarding constitutions, natural claims founded on the basic demands of men's nature as it actually exists will be seen to provide the only factual grounds both for presupposed "inalienable rights" and for the limitation of due process on a means-end basis. In crimes the relation of overt acts to the common good will be found to shape the legal meaning of a crime with implications regarding the distinction between malum in se and malum prohibitum, and the element of decision-making will eventuate as the cause of responsibility and punishment with direct bearing on insanity as a defense in criminal proceedings. In torts the same factor of responsibility consequent upon decision-making is likewise determinative, with the justification of liability with or without fault directly dependent upon it.

In property the original source of title, which is presupposed in the legal concept of property and which centers individual ownership within the social aspect of property, is the process by which ideas are transferred in labor from the mind of the worker to the materials he works. In contracts the means-end relation of contractual agreements, not only to commutative justice but also to contributive justice and the common good, will be seen to be the source of contractual obligation — not consideration. Finally, in equity it is from the demand for a recognized distinction between "mine" and "thine" that springs the quest for justice according to the spirit of man-made law, even though this results in going beyond the remedy afforded by the letter of the law as is evidenced in such situations as restitution and specific performance.

These are some of the more general applications. Other more specific ones will appear as our analysis proceeds.

II. Substantive Areas Only

The problems that we will examine pertain to substantive law only, both public and private. Substantive law, to recall, defines and specifies the claims of citizens that are to be protected or promoted. Procedural law (which is also known as adjective law since it exists for the sake of the substantive) prescribes the rules and methods to be followed in enforcing these claims or in obtaining redress for their violation. Substantive law includes constitutions, crimes, torts, property, contracts, equity, domestic relations and the like. Procedural law embraces administration, evidence, pleading, procedure and similar matters.

Substantive and procedural law, again to remember, are also regarded as private or public law depending on whether the claims under consideration pertain to individual citizens as individuals or to them as citizens composing political society. Private law regards the "private" claims of one citizen as against another. Public law is concerned with the "public" claims of citizens. Under public law are constitutional law, administrative law, municipal corporations, criminal law and procedure, as well as governmental law regulating the government's suing and being sued. Private law covers torts, property, contracts, equity, domestic relations and the like. Our inquiry, then, will cover the public law of constitutions and crimes; and the private law of torts, property, contracts and equity.

There are many other problems of substantive law that could profitably be examined besides those which we have selected. The ones that are studied, however, are for the most part key subjects that affect legal thinking in the whole area.

Without doubt some such application of principles and patterns of legal thinking should also be made to procedural law. This is a work yet to be done by others. "If Natural Law symbolizes the quest for justice, then those lawyers who claim to be adherents of Natural Law, or its equivalent, should not be content with improving the legal rules the better to reflect moral values. Those lawyers should also assiduously devote themselves to reforming our methods of trying cases, of training of future trial judges, of using the jury. For in our trial courts today 'is' and 'ought to be' remain too far apart. To separate ethics from the judicial process is to pervert the latter. We must ethicize the work of the courts. But that aim will come to relatively little unless we do so at the trial-court level." [1]

[1] Frank, Courts on Trial 371 (1949).

CHAPTER 13

Constitutions

The problem that concerns us regarding the Constitution is whether the "inalienable rights" presupposed by the Constitution, especially in due process, rest on solid ground and, if not, where such a foundation can be found. A lawman's attitude toward the interpretation of the Constitution and due process depends on this solution.

I. SUPREME AND PARAMOUNT LAW

The constitution of any political union is the groundwork of its legal structure. It is the basis for "government by law." It is the "fundamental and paramount law of the nation." [1] It states the working principles that will serve as guides concerning government, authority and the protection of claims.

That a formal setting forth of these matters in a written document is not absolutely necessary is attested by the fact that political unions and their governments have functioned fairly well in past centuries without such constitutions. In the last few hundred years, however, a written instrument has become the symbol of government of, by and for free men. It signifies government whose authority is defined and limited by law and to which governors are responsible. A constitution implies faith in the ability of free men to solve their own political problems without having someone do it for them at the price of their own political freedom.

A. *Establishes Type of Government*

It is the constitution that establishes the type of government that will direct the citizens to their common good. "The Constitution is the supreme law of the state, embodying the principles upon which the government is founded, regulating the division of the sovereign powers, and directing to what persons each of

[1] Marbury v. Madison, 1 Cranch 137, 177, 2 L. Ed. 60, 73 (1803).

these powers is to be confided, and the manner in which it is to be exercised." [2]

B. *Fixes Limit of Authority*

The constitution prescribes the extent and manner of exercising governmental authority. "The constitution fixes limits to the exercise of legislative authority, and prescribes the orbit within which it must move. In short . . . the constitution is the sum of the political system, around which all legislative, executive and judicial bodies must revolve. Whatever may be the case in other countries, yet in this, there can be no doubt, that every act of the legislature, repugnant to the constitution, is absolutely void." [3]

C. *Protects Claims*

The constitution declares that basic claims or rights of the citizens will be protected by this authority. "It grants no rights to the people, but is the creature of their power — the instrument of their convenience. Designed for their protection in the enjoyment of the rights and powers which they possessed before the Constitution was made, it is but the framework of the political government, and necessarily based upon pre-existing condition of laws, rights, habits and modes of thought." [4]

II. DUE PROCESS

The constitutional guarantee that claims will be protected is "due process." Due process is both procedural and substantive.

A. *Procedural Due Process*

Procedural due process is a guarantee that certain procedures prescribed by law will be carried out. "It may however be stated generally that due process of law requires an orderly proceeding adapted to the nature of the case in which the citizen has an opportunity to be heard, and to defend, enforce, and protect his rights. A hearing or an opportunity to be heard, is absolutely essential. We cannot conceive of due process of law with-

[2] Browne v. City of New York, 213 App. Div. 206, 211 N.Y. Supp. 306, 311 (1925).
[3] Van Horne's Lessee v. Dorrance, 2 Dall. 304, 310, 1 L. Ed. 391, 394 (1795).
[4] Hanson v. Vernon, 27 Stiles 28, 74 (Iowa, 1875).

out this. . . . 'Due process of law undoubtedly means in due course of legal proceedings according to those rules and forms which have been established for the protection of private rights.' . . . '[D]ue process of law' is not confined to ordinary judicial proceedings but extends to all cases where property is sought to be taken or interfered with." [5] "Fairness of procedure is 'due process in the primary sense.' " [6]

1. *Claims recognized as preceding written constitutions.* These prime norms of what is just are recognized as preceding written constitutions. "It is a rule founded on the first principles of natural justice older than written constitutions, that a citizen shall not be deprived of his life, liberty or property without an opportunity to be heard in defense of his rights, and the constitutional provision that no person shall be deprived of these 'without due process of law' has its foundation in this rule. This great guaranty is always and everywhere present to protect the citizen against arbitrary interference with these sacred rights." [7] "The right to life, liberty and property, was not conferred by society. The highest obligation of government is to defend and protect persons in their enjoyment. . . . For centuries the inviolability of person and property, against unusual and extraordinary invasions of power, has been the birthright of British subjects. From their magna charta, the principle has been transcribed into the American constitutions." [8]

In other words, at the origin of every written constitution there is an unwritten one. "There is, as it were, back of the written Constitution, an *unwritten Constitution,* if I may use the expression, which guarantees and well protects all the absolute rights of the people. The government can exercise no power to impair or deny them. Many of them may not be enumerated in the Constitution nor preserved by express provisions thereof, notwithstanding they exist and are possessed by the people, free from governmental interference." [9]

Due process is, then, a constitutional recognition that every man has elemental titles and claims and that these must be taken as the fundamental norms of what should be protected and pro-

[5] Stuart v. Palmer, 74 N.Y. 183, 191, 30 Am. Rep. 289 (1878). See also Anti-Fascist Committee v. McGrath, 341 U.S. 123, 161, 71 Sup. Ct. 624, 643, 644 (1951); State v. Rossi, 71 R.I. 284, 43 A.2d 323, 326 (1945).

[6] Anti-Fascist Committee v. McGrath, 341 U.S. 123, 161, 71 Sup. Ct. 624, 642 (1951).

[7] Stuart v. Palmer, 74 N.Y. 183, 190, 30 Am. Rep. 289 (1878).

[8] Brown v. Board of Levee Commissioners, 50 Miss. 468, 487 (1874).

[9] Hanson v. Vernon, 27 Stiles 28, 73 (Iowa, 1875).

moted in any legal structure. Due process guarantees that no man will be deprived of these claims without definite procedures being followed that are prescribed by law. These include assurance of no search without a warrant, of counsel, of no judgment being rendered without notice, of hearing the evidence against oneself, of an impartial trial, of a verdict before sentence is executed.

There may be reasons why a man should be deprived of his claims to life, liberty and property. He may be accused of committing a crime for the doing of which he shall have to suffer their loss as punishment. But before he is deprived of them, it must be certain that he is guilty. Until this is proved by evidence, his claims remain valid and effective.

2. *Magna Charta.* This aspiration of men to have their elemental claims so protected is not new. It is contained in Magna Charta, the great charter granted by King John of England to his barons in 1215, and it has been reaffirmed many times since as "the law of the land." Although honored with varying degrees of recognition throughout the centuries, it has remained a symbol of the claims of free men. In the Constitution of the United States of America "due process" is contained principally in the Fifth and Fourteenth Amendments.

B. *Substantive Due Process*

Due process may refer, not only to the procedure to be followed in protecting or promoting just claims, but also to the claims themselves. The phrase "law of the land" embraces both. "The phrase 'due process of law' in many decisions refers more particularly to the procedure prescribed by statute for the protection of life, liberty, and property, and the method of enforcing rights or obtaining redress for their invasion, while the phrase 'law of the land' includes the remedial law as well as substantive law. . . . The substantive law is that part which creates, defines and regulates rights as opposed to adjective or remedial law, which prescribes the method of enforcing rights or obtaining redress for their invasion." [10] Substantive due process is an application of the concept of due process in procedural law to problems in substantive law.

1. *Public vs. private claims.* The problem is always present of determining what the relation should be between a man's pri-

[10] Mix v. Board of Commissioners of the Nez Perce County, 18 Idaho 695, 112 Pac. 215, 220 (1910).

vate claims to his life, his freedom and his property and the public needs that may demand a part of these claims.   In striking
this balance judges, like any other human beings, are bound to be
influenced by the socio-economic theories prevalent at the time.

During the latter part of the nineteenth century great industrial expansion took place in the United States.   Laissez faire was
the prevalent economic doctrine.   What was sought was some
means of getting this economic theory into constitutional law as
a protection against regulation by state or federal legislation.
The due process clause of the Fourteenth Amendment was the
means at hand.   Hence, during this period due process was
gradually given a substantive interpretation and was used to protect vested interests.

After the turn of the twentieth century this "rugged individualism" began to show signs of having run its course and an economic
doctrine that had greater social concern for the people started to
assert itself.   Hence, as time went on an about-face took place
and "due process" was used by the courts less and less as a means
of protecting vested property rights.   It continued to be used,
however, as an instrument for protecting freedom in the form of
"civil liberties."

2. *Fluctuation.*   Court decisions of these years plot a wavering
and indecisive line.   They are, as is constitutional history itself,
"the record of a series of oscillations." [11]   The right of eminent
domain was consistently recognized.[12]   But the decisions regarding property in general and freedom of contract reflect vacillating
theories of economics and government control.

a. *Property.*   The preservation of property was said to be a
primary object of the social compact.[13]   Moneys collected by
public tax could not be put to private use and the individual
rights so protected were again related to the social compact.[14]
On the other hand, at this same time the Supreme Court was saying that state regulation of rates on grain storage was valid.
When private property was affected with public interest, it became subject to public regulation.[15]   After the turn of the century the Court was still concerned with vested rights.   An equali-
zation tax, whereby a board of assessors was empowered to examine returns on property and make whatever corrections seemed

[11] O'Brian, The Value of Constitutionalism Today, in Government Under
Law 507, 630 (Sutherland ed. 1956).
[12] Stuart v. Palmer, 74 N.Y. 183, 190, 30 Am. Rep. 289 (1878).
[13] Van Horne's Lessee v. Dorrance, 2 Dall. 304, 310, 1 L. Ed. 391 (1795).
[14] Loan Association v. Topeka, 87 U.S. 655, 663, 22 L. Ed. 455, 461 (1874).
[15] Munn v. Illinois, 94 U.S. 113, 126, 130, 24 L. Ed. 77, 84, 86 (1876).

necessary, was declared unconstitutional.[16] The attitude toward railroad rate fixing by statute was to find it invalid.[17] It is only later that the tendency is shown to allow states to put greater regulations on property through taxes.[18]

b. *Freedom of contract.* This fluctuation of Court opinion between private and public claims is perhaps more evident regarding freedom of contract. Just before the turn of the century a statute that regulated insurance company activities was found unconstitutional because it hindered such freedom.[19] The next year the Court held that a statute limiting the labor of men in mines, smelters and ore refineries to eight hours a day except in emergencies was constitutional.[20] A few years later, however, the Court decided that a statute was unconstitutional which limited employment in bakeries to sixty hours in one week or ten hours in any one day.[21]

Strong dissent, however, was voiced in a famous minority opinion in this last case on the grounds that ". . . [T]he Fourteenth Amendment does not enact Mr. Herbert Spencer's Social Statics . . . a Constitution is not intended to embody a particular economic theory, whether of paternalism and the organic relation of the citizen to the state or of laissez-faire. It is made for people of fundamentally differing views, and the accident of our finding certain opinions natural and familiar, or novel and even shocking, ought not to conclude our judgment upon the question whether statutes embodying them conflict with the Constitution of the United States." [22]

The opinion that due process should not be used to promote the laissez-faire doctrine of freedom of contract became preponderant in a short time. The Court held before long that a statute was constitutional which prohibited women from working in factories and laundries more than ten hours a day. Such limitation of freedom of contract was justified on the grounds that it was "for the benefit of all." [23]

This tendency to limit contractual freedom for a greater good became definite. A Workmen's Compensation Act had been held constitutional that provided compensation for accidental in-

[16] Turner v. Wade, 254 U.S. 64, 70, 41 Sup. Ct. 27, 29 (1920).
[17] Norfolk and Western Ry. Co. v. West Virginia, 236 U.S. 605, 608, 609, 35 Sup. Ct. 437, 438, 439 (1915).
[18] Madden v. Kentucky, 309 U.S. 83, 93, 60 Sup. Ct. 406, 410 (1940).
[19] Allgeyer v. Louisiana, 165 U.S. 578, 589, 17 Sup. Ct. 427, 431 (1897).
[20] Holden v. Hardy, 169 U.S. 366, 390, 18 Sup. Ct. 383, 386 (1898).
[21] Lochner v. New York, 198 U.S. 45, 58, 25 Sup. Ct. 539, 543, 544 (1905).
[22] Mr. Justice Holmes, in Lochner v. New York, 198 U.S. at 75-76.
[23] Muller v. Oregon, 208 U.S. 412, 422, 28 Sup. Ct. 324, 327 (1908).

jury or death of an employee without regard to fault except where the injury was self-willed or the result of drunkenness.[24]   Other aspects of freedom have been also interpreted under due process. Peaceful picketing in labor disputes has been viewed as containing an element of free speech.   Picketing is a laborer's means of communication.[25]   Finally the Fair Labor Standards Act fixing wages and hours was held constitutional.[26]

3. *Method of balancing.*   Due process, then, besides being a guarantee that claims will be protected by proper practices being followed in procedural law, has also come to mean a method by which private versus public claims may be decided and balanced in substantive law.

Perhaps a more logical place for the solution of such problems would have been under the "privileges and immunities" clause of the Constitution rather than under "due process."   For privileges and immunities have a cognate relation to claims or rights, as already noted.   But such has been the restricted interpretation put on the clause and the general development of constitutional law in the United States that attempts to strike a proper balance between proper and common goods have evolved by way of "due process."

C.   *Due Process Through Means-End Relation*

The main point to be noted regarding due process, however, as far as the philosophy of law is concerned, is that there has always been a constant principle at work.   In spite of fluctuations in the interpretations of due process caused by the inevitable tensions between private and public claims and differing socio-economic influences, the steady guide has been the norm of the means-end relationship.   Attempts to strike a balance between individual freedom and governmental restriction have to be made with one end in view — the common good.

Hence, it must be remembered that the Fifth and Fourteenth amendments ". . . do not prohibit governmental regulation for the public welfare.   They merely condition the exertion of the admitted power, by securing that the end shall be accomplished by methods consistent with due process.   And the guaranty of due process, as has often been held, demands only that the law shall

[24] Holden v. Hardy, 169 U.S. 366, 397, 18 Sup. Ct. 383 (1898).   See also New York Central R.R. Co. v. White, 243 U.S. 188, 206, 37 Sup. Ct. 247, 254 (1917).
[25] Thornhill v. Alabama, 310 U.S. 88, 102, 103, 60 Sup. Ct. 736, 744 (1940).
[26] United States v. Darby, 312 U.S. 100, 125, 61 Sup. Ct. 451, 462 (1941).

not be unreasonable, arbitrary or capricious, and that the means selected shall have a real and substantial relation to the object sought to be attained." [27]

III. SOURCE OF CLAIMS ASSUMED BY CONSTITUTION

Procedural due process takes for granted that there are certain "fundamental," "natural," "deep-rooted," "older-than-governments," "unwritten" principles of justice that should be protected for every man. Substantive due process, assuming this fact, goes further and attempts to determine the proper balance that should be set up between these private claims and public needs.

Common agreement regarding the existence of these rights is a necessary practical formula for legal thinking among men who differ theoretically as to how these rights are to be justified. But eventually, as far as the philosophy of law is concerned, the hard question has to be faced: what factually is the ground on which the validity of these "fundamental" principles of justice are based? For it is on this ground that the framework of the Constitution and our whole legal structure rests.

A. Not from a Hypothetical State of Nature

It has been contended that the Constitution of the United States is an archaic vestige of political and legal theories long since passed away. It is said to be as antiquated as are the notions it embraces.

Jarring and disconcerting though it may be to hear it and admit it, this statement is true if the concept of "natural rights" assumed by the Constitution rests on a historically untenable hypothesis. If the Constitution represents the embodiment of long since disproven political theories, its value as the fundamental legal instrument of the land is in question.

It seems to be a fact that the Constitution does assume a theory of "natural right" or "natural law" that has no factual foundation. This is the theory that relates the origin of "natural rights" to a "state of nature" that supposedly existed before the social compact to unite politically was agreed upon. The evidence points to the fact that the political theorists of the seventeenth century did not take as their point of departure the Aristotelian concept that man was by nature a political being. Their assumption was that men lived in an original state of nature that existed prior to the

[27] Nebbia v. New York, 291 U.S. 502, 525, 54 Sup. Ct. 505, 510 (1933).

existence of any political society.   In this state of nature, there was no government or man-made law and men's relations with one another were governed by a natural law contained in the nature of things.   For the more effective working of the natural law, according to these theorists, men covenanted together to create the "state" and to form governments whose function it was to enforce natural law — a responsibility, they said, originally inherent in each separate individual.

That the colonists had this theory of natural law in mind when they were working toward independence and a Constitution seems evident from the men they quote who professedly held this position.   "The state of nature — the state of 'men living together according to reason without a common superior on earth, with authority to judge between them' — was the point of reference around which Revolutionary thinkers grouped the principles of their political theory." [28]   "The colonists revealed the derivative quality of their political theory by quoting English and Continental definitions of the law of nature rather than seeking to define it for themselves.   Locke, Pufendorf, Vattel, and Burlamaqui were all called into service for this purpose, but Sir William Blackstone's definition was probably the best known and most widely cited." [29]

This idea of natural law and natural rights, which was held by Adams, Hamilton, Madison and Wilson, was that of Locke, Pufendorf, Burlamaqui and Montesquieu.[30]   That Jefferson depended on Locke for his political and natural law ideas seems well established.   The Declaration of Independence was principally the work of Jefferson, although Adams and Franklin had a minor part in it.   In the first paragraphs of the Declaration, "There are four fundamental political ideas . . . : the doctrine of natural law and natural rights, the compact theory of the state, the doctrine of popular sovereignty, and the right of revolution.   These conceptions were common to nearly all seventeenth and eighteenth century natural law theorists, but Jefferson's phraseology was closely modeled on John Locke's *Second Treatise*.   Several of Jefferson's most telling phrases were borrowed directly from Locke's essay.   Jefferson had in fact suc-

[28] Rossiter, Seedtime of the Republic 363 (1953).   The reference is to Locke's Civil Government, II, c. 3, §19.   By permission of Harcourt, Brace and Company.

[29] Rossiter, Seedtime of the Republic 367 (1953).   The reference is to 1 Blackstone, Commentaries 38-41.

[30] Wright, American Interpretations of Natural Law 88-89, 126-127, 281 (1931).

ceeded admirably in condensing Locke's fundamental argument into a few hundred words. . . . Jefferson's 'life, liberty, and the pursuit of happiness' was a variation from the expression 'life, liberty, and property' sanctioned by Locke." [31]

These political ideas found their way into church sermons. "After the Bible, Locke was the principal authority relied on by the preachers to bolster up their political teachings, although Coke, Pufendorf, Sydney and later on some others were also cited. The substance of the doctrine of these discourses is, except at two points, that of the *Second Treatise*. Natural rights and the social compact, government bounded by law and incapable of imparting legality to measures contrary to law, and the right of resistance to illegal measures all fall into their proper place." [32]

In this manner, the political and natural law ideas of Locke and others of like mind became part of the fabric of the Constitution. "A reference by a colonist to Locke's writing must not be considered a mere reference to a bookman who had been speculating about government; he was thought of as the expositor of the foundations of English constitutionalism, an authority on constitutional law. When the colonists of the Revolutionary days referred to him, they thought of him as putting forth, not theories of what *ought* to be, but pronouncements of what actually *was;* . . . they took the theories of the philosophers and the declarations of men like Locke and wove them into an actual constitutional structure." [33]

The implications, then, of this "state of nature" theory of natural law is that political union, government and man-made law are not natural to men. They are only unnatural expediencies and at best "necessary evils." But there is not the slightest evidence that men ever lived historically in such a state, as already noted. Hence, it is understandable when some say that "Locke's principles '. . . were embalmed in the Constitution of the United States which survives like an ancient family ghost haunting a modern skyscraper.' " [34]

[31] Kelly and Harbison, The American Constitution 90 (rev. ed. 1955). By permission of the W. W. Norton Company. The contention that Jefferson's political ideas were influenced by Bellarmine seems not to be supported by conclusive evidence. There is no proof that Jefferson used Bellarmine's ideas or that, if he did, he gave them Bellarmine's full meaning.

[32] Corwin, The "Higher Law" Background of American Constitutional Law 74-75 (reprint 1955). First published in 42 Harv. L. Rev. 149-185, 365-409 (1928-1929).

[33] McLaughlin, A Constitutional History of the United States 93 (1935). By permission of Appleton-Century-Crofts, Inc.

[34] Broad, John Locke, 31 Hibbert Journal 249, 256 (1933).

Looked at from this point of view, "natural rights," due process in protecting them, and the Constitution itself can be nothing but senseless skeletons of dead political theories.

B. *Not from International Law*

If the concept of "natural rights" assumed by the Constitution supposes a theory that is historically untenable, is there anything on which elemental rights can be founded? Attempts have been made to ground such rights on international agreements. Whatever nations agree to is said by some to be the norm of these rights. "Assuming the primacy of international law over national law, the problem of the basic norm shifts from the national to the international legal order. Then the only true basic norm, a norm which is not created by a legal procedure but presupposed by juristic thinking, is the basic norm of international law." [35]

International agreements are binding, it is said, because *pacta sunt servanda*. But why should agreements between nations be kept? In this theory the reason why agreements ought to be kept is simply: because they ought to be. "The States ought to behave as they have customarily behaved." [36]

But again, why should nations behave the way they customarily do behave? This question is left unanswered. The only ground that can be found is one that relates to the demands of men's nature. Unless agreements are kept, mutual confidence is destroyed among peoples and dealings among them are rendered suspect and uncertain. A condition of suspicion and fear will pervade the world. Trustful communication and intercourse are necessary if men are to live with one another in a condition of peace and security as demanded by their nature for their development. Hence, agreements ought to be kept because the keeping of them is a means necessary for the common good of all men.

C. *From the Demands of Men's Nature*

The foundation, then, for the "natural" or "inalienable" claims that the Constitution proposes to protect is the actual demands of men's nature. These claims are necessary for men because

[35] Kelsen, General Theory of Law and State 121-122 (1945). By permission of the author.
[36] Id. at 369.

men are structured the way they are. The claims are pre-supposed, not granted, by the Constitution.

It is because men are structured the way they are that they have definite basic drives. These drives demand certain things for their fulfillment. Men must live, their race must continue, they must own things, they must direct themselves. To the preservation of their lives, to the use of their sex functions, to those objects uniquely related to them, to the exercise of their freedom of inquiry and decision, they have a natural title. They are "theirs." Because of this natural title, they have a natural claim on others to fulfill their duty and justly respect this title.

In these claims is rooted procedural due process. It represents elemental justice in guaranteeing that no one will be deprived of them without certainty of his guilt. Substantive due process also is grounded on these basic claims. It takes them for granted and only endeavors to determine whether private or public claims should prevail in concrete instances. Substantive due process would be an invalid development, however, if it attempted to grant or withdraw these basic claims themselves to life, property and freedom. This would be tyranny.

The "natural rights" idea presupposed by the Constitution, then, can have a valid meaning. The Ninth Amendment to the Constitution says that "The enumeration in the Constitution of certain rights, shall not be construed to deny or disparage others retained by the people." These rights "retained by the people" are grounded on a fact. This fact is the nature of men as they actually exist.[37]

D. *Absolute and Relative Claims*

Hence, when the claims involved in due process are spoken of, it should be made clear regarding what claims one is speaking. To say that ". . . rights are no longer conceived . . . as categorical absolutes derived from the immutable law of nature; rather modern constitutional doctrine envisions private right as susceptible to growth and change in a process of continuous adjustment to the social order" [38] is certainly true if it refers to

[37] See Northrop, Philosophical Issues in Contemporary Law, 2 Natural Law Forum 41-63 (1957).

[38] Kelly and Harbison, American Constitution 828 (1948). It is interesting to note that in their revised edition (1955) the authors have dropped this passage and in its place say that, "Now it is possible to defend constitutional democracy against Soviet totalitarianism in absolute moralistic terms. If one accepts as true certain basic propositions about the nature and destiny of

private claims that must be restricted for the public welfare by substantive due process. It is also true, in a different sense, if it regards changing claims that are protected by procedural due process. But if it concerns the elementary claims to life, property and freedom themselves, such a statement courts disaster. For, if these fundamental claims may change, the whole purpose of a constitution is nullified — freedom for the individual person.[39]

Likewise, in discussions of the mutability and immutability of "fundamental law," it should be made certain in what sense "fundamental" is being taken. "The Constitutions are charters of governments, deriving their whole authority from the governed. By necessarily conclusive provisions incorporated in them the entertainment of any notion that the fundamental laws are immutable is entirely precluded. Freedom of speech, the right of assembly and petition, and the orderly processes designed to effect the revision or amendment of the Constitutions are among the provisions of the Constitutions particularly emphasizing the idea that these fundamental instruments were not established as the immutable expressions of supreme law." [40] "Fundamental" may mean something that is important, but relatively so, as a prerequisite for the functioning of democratic processes. Freedom of speech is certainly one of these and laws regarding its exercise are assuredly mutable. But "fundamental" may also refer to something that is an absolute requirement of men's nature. Such is men's claim to freedom in general and of which freedom of speech is only an area application. Laws proclaiming freedom itself are immutable. Otherwise a man's claim to lead a life of freedom as is expressed in law could be granted or taken away by the whims of other men without question of injustice.

---

man which are a fundamental part of the magnificent heritage of western culture, then it is relatively easy to show logically that constitutional democracy has a necessary and coherent relationship to that faith. The defense of constitutional democracy thus takes on an absolute moral justification. Lincoln and Jefferson certainly would have had it so, and for millions of Americans the moral foundations of constitutional democracy still provide the ultimate rationale of the system. For them it needs no other defense against Communist totalitarianism." (914-915.) By permission of the W. W. Norton Company.

[39] See Corwin, The "Higher Law" Background of American Constitutional Law, 42 Harv. L. Rev. 149-185, 365-409 (1928); Grant, The Natural Law Background of Due Process, 31 Colum. L. Rev. 56 (1931); Snee, Leviathan at the Bar of Justice, in Government Under Law 91-143 (1956).

On the political thinking behind the Constitution, see Gettell, History of American Political Thought 67-75, 134-141 (1928); Kelly and Harbison, The American Constitution 36-46, 165-166 (1955).

[40] Fairhope Single Tax Corp. v. Melville, 193 Ala. 289, 69 So. 466, 471 (1915).

C H A P T E R   1 4

Crimes

One of the main problems in crimes is to determine what the components of a crime are and what the source of a man's responsibility is. Dependent on this solution is a lawman's philosophy of crime and punishment as well as his view regarding the obligation of penal law.

I. Wrongs Directly Against the Common Good of Citizens

A crime in general is, to recall, a "public wrong." It is an act directly against the public good of the people considered as citizens united in political society. Such are homicide, assault and battery, larceny, embezzlement, robbery, forgery, arson, conspiracy and the like. "A 'crime' is a wrong which the government notices as injurious to the public, and punishes in what is called a criminal proceeding. . . . The terms 'crime,' 'offense,' and 'criminal offense' are all synonymous, and ordinarily used interchangeably, and include any breach of law established for the protection of the public, as distinguished from an infringement of mere private rights for which a penalty is imposed or punishment inflicted in any judicial proceeding." [1]

A. *Not Defined by Penalty*

The tendency to define a crime in terms of penalty is prevalent. "The act is made a crime by the terms of the penalty." [2] "A crime is conduct which is prohibited by state law and punishable by fine or imprisonment or both. Conduct punishable by a forfeiture is not a crime." [3]

However, as was pointed out above, a crime is a crime, not on account of the penalty attached, but because of the nature of the act committed. If it is against the public good it is a crime.

[1] In re Jacoby, 74 Ohio App. 147, 57 N.E.2d 932, 934, 935 (1943).
[2] State v. Allen, 129 La. 733, 56 So. 655 (1911).
[3] Wisconsin Criminal Code §939.12 (1955).

Whether it will be a grave crime (a felony) or a slight crime (a misdemeanor) depends on the gravity or slightness of the matter which is usually defined by statute. Robbing a man of $2500 is more grave than robbing him of $25. Besides, there may be crimes that have no penalty attached.

If legislators have well evaluated the gravity of wrongful actions against the common good and have assessed penalties accordingly, these penalties may be taken as an indication of whether the action in question is a grave or slight crime. Well-chosen penalties are signs of the nature of the act under consideration. They do not constitute it.

B. *Natural and Legal Crimes*

Crimes, like any wrongful conduct, may be contrary only to the demands of a man's nature. As such they are natural crimes. Or they may be a violation of a statute or judicial decision in which case they are also legal crimes. The kidnap-murder of a child is a natural crime even though there were no legislation covering it. The statute that recognizes it as a crime and makes it punishable by imprisonment or death constitutes it a legal crime. Although lawmen ordinarily understand crime to be acts declared such by statute or judicial decision, nevertheless the word admits of this wider meaning.

II. COMPONENTS OF A CRIME

The meaning given to crime should be consistent with the fact that a man is a being who governs himself. Involved in this are the broad issues of responsibility and punishment. But implied also are such notions as mens rea, malum in se and malum prohibitum and the part they play in "public welfare offenses" and "purely penal law." And, since "the general principles of criminal and civil liability are the same," [4] included too is the concept of liability, both relative and absolute, which pertains to torts. By reason of their history and importance, all of these ideas deserve to be subjected to the closest inspection.

The root from which these concepts draw their meaning is the nature of crime itself. Depending on what crime is said to be, they may or may not be valid. And since crime is a complex phenome-

---

[4] Holmes, The Common Law 44 (1881).

non composed of many factors, it may be well briefly to consider them.

A. *Prerequisites: Knowledge and Decision*

The activities of men that are distinctively human are those that are knowingly and freely directed. A man's powers of intellect and will are what make him different from animals. And one of the basic drives, as we have seen, is to use these powers of knowing and deciding. This means that every characteristically human action is caused by a knowing and free decision and on this basis rests all responsibility. Inasmuch as there is a defect of knowledge or free decision, the prerequisites for a crime are lacking.

Let us take the case of a man who backs his car out of the garage in the morning, runs over his wife who is standing in the middle of the driveway, and kills her.

1. *Knowledge.* Before this overt act can be matter for a crime the husband must have known that his wife was standing there. A man cannot intend what he does not somehow know. " 'Knowing' means conscious, cognizant. . . . 'Knowingly' is frequently used in contradistinction to 'ignorantly,' 'innocently,' or 'unintentionally.' It is sometimes used in the sense of 'intentionally.' " [5]

It is possible, of course, that he was *ignorant* of whether she was there or not because he wanted to be so. He intentionally made no effort to find out. If so, he would be responsible since he caused his ignorance. "Ignorance of facts exonerates from liability, unless such ignorance is culpable. Culpable ignorance is that which results from a failure to exercise ordinary care to acquire knowledge. Knowledge which could be acquired by the exercise of ordinary care is by the law imputed to the person, and he is held to have constructive knowledge." [6]

Or it could happen that he was ignorant of the fact that the accelerator was going to stick as he started to back out. In this case, the whole incident would have been *accidental* and no crime. " 'Accidental' is defined . . . as 'happening by chance, or unexpectedly; taking place not according to the usual course of things; casual; fortuitous as an accidental visit.' . . . 'Where the effect is not the natural and probable consequence of the means which produce it — an effect which does not ordinarily follow and cannot be reasonably anticipated from the use of the means, or an

---

[5] Cheffer v. Eagle Discount Stamp Co., 348 Mo. 1023, 156 S.W.2d 591, 595 (1941).

[6] Luck v. Buffalo Lakes, 144 S.W.2d 672, 676 (Tex. Civ. App. 1940).

effect which the actor did not intend to produce and which he cannot be charged with a design of producing — it is produced by accidental means.' " [7]

2. *Volition.* Following a man's knowledge, is his intention. "In their ordinary acceptation, the words . . . 'willfully, and knowingly,' when applied to an act or thing done, import knowledge of the act or thing so done, as well as an evil intent or bad purpose in doing such a thing." [8]

Implied in intention is freedom of choice and decision. " 'Willfully,' as used in connection with an act forbidden by law, means that the act must be done knowingly or intentionally, and that the act was committed with knowledge, and that the will consented to, designed, and directed the act." [9] ". . . [T]he word 'voluntary' means 'produced in or by an act of choice,' and it also means 'acting of itself,' or 'spontaneous.' " [10]

Freedom of choice may be affected by a number of factors. Some may merely reduce freedom, others may inhibit it completely. Perhaps the man ran over his wife in a fit of *passion* or rage caused by an argument with her as he got into the car. Such a state would affect the degree of freedom in his decision and therefore could lessen his responsibility. "By the expression, 'under the immediate influence of sudden passion,' is meant that the provocation must arise at the time of the killing, and that the passion is not the result of former provocation, and the act must be directly caused by the passion arising out of the provocation, if any, at the time of the killing. It is not enough that the mind is merely agitated by passion arising from other provocation, or a provocation given by some person other than the party killed. The passion intended is any of the emotions of the mind known as anger, rage, sudden resentment, or terror, rendering the mind incapable of cool reflection." [11]

Or possibly it was done out of *fear* that gripped him when he thought he saw her standing there with a gun aimed point-blank at him, and without any reflection he backed up as fast as he could. In such a circumstance, his ability to make a sufficiently free decision to be responsible, may have been lacking. For, in

[7] Norris v. New York Life Insurance Co., 49 F.2d 62, 63 (4th Cir. 1931). See also Murphy v. Travelers Insurance Co., 141 Neb. 41, 2 N.W.2d 576, 579 (1942).

[8] Erby v. State, 181 Tenn. 647, 184 S.W.2d 14, 16 (1944).

[9] Hutchman v. State, 61 Okla. Crim. 117, 66 P.2d 99, 102 (1937).

[10] Hartingh v. Bay Circuit Judge, 176 Mich. 289, 142 N.W. 585, 589 (1913).

[11] Stell v. State, 58 S.W. 75, 76 (Tex. Crim. App. 1900). See also Winton v. State, 151 Tenn. 177, 268 S.W. 633, 637 (1925).

some instances fear may be so great as to inhibit a sufficiently free decision for making the act a responsible one. Thus a girl's fear of being kidnapped, of having her face disfigured by cutting, of having her father's house blown to pieces if she did not marry the defendant was so great that it precluded the possibility of a responsible consent to a marriage contract. Hence, a court would find that it ". . . cannot sustain this contract under these conditions. . . . Under the evidence in this case, there can be but one conclusion, viz., that this plaintiff was forced into this marriage contract by duress; that this duress was occasioned by the defendant; that he uttered or instigated the threats of bodily harm to plaintiff and injury to property of the father and mother of plaintiff, and was cognizant of them when made; that at the time of the marriage these threats exercised a controlling influence over the will and conduct of this plaintiff and compelled her consent thereto; and that at the time of the marriage ceremony defendant knew, or had reason to believe, that plaintiff was impelled to marry him by fear that the threats so made would be carried into execution." [12]

It is possible also that he ran over her because of an *irresistible impulse*. This condition, if proved, would undoubtedly reduce or remove freedom of decision and responsibility. "It is not enough to relieve from criminal liability, that the doer be morally depraved. It is not enough that he has views of right and wrong that are at variance with those that find expression in the law. The variance must have its origin in some disease of the mind." [13]

Or perchance he followed his careless habit of never looking back as he backed out of the garage. If so, he would implicitly intend being *negligent*. "Willful negligence implies an act intentionally done in disregard of another's rights, or an omission to do something to protect the rights of another after having had such notice of those rights as would put a prudent man upon his guard to use ordinary care for the purpose of avoiding injury to such other person." [14]

Finally it could have happened that he backed up at a reckless speed and could not stop in time when he saw her. In this in-

[12] Fratello v. Fratello, 118 Misc. 584, 193 N.Y. Supp. 865 (1922).

[13] People v. Carlin, 194 N.Y. 448, 87 N.E. 805 (1909). On factors affecting freedom of decision, see: Hall and Menninger, Psychiatry and the Law, 38 Iowa L. Rev. 687-704 (1953); Hall, General Principles of Criminal Law 505-526 (1947); Guttmacher and Weihofen, Psychiatry and the Law (1952).

[14] Covert v. Rockford and I. Ry. Co., 229 Ill. 288, 132 N.E. 504, 505 (1921). See also Victor Coal Co. v. Muir, 20 Colo. 320, 38 Pac. 378, 385 (1894).

stance he would implicitly intend his *recklessness* and would be responsible for whatever resulted from it. For it has been held "that reckless driving meant such an operation as shows a 'disregard of the consequences which may ensue from the act and indifference to the rights of others' or '. . . operation of an automobile under such circumstances as to show a reckless disregard of the consequences.' Inferences may be reasonably indulged in. For instance, proof of excessive speed may supply an inference of reckless driving . . . but something more than the mere occurrence of an accident is unquestionably required." [15]

3. *Accountability.* Since a man's conduct is brought into existence by his creative free decision, he is the cause of the conduct. Since he causes it, it is *his*. Hence he is accountable, answerable, responsible for it. Hence, if the man knew his wife was standing in the driveway and intended to kill her, he is responsible for this overt act. "[R]esponsible . . . means to respond, and respond means to answer." Responsible means: "Answerable, legally or morally, for the discharge of a duty, trust, debt, service or other obligation; accountable, as to a judge, master, creditor, ruler, or rightful superior, subject to obligations; bound." [16]

B. *Factors Known and Willed*

Granting there is sufficient knowledge and free decision in an overt act, its factors still remain to be examined. In a crime, as in all overt acts all the objects of knowing and willing must be considered. These are principally two: what was done, with its particular circumstances; and why it was done.

1. *The "what" of a crime.* Analysis of the incident mentioned above will start first with *what* was done or the overt action, and the circumstances surrounding it that inevitably affect its meaning.

a. *The overt act.* The overt act here was running over the woman with a car. "An overt act, in criminal law, is an outward act done in pursuance and in manifestation of an intent or design." [17] Whether this overt, physical act proves to be the matter

[15] People v. Whitby, 44 N.Y.S.2d 76, 77 (1943).

[16] The Mary F. Barrett, 279 Fed. 329, 334 (3d Cir. 1922).

[17] United States v. Haupt, 47 F. Supp. 836, 839 (N.D. Ill. 1942). See also People v. Mills, 178 N.Y. 274, 70 N.E. 786, 790 (1904). The overt act in the law of conspiracy can be taken as part of the crime, as an indispensable mode of corroborating the existence of conspiracy, or as a device for affording a locus poenitentiae. See Braverman v. United States, 317 U.S. 49, 53 (1942).

of a crime, will depend on circumstances. It could have happened accidentally.

b. *Circumstances.* Knowing and willing an overt act necessarily include the circumstances in which it must inevitably take place. Circumstances may be of such consequence that they give to the overt act a definite form of goodness or badness. They make it specifically the kind of good or bad act that it is. Other circumstances do not so color the overt act. They merely attenuate the degree of goodness or evil the act already has.

The circumstances surrounding the overt act are usually grouped under the general facts of who did it, when and where, with what instruments and in what manner, with what results, and for what motive.

Who killed the woman in our present case? Not a complete stranger or her ten-year-old son, but her husband — a factor that may have a bearing on the motive. Where did he run over her? On his own driveway which he knows was too narrow to clear a person on the sides. By the instrumentality of what means was her death brought about? It was effected by the use of an automobile, a fact that does not preclude the possibility of accident as would the slashing of her throat. In what manner was it done? He ran over her once, and not several times, which still leaves accident as a possibility. When was it done? The incident happened before daybreak when neighbors could not see what was transpiring, a fact which could have a bearing on his intention.

What were the results that followed running over her? The wife died, leaving the husband free to marry again. This is an important effect that was caused by the event that occurred. For "when an event is followed in natural sequence by a result which it is adapted to produce or aided in producing, the result is a consequence of the event and the event is the result of a cause." [18]

2. *The "why" of a crime.* Granting such explorations have been made regarding knowledge and intention of what was done with its attendant circumstances, there still remains to be analyzed the other all-important circumstance of *why* the overt act was done. What was the motive behind what he did? What was his purpose in doing it? Did this man kill his wife because she had recently been diagnosed as having incurable carcinoma and he wanted to end her suffering? Or did he kill her for the reason

[18] Board of Trustees of Fireman's Relief and Pension Fund for City of Tulsa v. Miller, 186 Okla. 586, 99 P.2d 146, 147 (1940). See also Western Indemnity Co. v. MacKechnie, 214 S.W. 456, 460 (Tex. Civ. App. 1919).

that he wanted to be free to marry his secretary, which motive could increase the evil of the crime?

While the law is mainly concerned with what was done overtly and the intention to do it, nevertheless the reason why a deed is done is important not only in cases of circumstantial evidence but also in assessing the over-all rightness or wrongness of the whole act. " 'Motive' . . . is an inducement, or that which leads or tempts the mind to indulge the criminal act. It is resorted to as a means of arriving at an ultimate fact, not for the purpose of explaining the reason of a criminal act which has been clearly proved, but for the important aid it may render in completing the proof of the commission of the act when it might otherwise remain in doubt. With motives in any speculative sense, neither the law nor the tribunal which administers it has any concern. It is in cases of proof by circumstantial evidence that the motive often becomes not only material but controlling, and in such cases the facts from which it may be inferred must be proved. It cannot be imagined any more than any other circumstance in the case." [19]

Or, instead of being seized by fear when he thought he saw her with a gun, did the husband merely do what he did in *self-defense?* If this motive could be proved the overt act would not be murder, but it would be killing as a means of preserving his own life.

a. *Intent differs from motive.* In law, intent and motive are not the same. Intent refers to what is done, the overt act. Motive regards why it is done, the overall purpose. "Intent, in its legal sense, is quite distinct from motive. It is defined as the purpose to use a particular means to effect a certain result. Motive is the reason which leads the mind to desire that result." [20] The man's intent could have been to kill his wife and his motive could have been to put an end to her suffering.

b. *Purpose as intent.* Purpose in law is frequently used as synonymous with intent. " 'Purpose' means that which a person sets before him as an object to be reached or accomplished, an end, intention or aim." [21] "The word 'purpose' means that which one sets before him to accomplish." [22]

[19] People v. Lewis, 275 N.Y. 33, 9 N.E.2d 765, 768, 769 (1937).
[20] United Fidelity Life Ins. Co. v. Adair, 29 S.W.2d 940, 943 (Tex. Civ. App. 1928). See also State v. Logan, 344 Mo. 351, 126 S.W.2d 256, 260 (1939).
[21] State ex rel. Turner v. Patch, 64 Mont. 565, 210 Pac. 748, 750 (1922).
[22] Macomber v. State, 137 Neb. 882, 291 N.W. 674, 680 (1940).

C. *Twofold Object of Knowing and Willing*

Briefly, in any action, good or bad, there are two principal objects of knowing and willing. There is the end of the action, the aim which starts the train of actions and gives it motivation. In this case it is, let us say, the desire to stop the wife's suffering. And there is also the means used to accomplish this end, the channel through which motivation finds its expression. In this case, it would be running over the woman with a car to kill her.

To speak more precisely, what is primarily desired is the end, that is, the "why" which gives form to the willing. What is secondarily desired is the means, that is, the "what" or overt act with its particular cluster of circumstances, which constitutes the matter of will's act.[23]

Accordingly, it is all the things intended by a man that must be taken into account when any action of his is to be evaluated. If any of the things he wills is bad, his whole conduct is bad. For, he has a "bad will," a "guilty intention," a "guilty mind," a "mens rea."[24]

III. PUBLIC WELFARE OFFENSES

Criminal law usually limits the use of the word "intention" to the overt act, to "what" is done, as already mentioned. "Motive"

[23] ". . . [S]ome acts are called human inasmuch as they are voluntary. . . . In a voluntary act there is found a twofold act, namely, the interior act of the will and the exterior act. Each of these has its own object. The end is properly the object of the interior act of the will, while that about which the exterior act is concerned is its object. Therefore, just as the exterior act takes its form from the object about which it is concerned, so the interior act of the will takes its form from the end as its own proper object." Aquinas, 1-2 Sum. Theol. 18, 6.

[24] If knowledge and intention are necessary regarding all the aspects of a freely decided action, then why is not a man held to be excused before the law in cases where he is ignorant and could not therefore have the requisite intention — instead of being held not excused according to the maxim that "ignorantia iuris non excusat"? The answer seems to be that, although such a man is naturally and morally not guilty of committing any crime, nevertheless on account of *evidential expediency* he cannot be held to be excused legally. The evidence of his mere assertion that he was ignorant is too insubstantial to establish the fact that he actually did not know of the law. Such a defense could undermine all law. Hardship that may occur in individual cases is necessary in any system of law. Fortunately, though, there are means at hand to mitigate such hardship, for instance suspended sentence or pardon. See Allen, Legal Duties 195-196 (1931). See also Jerome Hall, Ignorance and Mistake in Criminal Law, 33 Ind. L.J. 1-44 (1957).

is used in reference to the end, the "why" of the action. Hence, "guilty intention," "guilty mind" or "mens rea" are used in law regarding overt acts that are evil.

A. Malum in Se and Malum Prohibitum

Overt acts that are evil are said to be of two kinds: those whose matter is evil in itself (malum in se) and those whose matter is evil solely because it has been prohibited by law (malum prohibitum).

Evils in themselves are said to be such actions as murder, rape, robbery, arson and the like.　Evil only because prohibited are said to be all other activities that have a public aspect about them. These may be either violation of laws pertaining to areas such as traffic or gambling, or of laws controlling certain manufacturing processes, for instance, drug regulations.　"Crimes from early days have been divided into things that are criminal because they are mala in se and crimes which are such because they are prohibited by statute or mala prohibita.　The former class embraces those acts which are immoral or wrong in themselves such as burglary, larceny, arson, rape, murder, and breaches of the peace, while the latter embraces those things which are prohibited by statute because they infringe upon the rights of others, though no moral turpitude may attach, and they are crimes only because they are prohibited by statute." [25]　"[T]hat category of statutes denominated 'malum prohibitum' . . . is made up of a vast number of acts which would not be wrong were they not prohibited by statute.　An offense 'malum prohibitum' is not naturally an evil, but becomes so in consequence of its being forbidden, as playing at games, which being innocent before, have become unlawful in consequence of being forbidden." [26]

Because such actions were "innocent" before being prohibited by statute, it is said that the offender does not have a "guilty mind."　"While the absence of any requirement of mens rea is usually met with in statutes punishing minor or police offenses (for which fines, at least in the first instance, are ordinarily the penalties), we think that interpretation of legislative intent as dispensing with the knowledge and wilfulness as elements of specified crimes is not to be restricted to offenses differentiable upon their relative lack of turpitude.　Where the offenses pro-

[25] Coleman v. State, 119 Fla. 653, 161 So. 89, 90 (1935).　See also State v. Trent, 122 Ore. 144, 259 Pac. 893, 898 (1927).

[26] People v. Boxer, 24 N.Y.S.2d 628, 632, 633 (1940).

hibited and made punishable are capable of inflicting widespread injury, and where the requirement of proof of the offender's guilty knowledge and wrongful intent would render enforcement of the prohibition difficult if not impossible (i.e. in effect tend to nullify the statute), the legislative intent to dispense with mens rea as an element of the offense has justifiable basis. Notable among such offenses are dealing in adulterated foods and drugs." [27]

According to these opinions there is no question of a guilty intention or mens rea in a whole segment of public activities because they are not evil in themselves. This being so, although they are technically legal crimes, because they involve no moral turpitude they are designated rather as "public welfare offenses" or "police offenses."

Further, it is said that since there is no crime involved in these "offenses," there can be no fault attached to them. Tort liability for any damages that may occur in these cases must be on another basis than fault and guilty intention.

B. *What Is Evil Because Prohibited?*

What is it that is malum in se or malum prohibitum as far as law goes? Malum in se refers in law to an act which, taken in the concrete with all its circumstances, is evil in itself whether prohibited by man-made law or not. The wrongful taking away of a thing without the right and with the intention of converting it to a use other than that of the owner and without his consent (larceny) or the wrongful killing of a human being by another with malice aforethought either expressed or implied (murder) are evil because prohibited by natural, man-discovered law. Such actions, therefore, involve moral turpitude.

Malum prohibitum, on the other hand, refers in law to all other actions which, again taken in the concrete with their circumstances, are not evil and therefore are said to involve no moral turpitude. The driving of a car beyond the limit prescribed by law (speeding) is not considered evil in itself by some or prohibited by natural, man-discovered law. It does not involve moral turpitude. It is said to be evil only because it has been declared so by statute or judicial decision.

With this concept of malum in se there is no significant prob-

[27] United States v. Greenbaum, 138 F.2d 437, 438 (3d Cir. 1943). See also United States v. Illinois Central R. Co., 303 U.S. 239, 242, 58. Sup. Ct. 533, 535 (1938).

lem. Here "in se" refers to the act itself taken in its circumstances and considered apart from any statute or judicial decision. But with the notion of malum prohibitum a problem of the first magnitude arises. Does the idea of malum prohibitum as used in law imply that some concrete overt actions taken in their inevitable circumstances have no relation to the common good and therefore have no quality of right or wrong about them before being declared so by man-made law? Or does malum prohibitum mean that these actions do have such a relation and quality but that it is in their detailed determination, which must necessarily be given them in the concrete by statutes and decisions, that they are evil?

If the meaning given to malum prohibitum in law is that some actions in their circumstances that are important enough to be made matter of law have no relation to the common good and can therefore be considered "indifferent" as to goodness or badness, this notion of malum prohibitum is at variance with the means-end philosophy of law expressed in this book. If, on the contrary, the meaning given to malum prohibitum is that such actions have some relation to the common good but that they can be evil regarding the specific determinations according to which they have been prohibited, then such an idea of malum prohibitum is consonant with a means-end philosophy of law, as well as with the part that such detailed determinations play in the formation of the prudential directives of lawmakers, in the relation of natural and legal obligation, and in the implementation of man-discovered by man-made law.

1. *Not overt acts in concrete circumstances.* From the viewpoint of the philosophy of law, malum in se has a more restricted meaning than it has in law itself. In law, as we have just seen, malum in se refers to the act taken with its circumstances. The "in se" means apart from a positive statute or decision. In the philosophy of law, malum in se refers to the act alone. The "in se" means apart from its circumstances — and all the more so, apart from any statute or decision.

a. *Overt acts impossible without circumstances.* According to the analysis of human acts made above, none can be taken in isolation from space-time conditions. Whatever is done must be done by this particular person and not that one, at a definite time and place, with certain instrumental helps and in a distinctive manner, with resulting effects especially on the public good. And it must be done on account of some specific purpose.

If the full force and implication of each of these facts are taken into account, it is evident that they cannot but affect the quality of an action. Even in a man's private actions, the chances would be slight indeed of an act taking place without being shaped by these factors into either a good or bad act. To take but one circumstance, and prescinding for the moment from the all-important circumstance of end and purpose, the very fact that a man must exercise his mental and physical powers whenever he acts implies that this exercise itself will affect him well or ill as an intrinsic sanction. It will have some relation to improving him or not, as would be true of any organism. Hence a quality of good or bad begins to appear immediately upon the decision to launch the act.

If it were possible, however, for none of the other circumstances to affect the goodness or badness of a man's act (which we are saying is not the case), the final circumstance of end would cause an otherwise indifferent action to be good or bad. The end on account of which a man acts cannot be indifferent. It must be either conducive to his final end or not. In a word it is impossible for a man's actions in the concrete to be indifferent. They must be either good or bad.

For, ". . . every individual act has some circumstance by which it becomes good or evil, at least from the intention of the end. Since it belongs to reason to direct, if an act proceeding from deliberate reason is not directed to a due end, by that very fact it is contrary to reason and has the character of evil. If, however, it is directed to a due end, it is in agreement with the order of reason and therefore has the character of good. But it is necessary that such an act either be directed or not directed to a due end. Hence, every act of a man that proceeds from deliberate reason, considered as an individual act, must be either good or evil." [28]

All the more is this true of a man's public activities, those that so touch others that they must be made the content of law. If the overt act is important enough to be incorporated into a law, it must be for the reason that in its circumstances it is affecting other people. Inasmuch as overt acts do this, they are either contributing to the common good of the people or detracting from it and, hence, have some aspect of good or evil about them.

---

[28] Aquinas, 1-2 Sum. Theol. 18, 9. For understanding the character of the criminal, the end may furnish a better indication than the means. ". . . [He] who steals that he may commit adultery is strictly speaking more of an adulterer than a thief." Aristotle, 5 In Ethicorum Aristotelis 2, 1130a24; quoted by Aquinas, 1-2 Sum. Theol. 18, 6. Criminal law, however, is and must be primarily concerned with what was done, that is, with the means, the overt act and its conditions.

a. *Circumstances specify.* The factual situation, then, is: with the exception of a few acts which are evil in themselves (blasphemy is one), most overt acts receive their specification and meaning from the circumstances in which they occur. Is the overt act of killing another man right or wrong? It depends entirely on the conditions in which the killing takes place. It could be done in self-defense or by an agent of the government in the execution of a convicted criminal, in which instances it would be right and good. For, in each case there was authority and a claim to act so. It could be done by a robber in the course of a bank holdup or by a gambler in the course of a heated argument, in which case it would be wrong and evil. Authority to take another's life is here absent. Or it could happen accidentally and there would be no question at all whether it was good or bad.

Is the overt act of taking what belongs to another good or bad? Again it depends on circumstances. It could be done with the explicit or implicit knowledge and consent of the owner. If so, the overt act would be one of borrowing and therefore not evil but good. It could be done by breaking and entering a dwelling of another at night with the intention of taking valuable jewelry. In such circumstances it would be burglary and evil. Or it could have been done by a man starving to death who took a loaf of bread to preserve his life. In such a circumstance, it would be a case of necessity of preserving his life, which would make the act good rather than evil.

This means that practically every overt act that is evil and is important enough to be made content of a law, is evil not because of what it is in itself (in the philosophical sense of the act alone) or because the law says it is evil. It becomes evil by dint of its concrete *circumstances.* The chief of these is the end and motive of the act. The end the law has in view is the common good. It is, however, in the recognition or determination of the detailed aspect of these circumstances by law that lies the possibility of an act being evil because prohibited, as will be seen shortly.

c. *Comment.* The meaning a lawman gives to malum prohibitum will depend on his background philosophy of human actions. If he holds that some acts can be indifferent in the concrete, he can logically maintain that they can become evil by prohibition. This was a position prevalent enough during the growth of the common law. According to it, the rightness, wrongness and obligation of acts depended on the positive precept and command of the divine will. If he holds, on the other hand, that it is impossible for acts to be indifferent factually, he can only conclude that these acts already are right or wrong to some degree before they are prohibited by law. This is the position maintained here. Rightness, wrongness and obligation have their basis in the means-end relation of human acts.

Even a cursory examination of the so-called mala prohibita contained in laws, discloses that they have been forbidden on some already existing grounds. Such a seemingly indifferent action as driving on the right or left side of the road shows, upon inspection, not to have been an arbitrary matter in its origin but to have been related to particular facts. Historically there were definite grounds or reasons why one or the other side was adopted.

On Roman roads, for instance, "The evidence . . . seems to indicate that the prevalence of the box wagon or postilion method of driving established the rule of the road in any given locality. In the country districts, where the box wagon was in general use, the practice was for the driver to sit on the extreme right side of the seat in order to permit the free play of his right whip hand. Thus he passed to the left so as to gage more accurately the clearance between the wheel hubs of his own and the approaching vehicle. In the city districts, however, where the postilion rode upon the left wheel, or rear horse, so as to permit the most direct use of the right whip hand, it was the custom to pass oncoming vehicles to the right." [29] Uniformity according to either the prevailing urban or rural custom was sometimes established by edict.

In North America during Colonial times ". . . although there was no generally accepted rule, the prevailing practice was to pass to the left in accordance with the English custom. The advent of the heavy Conestoga covered freight wagons in Pennsylvania, about the year 1750, with their postilion method of driving, began the establishment of right-handed rule of the road, which is now universally observed in the United States." [30]

Because it is impossible for an overt act to be indifferent, then, an act cannot be said to be evil merely because it has been prohibited by statute or judicial decision. The notion that there can be such acts and that malum prohibitum is based on them, has sired the further fictional distinction between crimes and "police offenses." The harboring of this misconception has impeded legislators and courts from seeing the need of a more accurate concept of evil and crime.

[29] Rose, *Via Appia* in the Days When All Roads Led to Rome, 1934 Smithsonian Report 347, 356.
[30] Ibid.

The speeding of automobiles, for instance, has been considered by some courts "not in itself criminal," even though facts prove that speeding automobiles are one of the greatest "killers" in modern living. "The unlawful act of exceeding the speed limit is not in itself criminal, but if done in a careless manner, in reckless disregard of the safety of others, and death results, the offender is guilty of involuntary manslaughter. . . ." [31] To say that a layman ". . . would apply the word 'criminal' to the act of one, who, under the circumstances here present, exceeded a speed limit or failed to stop before entering an arterial highway, is either to ignore the common usage of the term or else to imply that practically everyone who has ever driven an automobile is a criminal." [32]

Courts have spoken similarly concerning numerous other activities. Is discharging a deadly weapon within 300 yards of an inhabited house evil? If such an act is termed malum prohibitum as to the detail of 300 yards, it would seem to be a proper use of the phrase. However, it is not clear that courts always have this in mind. "The offense is not malum in se, but is malum prohibitum. There is nothing illegal or immoral in discharging a deadly weapon within 300 yards of an inhabited house, and the same is an offense against the law simply because the statute so declares." [33] But if there is nothing evil or immoral in shooting a gun within 300 yards of an inhabited house, why should it be made matter for a law? If, on the contrary, there is something evil about it, why say it is evil only because prohibited by law?

The pseudo distinction between crimes and "public welfare offenses," based as it is on an invalid notion of malum prohibitum, has fostered the opinion that crimes involve "inherent" moral turpitude and that "public welfare offenses" entail no moral wrong at all. A court in discussing the making of wine for home consumption, for example, takes for granted that there was nothing wrong with the production of this ancient and honorable beverage and that if there was anything evil about such an endeavor it derived from the statute which prohibited wine making.

It was the court's opinion that, "The above-mentioned violations of the National Prohibition Act were not felonies. The words 'involving moral turpitude,' as long used in the law with

[31] People v. Pavlic, 227 Mich. 562, 199 N.W. 373, 374 (1924). See also People v. Herbert, 6 Cal.2d. 541, 58 P.2d 909, 912 (1936).
[32] Van Ripper v. Constitutional Government League, 1 Wash. 2d 635, 96 P.2d 588, 591 (1939).
[33] State v. Adams, 24 N.M. 239, 173 Pac. 857 (1918). See also State v. Shedoudy, 45 N.M. 516, 118 P.2d 280, 286, 287 (1941).

reference to crimes, refer to conduct which is inherently base, vile, or depraved, contrary to accepted rules of morality, whether it is or is not punishable as a crime. They do not refer to conduct which, before it was made punishable as a crime, was not generally regarded as morally wrong or corrupt, as offensive to the moral sense as ordinarily developed. . . . Before the enactment of statutes on the subject, the making or possession of wine for the use of the maker as a beverage was not generally regarded as morally wrong. From the fact that those acts have by statute been made punishable as crimes it does not follow that they are inherently immoral, or involve moral turpitude, within the meaning of the provision in question." [34]

Undoubtedly crimes such as murder can legally be termed malum in se and can be considered to involve inherent moral turpitude in the sense that they are evil whether prohibited by law or not. But a searching philosophical analysis of overt acts reveals, as we saw, that all overt acts, with few exceptions, receive their specification of good or evil from their circumstances. Hence, the one fact that some overt acts called malum in se involve moral turpitude does not preclude the other fact that the other overt acts also have some aspect of right and wrong about them. The evil of one set of acts is only more easily and certainly known.

Concerning the type of judicial thinking represented in the above wine-making case, then, certain questions once more present themselves. If there was nothing evil about making wine at that particular time and in those circumstances before the statute was passed, what are the grounds on which the statute was passed? Was it purely arbitrary? And if it was not wrong to make the wine before the statute was enacted, why pass the statute? On the other hand, if there was something evil about making wine before the enactment of the statute, why deny it and say it was wrong only because declared so by governmental fiat? [35]

This failure to appreciate the relation between every overt act in its circumstances and the public welfare, and the consequent fostering of the fictional distinction between crimes and "police

[34] Coykendall v. Skrmetta, 22 F.2d 120, 121 (5th Cir. 1927).

[35] "In one generation we have witnessed the volatile character of public policy in relation to alcoholic liquor — going from almost unrestrained manufacture and sale to strict regulation, to the Prohibition Amendment, then to repeal of that constitutional amendment and back to regulation. It reflects in turn man's ambivalence toward the product of grape and grain." Pliakos v. Illinois Liquor Control Commission, 12 Ill. App. 2d 170, 177, 138 N.E.2d 863, 866 (1956).

offenses," is current. "It was not until recently that the Court took occasion more explicitly to relate abandonment of the ingredient of intent, not merely with considerations of expediency in obtaining convictions, not with the malum prohibitum classification of the crime, but with the peculiar nature and quality of the offense. We referred to 'a now familiar type of legislation whereby penalties serve as effective means of regulation,' and continued, 'such legislation dispenses with the conventional requirement for criminal conduct — awareness of some wrongdoing. In the interest of the larger good it puts the burden of acting at hazard upon a person otherwise innocent but standing in responsible relation to a public danger.' But we warned: 'Hardship there doubtless may be under a statute which thus penalizes the transaction though consciousness of wrongdoing be totally wanting.' " [36]

There is no doubt that acting "at hazard" or "at peril" has a place in torts where harm to the common good, if it does occur, is indirect. But there should be no question of acting "at peril" in crimes because injury to the common good is inevitable and direct.

Such "police regulations" have also been justified where emphasis is on social betterment rather than on punishment. "[A]s a rule there can be no crime without a criminal intent, but this is not by any means a universal rule. . . . Many statutes which are in the nature of police regulations . . . impose criminal penalties irrespective of any intent to violate them, the purpose being to require a degree of diligence for the protection of the public which shall render violation impossible. . . . [These are] regulatory measures in the exercise of what is called the police power where the emphasis of the statute is evidently upon achievement of some social betterment rather than the punishment of the crimes as in cases of mala in se." [37]

Again, the central point is not what is preferred — social betterment or punishment. The main issue is the relation between injurious acts and the common welfare. Punishment and social betterment take their meaning from this.

2. *Detailed determination of conditions.* But malum prohibi-

[36] Morissette v. United States, 342 U.S. 246, 254, 72 Sup. Ct. 240, 248 (1952).
[37] Id. at 246-247. For a discussion of the problem of mens rea and malum in se-malum prohibitum, see Levitt, Extent and Function of the Doctrine of Mens Rea, 17 Ill. L. Rev. 578-595 (1923); see also Notes, The Distinction Between Mala Prohibita and Mala in Se in Criminal Law, 30 Colum. L. Rev. 74-86 (1930), and Hart, The Aims of the Criminal Law, 23 Law & Contemp. Prob. 401-442 (1958).

tum does have a valid meaning in law, as mentioned, when it refers to acts considered as contrary to the specific details in which laws must necessarily be spelled out. As we have seen, such determinations are related to the distinction between natural and legal obligation.

Excessive speed is wrong, for it endangers life. No statute is needed to declare this to be so. But what is excessive speed? Some sort of detailed determination will have to be made by lawmakers. Once this is done, as scientifically as possible, some limit is arrived at beyond which speed is declared to be "excessive" — say 65 miles an hour. Perhaps it could have been 62 or 68 miles an hour. Approximations sometimes are the most to be hoped for. Nevertheless, the reason why a violation of a speed law so specified is wrong — gravely or slightly — is because 65 miles an hour has been prescribed by law. In this sense this violation as to the detail of 65 miles an hour is evil because prohibited.

Such is the situation regarding many other kinds of laws. Hence, in cases such as the one cited above regarding the use of deadly weapons, if the court means that there is nothing "immoral" or evil in endangering life by discharging a deadly weapon in the proximity of an inhabited house before a statute forbids it, his opinion is questionable. If, on the other hand, his meaning is that there is something wrong about this act but that the wrongness of shooting a gun at specifically 300 yards or closer derives from the fact that it has been determined in this detail by the statute, his use of the phrase malum prohibitum is valid.

C. *Crimes: From Grave to Slight*

In sum, since overt acts in criminal law have the inevitable relation to the public good that we have seen, it appears more accurate to speak of crimes as more or less serious, as greater or lesser, as extending from grave to slight, rather than to make the undiscerning division between crimes and "public welfare offenses." The idea of greater or lesser crimes is already present in the division of crimes into felonies and misdemeanors.

Crime, then, is more accurately represented when viewed as a "continuum." "The unfortunate effect of the judicial application of the mala in se — mala prohibita doctrine has been the setting up of a rigid dichotomy between traditional harms and the mass of petty misdemeanors which were declared to be amoral. This encouraged the most serious fallacies, namely, the legal theory that mens rea is not a material element of these offenses, and thence, that strict liability is therefore justified. . . . A sounder interpretation, in light of the above analysis, is suggested by the notion of a 'continuum' . . . The notion, 'moral continuum,' provides a common, connecting link unifying all criminal laws. . . . The differences throughout run in terms of degree, not of kind." [38]

The other type of so-called public welfare offenses, as mentioned, concerns certain dangerous and riskful enterprises.   In this kind of offense the overt act is said not to be evil in itself but only because prohibited.   Hence there can be no evil intention. Whatever liability there may be for unintended damages resulting from these enterprises must arise then, not from fault, but from some other source.   These assumptions will be examined under "Torts."

IV.   PURELY PENAL LAW

Closely related to the theory of public welfare offenses is that of "purely penal" law.   In fact it is the same problem looked at from the viewpoint of obligation.   Presupposing — as some do — that overt acts can be indifferent in the concrete and assuming that law and obligation derive from the will of the lawmaker, the theory of purely penal law holds that lawmakers must will that laws involving mala in se oblige in conscience; they may will, as they see fit, that the other laws entailing mala prohibita oblige or do not oblige.   The approach to purely penal law, then, is from the standpoint of obligation.   And because obligation implies the interaction of intellect and will (either as excluding the means-end relation as operative on the will or as including it) this theory has developed in a philosophical rather than a legal climate.   However, its importance to legal and civic thinking is great, as will be indicated shortly.

A.   *Penal Law*

The phrase "purely penal law" is not to be confused with what is commonly known in crimes as penal law.   Penal law in this sense usually refers to a statute that imposes a penalty for violation.   " 'Penal laws,' strictly and properly are those imposing a pecuniary or personal punishment for an offense against the state, and which are subject to the pardon power." [39]   "Penal

[38] Hall, General Principles of Criminal Law 297-298 (1947).
[39] Atlantic Coast Line R. Co. v. State, 73 Fla. 609, 74 So. 595, 600 (1917).

laws, strictly and properly, are those imposing punishment for an offense committed against the State, and which, by the English and American constitutions, the executive of the State has the power to pardon. Statutes giving a private action against the wrongdoer are sometimes spoken of as penal in their nature, but in such cases it has been pointed out that neither the liability imposed nor the remedy given is strictly penal." [40]

In view of the fact that a penal statute may, upon enforcement, afford some remedy to an injured individual, it can also have a remedial aspect. The determinant of whether it is penal or remedial is whether public or private wrongs are mainly redressed. "In determining whether a statute is penal in the strict and primary sense, a test is whether the injury sought to be redressed affects the public. If the redress is remedial to an individual and the public is indirectly affected thereby, the statute is not regarded as solely and strictly penal in its nature." [41] "Where a statute is both penal and remedial, as where it is penal in one part and remedial in the other, it should be considered as a penal statute when it is sought to enforce the penalty, and as a remedial statute when it is sought to enforce the remedy." [42]

B. *Purely Penal Law*

Purely penal law has an entirely different meaning than penal law or penal statute as used in crimes. It does not refer primarily to the fact that laws have penalties. Its main concern, rather, is with the way these laws *oblige*. According to this theory, a purely penal law, such as a pure food and drug law is said to be, obliges not to the observance of the law but to the payment of penalties inflicted after violation. Since such laws oblige merely to the payment of penalties, they are called "purely penal."

1. *Assumption*. The theory of purely penal law is based on two principal assumptions. These have to do chiefly with the nature of the will of the lawmaker as the source of law and obligation, and with the nature of overt acts.

a. *Will not necessitated*. The theory assumes first and foremost that the will of the lawmaker is of such a nature that it cannot be placed under any necessity by an objective means-end relation that is recognized by his intellect. Any necessity must come

[40] Huntington v. Attrill, 146 U.S. 657, 13 Sup. Ct. 224, 227 (1892). See also Kilton v. Providence Tool Co., 22 R.I. 605, 48 Atl. 1039, 1042 (1901).

[41] Atlantic Coast Line R. Co. v. State, 73 Fla. 609, 74 So. 595, 600 (1917).

[42] Collins v. Kidd, 38 F. Supp. 634, 637 (E.D. Tex. 1941). See also Diversey v. Smith, 103 Ill. 378, 42 Am. Rep. 14, 18 (1882).

from within the will itself, otherwise its freedom would be in jeopardy. Consequently, obligation originates in the will of the lawmaker.

b. *Overt acts indifferent.* The other philosophical assumption is that, although some overt acts are evil in themselves (mala in se), other overt acts are indifferent and not evil unless prohibited by law (mala prohibita). Acts like murder, robbery, adultery and the like are evil in themselves because they are prohibited by the natural law or by the Decalogue. All other acts are neither good nor evil unless declared so by law. As a result, it is said, lawmakers can enact statutes regarding indifferent overt acts without willing that subjects be obliged to obey the law. They may will to oblige them only to pay penalties if they are apprehended violating the law. By these penalties the common good is served.

2. *Acceptance.* Granted these assumptions, the theory of purely penal law is inevitable and logically consistent and there is no reason for multiplying the number of overt acts that oblige in conscience. This theory has found wide acceptance among those who are disposed to hold a "will" theory of law.

Among the many great legal philosophers who held this theory was Suárez. Purely penal laws obliged in his opinion, not in regard to the overt act, but only concerning the punishment. "There are laws that compel or oblige under the threat of punishment even though they do not oblige in conscience to the overt act, for the transgression of which they oblige to the punishment . . . A law is called purely penal which has only one, as it were, hypothetical precept 'if you do this or that,' even though the precept is not imposed regarding the act underlying this condition." [43]

Foremost among the lawyers who have held this theory is Blackstone. He held that "in relation to those laws which enjoin only positive duties, and forbid only such things as are not mala in se, but mala prohibita merely, without an intermixture of moral guilt, annexing a penalty to non-compliance, here I apprehend, conscience is no further concerned, than by directing a submission to the penalty, in case of our breach of those laws: for otherwise the multitude of penal laws in a state would not only be looked

[43] Suárez, 5 De Legibus 4, 2. Because the theory of "purely penal law" is not infrequently encountered in law work, the student would do well to acquaint himself with more than its mere outline which is all it is possible to give here. No better case has ever been made for the theory than that proposed by Suárez in his great work De Legibus. Selections translated into English are available in Scott, The Classics of International Law (1944). See also Davitt, The Nature of Law 86-108 (1951).

upon as impolitic, but would also be a very wicked thing; if every such law were a snare for the conscience of the subject. But in these cases the alternative is offered to every man; 'either abstain from this or submit to such a penalty': and his conscience will be clear, which ever side of the alternative he thinks proper to embrace." [44]

C. *Comment*

Because of the presence of the theory of purely penal law in legal opinions and because of the way it contrasts with the stand taken in this book, a comment seems called for. This will turn mainly on purely penal law's assumptions.

1. *Assumptions examined.* The assumptions made by this theory should be critically examined. For, regardless of the sort of case that can be made for the autonomous nature of men's will, it appears that no such case can be made for the indifference of overt acts.

a. *Will can be morally necessitated.* As we have already seen, the will of the lawmaker is not a blind or animal faculty. It takes its whole meaning from the fact that it is a "rational" will. If its choices are to be "rational" they must be made in conformity with the necessity of means for end as recognized by the intellect. Inasmuch as this is so, the will can be morally necessitated by the intellect presenting means-end relations.[45]

b. *Overt acts not indifferent.* The invalidity of the philosophical assumption that overt acts can be indifferent in the concrete has already been noted. It is factually impossible for an overt act that is important enough to be made content of law, taken in its actual circumstances, not to have some relation to the common good. This relation to the common good is determined by the nature of the acts themselves and not by governmental fiat. So also is the obligatory aspect of law determined by the nature of the facts involved and not by arbitrary ukase. An anti-smoke ordinance obliges because of the nature of various gasses and their relation to the public health.

Hence, in the light of the means-end relation of overt acts in their circumstances to the public good, the theory of purely penal law is wholly unintelligible. If law is a directive judgment in the mind of lawmakers formed according to objective public needs

[44] 1 Blackstone, Commentaries 57-58.
[45] On purely penal laws, see Davitt, The Nature of Law 1-6, 158-160, 219-229 (1951).

fulfillable by doing or refraining from certain overt acts, and obligation is the necessity of performing these acts as means necessary for the public good, then a lawmaker has no choice as to
whether laws oblige or not. If what a law demands is necessary
for the common welfare, by that very fact citizens are obliged to
obey the law.[46]

It is not pertinent to the main issue — of why overt acts are
obligatory — whether their number be small or great. If a large
number itself is sufficient reason for saying it would be too bur-
densome if they were considered obligatory, this same type of
reasoning could be indulged in regarding any other area of overt
acts whose number is also large.

2. *Court criticism of purely penal law.* Although there have
been courts who have adopted the theory of purely penal law,
nevertheless there are not wanting those who have rejected it.
"It is contended by the counsel for the plaintiff that there is a
distinction between malum prohibitum and malum in se; between things intrinsically and morally wrong, and things which
are made so merely by legislation. The inference he would make
from this distinction is, that when an act is merely malum prohibitum, it may conscientiously be done, provided only the party
be willing to incur the penalty. He considers it optional with the
party to do or to refrain from doing the act in question, and that
the alternative is presented him by the legislature, to abstain
from the act, or to do it and pay the penalty. If these premises
and this reasoning be correct, the courts, he says, cannot declare
the act to be illegal, for that would be infliction of a penalty beyond that imposed by the statute." [47]

In practice, the court continues, this means that a man is going
to be his own judge whether he ought to obey the law or not.
"But any person who should attempt to put this theory into practice, and to regulate his conduct by it, would find his path filled
with difficulties. In the first place, he must assume to judge for

---

[46] In the historical development of this question there has been a tendency
to confuse the status of purely penal laws in the political union with their
position in ecclesiastical unions. The primary end of ecclesiastical unions is
the proper good of the individual and whatever common good attaches to
these unions is secondary to this primary purpose. In such a union, rules
relate directly to the individual's proper good and not to the common good.
They can, then, be purely penal if it is the desire of the superior and the
inferior subjects himself to it. But this is not the situation in the political
union. Here the primary end is the common good and the content of all
laws, regardless of the lawmaker's desire, must have some relation to it.
Hence, these laws cannot be purely penal. See Davitt, id. at 22.

[47] Lewis v. Welch, 14 N.H. 294, 296-297 (1843).

himself what is right and what is wrong, irrespective of the law. He must test his obligation to obey the law, by a standard which exists in his own bosom. His moral sense must be so acute that he would never be in danger of mistaking his duty, and of sacrificing it to considerations of private advantage. Men differ in their views of right and wrong; the moral sense of one man is more obtuse than that of another. And just in proportion to its obtuseness will he be liable to overstep the line that separates right from wrong; and his reasoning may lead him into the commission of a felony when he fancies himself to be merely a trespasser, and that the payment of a fine which the statute might impose in a given case would make the balance even." [48]

Such a theory, this court concludes, promotes unequal operation of the law. "The subtle casuistry which self-interest teaches us, is a most unsafe guide in questions of morals, and peculiarly so in relation to those things which have been called duties of imperfect obligation, and whose performance might be enforced by penalties. The law would be extremely unequal in its operation, if its prohibitions were imperative on those only who should choose to be bound by it. If obedience to the law should depend entirely on the conscience of the individual, all legal restraints would soon be abolished." [49]

Another court, putting the matter a bit more pointedly, said: "I perfectly agree . . . in reprobating any distinction between malum prohibitum and malum in se, and consider it as pregnant with mischief. Every man is as much bound to obey the civil law of the land as the law of nature." [50]

3. *Attitudes toward law.* The theory of purely penal laws does not promote civic-mindedness and cooperative civic behavior for the common good. If a citizen believes he is not obliged to obey a tax law but is obliged merely to pay penalties if caught evading it, he can ignore the demands of such a law with a good

[48] Ibid.

[49] Ibid.

[50] Aubert v. Maze, 2 B. and P. 371, 375, 126 Eng. Rep. 1333, 1335 (1801). See also the editorial criticism of Blackstone's position on purely penal law (1 Blackstone, Commentaries 57-58) in the editions of both Sharswood (1856, p. 58, n.15) and Cooley (3d ed. 1884, p. 57, n.12). "Where an act is forbidden under penalty, it must in general be assumed that some degree of public mischief or private injury was meant to be prevented by the prohibition. The prohibition can have no other legitimate purpose. . . . '[I]t cannot be intended that a statute would inflict a penalty for a lawful act.' For example, it may appear that the penalty is imposed for the purpose of revenue merely, and that the act itself is matter of indifference if the penalty is paid." Cooley, ibid. See Cooley also for numerous cases supporting this criticism of the theory of purely penal law.

conscience. His only concern need be regarding the penalties he may incur. Nor could such a citizen be accused of contemning authority when he so disregards a law, since the lawmakers are supposed not to have intended to oblige him to obey the law in the first place.

The inevitable consequence of such a theory is that in vast segments of civic activities, citizens (at least those who are educated in schools where such subjects are considered) may feel they are not obliged in conscience to contribute to the common good by doing what the law decrees for the common good. Such an attitude inevitably is corrosive of the habit of contributive justice. The practical consequence of teaching such a doctrine in law schools is attested by those who, having evaded payment of taxes in good conscience, have paid the penalty in fines or are still paying it in prison.

4. *Focus on law's content.* Some who hold the theory of purely penal law claim that, on the practical side at least, it fits our law better. This claim is certainly well-founded in the sense that this theory is more congenial with the thinking of those courts that have accepted the cognate notions of malum in se as distinguished from malum prohibitum on the supposed basis of indifferent acts in concrete, public welfare offenses, no requirement of mens rea in some crimes, and the like. But whether this claim is true regarding fact situations is something else.

A type of problem frequently adduced to show the practicality of this theory is: "What is wrong with running through a red traffic light when you can see clearly that no car is coming in any other direction." The practical solution, it is said, is to hold that traffic laws are "purely penal laws" which oblige only optionally and that if the man runs through the red light under the conditions described he would not be guilty of any wrongdoing.

But is this the practical solution to the problem? Should the situation be passed off this easily? Before it can be decided whether running through the red light is right or wrong several factors should be examined. Is there any need of a traffic light at all at this intersection? If not, the law should be amended. If the light is needed, should drivers act as if it is not there and proceed at their own discretion? Obviously not, for this would nullify whatever good reasons there were for the light and the law in the first place. But perhaps at certain hours of the day or night there is little or no traffic. If so, the law should provide that at such hours the red-yellow-green light should be switched over to a red blinking light indicating "stop and proceed with caution" or to a yellow blinking light indicating "slow down and proceed with caution" as is commonly the practice in many localities.

In a word, the practical solution of such problems lies not in a ready satisfaction with the law as it is, possibly too undiscerning or outmoded, and in holding simply for an optional obligation. Rather the solution lies in a care for the practicality of the law's content and for bringing it into more accurate adjustment with actual needs. Focusing on the actual relation of the content of law to the public good, and not with the kind of wrong I commit if I break the law, is the best assurance of a just and well-working law.

This is also applicable to other areas covered by law such as taxes, emigration, import duties, subpoenaed witnesses, to mention but a few. Rather than immediately looking upon the law as adequate and having recourse to a split obligation, it is more practical and conducive to the common good to examine the law and work for changes if injustices are found. For, although laws are directive of means necessary for the public good, nevertheless these means are not inevitably known to be the absolutely best means. This would be the case only if the determination could be made by scientific methods. But, as already noted, this is not always possible in law. Law deals, not with constants, but with variables. The decision concerning the means to the common good is the result of the best possible prudential judgment of which the lawmakers are capable at the time. In the light of new data and further considerations, a new judgment may be needed that is directive of means more conducive to the common welfare.

V. RESPONSIBILITY AND PUNISHMENT

The meaning of punishment, as we have seen, is related to the meaning of crime. Crime, in the analysis of it made above, consists in the free decision to violate the ordering of means to end demanded by law. Crime is a misuse of the faculty of directing self according to what a man knows is right. By the very fact that a man refuses to observe what the law commands, he is deprived of the good the law is intended to bring him. This deprivation, as we saw, is the essence of punishment.

That there are certain factors which lessen the knowledge and freedom prerequisite to choice is obvious. Some are personal, such as ignorance, rage, fear, psychoses and vicious habits. Others are social, like educational systems, environments and social pressures.

A. *The Problem*

The actual impact of these circumstances on the criminal, however, gives rise to a problem. Is society so responsible for the presence of these conditions, that the criminal himself is no longer answerable? Has the center of responsibility shifted from the individual person to society in general?

This problem has meaning, of course, only for those lawmen who hold that man is a knowing and willing agent. For those others who believe that men are animals with only material powers, there can be no question of personal responsibility in the sense here explained. The place of knowledgeable free direction, responsibility and deprivation is supplanted by "all-embracing 'Determinism,' enigmatic 'Social Accountability' and euphemistic 'Treatment.' " [51] This will be adverted to later.

No extended examination of the subject of punishment is intended here. Accounts of the various schools of thought on this subject are prevalent. They are grouped under the misnomers of "classical," "neo-classical" and "determinist" schools. The classical school emphasizes freedom of the will and immutable penalties; the neo-classical view recognizes freedom but holds a variation of freedom and penalties; the determinist school denies all freedom and personal responsibility and proposes that the word "punishment" be dropped from criminal law altogether and the word "treatment" substituted in its place.[52] All that will be done here is to point out the position on punishment that is consistent with the principles held above.

B. *Society's Part*

It cannot be denied that responsibility for many of the conditions influencing crime rests with "society," which perhaps should be defined as "all of us." A "progressive" educational system has

[51] Hall, General Principles of Criminal Law 288 (1947).

[52] See Orme v. Rogers, 32 Ariz. 502, 260 Pac. 199, 200, 201 (1927), for a brief résumé of these positions. See also Saleilles, The Individualization of Punishment (1911); Sutherland, Criminology (1924) and Principles of Criminology (1947); De Grazia, Crime Without Punishment: A Psychiatric Conundrum, 52 Colum. L. Rev. 746-764 (1954); Yankwich, Changing Concepts of Crime and Punishment, 32 Geo. L.J. 1-24 (1943); Clark, Miller et al., A Symposium in Fitting the Punishment to the Criminal, 31 Iowa L. Rev. 191-236 (1946).

inculcated the notion that distinctions between right and wrong are mere fable, are harmful and only impede "self-development." This has inevitably resulted in arrogant disdain for lawful authority and its agencies which attempt to enforce what is "right." Contempt for such efforts is taken as a sign of mature self-development.

Certain mass media of communication at times have depicted as thrilling adventures what in criminal law are taken to be crimes. Sex perversion and promiscuity, kidnapping, torture, robbery and murder become acts whose wrongfulness is made to look dubious. Men in public life have taught by their example that still other crimes may after all not be so bad. Stealing through graft is viewed as part of being in government and brutality becomes a means justified by a good end.

Accompanying this deterioration of knowledge and respect for what is right, is a weakening of motivation. Ideals generate motivation. The ideals of right and wrong held high by "progressive" education, by some areas of mass communication and by many public officials are not the type that foster motivation on a national scale for doing what is right and avoiding what is wrong. On a local basis homes that have been completely, or partly broken, have also robbed youths of a source of ideals that is their birthright. The nadir is reached in the group or gang where the ideal is a life of crime, and the motivation is strongly tinged with hatred for law and right.

A further contribution to criminality is society's heedless reluctance to accept a man who has paid his penalty, without keeping in open display the brand: "former convict." No better way of keeping him from returning to society could be devised.[53]

For these and many other reasons the case against society is not without supporting evidence. Society is most assuredly responsible in some degree for the criminal's crime.

C. *Individual's Part*

In spite of the contribution to crime that society is guilty of making in diverse ways, the problem still remains of determining how much criminals are affected by it. To what degree is their knowledge and freedom lessened by these social forces?

The best source of evidence seems to be from the men and

---

[53] Such treatment of those who are attempting rehabilitation could be a violation of their claim to pursue happiness. Cf. Melvin v. Reid, 122 Cal. 285, 297 Pac. 91 (1931).

women themselves who are guilty of crimes. As everyone knows who has worked with prisoners, it is a rare case when a convict will claim that he did not know that what he did was wrong. He may claim that he did not know what he was doing at the time of the act, but that is an entirely different thing. Regardless of society's educational and environmental pressures on him, the average criminal has a correct enough knowledge of the wrongness of the common felonies and misdemeanors. Undoubtedly among certain underprivileged groups this knowledge may at times be hazy. But it is still clear enough so that they will know they should not have done what they did. Their very attempts to avoid apprehension indicate this.

This knowledge of right and wrong, notwithstanding the forces to the contrary, is only what is to be expected if the analysis of men's recognition of the demands of their basic drives made above is correct. For as noted, although education, environment and bad habits may influence the reasoning done from these elementary judgments, it will not affect the judgments themselves in a normal and sane man. If a man does not know that the main crimes are wrong, he is mentally abnormal. Society's fostering of ignorance, then, has not succeeded in keeping criminals from knowing the difference between right and wrong.

The criminal's ability to choose freely may have been influenced by society's failure to hold up ideals that engender motivation for right decisions. But to what degree has it been thus affected? This is not as easy to discern as is the impact on motivation of rage, fear, irresistible impulse and psychoses. There is no evidence, after psychiatric tests have proved an accused to be normal and sane, that the ability to direct himself is any more reduced in a man accused of a crime than it is in the average citizen who is not accused of a crime. That modern social conditions and pressures are producing more psychoses per capita than ever before, may be true. This is a medical problem. The important point is that even though more psychoses may be developing, a state of psychosis among men who commit crimes is not the prevailing condition. According to medical standards most men accused of crime are normal, sane men. Hence they have some degree of free self-direction and are proportionately responsible.

In sum, the individual criminal's knowledge and freedom of decision to do the overt act, reduced though it be, is still the lodestar of responsibility for crime. This is as it always will be unless the nature of man is changed. If this be not so, what men have talked about for ages as crime and punishment and its relation to the very purpose of living, will have passed from human thinking and from human discourse.

Society's responsibility, then, is peripheral in relation to the individual criminal's responsibility which is central. If society's responsibility is central, criminals should not be released on parole nor should rehabilitation be hoped for, until the criminal failures of society are corrected. Otherwise to what would they be rehabilitated? Then too if the main responsibility is society's, there would be the problem of accounting for the fact that only some men, and not all, become criminals — unless "stimulus-response" is to explain everything. The tendency in criminal law to look for responsibility for crimes in society has much in common with the inclination in tort law to pass liability for damages on to others better able to bear it.

D. *Irresponsibility and Insanity*

The relation between a lawman's legal thinking and his philosophical position is decisively shown in the matter of criminal (as well as civil) defense and responsibility. The change in opinion that has been occurring regarding the grounds for insanity as a defense in criminal cases is an instance of this.

1. *Change in grounds for irresponsibility.* From the middle of the past century to the first part of this one, the test for insanity has been the well-known "right-wrong" test. Originating in England, this test became law in the United States.

a. *Queen v. M'Naghten.* This test was expressed in the famous *M'Naghten* case. The judges in this case said that "Notwithstanding a party accused did an act, which was in itself criminal, under the influence of insane delusion, with a view of redressing or revenging some supposed grievance or injury, or of producing some public benefit, he is nevertheless punishable if he knew at the time that he was acting contrary to law.

"That if the accused was conscious that the act was one which he ought not to do; and if the act was at the same time contrary to law, he is punishable. In all cases of this kind the jurors ought to be told that every man is presumed to be sane, and to possess a sufficient degree of reason to be responsible for his crimes, until the contrary be proved to their satisfaction: and that to establish a defence on the ground of insanity, it must be clearly proved that at the time of commiting [sic] the act the party accused was labouring under such a defect of reason, from disease of the mind, as not to know the nature and quality of the act he was doing, or as not to know that what he was doing was wrong.

"That a party labouring under a partial delusion must be considered in the same situation, as to responsibility, as if the facts, in respect to which the delusion exists, were real.

"That where an accused person is supposed to be insane, a medical man, who has been present in Court and heard the evidence, may be asked, as a matter of science, whether the facts stated by the witnesses, supposing them to be true, show a state of mind incapable of distinguishing between right and wrong." [54]

b. *Smith v. United States.*   As the present century progressed, it was felt by some that the *M'Naghten* rules did not take sufficient account of compulsions in wrongdoers which overrode their knowledge of right and wrong.   The "irresistible impulse" rule, as a consequence, was added to the test of insanity.   "The modern doctrine is that the degree of insanity which will relieve the accused of the consequences of a criminal act must be such as to create in his mind an uncontrollable impulse to commit the offense charged.   This impulse must be such as to override the reason and judgment and obliterate the sense of right and wrong to the extent that the accused is deprived of the power to choose between right and wrong.   The mere ability to distinguish right from wrong is no longer the correct test either in civil or criminal cases, where the defense of insanity is interposed.   The accepted rule in this day and age, with the great advancement in medical science as an enlightening influence on this subject, is that the accused must be capable, not only of distinguishing between right and wrong, but that he was not impelled to do the act by an irresistible impulse, which means before it will justify a verdict of acquittal that his reasoning powers were so far dethroned by his diseased mental condition as to deprive him of the will power to resist the insane impulse to perpetrate the deed, though knowing it to be wrong." [55]

---

[54] Queen v. M'Naghten, 10 Cl. and Fin. 200, 201, 8 Eng. Rep. 718, 719 (1843).   The M'Naghten rules have been accepted by all states except New Hampshire.   See 1 Burdick, Law of Crimes 277-278 (1946) and Biggs, The Guilty Mind 111 (1955).

[55] Smith v. United States, 36 F.2d 538, 549 (D.C. Cir. 1929).   There is uncertainty regarding the number of states in which the irresistible impulse test is accepted.   "It is sometimes said that the test is law in fourteen states, but at other times the number of such states is alleged to be twenty-one.   It is uncertain whether in some of those states the courts have merely recognized that serious impairment of the cognitive functions is also expressed in a lack of normal self-control which, of course, is not acceptance of the irresistible impulse test."   Hall, Psychiatry and Criminal Responsibility, 65 Yale L.J. 778

c. *Durham v. United States.* Finally, as this present century passes the halfway mark, both the "right-wrong" test and the "irresistible impulse" test have been considered inadequate and in their place has been substituted the "diseased or defective mind" test. "We find that as an exclusive criterion the right-wrong test is inadequate in that (a) it does not take sufficient account of psychic realities and scientific knowledge, and (b) it is based upon one sympton and so cannot validly be applied in all circumstances. We find that the 'irresistible impulse' test is also inadequate in that it gives no recognition to mental illness characterized by brooding and reflection and so relegates acts caused by such illness to the application of the inadequate right-wrong test." [56]

The question to be decided by the jury, then, is whether the accused acted because of a mental disorder. "If you the jury believe beyond a reasonable doubt that the accused was not suffering from a diseased or defective mental condition at the time he committed the criminal act charged, you may find him guilty. If you believe he was suffering from a diseased or defective mental condition when he committed the act, but believe beyond a reasonable doubt that the act was not the product of such mental abnormality, you may find him guilty. Unless you believe beyond a reasonable doubt either that he was not suffering from a diseased or defective mental condition, or that the act was not the product of such abnormality, you must find the accused not guilty by reason of insanity. . . . The question will be simply whether the accused acted because of a mental disorder, and not whether he displayed particular symptoms which medical science has long recognized do not necessarily, or even typically, accompany even the most serious mental disorder." [57] The *Durham* decision admittedly follows the opinion expressed in the New Hampshire case of *State v. Pike.*[58]

This gradual change in the grounds for irresponsibility calls for an examination. The different philosophies back of the change, the need of a more critical attitude on the part of lawmen toward psychiatric theories, and the possibility of a workable rule for judges and juries should be looked at briefly.

---

n.62 (1956). The irresistible impulse test is not the law in England. See Biggs, the Guilty Mind 110 (1955).

[56] Durham v. United States, 214 F.2d 862, 874 (D.C. Cir. 1954).

[57] 214 F.2d at 875, 876. For an intersting discussion of the Durham case see the symposium entitled: Insanity and the Criminal Law — A Critique of Durham v. United States, 22 U. Chi. L. Rev. 317-404 (1955).

[58] 214 F.2d at 874. See State v. Pike, 49 N.H. 399 (1870).

2. *Divergent background philosophies.* Implied in the legal thinking represented in the cases just cited are divergent views of what a man is. A lawman should ask himself which of these philosophies is in agreement or disagreement with his own convictions — arrived at by reasoning or faith — on this matter.

a. *Man essentially a knowing decision-maker.* Broadly speaking there are two divergent philosophies back of these decisions. The one, already noted above,[59] holds that man is a unit of matter and spirit with powers of knowing and deciding. Implied in this statement, to explain somewhat more fully but with much oversimplification, is the fact that man has two principle powers — one is the power of apprehension or of knowing and the other is the power of appetition or of seeking the objects known. Since man is part matter, he has in common with animals the faculty of sense knowledge and sense seeking. But because he is also part spirit, unlike animals he has the capacity of intellectual knowledge and intellectual seeking.

The faculty of intellectual knowledge is sometimes called "intellect," "mind," or "reason." Or it may be referred to as the cognitive faculty. Its exercise is sometimes termed intellection. Since knowledge means "awareness" or "understanding" these words are at times used synonymously. The faculty of intellectual seeking is commonly called the "will." Its operation is known as volition. And because the will is "free," inasmuch as it is endowed with the power of choice, the capacity for "free decision" is frequently used with the same meaning as free will.

The appetitive is existentially integrated with the apprehensive inasmuch as it is the nature of the one to be related to the other. This is shown in the interrelation of intellect and will. The will can freely choose various objects because the intellect is capable of diverse concepts of them. The resulting composite act is knowing decision.[60] This does not mean, however, that the two powers are completely integrated operationally. The appetitive must be conditioned by habits that dispose it to follow the guidance of the apprehensive. A man may know what is forbidden by the directives of a certain law, but it does not follow automati-

[59] See Comment, page 14.

[60] The basic existential integration of man's intellect and will is well brought out in Aquinas' profound explanation of free decision. "The root of freedom is the will as its subject; but it is reason as its cause. For the will can tend freely to various objects precisely because reason is capable of diverse concepts of the good. Hence philosophers define free decision as being a free judgment arising from reason, implying that reason is the cause of freedom." 1-2 Sum. Theol. 17, 1. On this matter in general see Klubertanz, The Philosophy of Human Nature 158-321 (1953).

cally that he will choose to obey the law. Whatever assurance there is that he will follow cognized directives will depend on how well formed his appetitive habits are.

On the other hand, the appetitive can influence the apprehensive — for better or for worse. A man may judge theoretically — and in a way not immediately directive of his own actions — that adultery is wrong and that it should not be indulged in. He may have arrived at this judgment either because of his own reasoning on the matter, or because he has had a convincing course in ethics, or because of his faith in the Ten Commandments, or because it is forbidden by statute. But if the question should arise of his judging practically — and in a manner immediately directive of his own actions — whether or not he should commit adultery with this particular woman, his appetitive powers may influence the apprehensive. Although he knows and judges that adultery is wrong in general and should not be indulged in, nevertheless here and now he may judge that for him in particular it is somehow good and right and he will commit the act. It is this judgment of prudence, or imprudence as the case may be, that finally directs his own actions.

In other words, while the theoretical judgments (science) are not influenced by the appetitive, the practical judgments (prudence) may be. It is not the state of his theoretical knowledge alone that determines how a normal man will act. It is rather his knowledge as influenced by the disposition of his intellectual appetite — his will. It is in this practical directive judgment of prudence that the apprehensive and the appetitive cross with the result that we lead the kind of lives we do — wrong though they often may be and pursued with full awareness that they are so.

From this analysis of man and his powers certain points follow that pertain to the matter under discussion and will have an application shortly.

First, man's dominant power is his intellect because it guides his other powers. It is in terms of this power that he is defined as a "rational" being, and his will as a "rational" will. Though his other powers may influence the intellect, nevertheless their only source of guidance is knowledge had through the intellect. The actions of a man for which he is responsible are those that are caused by knowing decision.

Second, the presence in us of bad habits disposing us to do what we know is wrong is not a disease. Such dispositions in our powers — good or bad as they may be — are part of being a normal man — good or bad as he may be. And the manifestation of such wrong habits in bad intention or mens rea does not constitute physical or mental abnormality. Nor does it result in irresistible impulse. For, daily experience proves that such inclinations can be resisted. If this were not the case, all talk of a difference between a good and bad life and its corresponding reward and punishment would be so much nonsense.

Third, since knowing decision is a prerequisite for control and responsibility, whatever affects it affects the degree of control and responsibility. Fear, rage, passion, inherited defects, compulsions and disease are factors influencing knowing decision. But this does not signify that every time a man commits a crime one of these factors must have been the cause. When that is the case, it is the exception. In our ordinary, every day actions when we do what we know is wrong, it is the disposition of our appetitive power — bad will begotten of selfish love — that influences our judgment and inclines us to do what we do. Even though we know that the object of our desires is wrong and forbidden by some kind of law, we may be drawn by our own egocentric desires to judge or "know" what we want to: that this object is somehow "good" for us.

That men do act in this manner is attested by a massive block of evidence that has been a constant in human behavior since the beginning of history. What the possible root cause of this seemingly enigmatic tendency in men is should be investigated by lawmen, psychiatrists and criminologists — lest their efforts be spent ultimately on what is merely a chimera.[61] But it is this use of our apprehensive and appetitive powers that determines wherein will lie our destiny.

In this philosophy, knowing decision is the source of control of human actions and responsibility for them. It may be influenced by the disposition of our will — a normal condition — or it may be affected by compulsion, disease, and the like — an abnormal condition. The presence of knowledge and a healthy condition of mind is no assurance of virtuous action. They are only its sine qua non.[62] And the meaning of right and wrong, of which there

[61] See Chapter 5, note 16 and especially Chapter 8, note 38 on the actual state of human nature. Regarding this state, the fundamental question arises: if it is true that there was a historical event that has so effected men's apprehensive and appetitive powers that it is difficult for them to do always what they know is right and this fact can be known only through faith, can the final insight into men and their destiny be had from observable data alone?

[62] Ignorance (the absence of knowledge) and insanity (the absence of a healthy condition of mind) should be clearly distinguished. "[I]gnorance is not a state of the mind in the sense that sanity and insanity are. When the

may be question whether the accused had knowledge, is founded on the objective basis of men's dynamic drives, as explained above regarding man-discovered law.

b. *Man essentially a higher grade animal.* The other philosophy back of these decisions, and with still more over-simplification, is expressed in many ways but holds commonly that man is not a unit of matter and spirit. He is a material being only and is not essentially different from animals from which he has evolved. Somehow he has developed higher ways of acting than they. His integration is obvious and simple, since there is no problem of conjoining a spiritual element with a material one, as there is in the interpretation of man noted above.

The problem of getting a man to act rightly and lawfully in this position is not one of disposing his appetitive powers to being guided by his apprehensive. It is merely one of conditioning him, that is, of training or educating him. If he knows what is right, he will do what is right. The idea that "bad will" may interpose itself between knowledge and action in the normal man is not a controlling concept in this philosophy. For, the will as a spiritual power has been ruled out on the basis that man is composed of matter exclusively.

Free will is discarded as ". . . an expression of the narcissistic wish, or even the postulate of the moralists that the Super-Ego does, or should rule, supreme and unlimited in the psychic apparatus of men. . . . Psychoanalysis considers the human psychic apparatus as a system which is fully, and without a single gap, determined by psychological and biological causative factors." [63] Hence, the only cause for a man not doing what he knows is right, in this philosophy, would seem to be uncontrollable impulse or

---

mind is ignorant of a fact, its state still remains sound; the power of thinking, of judging, of willing, is just as complete before communication of the fact as after — the essence of the mind remains unaffected; but where insanity exists, its mysterious texture, so to speak, is impaired or for the time paralyzed — it is no longer subject to the will — its operations cease to be voluntary, its perceptions are impaired. Insanity is a state, a condition of the mind itself. Ignorance of a particular fact consists in this, that the mind although sound and capable of healthy action, has never acted upon that subject because it has never been brought to the notice of the perceptive faculties. The one is an incapacity to act perfectly, the other is the never having acted, although perfectly capable of so doing. Upon this theory all the presumptions of the law in relation to sanity and insanity are based." Meeker v. Boyland, 28 N.J. 274, 279, 280 (1860).

[63] Alexander and Staub, The Criminal, the Judge, and the Public 70, 71 (1931). The influence of Freud in this rejection of freedom of choice is unmistakable. See Freud, General Introduction to Psychoanalysis 97 (Riviere trans. 1935).

more especially mental disease or defect. These conditions are oftimes said to be caused by such biological factors as malfunctioning glands.

In this philosophy of man, then, there is no dominant power through which direction comes to the other powers with the possibility of guidance being opposed or affected by a rebellious will. Knowledge and sanity are, consequently, assurance of virtue. If a man knows what is right and is sane, he will do what is right. This philosophy also repudiates the distinction between right and wrong as lacking an objective basis. And for those lawmen of a legal, positivistic bent of mind, whose aim is to keep morals out of law, any meaning right and wrong may have is limited solely to what is permitted or prohibited by man-made law.

c. *Related philosophies.* It is not too difficult to discern which of these philosophies is back of the cases just noted. The *M'Naghten* rules are based on the philosophy which maintains that men's reason is their prime faculty inasmuch as it guides them in making free decisions. Hence, the main inspiration of these rules is congenial with a means-end philosophy of law which presupposes men endowed with intellect and will. However, these rules have certain shortcomings that call for reconsideration as will be noted shortly.

The *Smith* decision seems to rest on this same philosophy of man but it attempts to supply the inadequacy of the *M'Naghten* rules by saddling on them the notion of "irresistible impulse." Since the test of "irresistible impulse" has been rejected by many experts, as will be pointed out, the basis on which the decision rests is unsatisfactory.

Finally, the *Durham* opinion is grounded on a philosophy that denies to men's cognitive power a unique directive role. Consequently, free will ceases logically to be an important factor in human actions and the only cause of what we term crime is mental disease or defect, as will also be seen presently.

3. *Need of critical attitude.* There is need of a much more critical attitude on the part of lawmen toward the background of the insanity defense, both from the viewpoint of philosophy and of psychiatry. Not that lawmen should pretend to be psychiatrists and define mental disease, mental deficiency or irresistible impulse. That is a field for experts. But what must be avoided is an uncritical acceptance of supposedly established "facts" which are in reality a matter of controversy among eminent psychiatrists themselves.

a. *Irresistible impulse.* The validity of the notion of "irresistible impulse" as unrelated to the accused's mental condition has been seriously called into question. Prominent psychiatrists have said that they have ". . . never met a murder due to irresistible impulse unconnected with mental disease," [64] and have ". . . never known an irresistible impulse leading to a crime of violence except in association with other signs of insanity." [65] They report that the ". . . concept of 'irresistible impulse' test has been largely discredited . . . it is inherently inadequate and unsatisfactory." [66]

In other words, the type of legal thinking represented in the *Smith* decision is not scientifically well founded. "Irresistible impulse" cannot merely be added to the *M'Naghten* rules. It cannot be taken for granted that an accused can be without any disorder of understanding and still have an "irresistible impulse" to do what he knows is wrong. Hence, there is no justification for thinking that we have reached the point where we can accept the notion that a person of normal mentality may be "irresistibly" impelled to kill. The various kinds of impulses, their origin, and their interaction with men's mental faculties, as contrasted with a normal but rebellious will, are still in need of much more careful analysis, identification and classification.

Perhaps there is much to the contention that ". . . the law . . . is itself a subtreasury of time-tested psychology, most of it quite sound." [67] "Dealing as it does mainly with human behavior, the law very likely has more to teach psychology than to learn from it. The law has had a long history and very able students and practitioners." [68]

b. *Mental disease.* Legal thinking such as represented in the *Durham* decision should also be critically approached with an eye on the validity of its philosophical as well as its psychiatric assumptions. Theoretically there is no difficulty in considering mental disease as a valid defense in criminal proceedings. It is when mental disease is defined with questionable implications regarding the nature of man and his responsibility, that a problem arises.

[64] 1953 Report of the Royal Commission on Capital Punishment 96.
[65] Id. at 95.
[66] Id. at 109. This rejection of irresistible impulse by the Commission, along with its repudiation of the M'Naghten rules, was a source of influence on the Durham decision. See Durham v. United States, 214 F.2d 862, 870 (D.C. Cir. 1954). The Commission's Report, however, does not seem to have had a notable impact on English criminal law. See Hall, Psychiatry and Criminal Responsibility, 65 Yale L.J. 761, 763 (1956).
[67] Guttmacher and Weihofen, Psychiatry and the Law 12 (1952).
[68] Thorndike, Man and His Works 133 (1943).

First, it is doubtful that the *Durham* opinion rests on solid psychiatric grounds. "This opinion is a most revealing document. To the extent that it relies on and quotes current psychiatric authorities, it is on shaky ground. The publications cited contain serious errors, and discuss the question of legal insanity in the abstract without any substantial proof for their assertions. [The judge's] final conclusion is unfortunately based on the psychiatric vagaries found in some of these publications. He substitutes a new test for the *M'Naghten* rule. In essence it requires that the plea of legal insanity must be based on a demonstration that the crime was the product of mental disease. If he had had better psychiatric advice, [he] would have known that this is precisely how the *M'Naghten* rule has been interpreted in practice by experienced psychiatrists. In civil courts, before lunacy commissions, and in courts-martial of the Army and Navy, I have testified that if this particular mental disease had not existed there would have been no crime." [69]

Mental disease as the cause of a crime must be related to the cognitive state of the accused. "If crime is really the product, the result, the symptom of a psychosis, it is inevitable that the person who committed it cannot sufficiently distinguish between right and wrong and/or sufficiently know the nature and quality of his act. This fact is known to any psychiatrist who understands that the *M'Naghten* rule refers to the 'true capacity of the individual.' " [70]

Second, the notion of mental disease expressed in the *Durham* decision is based on a philosophy that runs counter to the firmly established position which holds that man is a being whose reason is the one faculty through which guidance comes to otherwise blind drives. This court's legal thinking assumes that a man's mental power is not his prime faculty and does not connote an essential difference between himself and all other creatures.

The court, in fact, goes out of its way to depreciate any such philosophy. "The modern science of psychology . . . does not conceive that there is a separate little man in the top of one's head called reason whose function it is to guide another unruly little man called instinct, emotion, or impulse in the way he

[69] Werthem, Psychoauthoritarianism and the Law, 22 U. Chi. L. Rev. 336 (1955).

[70] Werthem, id. at 337. On this point see also East, An Introduction to Forensic Psychiatry in the Criminal Courts (1927); Cleckley, Mask of Sanity (2d ed. 1950); and Davidson, Criminal Responsibility: The Quest for a Formula in Psychiatry and the Law (1955).

should go. . . .[71]   The science of psychiatry now recognizes that a man is an integrated personality and that reason, which is only one element in that personality, is not the sole determinant of his conduct.   The right-wrong test, which considers knowledge or reason alone, is therefore an inadequate guide to mental responsibility for criminal behavior." [72]

Undoubtedly reason in one sense is "not the sole determinant" of a man's conduct, as has already been discussed.   However, reason is the sole faculty of guidance.   Consequently, it is unique and cannot be reduced to merely "one element" in man's make-up.   If it is so reduced, then by what faculty is law itself known to men and how is this knowledge of law related to the subsequent direction of their lives?   But although reason is prime in the sense of being *the* directive faculty, nevertheless it is not without integration with the will.   A court's failure to do the necessary research on this difficult and subtle problem, either during pre-legal training or afterwards, can be the only explanation for its speaking of this most basic matter in superficial terms of "separate little men."   It is quite certain that the court would be hard pressed to adduce evidence of any eminent authority who ever held such a philosophy of man.

Lip service is also paid in the *Durham* decision to the part that free decision plays in the determination of criminal responsibility.   "The legal and moral traditions of the western world require that those who, of their own free will and with evil intent (sometimes called mens rea), commit acts which violate the law, shall be criminally responsible for those acts." [73]   But the importance of free decision has already been blocked off by the downgrading reason has received in the explanation proffered of the nature of men's powers.   As already seen, the will's freedom of choice is intimately related to the intellect's capacity for forming different concepts.   Decision and intent are meaningless when divorced from the directive function of reason.   Human self-control is an intellectual-volitional process.

Third, certain distinctions must be made.   There is a difference between a bad, mean, rebellious will and mental disease. The nonconformist, the man who refuses to follow "established social patterns of behavior," is not necessarily mentally defective.

[71] Durham v. United States, 214 F.2d 862, 871 (D.C. Cir. 1954), quoting Holloway v. United States, 148 F.2d 665, 667 (D.C. Cir. 1945).
[72] Durham v. United States, 214 F.2d 862, 871 (D.C. Cir. 1954).
[73] Id. at 876.

He may be so, but this must be proved by other evidence. In the absence of such evidence, the facile labelling of such a man as a "socio-path," and therefore a mental defective, is to betray shallow psychiatric insight and an inability to analyze human nature and probe beneath the surface of human conduct.[74]

A distinction should also be drawn between mental disease and criminal irresponsibility. They are not necessarily coextensive. A man may be suffering from a mental disease and still have sufficient control through knowing decision to be criminally responsible. However, as noted, this degree of control may be so reduced that the accused is no longer accountable for his actions.

Fourth, who is to be the trier of the facts? The *Durham* decision holds that an accused ". . . is not criminally responsible if his unlawful act was the product of mental disease or mental defect." [75] But any other reason why he would commit a crime — a rebellious will, for instance — has already been ruled out to all intents and purposes. Equivalently this means that the only reason why a man commits a crime is because he is mentally diseased or defective.[76] If this were the case, the sole fact to be determined would be whether or not the accused was laboring under such a disease or defect and whether his act was the "product of such abnormality." Such a determination supposedly is to be made by the psychiatrist or other expert.

But who ultimately is to determine whether the accused's mental state was the cause of his doing the act? "The requirement that the act be the product of the disorder is only a way of saying that there must be a causal connection. And presumably the rule requires *proximate* cause, as the law requires elsewhere. Medical men could perhaps testify in many cases that the defendant's mental condition was *a* cause of his criminal conduct; but will they be able to say it was *the* (the *proximate*) cause?" [77] Besides, it should be remembered that once a reputable expert testifies that the defendant has a mental disease or defect, it becomes ex-

[74] The question may well be raised whether there is not more evidence of the powers of intellect and will and of the condition of the will — cooperative or rebellious — than there is of the "Id," the "Ego," and the "Super-Ego."

[75] Durham v. United States, 214 F.2d 862, 874 (D.C. Cir. 1954).

[76] Not a few maintain that crime should not be treated as a moral problem but as a psychiatric one, that is, the same attitude should be had toward criminals as toward the insane. See Arnold, The Symbols of Government 167 (1935). This doctrine, if true, would in one sense prove consoling when extended to the theological implications of doing evil. For, if all evil doers are ipso facto insane they are not responsible; if not responsible they deserve no punishment; and if they deserve no punishment they cannot end up in hell.

[77] Weihofen, The Flowering of New Hampshire, 22 U. Chi. L. Rev. 356, 360 (1955).

tremely difficult for the prosecution to prove beyond a reasonable doubt that his act was not caused by his illness.

Hence, if mental disease and expert opinion are made the pivotal point around which the question of criminal responsibility turns, the psychiatrist or other expert assumes the authority of the judge and jury as trier of the facts. Thus, unless the testimony of experts is kept as ancillary to triers of the facts, the function of judge and jury will be materially changed. For, the ". . . purpose of expert testimony is to communicate to this body of ordinary persons [the jury] the wisdom and understanding necessary for the triers to exercise sound judgment in determining the issue in controversy." [78]

The whole matter of legal process and safeguards is at stake here. Hence, ". . . it would be a calamity if the disposition of criminal cases would be taken out of the hands of judges and given into the hands of psychiatric and other experts." [79] "It is sometimes suggested that the mental condition of an accused person should be taken out of the hands of the jury, and that a medical referee sitting with the presiding judge should determine the issue. I believe this suggestion is thoroughly mischievous . . . [A]n intolerable burden would be placed upon psychiatry in its adolescence if it had the last word in a criminal court." [80] Such decisions, being a matter of justice, should remain in the hands of judge and jury.

In a word, the *Durham* decision has the most serious objections against it. It does not rest on solid psychiatric grounds and it assumes a notion of man that is at variance with the long established concept of man on which western (and for that matter eastern) legal thought has been built. Courts have recognized the dangerousness of this decision faulted as it is with these radical defects. They have refused, for the most part, to adopt its rule and underlying philosophy. [81]

[78] Ladd, Expert Testimony, 5 Vand. L. Rev. 414, 428 (1952).

[79] Werthem, A Psychiatrist Looks at Psychiatry and the Law, 3 Buffalo L. Rev. 41, 48 (1953).

[80] East, Society and the Criminal 17 n.4 (1951).

[81] The Durham rule seems to have been applied only by the District of Columbia Circuit. See Kelly v. United States, 236 F.2d 746 (D.C. Cir. 1956); Douglas v. United States, 239 F.2d 52 (D.C. Cir. 1956); Fielding v. United States, 251 F.2d 878 (D.C. Cir. 1957). Another decision appears to approach the Durham rule. State v. White, 58 N.M. 324, 270 P.2d 727 (1954).

Other jurisdictions have refused to adopt the rule. See Howard v. United States, 232 F.2d 274 (5th Cir. 1956); Anderson v. United States, 237 F.2d 118 (9th Cir. 1956); Sauer v. United States, 241 F.2d 640 (9th Cir. 1957); Voss v. United States, 259 F.2d 699 (8th Cir. 1958); United States v. Smith, 5 U.S.C.M.A. 314, 17 C.M.R. 314 (1954); People v. Ryan, 140 Cal. App. 2d 412,

4. *Workable rule.* Judges and juries need a workable rule for testing insanity. It must be clear enough to be understood by any layman or laywoman who is a member of the jury and it must rest on a time-tested basis.

a. *Unsatisfactory rules.* None of the above mentioned rules is completely satisfactory. The rule of mental disease stated in the *Durham* case leaves much to be desired. Whether this ". . . new definition will improve the present unfortunate state of forensic psychiatry is doubtful. As a legal test this new definition is insufficient: it gives undemocratic leeway to the partisan and/or bureaucratic expert, and, on account of its wording, lends itself to grave abuse. It does not guide the jury as to the degree of mental disease, a term which includes psychosis and neurosis." [82]

The "irresistible impulse" test, adopted in the *Smith* decision and many others, is finally and deservedly being recognized as scientifically unsound. Its passing as a defense in criminal cases will not be lamented.

The "right-wrong" test embodied in the *M'Naghten* rules is also unsatisfactory as it stands. It does not take into explicit account the accused's ability to control his actions and make them conform to what he is aware — to some degree at least — is right and lawful. What is needed is a restatement of this test that will recognize the fact of control but as related to the cognitive state of the defendant.

b. *Rules suggested.* Several rules have been proposed for a legal test for insanity. One proposal is that "A person is not responsible for criminal conduct if at the time of such conduct as a result of mental disease or defect he lacks substantial capacity either to appreciate the criminality of his conduct or to conform his conduct to the requirements of law.

"The terms 'mental disease or defect' do not include an abnormality manifested only by repeated criminal or otherwise antisocial conduct." [83]

This proposal has much to recommend it, but it does seem open to criticism. For, in spite of the fact that it keeps the

---

295 P.2d 496 (1956); People v. Carpenter, 11 Ill. 2d 60, 142 N.E.2d 11 (1957); Flowers v. State, 236 Ind. 151, 139 N.E.2d 185 (1957); Thomas v. State, 206 Md. 575, 112 A.2d 913 (1955); Bryant v. State, 207 Md. 565, 115 A.2d 502 (1955); Commonwealth v. Chester, 150 N.E.2d 914 (Mass. 1958); State v. Kitchens, 129 Mont. 331, 286 P.2d 1079 (1955).

[82] Werthem, Psychoauthoritarianism and the Law, 22 U. Chi. L. Rev. 336, 337 (1955). See also Werthem's judicious review of Zilboorg, The Psychology of the Criminal Act and Punishment (1954), id. at 569-581.

[83] American Law Institute Model Penal Code, Tentative Draft 27 (1955).

M'Naghten rules as valid, what it appends to them results in little improvement over the *Smith* decision and the addition of "irresistible impulse." If the phrase ". . . either to appreciate . . . or to conform" connotes a separation of ability to conform from capacity to understand, no progress has been made. The matter is much more subtle than that, as we have seen. Perhaps, if the phrase were made to read ". . . to appreciate . . . *and* to conform" the necessary relation between ability to control and the cognitive state of the accused would be saved.

Another suggestion, offered as a substitute for the *M'Naghten* rules but admittedly retaining their essential structure, is that "A crime is not committed by anyone who, because of a mental disease, is unable to understand what he is doing and to control his conduct at the time he commits a harm forbidden by criminal law. In deciding this question with reference to the criminal conduct with which a defendant is charged, the trier of the facts should decide (1) whether, because of mental disease, the defendant lacked the capacity to understand the physical nature and consequences of his conduct; and (2) whether, because of such disease, the defendant lacked the capacity to realize that it was morally wrong to commit the harm in question." [84]

This suggestion has the merit of making the accused's awareness of what he was doing the central point of reference, while at the same time recognizing control as somehow related to this cognitive state.

E. *Punishment*

Criminals are responsible for evil overt acts to the degree that they have caused them through knowing decision. Deprivations that follow such decisions are penalties for having made them.

The degree of punishment should be proportioned to the crime. Crimes vary in themselves, as already mentioned, since the matter of the overt act admits of degrees. Slitting a man's throat is not the same as shooting his dog. These variations are recognized in the gradation of misdemeanors and felonies. So also does the amount of knowledge and free decision involved in deciding to do the overt act vary. Hence the evaluation of any crime and its punishment must take these varying factors of the matter and form of a crime into account.

1. *Matter and form of crime vary.* It would be an error to

[84] Hall, Psychiatry and Criminal Responsibility, 65 Yale L.J. 761, 781 (1956).

hold, therefore, that while the matter of the overt act varies, knowledge and freedom never do. This would mean that punishments should vary but responsibility never is lessened. Contrariwise, it would be equally a mistake to say that, while the matter of the overt act never varies, knowledge and freedom vary so widely that often they are not even present. This would imply that punishment would always be the same but it should practically never be inflicted.

2. *Punishment is primarily retributive.* Punishment, then, as a deprivation is primarily retributive as we saw. It is a price that is exacted by the very act of disobedience. It may also be said to be a vindication of the law. Hence to ask what the purpose of punishment is may betray a misunderstanding of its profound nature as intrinsic sanction. It would scarcely make sense to ask the purpose of the reckless driver's ending up in the ditch as a consequence of his violating the speed limit. But it would be his punishment as the intrinsic sanction of the law.

3. *Punishment is deterrent and corrective.* Besides being retributive, to repeat, deprivation may be a deterrent and a corrective. Fear of loss can keep men from taking chances they otherwise would take, and the tendency to decide to take these chances is thereby corrected. "It [the state] may inflict a deserved penalty merely to vindicate the law or to deter or to reform the offender or for all of these puposes." [85] "Generally, punishment is imposed for crime for [the] twofold purpose of reformation of the convicted offender and a deterrent to others who might be disposed to commit such a crime." [86] Those who are of the opinion that it is not the threat of punishment that deters criminals but the fear of apprehension, should remember that loss of liberty by apprehension is a form of punishment.

Deprivation as corrective or reformative implies the idea of education. Education here connotes that the criminal learns to use his power of decision in a manner demanded by law. "I'll never do that again" and "I have learned my lesson" are statements which, if true, indicate progress toward rehabilitation. "In deciding upon a sentence . . . the court has in mind the objectives of punishment under the Penal Law of this State, to wit: That others may be deterred from similar crimes; that one convicted should be deterred from future crime; and that an en-

[85] Pennsylvania ex rel. Sullivan v. Ashe, 302 U.S. 51, 55, 58 Sup. Ct. 59, 60 (1937).

[86] Law v. State, 238 Ala. 428, 191 So. 803 (1939). See also Yates v. State, 31 Ala. 404, 17 So.2d 594, 595 (1944).

deavor should be made to return the one convicted to society as a useful member." [87]

4. *Treatment of criminals.* In addition to the retributive, deterrent and corrective effects of punishment, there is the matter of the treatment of criminals. The treatment of criminals may refer to many different things. It may refer to the segregation of juveniles from older men and first offenders from multiple "losers," to the living conditions of the prison, to ordinary medical care, to the disciplinary measures employed, to the good behavior and parole arrangements.

Treatment may have reference to psychiatric treatment of prisoners. They may have been normal enough to commit a crime but now are in need of aid in adjusting themselves to prison life in such a way as to prepare for future rehabilitation.

The treatment of prisoners may also mean educating them in a formal sense. This entails libraries with well-chosen holdings and lectures especially on the purpose of life and the meaning it can have, on the blocking effect of crime on the prisoner himself and others, and on the place he can still have in society.

5. *Education is not punishment.* What must be marked well, however, is that education in this formal sense is not punishment, any more than psychiatric therapy is. Knowledge and the ability to decide between right or wrong are prerequisites to a criminal act. A lack of them is not a crime. Neither education nor therapy are types of punishment.

The view that education is punishment is based on the Socratic illusion that "knowledge is virtue," that if a man knows what is right he will do what is right. But this is to confuse what a man knows with what he will do. Science is not prudence.

Only when the meaning of crime is put on an entirely different basis can education be called "punishment." "Penalties are compulsory measures by which the government protects a certain order of social relations against future infractions by the criminal himself or by others. Apart from their deterrent effect, they achieve this purpose by re-education as well as by the isolation and, in extreme cases, by the extermination, of the criminal. Crime, in a class-divided society, originates from the latter's social structure, not from the personal 'guilt' of the criminal. Thus, punishment ought not to redeem the 'guilt.' It ought to be restricted to the demands of expediency without inflicting upon the criminal injurious and needless sufferings. In this rejection of a specific 'penal' character of what is called 'penalty,' the leading

[87] People v. Smith, 163 Misc. 469, 472, 297 N.Y. Supp. 489 (1937).

principles of 1919 went to the length of including in the catalogue of suggested 'penalties' compulsory acts which involved no suffering of any kind and which were in no way deterrent to reasonable beings, such as compulsory attendance at evening classes. Of the alternative of re-education and complete isolation (of which extermination is the extreme form), the Leading Principles, being destined for the ordinary courts, emphasize the former." [88]

6. *Therapy is not punishment.* Similarily psychiatric therapy is not punishment. A sane state of mind, like knowledge, is a prerequisite to the commission of a crime. The absence of it is not a crime and its therapy is not a punishment.

To hold the notion that therapy is punishment is only to ring a change on "knowledge is virtue" by saying "sanity is virtue," that is, if a man is of sound mind he will not commit a crime. This, however, is to go contrary to scientific findings. For, psychiatric tests prove there can be criminals of perfectly sound mental faculties who, with a considerable margin of self-direction, decide to do what they know is wrong.

7. *Punishment of criminal promotes public good.* Finally it may be well to recall that deprivation, while a physical evil to the criminal, may be a good in relation to social and political needs. For, punishment is a necessary means of promoting the public welfare. As a deterrent it promotes the observance of laws and therefore the common good. Some penalties do this directly. What a criminal is deprived of by way of fine or confiscation (not just restitution) is a public gain. Hence if the question be raised whether punishment is an evil to the criminal or a good to society, the answer is that it is primarily a loss and a physical evil to the criminal, and secondarily a gain and a good to society.

F.   *Capital Punishment*

Punishment is supposed to fit the crime. In some jurisdictions murder in the first degree, rape, and kidnapping are crimes for which the penalty is death. In others these same crimes are punishable by life imprisonment or less. Hence the question arises, is capital punishment a condign penalty for such crimes?

Though this is perhaps an ethico-moral problem and as such pertains to a specialized treatment of the content of law as noted above, nevertheless it seems worthy of parenthetical note here because of its immediate relation and importance to crimes.

[88] Schlesinger, Soviet Legal Theory 74-75 (1946). By permission of Routledge and Kegan Paul Ltd.

1. *Justifying circumstances.* Taking the life of another can be justified when it is a means necessary to preserve life or other values of equal importance. For, if the elementary demand expressed through a man's basic drive that he preserve himself in existence means anything, it means that he has a claim to use means that are necessary to protect himself.

a. *Self-defense of individual as individual.* If I am attacked, I may defend myself even to the point of killing my assailant should conditions warrant it. The rule is well settled "that the killing of one who is an assailant must be under a reasonable apprehension of loss of life or great bodily harm, and the danger must appear so imminent at the moment of the assault as to present no alternative of escaping its consequences but by resistance. Then the killing may be excusable, even if it turns out afterwards that there was no actual danger. . . . The law of self-defense is a law of necessity, and that necessity must be real, or bear all the semblance of reality, and appear to admit of no other alternative, before taking life will be justifiable or excusable. Whenever it is set up, the case will always call for a most careful and searching scrutiny, to be sure that it rests, where alone it can rest, on the ground of real or apparently real necessity." [89]

Certain requisites must be present to justify self-defense. "The essential elements of self-defense are: (1) The defendant must be free from fault; that is, he must not say or do anything for the purpose of provoking a difficulty, nor must he be disregardful of the consequences in this respect of any wrongful word or act. (2) There must be a present impending peril to life, or of great bodily harm, either real or so apparent as to create the bona fide belief of an existing necessity, and the defendant must have been so impressed. And (3) there must be no convenient or reasonable mode of escape by retreat or declining the combat." [90]

In attacking me and not respecting my claims to life, my assailant has already violated his duty to preserve peaceful living conditions. Hence I am under no obligation not to react. Since my action is in direct accord with the demands of my nature, it is right and good. Hence killing another in self-defense is justified if it is a means necessary to preserve my life.[91]

[89] Logue v. Commonwealth, 38 Pa. 265, 80 Am. Dec. 481, 484 (1861).

[90] Hayes v. State, 225 Ala. 253, 142 So. 675, 677 (1932). See also People v. Keys, 62 Cal. App. 2d 303, 145 P.2d 589, 596 (1944); Cooke v. State, 18 Ala. App. 416, 93 So. 86, 88 (1921).

[91] It is sometimes mooted whether I may directly intend to kill my assailant in defending myself, or only intend to render him "quiescent" even though he is thereby killed. It seems that if killing the assailant is clearly necessary,

b. *Self-defense of individuals as politically united.* The case seems clear enough for one man justifiably taking another's life in self-defense on an individual basis, given circumstances of necessity. May men, however, as citizens united in a political union take the life of another for a serious crime already committed? Is this still a form of self-defense?

Suppose kidnap-murders of children are occurring in a community, say in an early New England town, where the citizens act together in governing themselves democratically. These crimes are happening not in isolated instances but in such numbers that it is dangerous and unsafe for children to attend school or even be out of their homes. One of the kidnap-murderers is apprehended and convicted. The citizens have good reason to suspect that there are others who plan on getting ransom money in the same easy way. They must be deterred from such acts. It is judged that the only way of discouraging them is by taking the convicted man's life and thereby giving an object lesson to the others. If the price of kidnap-murder is put high enough, the odds may not seem worth taking by other potential kidnap-murderers. Again, is the killing of this criminal a means necessary for saving life? Is it therefore a form of self-defense?

The overt act, as already noted, receives part of its meaning from the circumstances in which it is done. One of these is the consequence it causes. Kidnap-murder successfully accomplished

---

it can be directly willed. For instance, a man may be in circumstances in which he will be killed unless he kills another first. I am shipwrecked with another man on an uninhabited island. We both have guns. He assures me that as soon as I fall asleep — which I am most certain to do before he does, because he is strong and vigorous and I am weak and exhausted — he will shoot and kill me in order that he may have what food and water there is for himself and thereby increase his chances of survival and eventual rescue. If I attempt merely to incapacitate him or render him "quiescent," I will eventually be killed. For as long as he is alive he will try to kill me. What is it licit for me to do? If my obligation to preserve my life is not to be made self-contradictory, I may kill or at least attempt to kill this man in self-defense. Further, if the killing is a necessary means of preserving my life, then I may intend it — although reluctantly. See John De Lugo, De Justitia et Jure (1652), Disp. X, Sect. VI, n. 149-153 (Vives ed. 1869), Vol. VI, 85-86, for a thorough-going analysis of this question. The same position was held by Soto, Molina, Vasquez, and Lessius.

Therefore "in the case of legitimate self-defense even a direct killing is morally justifiable." Fagothy, Right and Reason 291 (rev. ed. 1959). Aquinas' treatment of this problem (2-2 Sum. Theol. 64, 3 and 7) does not take into account situations such as the one just described (which, though not ordinary, may nonetheless occur and therefore should be considered) or the possibility of weapons (such as shotguns) whose deadliness could not be controlled as could that of swords and daggers.

and left unpunished is an encouragement to others to acquire money in this same effortless manner. An example is set, in this case one of encouragement. In other words, not only is kidnap-murder the taking of a person by force or threat of force from one place to another without his consent and with the intention of secretly confining him and then killing him, but it is also the setting of an example of an easy way to obtain money to other members of the community with criminal bent thus constituting a threat to security. Since punishment is proportioned to the crime, the penalty for kidnap-murder in this community should be such that, not only the law be vindicated, but also that the encouragement given to others to commit crime be offset and they be deterred from perpetrating such crimes in the future and the security of the community be thereby promoted.

Hence if the killing of a criminal is a necessary means of preventing further kidnap-murders, it is justifiable protection of the community. It is a defense against further killing. Men's claim to defend themselves does not cease on the political level. They still may justly use means necessary to protect their lives.

True, this kind of self-defense on the political level differs in some respects from that conducted on an individual basis. In individual self-defense by killing an assailant, the attack is more imminent, it is against a definite person, and the attacker is committing a crime at the time he is killed. In political self-defense by deterring others through the death of an already convicted criminal, the attack of potential kidnap-murderers is in the indefinite future, the object of their attack could be any person, and the attackers have not yet committed the crime. Nevertheless these are differences of degree not of kind. In both situations the threat to life and the need for self-protection is actual and real.

c. *Accepted doctrine.* For solid reasons, then, this has been the accepted doctrine in Anglo-American law. Only cruel and unnecessarily painful ways of executing the sentence have been the subject of question. "We find nothing in what took place here which amounts to cruel and unusual punishment in the constitutional sense. The case before us does not call for an examination into any punishments except that of death. . . . The traditional humanity of modern Anglo-American law forbids the infliction of unnecessary pain in the execution of the death sentence. Prohibition against the wanton infliction of pain has come into our law from the Bill of Rights of 1688. The identical words appear in our Eighth Amendment. The Fourteenth would prohibit by its due process clause execution by a state in a cruel manner." [92]

Whether or not the fixing of the alternative between death or life imprisonment should be left to a jury is a subject open to much good debate. "The law of this state provides that every person guilty of murder in the first degree shall suffer death, or confinement in the state prison for life, at the discretion of the jury. If you find that the defendant is guilty of murder in the first degree it will be your duty to fix the penalty. It is entirely for the jury to determine which of two penalties is to be inflicted in case of murder in the first degree, the death penalty or confinement in the state prison for life. If the jury should fix the penalty as confinement in the state prison for life, you will so indicate in your verdict. If, however, you fix the penalty at death, you will say nothing on this subject in your verdict, nor will you specify the death penalty in your verdict. In the exercise of your discretion as to which punishment shall be inflicted you are entirely free to act according to your own judgment." [93]

In summary, capital punishment may be justified as a necessary means of self-defense on the political level if circumstances warrant it.

2. *When are these circumstances present?* It is one thing to say that capital punishment is justified if circumstances are such that it is a necessary means of self-defense of individuals united politically, and it is entirely another thing to say when such circumstances are actually present. In the hypothetical situation just examined, it was supposed that the means necessary to prevent kidnap-murders was the threat of death. Are there now or have there ever been such situations actually in which such a threat was necessary?

a. *A historical instance.* One such instance seems to be the hanging of horse thieves in the early days of the development of the western part of the United States. Horses were the only means of transportation and without them the procuring of food and water was extremely difficult or practically impossible. To take a man's horse in many instances was the equivalent of taking his life. Present also in no small numbers in the area were men of uncertain honesty and trustworthiness who would not hesitate to steal a horse for whatever gain it might bring, even though it might inflict fatal hardship on the owner. Hence stringent measures were needed to keep men from stealing horses. Under fron-

[92] State ex rel. Francis v. Resweber, 329 U.S. 459, 463, 67 Sup. Ct. 374, 376 (1947).
[93] People v. Martin, 12 Cal. 2d 466, 85 P.2d 880, 883 (1938).

tier conditions there was no other effective way of doing this than for lawfully constituted authority to hang those who stole horses.[94] Hence it seems that in this instance of horse thieving we have a case wherein the circumstances were present which made capital punishment a necessary means of self-defense. There have undoubtedly been situations in other parts of the world warranting such drastic actions.

But are such circumstances present in any criminal situation today? Perhaps they are; perhaps they are not. The main thing to avoid before trying to answer this question, is the naïve notion that the answer is easy. No attempt will be made to answer it here; but some of the facts that will have to be ascertained before it can be scientifically answered will be indicated.

b. *Factors to be considered.* An attempt to ascertain whether the threat of death has a deterrent effect on criminals is an attempt to know the mind and feelings of men who are likely to perpetrate crimes. This means that the temper and outlook of the people of the particular country under consideration, or a particular part of it, will have to be known. The education and the economic, social, moral and religious environment will have to be essayed. The present effects of other types of punishment will have to be studied. Whether conditions are normal or abnormal, as in a state of war, will have to be taken into consideration. The possibility that schedules regarding time off for good behavior and the parole system are putting killers back on the streets with guns in their hands, will have to be hard-headedly examined.

If, after research into these and like facts, a governing body decides that the fear of losing their lives is a deterrent to criminals and that it is necessary to threaten them with it, capital punishment would be justified. The possibilities that the wrong man may be executed and rehabilitation thereby rendered impossible when the mistake is discovered, is not of overriding importance. There is a margin of possible error in the administration of all justice. Such a miscarriage could as well occur to a man wrongly sentenced to life imprisonment and discovered only in his advanced years and close to his death. The main consideration regarding capital punishment is whether in a given set of circumstances it is a necessary deterrent. If it is, it can be justified.

[94] This, therefore, is not a justification of hangings by irresponsible mobs.

CHAPTER 15

Torts

The problem facing us in torts is to ascertain whether or not there is a basis for responsibility and liability that is consistent not only throughout torts but also crimes, and to decide how far liability extends under certain conditions in aiding others. The solution to these problems is of extreme importance because on it depends a lawman's attitude toward "liability without fault" with all its implications, as well as his view of the duty to aid others in times of distress.

I. WRONGS INDIRECTLY AGAINST THE COMMON GOOD OF CITIZENS

A tort is, to remember, a private wrong implying injury to another's person or property independent of contract. "Ordinarily, the essence of a tort consists in the violation of some duty due to an individual, which duty is a thing different from the mere contract obligation." [1] ". . . [A] tort in contemplation of law consists in a violation of a duty imposed by general law or otherwise upon all persons occupying the relation to each other which is involved in a given transaction." [2]

Because of the nature of a tort, the injury to the common good is indirect. Such are injuries sustained as the result of negligence, trespass, false imprisonment, defamation, slander, dangerous enterprises, and the like.

A. *Tort Distinguished from Crime*

A tort is distinguished from a crime inasmuch as a tort is a private wrong and a crime is a public wrong. A tort is an act indirectly against the public good. A crime, as noted above, is an

[1] Rich v. New York Central and H.R.R.R. Co., 87 N.Y. 382, 390 (1882).
[2] Coleman v. California Yearly Meeting of Friends Church, 27 Cal. 2d 579, 81 P.2d 469, 470 (1938). See also Diver v. Miller, 34 Del. 207, 148 Atl. 291, 293 (1929); City of Mobile v. McClure, 221 Ala. 51, 127 So. 832, 835 (1930); Mitchell v. Health Culture Co., 349 Mo. 475, 162 S.W.2d 233, 237 (1942).

act directly against the public good of the people taken as members united in a political society. To put it another way, a crime is a violation of public claims that directly affect the whole community as such; a tort is a violation of private claims that directly affect the individual citizen as an individual and thereby indirectly affect the whole community.

B. *One Act May Be Both Tort and Crime*

An act may be both a tort and a crime, for instance, assault and battery or arson. The burning of a building not only directly injures the individual owner but also affects the public interest as well. Damages will be sought by the individual owner and punishment will be inflicted by the government. "In a general way, it may be said that a crime is an offense against the public, while a tort is a private injury. The distinguishing feature, however, between a crime and a tort is in the manner in which they are respectively pursued. An offense which amounts to a crime is pursued by the sovereign; an offense which amounts only to a civil injury is pursued by the injured party. In many instances, however, the same act constitutes both a crime and a tort, and the wrong is both to the public and to an individual. In this case, the act committed possessed a dual nature. It was a crime against the state, and it was also a wrong against the owner of the building that was burned." [3]

A tort may involve failure to fulfill an obligation toward the proper good of an individual citizen. Such, for instance, would be the failure to respect his claim to privacy by harmful publication of his picture.[4] Or a tort may imply failure to fulfill an obligation toward the common good of citizens from which dam-

[3] Bergman v. State, 187 Wash. 622, 60 P.2d 699, 701, 106 A.L.R. 1007, 1009 (1936). The law of torts, contracts, property, equity and the like which protects private claims is called civil law in distinction to criminal law. However, "civil law" is also used in distinction to *common* law insofar as civil law is the law of Continental Europe and common law is the law of England and the English speaking countries. "Civil law" is further used in distinction to *canon* law inasmuch as civil law is made by men with political authority and canon law is made by men with ecclesiastical authority. More recently "civil law" has been used in distinction to *military* law insofar as civil law issues from civil authority and is intended for civilians and military law emanates from military authority and pertains only to military personnel. Finally "civil law" in the sense of positive law is sometimes used in distinction to *natural* law inasmuch as civil law is man-made and natural law is not man-made but is discovered by men as expressed in their very nature.

[4] See Munden v. Harris, 153 Mo. App. 652, 134 S.W. 1076, 1078 (1911); Themo v. New England Newspaper Pub. Co., 306 Mass. 54, 27 N.E.2d 753, 755 (1940).

age results to an individual. Failure to label a deadly drug "poison" could be such a tort.[5]

II. Basis of Liability

Liability for injuries is a main problem in torts somewhat as guilt and punishment are central difficulties in crimes. For, regardless of whatever solution is arrived at, it will entail principles that cut to the heart of human living.

A. *Responsible — Answerable*

To be liable connotes in general to be "justly or legally responsible or answerable" for something.[6] "The word 'liable' is defined as 'bound or obligated in law or equity; responsible; answerable.' "[7] Liability then "includes responsibility for torts, and 'is applicable to all actions at law not specially mentioned in statute[s].' "[8]

B. *At Fault — At Peril*

The basis for tort liability has been acting either "at fault" or "at one's peril." How these have varied in prominence and interpretation will be noted presently.

1. *At fault.* Some torts, like crimes, are wrongs done intentionally. I intentionally assault my neighbor. Because I knowingly and willingly direct myself to do this overt act in these circumstances, it is uniquely related to me. I and not any other person have initiated the overt act. I caused it. " 'Caused . . . has been employed as synonymous with contributed, or occasioned, and as equivalent to initiated.' "[9] Since I caused it, it is *my* act. Hence whatever evil there is about it, is imputable to me. I am responsible. I am liable.

It is because some torts are wrongs knowingly and intentionally done, that committing them is a fault. ". . . [F]ault . . . must

---

[5] Osborne v. McMasters, 40 Minn. 103, 41 N.W. 543, 544, 12 Am. St. Rep. 698 (1889).

[6] Breslaw v. Rightmire, 119 Misc. 833, 196 N.Y.S. 539 (1922).

[7] State v. Albert, 125 Me. 325, 133 Atl. 693, 694 (1926). See also Homan v. Employers Reinsurance Corp., 345 Mo. 650, 136 S.W.2d 289, 298 (1939).

[8] Italiani v. Metro-Goldwyn-Mayer Corp., 45 Cal. App. 2d 464, 114 P.2d 370, 372 (1941). See also Mayfield v. First National Bank of Chattanooga, 137 F.2d 1013, 1019 (6th Cir. 1943); Eberhard v. Aetna Insurance Co., 134 Misc. 386, 235 N.Y.S. 445, 448 (1928).

[9] Hill v. Montgomery, 352 Mo. 147, 176 S.W.2d 284, 287 (1943).

be taken as having application only to willful, deliberate and intentional acts or to negligence, so gross as in law to amount to willfulness and intention." [10] "The term 'fault' has the meaning of bad faith or mismanagement, neglect of duty, or a deviation from prudence, rectitude or duty." [11] "Fault means wrongful act or default." [12] To be at fault is to be culpable,[13] and to be culpable is to be blameworthy. "Culpable means that which is deserving of moral blame." [14] "The word 'culpable' is not objectionable in the sense of . . . 'blamable.' " [15]

Other torts may be wrongs, not directly intended like assault, but for which the tortfeasor is nevertheless culpable because of his negligence. The owner of a painters' scaffold is liable for damages resulting from his neglect to keep the ropes in fit condition. "Actionable negligence consists in the neglect of the use of ordinary care or skill towards a person to whom the defendant owes the duty of observing ordinary care and skill, by which neglect the plaintiff, without contributory negligence on his part, has suffered injury to his person or property." [16]

One who is negligent is "at fault." "[F]ault in legal literature is the equivalent of negligence." [17] "If the defendant was negligent, as contemplated, then . . . [his act] was certainly culpable, — i.e., 'blamable.' " [18]

2. *At peril.* There are other torts that are wrongs, not because the overt act in its circumstances is necessarily wrong, but because of a harm that will eventuate as a result of the act. Hazardous enterprises in general are a source of this type of tort. The keeping of wild animals, the escape of dangerous substances, and the pursuit of inherently precarious undertakings are activities of this nature.

The keeper of a bear is responsible for any harm the animal may do, because in engaging in this occupation the keeper "takes the risk" involved.[19] Those who maintain a water reservoir are

[10] Continental Insurance Co. v. Sabine Towing Co., 117 F.2d 694, 697 (5th Cir. 1941).

[11] Continental Oil Co. v. Horsey, 175 Md. 609, 3 A.2d 476, 477 (1939).

[12] Cochrane v. Forbes, 257 Mass. 135, 153 N.E. 566, 570 (1926).

[13] The Latin word for fault is "culpa."

[14] Mercury Motor Transport v. State ex rel. Motor Vehicle Commissioner, 197 Miss. 387, 21 So.2d 25, 28 (1945).

[15] Peoria and Pekin Union R.R. Co. v. Clayberg, 107 Ill. 644, 651 (1883).

[16] Heaven v. Pender, L.R. 11 Q.B.D. 503, 507 (1883).

[17] Continental Ins. Co. v. Sabine Towing Co., 117 F.2d 694, 697 (1941).

[18] Peoria and Pekin Union R.R. Co. v. Clayberg, 107 Ill. 644, 651 (1883).

[19] Bottcher v. Buck, 265 Mass. 4, 163 N.E. 182, 183 (1928). See also City of Tonkawa v. Danielson, 166 Okla. 241, 27 P.2d 348, 349 (1933); Panorama Resort v. Nichols, 165 Va. 289, 182 S.E. 235, 238 (1935).

"prima facie answerable" for damage done by escaping waters, because in engaging in such an enterprise they act "at their peril." [20] One who engages in blasting operations is also "responsible" for damage done to adjoining property regardless of care exercised.[21]

In view of the fact that these overt acts in their circumstances are good and not evil — otherwise no one could be allowed to engage in them — they are blameless and without fault. Liability for such acts is logically called liability "without fault." Since this liability is not related to fault, it has also been termed "absolute liability." Because it is incurred regardless of intent and negligence, it is also known as "strict liability." The grounds for liability for such acts, therefore, must be something besides fault. Of late years this ground has been said to be the defendant's "ability to pay." This will be adverted to presently.

3. *Historical development.* The growth of tort liability has been marked by the prominence of first one basis of liability and then the other. The earlier periods of torts were characterized, it is generally thought, by liability from acting at one's peril. Whether or not fault was present on account of wrongful intention or negligence, the doer of a deed was considered responsible simply because he did it.[22]

Reaction to the inequities brought about by this disregard of intention and negligence caused a swing to fault as the decisive factor in tort liability.[23] "No liability without fault" was the guiding norm.[24] If the defendant was held liable, it was because he was at fault.

What with the growth of modern enterprise, however, intention and negligence have been hard to prove. Hence, there has been a shift back to liability without fault.

Whether liability based on acting at one's peril, then liability because of fault, and again liability from acting at peril have succeeded one another as clean cut historical periods and over how long a time, is not entirely certain. It has been maintained that the succession is one of recurring cycles.[25] It is possible that more extensive research into the entire history of this matter would reveal that liability without fault and liability with fault

[20] Fletcher v. Rylands, L.R. 1 Ex. 265, 279 (1866).
[21] Colton v. Onderdonck, 69 Cal. 155, 10 Pac. 395, 397 (1886). See also Madsen v. East Jordan Irrigation Co., 101 Utah 552, 125 Pac. 794 (1942).
[22] Harris, Liability Without Fault, 6 Tulane L. Rev. 337, 343-348 (1932).
[23] Ibid.
[24] See Brown v. Kendall, 6 Cush. 292, 298 (Mass. 1850).
[25] Isaacs, Fault and Liability, 31 Harv. L. Rev. 954-979 (1918).

have always been present together in the same period, but with now one, now the other receiving the emphasis when practicable.[26] What is certain, though, is that the interpretation of liability without fault as able-to-pay liability is of recent origin.

III. PROBLEM

In torts, then, there are three kinds of liability but they do not rest on one and the same grounds. Liability for intended harms and liability for harms that are unintended but blameworthy because of negligence are based on fault. Liability for the harms that are not intended and regarding which there is no negligence as happens in dangerous enterprises, rests on grounds that are without fault. Is such a double standard of liability admissible?

This problem touches the very nerve of tort liability. "It is a practical question of the first importance, as well as a theoretical question of interest, whether we are to generalize our whole system of tort liability by means of one principle of liability for fault and for fault only . . . or on the other hand, are to admit another source of delictual liability alongside of fault. . . . For in our law as it stands one may perceive readily three types of delictual liability: Liability for intentional harm, liability for unintentional culpable harm, liability in certain cases for unintended non-culpable harm. The first two comport with the doctrine of no liability without fault. The third cannot be fitted thereto. We must either brand cases of the third type as historical anomalies, of which we are gradually to rid ourselves, or else revise our notions of tort liability." [27]

But compounding an already difficult problem is the added factor of the interpretation put on liability without fault. For if liability without fault is to be taken to mean "able-to-bear" liability as it has in recent years, then the inconsistency of tort liability is still greater. One part rests on the personal factor of fault, the other on the impersonal factor of resources. The problem is the issue between personal and impersonal liability. ". . . [T]o oversimplify: are there situations in which society today is better served if certain kinds of conduct involve legal liability, absolutely, and without regard to moral fault, or is our society, as at present constituted, better served by a system and theory of

[26] See Winfield, The Myth of Absolute Liability, 42 L.Q. Rev. 37 (1926).
[27] Pound, Introduction to the Philosophy of Law 84-85 (1954). By permission of the Yale University Press.

legal responsibility which is personal and moral in its implications?" [28]

This is no quest of consistency merely for consistency's sake — jewel though it be. It is the search for a basis of responsibility which, when applied to other areas of torts and crimes, will result in the distinction between tortfeasor and non-tortfeasor, between criminal and non-criminal remaining intact. Although strict liability at the present time is confined to limited areas, the possibility of its being extended to others in the future warrants its examination here.

IV. SOLUTION

Preliminary to finding a consistent base for tort liability, a misconception must be cleared away. This regards the value of the phrase assumed in torts, "No liability without fault."

A. *Misapplication of Axiom from Crimes*

This phrase seems to be a misapplication in torts of the axiom in crimes, "Nulla poena sine culpa," that is, no punishment without fault. Such a principle is valid in crimes where by definition the overt act in its circumstances is evil and its commission is necessarily a fault. Hence, no man should be punished if he is not guilty of a fault. In torts, however, the situation is different. The word "wrong" or "harm" is here used analogously. In one meaning it refers, not to overt acts that are culpable, but to harms resulting from these non-culpable acts. Hence, a broader base than "fault" for liability in torts must be found if its explanation is to be consistent.

B. *Intended Acts and Responsibility*

The solution to this problem lies in adopting the same ultimate basis for liability in torts as is the basis of responsibility in crimes. The ultimate basis for responsibility in crimes is the criminal's *knowing intention* to do a certain overt act that in its circumstances is evil. His knowing decision makes the act his and the responsibility for it his.

So also in torts the basis for the three kinds of liability is the fact that the tortfeasor knowingly intends either to harm some one directly, or to be negligent, or to engage in a riskful enterprise for

[28] Bohlen and Harper, Cases on the Law of Torts 1 (5th ed. 1953).

the results of which he assumes responsibility.[29]   In the first two instances he intends to do something that is a fault.   In the last instance he intends to do something that is not a fault, true enough, but he also intends to assume risk and responsibility for any damages that may follow.

In a word, although absolute or strict liability is liability without fault, it is not liability without knowing intention.   On this point turns the solution to the problem of tort liability.[30]

C.   Overt Acts with Harmful Consequences

Important in understanding liability for actions done "at peril" and without fault wherein the doer intends to assume responsibility for the risk is a recognition of the nature of overt acts that have a double consequence — one good, one evil.

Justification for doing an overt act that may or may not have a harmful consequence is found in the specification of human actions as noted above.   If the circumstances of an overt act render it evil, it is illicit to do it whether it be a tort or a crime.   Such would be assault and battery or robbery-murder.   If the circumstances make the overt act not evil but good, it is licit to do it. Killing in self-defense is an example.   At times the circumstance of "consequences" may be determinative.   A known homicidal tendency in a man when he is drunk, makes his drinking seriously wrong.

1.   Double consequences in crimes.   Sometimes overt acts have a double consequence, one good and one evil.   Surgery is indicated in the case of carcinoma of the cervix of a gravid uterus. The fetus is not viable, that is, old enough to live outside the

[29] In moral philosophy a person is responsible for the consequences of his negligent act if he *actually foresees* that harmful consequences may follow therefrom.   In tort law a person is legally responsible if, in these circumstances, the ordinary reasonable man *could have foreseen* that such consequences could or would follow.   In other words, imputability for negligence is wider in law than in moral philosophy.   See the principle of "double consequence" below.

[30] The notion is not uncommon that individual fault and liability must be based on a theory of the "autonomy of the will," and since this theory has been discredited the only alternative to individual liability is social or strict liability.   See Takayanagi, Liability Without Fault in the Modern Civil and Common Law, 16 Ill. L. Rev. 163-173, 268-303 (1921); 17 Ill. L. Rev. 187-210, 416-439 (1922).   See also Feezer, Capacity to Bear Loss as a Factor in the Decision of Certain Types of Tort Cases, 78 U. of Pa. L. Rev. 805-841 (1930); 79 U. of Pa. L. Rev. 742-767 (1931).   However, as exemplified in this book, the alternative to an "autonomy of the will" theory is not positivistic socialism, but rather a philosophy of life in which knowledge and free decision guide the responsible choice of means to end.

uterus. Two consequences will result from the operation. The good one is the excision of the cancer, the bad one is the loss of the fetus. Will the circumstance of one evil consequence render the overt act of surgery evil, even though there is another consequence that is good? The solution will depend on whether one consequence outweighs the other and therefore will be preponderant in determining the goodness or badness of the overt act, and also whether the evil consequence is the means of obtaining the good one.

In the present case, the evil consequence of losing the fetus does not outweigh the good consequence of saving the mother's life; hence the overt act of surgery is good and licit. Nor is the mother's life saved through the killing of the fetus. It is saved by the excision of the cancer. The excision of the cancer and the expulsion of the fetus follow independently of each from the one overt act of surgery. It is taken for granted, of course, that the intention of the surgeon is to save the mother's life. Otherwise his action would be illicit.

On the other hand, if this proportionate balance is lacking or if the good consequence is attained by means of the evil consequence, the overt act of surgery becomes evil. Such is the situation when an unmarried girl has an abortion performed to save her reputation. The overt act of surgery has two consequences: the good one of saving her reputation and the evil one of killing the child. But the good of saving her reputation is accomplished by the evil of directly killing the child. There is no pathology present to which the surgery can be directed. This makes the overt act of surgery evil. The end does not justify the means regardless of what the intention of the surgeon may be. This overt act is recognized as evil in criminal law and is the crime of abortion.

2. *Double consequences in torts.* In torts somewhat similar situations can arise, with the added factor of possible cause for damages. In a case of menorrhagia the physician may feel that irradiation of the ovaries is indicated, with the result that the girl is rendered sterile. In the contractual relation between the patient and the physician, the patient implicitly consents to the administration of whatever therapy the physician thinks is indicated. This fact and the fact that he will apprize the patient of possible injurious side effects and the risk involved before acting, takes his act out of the category of acting at his peril and of assuming responsibility for possible harm.

But in the conduct of dangerous pursuits, say blasting, there is no such contractual agreement. In such situations there is intent to act at peril and assume responsibility. There is no question of the overt act being evil, because if it were no one would ever be permitted to blast. Nor is there question of the bad consequence rendering the overt act evil. First of all, the injurious consequence may never occur. Secondly, the good result of the blasting, opening the way for a road, does not come through its evil result, the destruction of adjacent property. Both result from the blasting independently of each other. Thirdly, there is a proportionate reason for running the risk.

This pattern (overt act with double consequence) of evaluating fact situations (more commonly known as the principle of the double effect) has not been as operative in tort thinking as it should be. For it furnishes the rationale for liability without fault understood as including intention to assume responsibility.

3. *Consistent basis.* The consistent basis for responsibility for both crimes and torts, then, is the knowing intention of a man to do a certain thing. This may be an overt act which in its circumstances is wrong and bad, whether a tort or a crime. The doer of such an act is responsible for a blameworthy act. He is at fault and therefore liable for the consequences. Or it may be an overt act which in its circumstances is right and good but which has one consequence advantageous to the enterpriser and another consequence injurious to others. The doer of such an act is not at fault since the overt act is not evil or wrong, but he is liable for damages inflicted on others because he initially assumed responsibility for them, when he decided to engage in this enterprise at his peril.[31]

Since in human activities men knowingly intend to act either at fault or at peril it is not surprising to find these two aspects of intended overt acts in the development of tort law — when the tortfeasor is at fault and when he is acting at his peril. This is but a manifestation of men's natural instinct to judge that a man is responsible and liable for the actions he intentionally causes whether this be because he intended to do what was blameworthy or simply because he intended to do what he did, blameless though he be but responsible for the results.

[31] It would seem that even the man given to sleepwalking or epileptic fits, once he knows he is subject to such eccentricities, leads his life at the peril of their taking place and therefore assumes responsibility for whatever damage he may cause while in these states — even if there is no provable negligence.

D. *Absolute Liability Implies Assumed Responsibility*

The interpretation of liability without fault, that is, absolute or strict liability, as implying assumed responsibility is the tenor of many courts' dicta. "The very essence of fairness seems to suggest that if one, in order to obtain a certain type of use or enjoyment of his own property, is compelled to blast, he must, as part of the cost of such use or enjoyment, pay the damages he causes to his innocent neighbor. . . . It is conceded that the rule of absolute liability prevails when one uses explosives and the blasting of said explosives results in hurling of rock, earth or debris which causes injury to another." [32]

Disclaimers of liability and negligence in riskful enterprises is further evidence that those who engage in them are considered to assume responsibility for whatever damages ensue from their activities.[33]

1. *Rylands v. Fletcher.* In fact, assumed responsibility, and not liability without fault much less able-to-pay liability, is what is contained in the case that is supposed to be its fountainhead, and is controlling in many jurisdictions.

a. *At peril.* *Rylands v. Fletcher* is the well-known case of escaping waters wherein the defendant was held liable, not because he was negligent or at fault but because he acted at his peril. The court speaks of the defendant as being "prima facie answerable for all the damage" because he acted "at his peril." This controlling factor of "at peril" is repeated in the final confirming opinion. ". . . [If] the defendants, not stopping at the natural use of their close, had desired to use it for any purpose which I may term a non-natural use, for the purpose of introducing into the close that which in its natural condition was not in or upon it, for the purpose of introducing water either above or below ground in quantities and in a manner not the result of any work or operation on or under the land; and if in consequence of their doing so, or in consequence of any imperfection in the mode of their doing so, the water came to escape and to pass off into the close of the plaintiff, then it appears to me that that which the defendants

[32] Madsen v. East Jordan Irrigation Co., 101 Utah 552, 125 P.2d 794, 795, 796 (1942).

[33] Prosser, Law of Torts 303 (2d ed. 1955). On the position that liability should not be absolute but should be related to negligence see Plant, Strict Liability of Manufacturers for Injuries Caused by Defects in Products — An Opposing View, 24 Tenn. L. Rev. 938-951 (1957).

were doing they were doing *at their own peril;* and, if in the course of their doing it, the evil arose to which I have referred, the evil, namely, of the escape of the water and its passing away to the close of the plaintiff and injuring the plaintiff, then for the consequence of that, in my opinion, the defendants would be liable." [34] Not once does the idea of liability without fault or ability to pay appear in these opinions.[35]

b. *Assumed responsibility.* It is now conceded that the principle of law expressed in *Rylands v. Fletcher* and similar cases is assumed responsibility. "The principle of law behind all these cases is, it is submitted, that if a man takes a risk, which he ought not to take without also taking upon his own shoulders the consequences of that risk, he shall pay for any damage that ensues. . . . In every case the question really is: Was the risk one which the defendant was entitled to take only on condition of paying compensation to those injured thereby irrespective of any negligence on his part? And the answer to that question will not depend upon whether the thing in question was dangerous *per se,* but upon whether it was dangerous in the circumstances of the particular case." [36]

The evidence shows that liability without fault originated, not in England, but in America. It may be commented that it is not without significance that the reputed originator of liability without fault, if so he be, is on record as the proponent of a non-moral basis for torts as well as crimes.[37]

[34] Rylands v. Fletcher, L.R. 3 H.L. 330 (1868). (Emphasis added.)

[35] "One phrase which has clung to the doctrine of Rylands v. Fletcher, enshrouded it in darkness and tended to some considerable extent to cast it into discredit, is 'liability without fault.' No such phrase or idea is to be found anywhere in the three opinions in the original case; nor can I find it in any subsequent English decision, or in any discussion by any English writer. They have said that the defendant acts at his peril, and that he is liable without proof of negligence in the manner in which the act is done, but they have not said that he is not at fault in doing the act at all. On the contrary, the repeated emphasis upon the extraordinary, abnormal, unnatural, inappropriate and tortious character of the activity and the undue danger to its surroundings seems to make it fairly clear that, although it is not called negligence, fault of some kind is very definitely there." Prosser, Law of Torts 179 (2d ed. 1955). By permission of the West Publishing Company. According to our analysis, it is not correct to say "fault of some kind is definitely there." Rather, liability for damage is there based on assumed responsibility. Assumed responsibility is not fault.

[36] Stallybrass, Dangerous Things and the Non-Natural User of Land, 3 Camb. L.J. 376, 387 (1929).

[37] Mr. Justice Holmes is the man at whom the finger of suspicion has been pointed. Prosser, Selected Topics on the Law of Torts 179-180 (1953). In 1881 Holmes was saying that ". . . in the main the law started from those intentional wrongs which are the simplest and most pronounced cases . . .

2. *Able-to-bear liability.* The alternative to interpreting absolute liability as implying intended responsibility is to read into it liability assessed on the grounds of ability to bear the loss. Such an interpretation is of relatively recent origin.

Since the Industrial Revolution and the prevalence of the machine, new and varied harms have occurred and in proportionately increasing numbers. These injuries to men have become as inevitable as breakage of machines. Intent and negligence in many cases are either absent or hard to prove. If liability without fault is feasible, it has been reasoned, the enterpriser is the obvious one better able to bear the loss. He can spread it over price increases or cover it by insurance. The tendency of courts has been to make those strictly liable who are best able to pay. In a case of flooding from broken water mains, it was held that "even though negligence be absent, natural justice would seem to demand that the enterprise, or what really is the same thing, the whole community benefited by the enterprise, should stand the loss rather than the individual. It is too heavy a burden upon one. The trend of modern legislation is to relieve the individual from the mischance of business or industry without regard to its being caused by negligence. Our safety appliance acts and workmen's compensation acts are examples." [38]

This tendency to interpret liability without fault as meaning best-able-to-bear liability is said to be justified on the basis of a social philosophy that calls for the shifting of liability from individual persons and placing it on society at large. "Until about the close of the nineteenth century, the progress of the law was in the direction of limiting liability in tort to 'fault,' in the sense of a wrongful intent or a departure from a community standard of conduct. Modern law is developing a policy of imposing liability without regard to 'fault,' particularly in cases where the defendant's activity is an unusual one involving abnormal danger to others, even though it is carried on with all possible precautions. The basis of this policy is a social philosophy which places

---

It thus naturally adopted the vocabulary, and in some degree the tests, of morals. But as the law has grown, even when its standards have continued to model themselves upon those of morality, they have necessarily become external, because they have considered, not the actual condition of the particular defendant, but whether his conduct would have been wrong in the fair average member of the community, whom he is expected to equal at his peril." Holmes, The Common Law 161-162 (1881). See also Holmes, The Path of the Law, 10 Harv. L. Rev. 457-478 (1897) and Fridman, The Rise and Fall of Rylands v. Fletcher, 34 Can. B. Rev. 810 (1956).

[38] Bridgman-Russell Co. v. City of Duluth, 158 Minn. 509, 511, 197 N.W. 971, 972 (1924).

the burden of the more or less inevitable losses due to a complex civilization upon those best able to bear them, or to shift them to society at large." [39]

a. *Personal problem for lawmen.* Liability based on ability to pay presents a problem of the first magnitude to lawmen who subscribe to a philosophy of human responsibility such as is maintained in this book. Many who are committed to such a philosophy — because of their convictions based either on reasoning or on faith — do not seem to realize the inconsistency that accepting such a basis of responsibility introduces into their own lives. The lawman who is convinced that he himself is a knowing and freely deciding being; that he is responsible for his own actions as he believes his family and his friends are because they somehow and to some extent cause them; that the ultimate success or failure of his life, as well as of others' lives, turns on this axial point and will be so evaluated; should take a long and hard look at able-to-pay liability before accepting it as a moral and legal principle of responsibility and liability. For, once he accepts it, he will have introduced even into his own life a double standard of morality. Some faults or wrongs will be individual, others will be social;[40] and logically the responsibility for these wrongs will be individual, for others it will be social.

b. *Causal link.* The question is: is a man responsible because of what he has, or because of what he does. According to the analysis of responsibility outlined in this book, a man is responsible for the actions he causes either directly or indirectly. The source of responsibility is found *within* his own person. In able-to-bear liability, the source is not within the person; it is found in something *outside* the person, namely in resources possessed, as in the case of insurance. Able-to-pay liability originates in an economic fact, possessions, which may be completely divorced from the person committing the tort. In a word, the source of this kind of liability is no longer the moral act of a person; it is the non-moral condition of things. Such a justification of liability breaks the link between the doer and the thing done. The causal relation between the actor and what should be his act is broken. Perhaps those who are able to pay should assume responsibility for their enterprises. But this is beside the point. The issue is whether a man is liable simply because he is better able to pay than others.

[39] Prosser, Law of Torts 315 (2d ed. 1955). By permission of the West Publishing Company.
[40] Id. at 16 and 316.

A lawman's convictions about the responsibility for human actions is what it is regardless of whether he is functioning as a private citizen or as a judge or legislator. He cannot admit a double standard if he is to be true to his deepest convictions. Fortunately, the lawman who wishes to be consistent in his principles of responsibility and keep them integrated need not adopt ability-to-pay as a ground of liability. As we have already seen, in all cases of acting at peril and risk there is the element of assumed responsibility.

V. The Difference It Makes

At this point the question may well be asked: what difference does it make whether plaintiff's recovery is based on defendant's assumed responsibility or his ability to pay? The amount of damages awarded would probably be the same in either case. Since this is obviously true, the difference at stake does not necessarily relate to remedy. It goes far beyond this.

One difference it makes has already been mentioned: the inconsistency that the adoption of a non-personal basis of responsibility and liability introduces into the individual lawman's private life as well as into his legal life. The reverberations this principle would cause even regarding his own family and acquaintances is well worth a moment's reflection.

A. Torts and Crimes

But the great difference it makes whether an impersonal basis of responsibility be adopted is the chaotic and blurring effect that its logical extension would have in other areas of torts and throughout crimes. For, if responsibility can be put on an impersonal, economic basis and shifted to society in one segment of torts, why cannot it be extended to others? And if this process is valid, why cannot it be further extended to crimes, since "the general principles of criminal and civil liability are the same." [41]

Such an application has already been made, of course, in Workmen's Compensation Acts and it is being suggested in traffic cases. But why stop there? If intention and negligence can be declared immaterial and responsibility shifted to society in these instances, why can it not be done with regard to all manufactured articles, independent contractors, and various kinds of negligence and trespass?

[41] Holmes, The Common Law 44 (1881).

That such a shift is already present in crimes was noted above. In many types of crimes, especially those of first offenders, the philosophy is flatly expressed that the criminal is not to blame but society is. In such thinking, intent and negligence have already been abandoned as immaterial. The logical consequence has to be that responsibility should be shifted to society.

In fine, if tort liability is handed on to the public and criminal responsibility is passed on to society the already confusing question of responsibility for our actions is worse confounded by the added baffler of whether we or society are responsible for our overt acts. This supposition would lead to a condition in which the majority of the people who lead good lives will have to bear the responsibility of the minority who lead bad lives. This minority, however, because society is ultimately responsible, are actually not bad. At this point the line between good and bad, innocent and guilty becomes hopelessly blurred and indiscernible. In place of the vital difference between who is guilty and who is not, we have the lifeless distinction between who has more and who has less.

A point not to be overlooked in this context is that if men are merely material units of the political economy and not beings endowed with the power of knowing decision, able-to-pay liability makes excellent sense. For in that case to take from the "haves" and give to the "have nots" is but a laudable way of distributing the wealth regardless of how it is done. But if men are more than such economic units, the justice of such a procedure and how it is promoted has to be re-examined.

B. *Workmen's Compensation*

A practical example of the extension of able-to-pay liability is Workmen's Compensation. It is but a step from holding an enterpriser strictly liable for the results of his dangerous activities to holding the employer strictly liable for the injuries sustained by his employees during their work. There is the same justification for the one as for the other.

1. *Origin.* To engage in modern industry means the employment of machines and men. Inevitable in such industrial activity is breakage of machines and injuries to men as noted above. The cost of these, it is said, can best be borne by the employer, who can either spread it over an increase in commodity prices or cover it by insurance and thereby pass it on to the public. The basis of the employer's liability, as workmen's compensation now

stands, is his ability to sustain these losses better than the employee. The advantages of making the employer strictly liable are supposed to be: proper care of injuries and compensation for losses sustained by the worker, avoidance of costly trials at which negligence is difficult to prove, and rendering the employer more apt to take precautions to prevent injurious accidents.

Consideration for the workman as shown in workmen's compensation represents a hard-won and much-deserved victory over the injustices to labor caused by the rigid "freedom of contract" theory which was part of the socio-economics of laissez faire and rugged individualism. Its need is universally recognized. "The fundamental principles of the law of workmen's compensation were unknown to the people and the times that produced our common law. Workmen's compensation is the natural product of necessity. The numerous hazards which accompanied the growth of industry with the development of power-driven machinery antiquated the common law. Need for a new method and means of giving greater protection and security to the worker and his dependents against injury and death occurring in the course of employment gave birth to legislative law. This creature of the legislature with improvements and refinements is now commonly called workmen's compensation." [42]

There have been objections to workmen's compensation on the score that it deprives employers of property without due process of law. But the weight of judicial opinion has not sustained this contention.[43]

2. *Grounds.* Granting the nobility of motive of workmen's compensation (care of the worker) there are still certain factors that demand the lawman's careful consideration. Why should the worker be considered as merely an economic unit in industry whose negligence is immaterial in accident cases? If the employer is to be held liable, must it be solely on an able-to-pay basis? Admitting that negligence, contributory or comparative, may be hard to prove in industrial cases, is there any other ground for even considering the employees' responsibility? Does it make any difference ultimately what answers are given to these questions?

3. *Latent misevaluation.* There is a possibility of latent misevaluation of the human worker in Workmen's Compensation Acts. A warning has been sounded in this regard. "In the series

[42] United Airlines Transport Corp. v. Industrial Commission, 107 Utah 52, 151 P.2d 591, 594 (1944).
[43] Ibid.

of Workmen's Compensation Acts, the workman is conceived as a mere unit of earning capacity, and a being who is not fully responsible in law for his own acts and defaults. Thus, if an accident is due to negligence or default on the part of the workman, his claim for compensation is not affected unless the negligence or default amounts to serious and wilful misconduct. And gross negligence, it seems, does not necessarily amount to serious and wilful misconduct." [44]

4. *Suggestions.* If negligence is the *bête noire* in compensation cases that is difficult to lay hands on and the employer is to be made liable, should his responsibility not be based on assumed responsibility? Although the amount of compensation might be the same whether the employer be held liable because he is able to pay or because he has assumed responsibility, nevertheless it is vital that his liability be justified on correct grounds for the reasons given above. With justification can the employer be said to assume liability. He is the enterpriser who is engaging in a pursuit that undeniably involves conditions dangerous and injurious to the workers. To this extent he is acting at his peril and assuming responsibility. Besides, he is the one who reaps the greater part of the profits and hence is in a position to handle the cost.

On the other hand, is there not a case to be made for the workers' responsibility? The workers' relation to the employer is one of free contract, albeit negotiated ordinarily by a labor union. Workers are not actually in a master-servant status but are declared to be so only by legal fiction. In the ordinary cases of riskful activities the plaintiffs have had no causal part in the activities that resulted in harm to them. In compensation cases, however, the workers as intelligent and free beings, have had a causal part in the occurrence that brought on their injuries, if it was not purely accidental.

Hence, it seems only logical that workers should assume some responsibility for their own injuries. This would imply a balancing of employer and employee responsibility. If this were done, insurance of the workers themselves would be a prerequisite to labor. The cost could be covered by raises in wages and, as now, could be spread over commodity price increases. Better legal representation would be required. Precautionary measures against hazardous working conditions could be the aim of legislation, inspection and even strikes. More careful work could not help but ensue.

[44] O'Sullivan, The Bond of Freedom, 6 Mod. L. Rev. 177, 182 (1943).

5. *Realization of aims.*   It is questionable whether Workmen's Compensation Acts have realized some of the important aims their framers envisioned, such as avoidance of delays and good medical service.   "Two of the most fundamental and important concepts of the framers of our Workmen's Compensation Law in its present amended form — the avoidance of the delays of litigation following industrial accidents which deprive workers of means of subsistence when most needed, and the assurance of skilled and unbiased medical service — have failed of realization." [45]   How widespread this condition may be is uncertain in the absence of statistical evidence.   However, because of known shortcomings of Workmen's Compensation Acts, it does seem that our minds should not be closed to the possibility of further developments regarding the manner in which workmen can be compensated for injuries.

6. *The gain.*   To what extent assumed responsibility balanced between employer and employee would alleviate such conditions is of course a matter of conjecture.   But one thing is certain: such a sharing of responsibility would recognize and dignify the worker as a freely contracting human being.   Workers were at one time in the status of slaves or servants.   They have left that condition in many countries.   But whether their line of progress will continue to be straight away from this status or whether it will become circular and lead them back to it will be determined in large part by the content of law regarding employer-employee relations.

It assuredly is worth remembering that it was through the vigorous advocacy of the freedom and responsibility of the worker over the centuries and through a representation of himself that was unknown in ancient times, that "the unfree class of slave and serf and villein was finally emancipated and in the course of time Everyman was established in dignity and status as a free and responsible person living in the fellowship of a free country." [46]

C. *Insurance Not a Basis of Liability*

As strict liability has become more widespread, insurance has grown in importance as one of its necessary concomitants.   As a ready way of passing ability to pay on to the public, it demands close scrutiny.

[45] Report to the Governor of New York under §8 of the Executive Law, (1944); reprinted in Riesenfeld and Maxwell, Modern Social Legislation 339 (1950).

[46] O'Sullivan, The Bond of Freedom, 6 Modern L. Rev. 177, 182 (1943).

1. *Necessary protection.* It is only good business for the employer or the employee to insure himself against injury and loss, depending on who is going to be held liable. There is nothing morally or legally wrong with a man insuring himself against possible loss. Insurance is simply "a contract 'whereby one party called the "insurer," for a consideration undertakes to pay money or its equivalent, or to do an act valuable to another party called the "insured," or his "beneficiary," upon the happening of the hazard or peril insured against, whereby the party insured or his beneficiary suffers loss or injury.' " [47]

2. *Not a basis of liability.* Insurance becomes a matter of concern in torts, however, when it is taken as an indication of where liability should be located. For the theory of able-to-pay liability most certainly takes dead aim at the insurance carrier.[48] Looked at in this manner, insurance becomes the obvious means of passing loss "on to the public."

To hold a defendant liable merely because he is insured, is open to the same criticism that may be leveled against liability without fault or strict liability when it is construed as able-to-pay liability. Unless assumed responsibility of the defendant be the basis of his liability in cases where there is no fault (even though he has contracted with an insurance company to reimburse him if he has to pay), the non-moral basis of economics is substituted for the moral basis of knowing and free cause. When this is done the intrinsic causal relation between person and responsibility is broken.

Even the most ardent proponents of "social engineering" have come to see the oversetting consequences of able-to-pay liability. ". . . [A] judge of one of our most important courts intimates that the requirement that one who is required to repair a loss must have caused it is artificial and should be abrogated. See what this means. Suppose X determines to commit suicide but wishes to provide for his dependents. He stands at the corner waiting for a bus or heavy truck as the chosen agent of self-destruction. When one comes along he throws himself beneath its wheels and is killed. If causation and fault as prerequisites of liability are eliminated must not the transportation company or trucking company repair the loss to the widow and children?

---

[47] Commissioner of Banking and Insurance v. Community Health Service, 129 N.J.L. 427, 30 A.2d 44, 46 (1943). See also Clardy v. Grand Lodge of Oklahoma, 132 Okla. 165, 269 Pac. 1065, 1066 (1928).

[48] Becker and Huard, Tort Liability and the Atomic Energy Industry, 44 Geo. L.J. 58, 66 (1955).

Thus we achieve high humanitarian purposes by the easy method of using the involuntary Good Samaritan as the Greek playwright used the god from the machine. It may be that we shall call this justice. But the morals are those of Robin Hood or of the pickpocket who was so moved by the eloquence of the preacher of the charity sermon that he picked the pockets of every one in reach and put the contents in the plate." [49]

3. *Loss passed on?* Insurance is looked on as a way of passing loss on to the public. What is implied in this "passing on"? Who is the "public"? Certainly loss is not passed on till we lose it some place, simply because we use a phrase that declares that this is so.

Behind these deceptive words lurks an economic poser that deserves careful inspection. According to this idea, loss is to fall on whomsoever is in a position to pass it on. But in the present organization of governmental agencies it is open to question whether this actually takes place. Agencies work independently of each other. One determines rates, another fixes prices, a third sets wages. Still another assesses damages or compensation. Each works with its own particular interests in mind. In view of this lack of coordination, losses are shifted to the most available bearer. Hence, factually there is little meaning to the phrase that loss is "passed on to the public." "But the deceptive doctrine that we are all of us insuring each of us by imposing loss and damage on an involuntary Good Samaritan makes for growing acceptance of absolute liability." [50]

Although negligence seemingly has been hurled far beyond the pale of materiality by court judgments leveled against defendants simply because they are insured and therefore better riskbearers, nevertheless it comes whirling back boomerang-like when the insurance company penalizes the policyholder for negligence in allowing repeated accidents to occur. In some types of cases, automobile insurance for instance, repeated accidents are followed by higher premiums or cancellation of policies altogether. This could eventually mean insurance costs that are prohibitive.

[49] Pound, Justice According to Law 14 (1951). By permission of the Yale University Press.
[50] Pound, id. at 12-13. See the interesting and informative article by Benson, Preservation of Our System of Administering Justice in Personal Injury Cases, 30 N.Y.S.B.A. Bull. 103-116 (1958). See also Marx, A New Approach to Personal Injury Litigation, 19 Ohio L.J. 278-289 (1958) and Greene, Must We Discard Our Law of Negligence in Personal Injury Cases? 19 Ohio St. L.J. 290-312 (1958).

D. *Boards of Adjustment*

In the complexity of modern living intent and negligence are hard to prove, as mentioned. Cases of industrial and traffic accidents are evidence of this. Backlogs of cases become too great to be handled by existing courts. Hence, in order to expedite recovery for damages, especially from insurance carriers, the tendency is growing to regard intention and negligence as immaterial. But the implications of such thinking should be squarely faced.

To locate intent and negligence pertains to the heart of justice in tortious and criminal actions. If these elements of justice are to be abandoned, the subsequent process by which liability is assessed is not one of justice. Hence, it seems that if a double standard of settling disputes is admitted, the implementation of this double standard should assume a two-fold aspect. Cases in which responsibility is based on knowing intention, negligence or assumed risk are within the realm of justice and should be adjudicated by a court of law. Cases in which liability is based, not on these personal factors, but on the impersonal one of resources are in the area of adjustment and awards should be fixed by a board of adjustment. These boards should be recognized for what they are. Their duty would not be to reach "just" decisions. Their goal would be merely to settle cases by assessing damages, whether these be paid for by the "guilty" party or not.

The creation of such boards functioning alongside of courts of law in an attempt to meet the needs of the times in the United States could seemingly be compared to the former rise of the courts of equity beside the courts of law in England. But there is this disconcerting difference: the courts of equity were in pursuit of justice based on personal responsibility.

VI. Duty to Aid

Duty to aid is another section of torts in which there is a problem to be examined.[51] It arises from the discrepancy between the demands of natural obligation and the provisions of law. Involved here is principally the question of whether or not duty-to-aid pertains to justice and therefore to law.

---

[51] The more logical place to treat duty to aid is, perhaps, under crimes. But because it has been treated under torts in the United States, it is so considered here. Besides, duty to aid does have a tort aspect inasmuch as there may be question of damages or remedy.

A. No-Duty-to-Aid Decisions

Cases in which the defendant was held to have no duty to aid
are numerous. A family physician was held not liable for arbitrarily refusing a call, though he was the only physician available.[52] A defendant who rented a canoe to an intoxicated cus-
tomer was declared to be under no legal obligation to come to his
aid when he overturned and was drowning, even though he could
have done so without danger to himself.[53] A railroad signal
tower operator was declared to be under no duty to a motorist
stalled on a nearby crossing to stop the train that was about to
strike the motorist.[54] The employer of a painter who fainted
and became entangled in a rope was held to be under no duty to
come to his aid. "No legal duty rests upon a person to exercise
any degree of care or diligence to protect another against the
hazards of a perilous situation brought about through no fault of
the former. . . . [H]is employer, who is in control of the premises, is, upon becoming acquainted with the situation, under no
legal duty to exercise any degree of care or diligence to extricate
the hapless man from his perilous condition." [55]

B. Discrepancies Recognized

This difference between the provisions of law in this regard
and the elementary demands of human nature, has been fully perceived. In holding that the failure of railway employees to care
for a trespasser who was injured was not a violation of any legal
duty for which the company was liable, the court in a well-known
railroad case stressed that it was not concerned with what was
merely "humane." "With the humane side of the question courts
are not concerned. It is the omission or negligent discharge of
legal duties only which come within the sphere of judicial cognizance. For withholding relief from the suffering, for failure to
respond to the calls of worthy charity, or for faltering in the
bestowment of brotherly love on the unfortunate, penalties are
found not in the laws of men, but in that higher law, the violation of which is condemned by the voice of conscience, whose sen-

[52] Hurley v. Eddingfield, 156 Ind. 416, 59 N.E. 1058 (1901). See also Ran-
dolph's Administrator v. Snyder, 139 Ky. 159, 129 S.W. 562, 563 (1910).
[53] Osterlind v. Hill, 263 Mass. 73, 160 N.E. 301, 302 (1928).
[54] Toadvine v. Cincinnati, N.O. & T.P.R. Co., 20 F. Supp. 226, 227 (E.D.
Ky. 1937).
[55] Ficken v. Southern Cotton Oil Co., 40 Ga. 841, 151 S.E. 688, 689 (1930).

tence of punishment for the recreant act is swift and sure." [56]

Other decisions admit that statutes decreeing no duty to aid in similar cases are against the "instincts of humanity." "Actionable negligence is the neglect of a legal duty. The defendants are not liable unless they owed to the plaintiff a legal duty which they neglected to perform. With purely moral obligations the law does not deal. For example, the priest and Levite who passed by on the other side were not, it is supposed liable at law for the continued suffering of the man who fell among thieves, which they might, and morally ought to have, prevented or relieved. Suppose A, standing close by a railroad, sees a two-year-old babe on the track, and a car approaching. He can easily rescue the child, with entire safety to himself, and the instincts of humanity require him to do so. If he does not, he may, perhaps, justly be styled a ruthless savage and a moral monster; but he is not liable in damages for the child's injury, or indictable under the statute for its death." [57]

Such decisions surely are revolting to any moral sense. Legal writers have gone to great lengths to stress this point. "The limits of the law on this head seem, however, to be capable of being extended a good deal farther than they seem ever to have been extended hitherto. In particular, in cases where the person is in danger, why should it not be made the duty of every man to save another from mischief, when it can be done without prejudicing himself, as well as to abstain from bringing it on him? This accordingly is the idea pursued in the body of the work. A woman's headdress catches fire: water is at hand: a man, instead of assisting to quench the fire, looks on, and laughs at it. A drunken man, falling with his face downwards into a puddle, is in danger of suffocation: lifting his head a little on one side would save him: another man sees this and lets him lie. A quantity of gunpowder lies scattered about a room: a man is going into it with a lighted candle: another, knowing this, lets him go in without warning. Who is there that in any of these cases would think punishment misapplied?" [58]

C. *Cause of Discrepancies*

The inconsistency between what is demanded by human inclinations and what is decreed by statutes and precedents in duty-

[56] Union Pacific Ry. Co. v. Cappier, 66 Kan. 649, 72 Pac. 281, 282 (1903).
[57] Buch v. Amory Mfg. Co., 69 N.H. 257, 260, 44 Atl. 809, 810 (1898).
[58] Bentham, An Introduction to the Principles of Morals and Legislation, c. 17, XIX, note 1 (Lafleur ed. 1948).

to-aid cases is so striking that an attempt to explain its cause is called for. Why has one been excluded by the other? Two factors seem to be at work in the thinking that concludes in no-duty-to-aid statutes and decisions. One is the preconceived notion that morals have no place in law, which entails a misunderstanding of what is embraced by morals; and the other is the failure to recognize that duty to aid pertains to justice and not merely to love.

1. *Morals in law.* The notion that moral principles have no place in law was given a philosophical setting, as we have seen, by certain philosophers. The idea was embraced in this country by prominent jurists. Many courts, perhaps without examining its possible inconsistencies or caring about the circumstances of its origin,[59] blandly assumed that it represented a "critical" philosophy of law and allowed it to guide their legal thinking.

According to this notion, as we have seen, morals refer to obligation and conscience which originate in the inner necessity of the will of doing what is right and just, simply because it is right and just. The possibility of obligation and conscience being related to the extrinsic necessity of means to end is excluded from consideration. Law, in this theory, is not concerned with obligation and conscience, but only with sanction and punishment.

Courts of this frame of mind have logically eliminated any consideration of moral duty to aid. In a case in which a man and his paramour had been together intoxicated for several days and she took morphine, became unconscious and died, the defendant was found not liable for her death although he had made no attempt to render her aid. The court said: "Seeking for a proper termination of the case at bar by the application of the legal principles involved, we must eliminate from the case all consideration of mere moral obligation and discover whether respondent was under a legal duty. . . . 'In the absence of such [legal] obligations, it is undoubtedly the moral duty of every person to extend to others assistance when in danger . . . and, if such efforts should be omitted by any one when they could be made without imperiling his own life, he would by his conduct draw upon himself the just censure and reproach of good men; but this is the only punishment to which he would be subjected by society.' " [60]

According to our analysis made above, morals must take ac-

[59] "There are Kantians and Hegelians in the world who have never heard of either Kant or Hegel." Radin, The Permanent Problems of Law, in Jurisprudence in Action 444 (1953).

[60] People v. Beardsley, 150 Mich. 206, 113 N.W. 1128, 1131 (1907).

count of things and persons as they are if it is to have a factual basis. Law, obligation, sanction, and conscience take their meaning from the same fact situations and are based thereon. Facts are the obvious point of departure for the average lawman's thinking, unless he has been predisposed to think that facts and a knowledge of them are beyond his reach. Morals, therefore, are concerned with the goodness and badness, rightness and wrongness, justice and injustice of the same human actions that law is. These actions are just or unjust on the same basis of a means-end relation.

2. *Duty: In justice — In love.* The other factor that seems to have contributed to the legal thinking behind no-duty-to-aid decisions, is the failure to distinguish between what is due in justice and what is due in love.

Justice, as defined above, is the habit of will that disposes a man to give to others what is their due. What is due or owed is decided, not arbitrarily, but by the existence of certain facts. Thus others owe me respect for what is mine; a contract specifies what one man owes another; the needs of the people determine what all owe to each other and should contribute to the common good. The demands of justice are impersonal inasmuch as its determining norm applies to all without favor. Justice typically is blindfolded when her scales are being balanced.

Love, on the other hand, is also a habit of the will but it is one that disposes one person to be united to another as noted above. Love admits of degrees. To speak of something "due" or "owed" on account of love, would be to use the words analogously if not equivocally. There is no objective norm for what is due in love as there is in justice. What is owed in love is limited only by the degree of love of the lover for the one loved, and vice versa in reciprocation. Even life itself may be given by a man simply because he loves someone.

The demands of love, then, are personal and not impersonal as is the case in justice. But like justice, love can exist only between two persons and "love" of things is, strictly speaking, a euphemism.

D. *Duty to Aid Is a Matter of Justice*

What of a man's duty to aid in cases where another's life is in peril and aid can be given without danger or great inconvenience? Even prescinding from cases of employer-employee relations, trespass, negligence, and the like, the duty to aid another human being in the above circumstances is one of justice. It is not a matter of love only — brotherly or otherwise, natural or supernatural.

Men live in political society in order to obtain their common good of peace and security. Consequently, as already observed, each member has an obligation in justice — in contributive justice — to cooperate in the attainment of this end. Basic in the pursuit of peace and security is the preservation of life. This is, in fact, one of the elemental reasons why men live in the society of other men. The degree and kind of actual cooperation that may be needed in the preservation of other men's lives, insofar as it has a public aspect about it, is ordinarily provided for by statutes and decisions. The security of a member of society who is in danger of death, however, which can be contributed to by a fellow member aiding him at no great cost to himself, certainly seems to be one of the "common necessities" to which "each member shall contribute his share." [61] Hence the duty to aid another under such conditions would seem to be one of justice and therefore proper matter for law.[62]

[61] Mott v. Pennsylvania R.R. Co., 30 Pa. 9, 35 (1858).

[62] In moral philosophy and moral theology, aiding another in danger of death has been emphasized as a duty in love more than it has as a duty in justice. As a duty in love it is said that ". . . in extreme spiritual necessity we must assist our neighbor even at the risk of our life. . . . In extreme temporal necessity our neighbor must be helped even at our great personal inconvenience, but not at the risk of our life, unless our position or the common welfare demand the safety of the threatened party." Jone, Moral Theology 80 (Adelman trans. rev. ed. 1955).

It is considered to be a duty in justice, on the other hand, to give another in extreme need whatever of my goods is necessary to save his life. Because of his perilous condition he has a natural claim to this aid, the correlative of which is my duty to give it. "One may take the property of another without being guilty of moral fault . . . in the case of extreme necessity. . . . Necessity is extreme when life is in danger or some comparable evil is imminent, and the person in need cannot extricate himself from it unaided. A person in such necessity may take as much of the goods of another as will relieve present need, unless that other is in a like necessity. In such need, the goods of the earth are common property; rights of exclusive private ownership lapse; there is, in fact, an obligation to preserve life, which is a higher good than property." (2 Davis, Moral and Pastoral Theology 310-311 (4th ed. 1943).)

But by the same token there would seem to be a duty in justice to aid such a man in other ways. If there is a duty to aid by giving him some of my property, it is only reasonable that there is also a duty in justice to aid him by rendering whatever other forms of aid I can — without great inconvenience to myself — that will save him from possible death. There are indications that thinking in this regard is swinging toward recognizing such a duty as one in justice. "In grave spiritual or temporal need our neighbor must be helped in as far as this is possible without a serious inconvenience to ourselves. Position, *justice,* or piety may oblige one to make such a sacrifice." Jone, Moral Theology 80 (Adelman trans. rev. ed. 1955) (emphasis added).

An aspect of the common good that is accomplished by recognizing legally the natural duty to aid, besides the actual help of those in distress, is the assurance of mind that results from the realization that aid will be forthcoming in case of accident or disaster. No little part does this confidence play, for instance, in the esprit de corps of branches of the armed services. Certainty that every effort will be made to aid those in distress, such as a plane down at sea, creates an assured attitude in the members at large toward the pursuit of their objective. Such an assurance in the mind of the citizenry in general regarding civic duty to aid is a distinct need in the hazardous living of modern society.

It is possible that I may aid another person because I know him personally and love him. Or it may also happen I believe that "whoever does it to the least of these, does it to Me" and I aid another for the love of God. Laudable and meritorious though these reasons for aiding be, they are not the reason why statutes and decisions should recognize this duty. This reason is, to repeat, because it is a matter of contributive justice.[63]

It is true that law and the courts do not have to enforce all natural obligations in order that the common good of peace and security be promoted. But the natural obligation to aid others in mortal danger is so closely related to the very elementary purpose of social living — the preservation of life — that it is one natural obligation that still stands in need of legal acknowledgment and enforcement in this country.

E. *Recognition of Natural Duty to Aid*

The law is beginning to recognize natural duty to aid and that the existence of natural duty produces a legal effect even though it is not legally required.

1. *United States.* The failure of railroad employees to aid a man struck by an engine was declared to be against "the laws of humanity." "We are next brought to the question whether the defendant be liable for the negligence of its agents in their treatment and disposition of the deceased subsequent to the collision.

---

[63] The incident of the man who was robbed and beaten and who was ignored by the priest and the Levite and helped only by the Samaritan (10 Luke 30-37), it must be remembered, was used by Christ primarily to show the Jews that their neighbors were not only those who were faithful Jews but also all other men — any man. Christ was saying that all men are "our neighbors absolutely. For these are closely related to us by the sharing of the same human life." The relation of neighbor "is reckoned from nature, not from virtue, substance, dignity, compassion or place." Cornelius à Lapide, 8 Comment. in Script. Sacram 749, 751 (1875) (my trans.).

This we think free from doubt or difficulty. From whatever cause the collision occurred, after the train was stopped the injured man was found upon the pilot of the defendant's engine in a helpless and insensible condition, and it thereupon at once became the duty of the agents in charge of the train to remove him, and to do it with a proper regard to his safety and the laws of humanity, and if in removing and locking up the unfortunate man, though apparently dead, negligence was committed, whereby the death was caused, there is no principle of reason or justice upon which the defendant can be exonerated from responsibility. To contend that the agents were not acting in the course of their employment in so removing and disposing of the party is to contend that the duty of the defendant extended no further than to have cast off by the wayside the helpless and apparently dead man, without taking care to ascertain whether he was dead or alive, or if alive, whether his life could be saved by reasonable assistance timely rendered. For such a rule of restricted responsiblity no authority has been produced, and we apprehend none can be found. On the contrary, it is the settled policy of the law 'to give such agents and servants a large and liberal discretion, and hold the companies liable for all their acts, within the most extensive range of their charter powers.' " [64]

In a similar case involving injury on a railroad the court spoke of the requirements of "common humanity." "This being true, they owed him one of two alternative duties — either to see him safely out of the yard, which common humanity required, or, failing in this, to watch out for him as the engine was moved about in the corporation's business. . . . Under these circumstances, we think they, after having discovered his perilous condition, owed him the duty of refraining from injuring him by exercising the care for his safety which we have indicated." [65]

A cattleman, who forced a desperately ill guest to leave his home in extreme cold with the consequence that the plaintiff was severely frozen, was found to have acted against the demands of "humanity." "In the case at bar defendants were under no contract obligation to minister to the plaintiff in his distress; but humanity demanded that they do so, if they understood and appreciated his condition. And though these acts which humanity demands are not always legal obligations, the rule to which we have adverted applied to the relation existing between these

[64] Northern Central Ry. v. State, 29 Md. 420, 96 Am. Dec. 545, 552 (1868).
[65] Cincinnati, N.O. & T.P. Ry. Co. v. Marrs, 27 Ky. L. Rep. 388, 85 S.W. 188, 189, 190 (1905).

parties on this occasion and protected plaintiff from acts at their hands that would expose him to personal harm. He was not a trespasser upon their premises, but on the contrary, was there by the express invitation of Flateau, Sr. He was taken suddenly ill while their guest, and the law, as well as humanity, required that he be not exposed in his helpless condition to the merciless elements." [66]

Even where there is no previous relation such as mentioned in the above cases, defendants have been held liable for not rendering aid. Such is the maritime duty to rescue anyone found in distress at sea. ". . . [T]he master or person in charge of a vessel shall, so far as he can do so without serious danger to his own vessel, crew, or passengers, render assistance to every person who is found at sea in danger of being lost; and if he fails to do so, he shall, upon conviction, be liable to a penalty of not exceeding $1,000 or imprisonment for a term not exceeding two years, or both." [67]

Hit and run statutes and decisions, although pertaining to the driver who caused the injury and not to another driver who happens to be passing by, are becoming prevalent examples of the incorporation of natural and moral duty into legal duty to aid. Negligence in these cases is prima facie. "The conduct of a hit and run driver of an automobile in failing to stop and give his name, etc., and render assistance to the person injured by him in the operation of his automobile along a public highway may, in that it is in violation of a statute . . . , be regarded as negligence as a matter of law. Although when taken alone, such conduct may have no causal connection with the act which caused the injuries, the conduct of the driver in hitting, running, and failing to stop, etc., is a circumstance which may be considered, in connection with his other acts preceding the injury, as tending to establish his conduct in causing the injury as being negligence." [68]

Drivers are under duty to give aid even though they are not responsible for the accident. ". . . [T]he Vehicle Code requires an automobile driver who injures another to stop and render aid. This duty is imposed upon the driver whether or not he is responsible for the accident, and a violation gives rise to civil liability if it is a proximate cause of further injury or death. . . . Failure to stop and render aid constitutes negligence as a matter of

[66] Depue v. Flateau, 100 Minn. 299, 111 N.W. 1, 3 (1907).

[67] 37 Stat. 242 (1912), 46 U.S.C. §728. See Warshauer v. Salbaudo, 71 F.2d 146, 148 (2d Cir. 1934).

[68] Battle v. Kilcrease, 54 Ga. App. 808, 189 S.E. 573 (1936). See also Hallman v. Cushman, 196 S.C. 402, 13 S.E.2d 498, 500 (1941).

law, in the absence of a legally sufficient excuse or justification." [69]

2. *Continental Europe.* The natural, moral duty to aid has for some time been incorporated into law in Continental Europe. For instance in Holland the law provides that "One who, witnessing the danger of death with which another is suddenly threatened, neglects to give or furnish him such assistance as he can give or procure without reasonable fear of danger to himself or to others, is to be punished, if the death of the person in distress follows, by a detention of three months at most and an amends of three hundred florins at most." [70] France has a similar statute decreeing that "Whoever abstains voluntarily from giving such aid to a person in peril that he would have been able to give him without risk to himself or to third persons by his personal action or by calling for help . . ." shall be punished by imprisonment of a month to three years or a fine.[71] Other countries also show a trend in this direction.[72]

3. *The future of duty to aid.* Unquestionably the natural duty to aid is being recognized legally more and more. There is a definite trend to incorporate into law the duty in justice of every citizen to aid anyone he knows is in great danger of serious injury or of death, providing this can be done with no great inconvenience to himself. The legal requirement of this duty is to be hoped for.[73]

[69] Summers v. Dominguez, 29 Cal. App. 308, 84 P.2d 237, 239 (1938). See also Brooks v. Willig Truck Transp. Co., 40 Cal. 2d 669, 255 P.2d 802, 808, 809 (1953).

[70] Dutch Penal Code, Art. 450.

[71] French Penal Code, Art. 63 (1945).

[72] The legal requirement of duty to aid has been adopted, for example, in Russia. The basis for this adoption, however, is entirely different from the one maintained in this book. See Notes, The Failure to Rescue: A Comparative Study, 52 Colum. L. Rev. 631-647 (1952).

[73] "In this growing doctrine of the Common Law, then, we may see a recognition of the fact — which, as I have said, a hundred years ago would probably not have been admitted as a circumstance which the law could safely assume — that, at least where human life is at stake, the impulse to purely altruistic conduct is part of the morality of the average man . . . [I]t seems not at all improbable that some day the law may imperatively require of human nature at least that minimum of altruism which Bentham, and most sensible persons with him, considered not in excess of the plain man's plain duty." Allen, Legal Duties 220 (1931).

CHAPTER 16

Property

The root problem in property is to find justification for the concept of ownership that is presupposed by man-made law in one half of the world and which is completely rejected in the other half. At stake is a lawman's attitude toward property as having both individual and social facets, as well as his understanding of labor's relation to property. The world-wide economic, political and legal implications of this problem should be obvious.

I. CONCEPT OF PROPERTY

Property is a fundamental concept. It is the main anchor to windward of the life and liberty of free men. These three are inextricably bound together. Life without liberty is slavery and the main assurance of liberty is property.

It should be remembered ". . . that of the three fundamental principles which underlie government, and for which government exists, the protection of life, liberty, and property, the chief of these is property; not that any amount of property is more valuable than the life or liberty of the citizen, but the history of civilization proves that, when the citizen is deprived of the free use and enjoyment of his property, anarchy and revolution follow, and life and liberty are without protection."[1] The concept of property in law rests on non-legal assumptions that derive directly from the nature of man.

Property, as we briefly saw,[2] involves many factors: the things, tangible or intangible, that are uniquely related to me and to no one else; the relation of title between these things and myself; others who have the duty to make this relation exclusive; my claim on them to do so; and my resulting freedom to enjoy these things.

A. As a Thing — As a Claim

Property has often been conceived to be either the thing owned or the claim to the thing. " 'Property,' in the strict legal sense,

[1] Children's Hospital v. Adkins, 284 Fed. 613, 622 (D.C. Cir. 1922).
[2] Chapter 3.

is an aggregate of rights which are guaranteed and protected by government. In the ordinary sense, it is used to indicate the thing itself, rather than the rights attached to it. Whether or not we employ the term in one or the other of these senses, the result is the same, so far as the interference with property is concerned; for, while in the former attention is directed to the rights which make up the thing, in the latter the thing which constitutes the aggregation of these rights is emphasized. In both cases the rights attached to the thing are the subject of concern." [3]

Property can have a broad as well as a narrower sense. "The term 'property' is said to be a nomen generalissimum and to include everything . . . corporeal or incorporeal, tangible or intangible, visible or invisible, real or personal; everything that has an exchangeable value, or which goes to make up one's wealth or estate. . . . In a narrower sense, property implies exclusive ownership of things, as where a man owns a piece of land or a horse; in the broader sense, property includes, in the modern legal systems, practically all valuable rights . . . including various incorporeal rights as patents, copyrights, rights of action." [4]

B. *As a Relation of Title*

Because the rights spoken of in describing property usually are "rights attached to a thing," according to the analysis of right made above property is more accurately defined as the relation of title that exists between a thing and myself. It is this that makes the thing "mine" and which may be the object of conveyance. It is because of this relation that I can claim the non-interference of others. Emphasis here is on the fact that the thing is "mine" regardless of its exchange value.

It is in terms of such a relation that property is defined in the Restatement. "The word 'property' is used sometimes to denote the thing with respect to which legal relations between persons exist and sometimes to denote the legal relations. The former of these two usages is illustrated in the expressions 'the property abuts on the highway' and 'the property was destroyed by fire.' This usage does not occur in this Restatement. When it is de-

[3] Fulton Light, Heat and Power Co. v. State, 65 Misc. 263, 121 N.Y. Supp. 536, 553 (1909).

[4] State v. Cowen, 231 Iowa 1117, 3 N.W.2d 176, 180 (1942). On property as referring to "interests" or "estate," see Samet v. Farmers' & Merchants' National Bank, 247 Fed. 669, 671 (4th Cir. 1917); on the inclusiveness of "property" see Felix S. Cohen, Dialogue on Private Property, 9 Rutgers L. Rev. 357-387 (1954); for various judicial definitions of property see Globe Indemnity Co. v. Bruce, 81 F.2d 143, 150 (10th Cir. 1935).

sired to indicate the thing with regard to which legal relations exist, it will be referred to either specifically as 'the land,' 'the automobile,' 'the share of stock,' or, generically, as 'the subject matter of property' or 'the thing.'

"The word 'property' is used in this Restatement to denote legal relations between persons with respect to a thing. The thing may be an object having physical existence or it may be any kind of an intangible such as a patent right or a chose in action." [5]

As noted before, although it may be difficult to determine in many instances what is included under "mine" and what is not, nevertheless comprehended are not only tangible things but such intangibles as ideas. If they are original and concrete enough, they can be the object of a property right.

An idea for a new type of radio program was thus held to be the matter of such a claim. "Originally at common law such a property right did not exist. . . . The law has recognized a qualified property right in trade secrets, and grants injunctive relief against their use or disclosure by a breach of contract or a violation of confidence. It is but one short step further to extend to ideas at least a limited property right. This step has been recently taken. The law now gives effect to a property right in an idea even though the idea may be neither patentable nor subject to copyright. Such a concept, however, in order to receive the protection of the law, must be more than a mere abstraction. It must be reduced to a concrete detailed form. It must, of course, be novel. For the appropriation of such an idea, if it has not been published and thus placed in the public domain, compensation may be recovered either on the theory of a tort, or on the theory of a contract implied in law or quasi-contract." [6]

In other words, if there is a definite object — whether it be tangible as a sea shell or intangible as an idea — between which and myself there is a unique relation of title, it is "my" property. I can lay claim on others' obligation to respect it. This being the case, the so-called "right to freedom," for instance, is not a property right. The "right to freedom" of speech, of vocation, of travel, of worship and the like, rests on a different foundation. My claim on others to be allowed to speak my mind, to engage in the kind of occupation I choose, to go from place to place, to worship as I see fit, is not based on a unique relation of title that I have to these things as a definite object such as is the situation

[5] Restatement of the Law of Property 3 (1936).

[6] Belt v. Hamilton National Bank, 108 F. Supp. 689, 691 (D.D.C. 1952).

regarding a sea shell. They are not definite objects in this sense. They are, rather, modes of action in which I must engage if I am to fulfill the basic demand that I so use my powers of reason and free decision concerning life and property that I progress in my own development and perfection.

In fine, property may refer to the thing owned, to my claim regarding it, or to the relation of title which is the initial link between it and me. Of these three, it is the relation of title that is constitutive of property.

II. TITLES TO THINGS

The result of the process by which a relation is created between a thing and me is, then, a title. Title literally connotes a sign of something. Markers used to indicate boundary limits of claims established in undeveloped territories were titles in this root sense of the word. They were signs that someone had "staked out a claim." They proclaimed that a unique relation had been created between the piece of land and a particular person because it had been first occupied by him.

This rudimentary meaning of title underlies the usual descriptions given of it. "Title is the means whereby the owner of lands has the just possession of his property." [7] " 'Title' is the means by which an estate is acquired." [8] Because of the part played by titles in the justification of "private property," they will be discussed briefly.

A. *Original Titles*

The process by which a relation of title is created may, from the viewpoint of the philosophy of law, presuppose a previous title or it may not. If it does not, it results in a primary or original title. If it does, it results in a secondary or derived title.

1. *Occupancy.* Occupancy is, in the order of time, the first of the original titles. In situations where things are not possessed by anyone, it is an elemental way of establishing ownership. ". . . [A] rule alike ancient and of undoubted merit — that of 'title of occupancy' — [is] as follows: 'Occupancy is the taking possession of those things which before belonged to nobody' and 'whatever movables are found upon the surface of the earth, or in the sea, and are unclaimed by any owner, are supposed to be

[7] Horney v. Price, 189 N.C. 820, 128 S.E. 321, 323 (1925).
[8] Case v. Mortgage Guarantee and Title Co., 52 R.I. 155, 158 Atl. 724, 726 (1932).

abandoned by the last proprietor, and as such are returned into the common stock and mass of things, and therefore they belong, as in a state of nature, to the first occupant or finder.' " [9]

2. *Labor.* Labor is also an original process by which title to things is acquired. It is not original in the same sense as occupation, for labor works on materials that are already possessed by someone. It is, however, truly original in the sense that the laborer, who works on materials owned by another, acquires a title to part of the product without previous possession of any kind.

By labor a relation of title is created between the product and the laborer. Courts have always recognized labor as a title to property. "By the law of nature every person is entitled to the fruit of his own labor and skill." [10] The paramount position of the process of labor (not the contract of labor which is based on the process), as the key to the justification of "private" property, deserves separate analysis which will be made shortly. All the other titles, including occupancy, will be seen to depend ultimately on labor for their validity as titles to property from the standpoint of the philosophy of law.

B. *Derived Titles*

Derived titles to property are, as noted, the result of those processes of creating a relation of ownership that presuppose a previous title to the object under consideration.

1. *Contract of sale.* Contract, especially contract of sale, is the most common and important process of derived titles from the standpoint of the philosophy of law. In the process of contract, it is taken for granted that the thing offered in exchange is something to which the contractor already has title. Along with labor, contracts of buying and selling are the most prevalent ways of creating new relations of property. For, contracts are "the concurrence of two or more persons in a common intent to affect their legal relations." [11] Contracts will be considered at greater length in the next chapter.

2. *Gift inter vivos.* Gift is also a process by which title to things is acquired. "A gift is but the transfer of personal property

[9] Goddard v. Winchell, 86 Iowa 71, 52 N.W. 1124 (1892).

[10] Atwood v. Holcomb, 39 Conn. 270, 274, 12 Am. Rep. 386, 388 (1872). On the relation of the right to work and property see Dorrington v. Manning, 135 Pa. 194, 4 A.2d 886, 890 (1939).

[11] Buffalo Pressed Steel Co. v. Kirwan, 138 Md. 60, 113 Atl. 628, 630 (1921). See also Anson, Principles of the Law of Contracts 10-11 (1939).

made voluntarily and without consideration." [12]   "As a gift is a parting by the owner with his property without pecuniary consideration, the law scrutinizes such transactions very closely, and to establish such a gift there must be a donor competent to make it, and an intention on his part to make it; a donee capable of taking a gift; the gift must be complete with nothing left undone; the property must be delivered by the donor, must be accepted by the donee, must go into immediate and absolute effect, must be gratuitous, and, in the case of gifts inter vivos, must be irrevocable." [13]

3. *Wills and intestate succession.*   Another manner in which title to things may be acquired is by wills and intestate succession. Will or bequest results in a title to things inasmuch as it is a gift of personal property.   "The words 'bequest' and 'legacy' properly and ordinarily mean testamentary gifts of personal property." [14] "The word 'bequest' is commonly defined as a gift of personal property by will." [15]   Title is likewise acquired by intestate succession.   "The word 'intestate' signifies a person who died without leaving a valid will." [16]   "Where such intestate shall leave a spouse surviving or other kindred, but no issue, the surviving spouse shall be entitled to the real or personal estate or both." [17]

4. *Accession.*   Accession is a process resulting in title to what is produced by adding value to another's property through additional material or labor.   ". . . '[A]ccession' is defined as the right to all which one's own property produces, whether that property be removable or immovable, and the right to that which is united to it by accessory, either naturally or artificially.   The nature of this right to acquire the property of another by its joinder with the owner's own property is complex and no rule, general and precise, to cover all cases has ever been formulated. In some instances the relative value of the principal property to that which is added to it is the decisive element.   One test frequently applied is whether the added property or materials can be identified.   An important and controlling consideration often is whether the addition is such that it is separable and severable from the principal thing without damage." [18]

[12] Gordon v. Barr, 82 P.2d 955, 957 (Cal. Dist. Ct. App. 1938).
[13] Hays' Administrators v. Patrick, 266 Ky. 713, 99 S.W.2d 805, 809 (1936).
[14] In re Wood's Estate, 232 Iowa 1004, 6 N.W. 2d 846, 848 (1942).
[15] United States v. Merriam, 263 U.S. 179, 184, 44 Sup. Ct. 69, 70 (1923).
[16] In re Cameron's Estate, 47 App. Div. 120, 62 N.Y. Supp. 187, 188 (1900).
[17] In re Shestack's Estate, 267 Pa. 115, 110 Atl. 166, 167 (1920).
[18] Franklin Service Stations v. Sterling Motor Truck Co. of N.E., 50 R.I. 336, 147 Atl. 754, 755 (1929).

Title to land resulting from a shift in the course of a river is an example of title acquired by the process of accession.[19] So also is the title to property caused by labor, as will be seen later.

5. *Adverse possession.* Adverse possession is another process by which title is acquired to property. It commonly involves the occupancy of corporeal hereditaments, for instance land, for a time the limitation of which is determined by statute.[20] Prescription is similar to adverse possession but is usually concerned with incorporeal hereditaments, for example an easement.[21]

Both adverse possession and prescription differ from custom. "Prescription may be defined to be a mode of acquiring title to incorporeal hereditaments by continued use, possession or enjoyment had during the time and in the manner fixed by law. The term properly applies only to incorporeal rights. An interest in the land of another greater than an incorporeal hereditament, such as the possession and use of a building thereon, cannot be established by prescription. Prescription is distinguished from custom in that the former is a personal usage or enjoyment confined to the claimant and his ancestors or those whose estate he has acquired, while the latter is a mere local usage, not connected to any particular person, but belonging to the community rather than to its individuals. Adverse possession is distinguished from prescription in that it is, properly speaking, a means of acquiring title to corporeal hereditaments only, and is usually the direct result of the statute of limitations; while prescription is the outgrowth of common-law principles, with but little aid from the legislature, and has to do with the acquisition of no kind of property except incorporeal hereditaments." [22]

The derived titles to property presuppose the primary titles. Of the primary titles, labor is the most basic. If a root justification of "private property" is to be found, it will have to be located in the process of labor.

III. Private Ownership

The concept of property is basic in law as it is in life. The claim to own things privately, as opposed to owning them only commonly, marks off one part of the philosophical, economic, political and legal world from the other.

[19] Manry v. Robison, 122 Tex. 213, 56 S.W.2d 438 (1932).
[20] Lowery v. Garfield County, Mont., 122 Mont. 571, 208 P.2d 478, 486 (1949).
[21] See Zetrover v. Zetrover, 89 Fla. 253, 103 So. 625, 627 (1925).
[22] Hester v. Sawyers, 41 N.M. 497, 71 P.2d 646, 649 (1937).

A. *Need of Justification*

Wherever the law protects the claims to own things as private property,[23] it is generally taken for granted by lawmen that such a claim is well-founded. Continued reference to it in the assuring language of "inherent" and "inalienable" rights engenders confidence in its validity.

However, the justification of private ownership is admittedly extra-legal, inasmuch as it is "inherent in human nature" and "inalienable" from it. Hence it behooves lawmen to examine critically this non-legal assumption, if they are to understand their own position on this problem of world-wide implications.

For those lawmen who are convinced that men are beings singularly endowed with power of conceiving and expressing ideas, a rationale for private ownership is possible that is solid and irrefragable. For the others who do not share this conviction, the quest for reasons justifying private ownership must ever be uncertain and beset with doubts. The search will be endless and in the meantime only common ownership will seem logical.

B. *Appropriation in General*

Before the problem of private ownership can be tackled, it must be seen that it is right and not wrong for men to appropriate external things in general for their use. This can be discerned from either of two viewpoints.

1. *Reductio ad absurdum.* By way of a reductio ad absurdum, it is not difficult to perceive that the use of external things is necessary for men's sustenance. If it were absolutely wrong for men to appropriate such things for their own use and all men would accordingly refrain from doing so, it would be only a matter of days until the human race would be extinct. Hence the appropriation of external things by men must be considered right and good if men are to continue to exist.

2. *Plan of creation.* The other way this appropriation may be seen to be right, is from the plan of creation. There is implied in creation a subordination of the lower to the higher. The lower is for the use of the higher. The inorganic serves the organic. Vegetative life serves animal life and both vegetative and animal life serve intellectual life — men. Hence the right-

---

[23] The phrase is redundant, since property (from the Latin "proprius") means proper to the individual, that is, private.

ness of appropriating external things derives from the purpose of the creation of the subordinated levels.

Whether the question of appropriation in general, then, is approached from a non-creationist standpoint such as a reductio ad absurdum or from a creationist point of view, its rightness is clear enough. It is only from the creationist standpoint, however, that all beings — including men — appear in their correct perspective.

C. *Individual Appropriation*

Though it be right and licit for men to appropriate external things in general, appropriation must be particularized if it is to be of practical use. Whether it be a question of consumer or productive goods, a man does not sustain himself by living on the world in general. He must maintain himself by eating this bread, by working this land.

Hence, granted that I may appropriate an external thing for my use (say by occupancy which others are obliged to respect in order to avoid a state of animal struggle), the problem still remains of determining what the ground reason is why I may claim it as "mine."

1. *Socio-economic necessity.* One reason why I may make such a claim is that it is a socio-economic necessity to have possessions that are "mine." Unless a man can look upon certain things as his, incentive, initiative and satisfaction will be lacking in his life. If he cannot manage and administer things as his own, he will not be solicitous about the work he puts on them, he will not be orderly in his dealings with others, and he will not lead a contented and peaceful life. Rather he will be careless, disorderly, discontented and rebellious.[24]

The advantages of private ownership have been recognized these many centuries. "Property should be in a certain sense common, but as a general rule, private; for, when every one has a distinct interest, men will not complain of one another, and they will make more progress, because every one will be attending to his own business. . . . And further, there is the greatest pleasure in doing a kindness or service to friends or guests or companions, which can only be rendered when a man has private property. These advantages are lost by excessive unification of the state. The exhibition of two virtues, besides, is visibly annihilated in such a state; first, temperance towards women (for

[24]Aquinas, 2-2 Sum. Theol. 66, 2.

it is an honourable action to abstain from another's wife for temperance' sake); secondly, liberality in the matter of property. No one, when men have all things in common, will any longer set an example of liberality or do any liberal action; for liberality consists in the use which is made of property." [25]

Such necessity of private ownership is undoubtedly a valid reason why men should possess things as their own. The evidence of the centuries supports it. It is, however, a reason that is extrinsic to me and the thing that is "mine." Consequently it leaves as arguable the question whether the same solicitude, care and contentedness could not be brought about by a benevolent government distributing proportionate rewards for initiative from publicly owned property. The justification of individual ownership, to be irrefutable, must rest on something intrinsic to me and what is mine. If this can be identified, the basis of individual ownership will be located primarily in the process of one of the titles, and secondarily in its socio-economic necessity.

2. *Process of labor.* Since the derived titles to property depend on the original titles, the problem of finding a title whose relation is based on something intrinsic to me and what is mine, narrows itself to occupancy and labor.

Occupancy, as observed, creates a unique relation between the thing occupied and me. Others should respect this relation. But the basis of the relation is at best a spatio-temporal one. It derives from the simple fact that I was in this particular place first. There is nothing of me in the thing I occupy.

Labor also establishes a unique relation between the laborer and his products. It appears to come closer than occupancy to furnishing an intrinsic basis for this relation. The laborer expends his time and his effort in making the product. But again, time is an extrinsic factor; and effort, if it is taken as physical energy, also remains extrinsic to the product. Time and energy expended do not appear specifically as something intrinsic to the thing made. Besides, the horse plowing the field expends time and energy but he has never been considered to have thereby acquired any ownership of the field. Hence, when courts say, "By the law of nature every person is entitled to the fruit of his own labor and skill" the question remains: why is this statement valid?

a. *Phenomenon of elaboration.* It is only in labor seen as a process by which men project ideas that are theirs into things they are making, that there is an intrinsic basis for the relation of

[25] Aristotle, 3 Politics 5, 1263a-1263b (Ross trans. 1941).

mine. It is only in the amazing phenomenon of intellectual beings elaborating material things that the indisputable justification of individual ownership is found.

A potter, to use a primitive example, takes a mass of clay and by working it gives it a form that it did not have before. It now has the form of a beautiful, symmetrical jar. The clay, which before was a formless clod, is now formed into a jar.

Whence came this form? It came from the laborer himself who, so to speak projected *his* idea of a jar into the clay, with the result that it now has the form of a jar. The worker has made the jar according to his own image of a jar. He has stamped it with the seal of "mine." Or, to put it more technically, he has educed the form of "jar," of which his own idea was the exemplar, from the potency of the matter he was elaborating.

In the process of "e-labor-ation," then, there is an intrinsic basis for the unique relation of title between me and the product; the basis is my *idea* and its expression in the thing made. In terms of cause and effect, the form of the jar is an effect that pre-existed in my idea as cause. "Our effects, in other words, before existing in themselves as effects, exist in us as causes, and partake of the being of their cause. The possibility of the typically human mode of causality, that of the *homo faber,* rests precisely on the fact that man, being gifted with reason, is capable of containing within himself, by way of representation, the being of possible effects which shall be distinct from himself. And that, moreover, is why what we do or produce is ours; for if we are responsible for our acts and legitimate owners of the works of our hands, it is because, as these effects were at first but ourselves as cause, so it is still we ourselves who exist in them in their being as effects. The plays of Shakespeare, the comedies of Molière, the symphonies of Beethoven *are* Shakespeare, Molière, Beethoven; so much so that we might reasonably ask whether they do not constitute the best part of their authors' being, the very summit of their personality." [26] In a word, in the process of elaboration, the proprietorship that a man has over himself is extended to external things.

b. *Title to increased value.* In the process of elaboration, the value of what was mere clay is enhanced to the extent that it now is a jar. Who has the title to this increased value? Who owns it? Whose property is it? Answers to these questions have a direct connection with the labor contract.

[26] Gilson, The Spirit of Mediaeval Philosophy 88-89 (1936). By permission of Charles Scribner's Sons.

If the potter owns the clay before he formed it into the jar, the jar with its added value is totally his; because the idea which was the exemplar of the form was his. He conceived it in his own mind and he is the one who caused the clay to become a jar. He and no one else, therefore, owns it.

If the potter did not own the clay but another owned it and he has agreed to work for the other as is the case in employer-employee relationships, he and the other both have a title to the jar. They are co-owners; the other because he owned the clay, the potter because he owned the idea according to which form and added value were given to the clay. The percent of ownership to which one or the other has title is difficult to determine with accuracy and justice. Hence, a practical solution is for the laborer to transfer his title to the other for an amount determined on a time basis, say one dollar an hour. Thus the potter's title to the added value created by his labor, is the basis of the labor contract. The labor contract is in essence a substitute for co-ownership.[27]

With men instinctively conscious of the unique relation that exists between themselves and what they make, it is not surprising that they judge such things to be "mine." "In a historical examination of the question we find that man in the rudest state of nature was not without some notions of exclusive property, and that jurists in every age, as civilization advanced, have maintained that what a man has obtained by the honest exertion of his own mind, or his own hand, is by natural right his own property. Indeed, it may be said that the protection of this right is the main security to the enjoyment of life." [28]

Through the process, then, of labor — the elaboration of material things — the worker acquires title to property. This phenomenon is possible because men have minds. Hence, the concept of private property, so basic to western legal thought, has its rationale in the intellectual nature of men.[29]

[27] This presupposes some agreement between the owner and the laborer. If there is no such agreement and the laborer knowingly and willingly violates the rights of another in working on his materials or if he does so by mistake, the situation is different. See, for instance, Baker v. Mersch, 29 Neb. 227, 45 N.W. 685, 688 (1890).

[28] Atchison and Nebraska R.R. Co. v. Baty, 6 Neb. 40, 29 Am. Rep. 356, 357 (1877).

[29] For a more detailed discussion of this point see Maritain, Freedom In The Modern World 193-214 (1936). Aquinas does not develop the concept of elaboration. Perhaps it is implicit in his statement regarding the use of external things that ". . . man has a natural dominion over external things, because by his reason and will he is able to use them for his own utility." 2-2 Sum. Theol. 66, 1. His statement regarding the relation of dominion to

c. *Occupancy ordered to elaboration.* Even raw materials which are the means of production, such as coal, oil, iron ore, uranium and the like, are occupied by men for use that is distinctly human. Human occupancy implies human use and human use ultimately connotes, not only use that is wise and prudent, but use that bears the stamp of art, of making. It entails the imprint of ideas. And although occupancy does not establish a relation of title based on something intrinsic to me and the object, nevertheless the thing occupied is destined for such a relation. That is why it is occupied.

The relation of title created by the originative process of elaboration between product and worker is, along with contract, the most common basis for new jural relations. All jural relations towards the worker have this relation of title as their ultimate base.

3. Basis of labor agreements. The relation of title which is created by the process of labor is the basis for the labor contract. This is the ground for all bargaining.

a. *Wages a substitute for title.* The title to the increased value given to a thing by the laborer's elaboration of it is the laborer's. In situations wherein the materials he works are already owned by another, his labor results in co-title or co-ownership. On account of the practical difficulties of determining what percentage belongs to whom in co-ownership, the problem is solved by the worker relinquishing his title and accepting in its

---

creation (". . . natural dominion over other creatures, which belong to man because of his reason in which consists the image of God, is manifested in the very creation of man [Gen. 1:26] where it is said: 'let us make man to our image and likeness; and let him have dominion over . . . the whole earth.'" 2-2 Sum. Theol. 66, 1.) could contain in germ the idea that just as God made man to his image (an intellectual-volitional being) so man makes things to his image (his own ideas).

However, Aquinas' further analysis does not proceed along this line of man as "maker" but rather along the lines of the necessity of private possession. "If a particular piece of land be considered absolutely, it contains no reason why it should belong to one man more than to another; but if it be considered regarding its adaptability to cultivation and the unmolested use of the land, it has a certain commensuration to be the property of one and not of another man." 2-2 Sum. Theol. 57, 3.

His further explanation of how individual as well as common ownership can be justified seems to be in terms of natural titles but recognized and specified by man-made law. "Community of things is attributed to natural right, not because natural right dictates that all things should be possessed in common and that nothing should be possessed as one's own; but because the distinction of possessions is not according to natural right but rather according to human agreement which belongs to positive law. . . . Hence, private possession is not contrary to the natural law but an addition thereto devised by human reason." 2-2 Sum. Theol. 66, 2, 1.

stead remuneration computed on a flat, time basis. In a word, the laborer's title to the added value created by his labor is the basis of the labor contract, as we have noted.

A conclusion follows regarding the matter of the labor contract that has extremely important implications. The object of the contract is neither the laborer himself, nor his activity, nor his time. If the laborer or his activity were the matter of the contract, the laborer would be actually selling himself. In such a case, labor by its very nature would have the status of slavery. Labor would be a commodity that could be bargained for on the open market like any "thing." A laborer, however, is not a thing. He is a man. He is a person. His relation to his employer is a contractual one entered into by a free man.[30] Nor is the time expended by the laborer the object of the labor contract. For, the laborer's title to the added value he creates does not derive from something extrinsic to the product, such as the time element, but from something intrinsic to it, his ideas as embodied in the product. Time is merely the extrinsic condition of labor. The basis of the labor contract is, then, the laborer's title to that part of the product which can be said to be his.

b. *Determined by worker-owner agreement.* It follows, therefore, that the determination of the terms of the labor contract is a matter that pertains primarily to the worker and the owner. This is not to say that the government may not rightly intervene in situations where satisfactory employer-employee relations cannot be established and the public welfare is thereby jeopardized. What is implied is that such intervention is merely the reconciling of conflicting claims that relate basically to the individual persons involved.

The claims of workers and owners do not come from the government. They are the birthright of the people. "The right to the free use of his hands is the workman's property, as much as the rich man's right to the undisturbed income from his factory, houses, and lands. By his work he earns present subsistence for himself and family. His savings may result in accumulations which will make him as rich in houses and lands as his employer. This right of acquiring property is an inherent, indefeasible right of the workman."[31]

Like any other group of men who have some common end they

---

[30] See discussion of workmen's compensation, Chapter 15. But see Coppage v. Kansas, 236 U.S. 1, 10 (1914), on "selling labor."

[31] Erdman v. Mitchell, 207 Pa. 79, 56 Atl. 327, 331 (1903).

desire to pursue, laborers may rightly unite to promote their common good. This is mainly higher wages and better working conditions. Such a union is a natural means of obtaining a necessary end and the right to do so is fundamental. "So far as the question now before us goes it is of no consequence whether the right to pursue one's calling (whether it be of labor or of business) is a common law right or a constitutional right, since the violation of it here complained of is on the part of individuals and not on the part of the legislature. What is of consequence here is that such a right exists. In article 1 of the Declaration of Rights it is declared that 'all men are born free and equal, and have certain natural, essential, and unalienable [sic] rights; among which may be reckoned the right of . . . acquiring, possessing, and protecting property; in fine, that of seeking and obtaining their safety and happiness.' It is in the exercise of this right that laborers can legally combine together in what are called labor unions." [32]

c. *Labor and Marx.* The difference between this analysis of the relation of a laborer to the product of his labor and the labor theory of Karl Marx should be carefully noted. In the present explanation, it is the specifically human element in labor — ideas — that is controlling. In Marx's theory, it is a non-human factor — time — that is paramount. ". . . [T]he price of labor is regulated by its cost of production, that is, by the *duration* of labor which is required in order to produce this commodity, labor-power." [33]

In our analysis, to repeat, it is neither the laborer's time nor his physical effort that is the ultimate basis of his title to the product of his work. It is specifically the ideas that are his and which he causes to be embodied in the product that give him title to the end result as in some part his.

d. *The extent of "labor."* The relation between an idea in the mind of the maker and the form or structure of the thing he makes, is more evident in the "higher" arts than it is in the "lower" arts. It is easier to discern it in a symphony, a painting or a poem than it is in the digging of a ditch or the running of a punch press.

[32] Pickett v. Walsh, 192 Mass. 572, 78 N.E. 753 (1906).
[33] Marx and Engels, Wage-Labor and Capital (1849) in Essentials of Marx 91-92 (Moore trans. 1946) (emphasis added). See on this subject, 1 Marx, Das Kapital 185-559 (1867), or 1 Capital 197-585 (Moore and Aveling trans. 1906); Kautsky, The Economic Doctrines of Karl Marx 64-231 (Stenning trans. 1936); Gray, The Socialist Tradition 297-332 (1947).

However, the imprint of an idea is present in everything that men make. Human making is art, that is, "the human ability to make things." Hence, as long as the product is something animals cannot make, the principle of elaboration is at work. There is present the human contribution of an idea. This is "human making." In modern living it is almost impossible to be out of sight of an artifact — an object that once pre-existed as an idea in the mind of a man.

Ordinarily in this context no distinction is made between labor and work as long as they include both the physical and mental aspects of a man's activities. "We find no clear-cut distinction between the terms of 'labor' and 'work'. . . . Both of these terms include both mental and physical effort. Among the preferred definitions of the term 'work' is that it consists of 'physical or intellectual effort.' And the term 'labor' is defined as 'physical or mental toil; bodily or intellectual exertion.' "[34]

Where the effort is predominantly mental, it is not labor or work in the sense that elaboration or making is. The communication of ideas by a schoolteacher is not work in the technical sense. Nor would the services of foremen, superintendents, messengers and watchmen be.

Courts, however, confronted with practical problems, have found differently in some cases. "There are many definitions of the term 'labor.' This court . . . held that a school teacher was not a laborer . . . [another court] holds that under some circumstances a foreman does not perform labor within the meaning of a similar Act. . . . [A]mong other definitions labor [is defined] as 'the service rendered or part played by the laborer, operative and artisan in the production of wealth, as distinguished from the service rendered by capitalist or by those whose exertion is primarily and almost entirely mental. . . . The school teacher's work is almost entirely mental exertion, while in the case of the respondent his work required bodily exertion, whether at the moment he was repairing the mine, acting as messenger or watching the mining properties. It is apparent that while he was repairing the mine or acting as messenger, he was performing labor. . . . Certainly, that work involved physical exertion rather than mental. That is also true as to his services as a watchman. . . . In the . . . case [cited] the court construed a statute providing for certain exemptions to laborers on garnish-

[34] Christie v. Commercial Casualty Ins. Co., 6 Cal. 2d 710, 45 P.2d 263, 266, (1935).

ment of their wages, and the court held that a night watchman was a laborer within the meaning of the statute." [35]

e. *Labor and service.* Strictly speaking, however, there is a great difference between the process of making a thing according to ideas and skills previously had as is done in labor and in the trades in general, and the process of assisting other persons by reason of more or less specially acquired knowledge and skills as occurs in the various service occupations. The claim of the carpenter or machinist to new property in the form of wages rests on a different basis than does the claim of the teacher, the physician and the public official to their salary. The basis of the former's claim is an originative making; the ground of the latter's claim is a derivative contract.

Service occupations, then — whether of the director-governor type such as executives, judges, legislators, or of the professional kind such as teachers, physicians, lawyers — acquire property by the secondary title of contract. Their titles presuppose the society of workers who acquire property by the primary title of labor. For, governors are concerned with the good that is common to all and the professions hold as their ideal the service of humanity.[36]

The professions are often distinguished from the trades on the score that the professions have for their admitted prime purpose the service of humanity, which the trades do not. True though this may be, there is a more profound way the trades differ from the professions: their title to property derives from a transformation of material things by the embodiment of ideas.

IV. Social Versus Individual Aspects of Property

The appropriation of external things has, then, both a social and individual facet. Because of this, both public and private ownership are right and just. The common need, as we saw, determines which is better at any one time. However, it is inevitable that a more fundamental question be asked: which is more according to the demands of men's nature, social or individual appropriation?

[35] Britt v. Cotter Butte Mines, 108 Mont. 174, 89 P.2d 266, 267 (1939); United States Fidelity and Guaranty Co., for Use of Reedy v. American Surety Co., of New York, 25 F. Supp. 280, 284 (M.D. Pa. 1938).

[36] "The prime object of the medical profession is to render service to humanity; reward or financial gain is a subordinate consideration." Principles of Ethics of the American Medical Association 5 (1954).

A.　*The Social Aspect*

This question can best be answered according to the two steps of appropriation already established, the general and the particular. The starting point of the analysis of appropriation is that "all things are for the use of all men." Hence insofar as things external to men are appropriable by no one in particular but by anyone, appropriation is communal and social. There is no designation according to the nature of men and things as to who should appropriate what. This particular piece of land is not destined by nature for this man rather than that man. Such a relation must be established by human enterprise.

B.　*The Individual Aspect*

In view of the fact that particular things must be appropriated by particular men, however, individual appropriation follows as a matter of necessity. The laborer creates a unique relation of title between his product and himself. Occupancy and contract also exemplify this. Hence, although appropriation is social insofar as things are potentially appropriable by anyone, it is individual inasmuch as they must actually be appropriated on a this-thing, this-man basis.

C.　*Individual Limited by the Social*

Individual appropriation in the final analysis, then, is not absolute and unlimited. It is qualified by appropriation's social aspect.

This limitation may assert itself, for instance, when the holder of surplus property is obliged in justice to aid one in extreme need. A starving man would be justified in demanding from such a one what was necessary to preserve his life. His claim would be founded on the primal fact that "all things are for the use of all men."

Because individual appropriation of things is limited by their overall social purpose, the word "ownership" must have a qualified connotation. If men do not have an unlimited use and control over what they possess, they do not have absolute ownership. Hence, in this larger context, such expressions as the "management" or "stewardship" of things are more accurate.

This socio-individual nature of property is the explanation of

why there has been constant interplay and tension throughout
the ages between individual and social, private and public ownership.   It is also the reason why constant vigilance must be
exercised to avoid the extremes of engulfing socialism on the one
hand and rugged individualism on the other.   Here lies the
justification of legislators' and courts' actions limiting or supporting private ownership.   The more human mode of limitation
is one self-dictated by love and friendship; but the more certain
and effective way seems to be the one imposed by justice and law.

The full meaning of property, then, can be got only from the
purpose of material things.   And since material things take on a
particular meaning and value from the elaboration they receive
from the rational being man, the ultimate nature of property can
be known only through an insight into the nature of men.

CHAPTER   17

Contracts

The problem which concerns us in contracts is to find the ground for contractual obligation and also to ascertain the jural relations that are created by contracts.   Upon these solutions depends a lawman's evaluation of consideration in contracts and his understanding of the relations of union that result from contractual agreements.

I.   The Nature of a Contract

Contracts, along with labor, are the most common way of acquiring new property.   It is through this process that we acquire most of the things that are new to us.   A contract may be considered as to its origin or as to the resulting relations between the parties.   Its origin is a promissory agreement and, if it is bilateral, it results in a union of the parties.[1]

A.   *Contracts Are Promissory Agreements*

Most definitions of contract stress the aspect of agreement.   "A contract has been defined as an 'agreement which creates an obligation' . . . and such an agreement may be defined as the concurrence of two or more persons in a common intent to affect their legal relations."[2]   Or it is "an agreement enforceable at law, made between two or more persons, by which rights are acquired by one or more, to acts or forebearances on the part of the other or others."[3]   A contract is also defined as "A promise or set of promises for breach of which the law gives a remedy, or the performance of which the law in some way recognizes as a duty."[4]

Agreement implies consent or assent.   "An agreement in the broadest sense of the word is a manifestation of mutual assent by

1 Contract is from the Latin *con-trahere:* to draw together.
2 Buffalo Pressed Steel Co. v. Kirwan, 138 Md. 60, 113 Atl. 628, 630 (1921).
3 Anson, Principles of the Law of Contracts 10-11 (1939).
4 1 Williston, A Treatise on the Law of Contracts 1 (1936).

two or more persons to one another. Agreement in its narrower sense as an essential element of a contract may be defined as a manifestation of mutual assent by two or more persons to affect their legal relations by means of a bargain concluded between them consisting of an exchange of mutual promises or an exchange of a promise for a performance." [5]

For the purposes of contract, "consent," and "assent" may be taken as synonymous, although a difference may be drawn between them. "An assent indicates the meeting of the minds of the contracting parties. 'Assent' means to approve, ratify, and confirm. It is the very language of contract." [6] "Consent in law means a voluntary agreement by a person in the possession and exercise of sufficient mentality to make an intelligent choice to do something proposed by another. Consent differs very materially from assent. The former implies some positive action and always involves submission. The latter means more passivity or submission which does not include consent." [7]

Looked at as a state of the parties resulting from their mutual promises, a bilateral contract is also defined in terms of a union. A contract in this sense has been said to be "The union of several persons in a coincident expression of the will by which their legal relations are determined." [8]

Or emphasizing the end and purpose of the promissory union, a contract may be defined as: a union of two or more persons, originating in their mutual promises enforceable in law, for the reordering of their relations of title, duty and claim regarding something to be done or not to be done.

B. *Requisites for a Promissory Agreement*

The conditions of contracts, as well as the kinds, are too well known to bear repetition here. Suffice it to point out briefly

[5] Simpson, Law of Contracts 4 (1954).

[6] People v. Consolidated Indemnity and Insurance Co., 233 App. Div. 34, 251 N.Y. Supp. 566, 569 (1931).

[7] People v. Kangiesser, 44 Cal. App. 345, 186 Pac. 388, 389 (1919).

[8] Von Savigny, Obligationenrecht (1853) ii, 7. This definition of contract properly identifies the essence of a contract as a union. However, due to the author's philosophical predispositions, this union is said to consist in "a coincident expression of the will." This union is rather, if one takes a factual means-end view of things, one of relation of persons united in their pursuit of a common end — the exchange of jural relations. It is initiated by their mutual agreement of wills. Note the similarity between Savigny's definition and Kant's: "The act of the united wills of two persons by which in general what is one's own is transferred to another." Kant, The Philosophy of Law 101 (Hastie trans. 1877).

the relation between some of these and the prerequisites for rational acts.

The main requirement for making a promissory agreement is that the person be capable of sufficient knowledge and consent. Hence, contracts entered into by infants, the inebriated and the insane (unless adjudicated insane), though not void, are voidable. Regarding the terms of a contract, the knowledge must be substantially correct; accidental error alone will not void the agreement. The presence of duress, mistake and the like, though not rendering the agreement void, can again make it voidable. The terms must be recognized as just both naturally and legally — a condition that has a bearing on restitution in equity. The notions of malum in se and malum prohibitum, when used to show the illegality of some terms of contracts, should be subjected to the same criticism as was made of it above in crimes.

C. *Natural and Legal Promissory Agreements*

Some promises are not enforceable in law, others are. Hence promises are either natural or legal.

1. *Natural promissory agreements.* Natural promissory agreements are the fabric of our everyday life. A and B agree to meet at the country club for a round of golf; C and D consent to have lunch together tomorrow; E, in an unguarded moment of expansiveness, promises his wife a fur coat; and so forth.

Or, as may happen for instance in aboriginal territory where there is no law enforcement, F and the natives agree to exchange trinkets for food. Although this agreement is a natural and not a legal one, it involves nonetheless an exchange of jural, though not legal, relations. Such a natural agreement is a natural contract.

2. *Legal promissory agreements.* The word "contract," however, is ordinarily used in the sense of a legal promissory agreement. Besides the prerequisite conditions of a natural contract, such a legal promissory agreement must fulfill certain other conditions stipulated by law. It must have a specified form, which may include a writing, witnesses, seal and consideration.

One of the chief differences between a natural and legal contract, is that the latter is enforceable by law. The law will see to it that the terms of such a contract are fulfilled or that a remedy is forthcoming.

D. *Freedom of Contracting*

Before examining the obligation of contracts, it may be well to point out briefly the different meanings the ambiguous word "freedom" may have in relation to contracts and some of their implications.

1. *Freedom from intrinsic influences.* Freedom, when used concerning contracts, may have reference to the background power that is prerequisite for all agreements inasmuch as they are human acts. This is the power to decide and consent freely to some act which, in the case of a contract, is the promissory agreement. This power may be reduced or nullified by duress, fear and the like, as is presupposed in crimes and torts. To the degree that these factors influence a man's ability to decide and choose, his freedom proportionately is limited.

Freedom in this sense, then, connotes the absence of intrinsic factors that affect a man's power of decision and choice.

2. *Freedom from extrinsic limitations.* Freedom of contract, however, may also have another meaning. In this connotation it refers to extrinsic factors that may limit a man's ability to control the terms of a contract.

a. *Economic doctrine.* Within the context of economics, freedom of contract has a particular meaning. As the consecrated shibboleth of laissez-faire economists, it meant that enterprisers should enjoy unlimited contractual freedom in the conduct of their business. Regardless of how inhuman the hours, wages or conditions of labor, there should according to this doctrine, be no governmental interference by regulative measures.

b. *Control of terms.* Freedom also has another meaning when used with reference to contracts. It may refer to a man's ability, or lack of it, to manipulate the terms of the contract in concrete circumstances before he agrees to them. This exercise of freedom is common in a wide range of activities that run throughout the law of contracts.

There are other areas, however, wherein the terms of contracts cannot be so easily controlled. Such is the case where prices and rates are established by the economic laws of supply and demand or, when necessary, by governmental controls. The prices of food, clothing, housing and the like, and the rates of water, gas, oil, electricity and transportation are examples of contractual terms in the management and control of which the individual man has limited freedom.

Parenthetically, another example may be mentioned of this type of contract where the terms are pre-determined — in this particular case by the nature of the terms themselves. This is the contract of marriage. In the marriage contract the terms are claims regarding each other's body and sexual acts of their nature conducive to reproduction, the exclusion of a third party, and permanence of the contractual union. These claims are not arbitrarily determined. They derive from the very nature of the subject matter of the institution of marriage.[9] Such contracts, whose terms are somehow completely or partially prescribed, have been called contracts of acceptance or *contrats d'adhésion*.

3. *Evaluation*. When the question is asked, therefore, whether freedom of contract is disappearing from the economic and legal world, it is necessary to answer it in the light of the above distinctions.

a. *Power to decide*. Individual men are seemingly as free to make decisions as they ever were with only the same internal factors influencing them as always. Whatever emotional disturbances there may be that reduce freedom in the commission of crime or a tort, certainly they do not have the same effect in the closing of a contract. Freedom of contract in the sense of the power to decide freely cannot be said to be disappearing.

b. *Laissez faire*. As for the freedom of contract of laissez faire, it is undoubtedly disappearing to a great extent. Fortunately and with good reason the courts have seen to it that this bar to common justice has in great part been removed.

c. *Terms*. Freedom to manipulate terms of contracts in general is not decreasing as everyday experience will testify. In spite of undercover price fixing, for instance, and illegal though it be, terms of contracts are still the subject of some adjustment. Contractual bids submitted in open bidding are evidence of this.

There can be no doubt, however, that the amount of freedom to manipulate terms of contracts, where prices and rates are fairly well fixed in particular fields, has lessened since the Industrial Revolution. The terms of such contracts have to be accepted as they are offered or attempts made to change them.

There are certain means to which men are still free to have recourse in some places whose purpose is to affect the terms of price and rate contracts. Strikes, boycotts, and the like are designed to bring about a change in the contractual terms of prices and rates. As long as such conditions of bargaining prevail, there

---

[9] See Leclercq, Marriage and the Family (Hanley trans. 1941).

is still some freedom, however qualified, of contracting in these fields.

d. *Use of phrase.* Hence, lawmen would do well to use the phrase "freedom of contract" with discernment. To say that freedom of contract "is politics masquerading as jurisprudence, the ideology of vested interests deemed useful as a weapon against collectivism" [10] may be true if it refers to laissez-faire economics. Otherwise it is most assuredly false. Again, the truth of the statement that contract based on agreement or a "meeting of the minds" is "in danger of becoming a legal fiction" in planned society in which economic terms are dictated by governmental authority,[11] depends for its validity on the degree to which such terms are dictated. Certainly the setting up of a limited amount of regulations such as those mentioned regarding the wages, hours and conditions of labor cannot be construed as rendering contracts a matter of "legal fiction."

II. OBLIGATION OF CONTRACTS

Since a contract is essentially a promissory agreement or union, the reason why a contract obliges is related to why a promise obliges.

A. *Consideration*

There must be some way of distinguishing between promises that are not enforceable legally and those that are. An agreement to go sailing with a friend would not be enforceable in a court of law. There must be some particular characteristic about a legally enforceable promise that sets it apart from those that are not so enforceable. There must be a norm for judging which are and which are not legally sanctioned and enforceable. It must be certain that the parties intended to enter upon a legal contract. To prevent fraud clear evidence is necessary. In Anglo-American law the mark of this difference is said to be "Sufficient bargain and exchange consideration," an idea that received great impetus from the laissez-faire economics of the eighteenth and nineteenth centuries.

1. *Price of a promise.* Consideration is, in general, the price bargained and paid for a promise. This may be some act, or the refraining from some act, or a return promise itself. If these result in a legal benefit to the promisor or a detriment to the

[10] Kelsen, 2 Annales de L'Institut de Droit Comparé 30 (1936).
[11] Keeton, The Elementary Principles of Jurisprudence 407 (1949).

promisee, the consideration is "sufficient." Legal benefit or detriment does not necessarily imply an economic benefit or detriment. Rather, a legal detriment is what is incurred by the promisee when, as the bargained-for price of the promise, he has promised to do any act or refrain from any act however inconsequential to which he was not already bound. Even the possibility of a detriment bargained for is sufficient consideration to support a promise.[12]

This, in the large, is the notion of consideration that has been adopted by the courts. "A 'consideration' is the reason which moves contracting parties to enter into the undertaking. It may be a forebearance or the promise thereof, which is offered by one party to the agreement and accepted by the other. It is the price, motive, the matter of inducement to contract, whether it be compensation which is paid or the inconvenience which is suffered by the party from whom it proceeds. . . . A consideration may be a benefit to one and a detriment to the other party to the contract. . . . The alteration or modification of a contract to be effective must be supported by a consideration, which need not be the payment of money or delivery of property, but it may be anything which is of benefit to the promisor or detriment to the promisee." [13]

Even refraining from action has been held to be sufficient consideration. "If A. promise B. to pay him $5 if he will not eat a dinner or $10 if he will not wear his best coat for a day, B's abstaining from eating his dinner and refraining from wearing his coat is sufficient to support A's promise, for B. has a legal right to do both of these things. In a New York case, an uncle promised a nephew that if he would refrain from drinking liquor, using tobacco, swearing, and playing certain games for money until he came of age, he would pay him $5000. The nephew kept his side of the bargain, but, when sued for the money, the uncle claimed that the agreement was not founded on a valid consideration. But the court said: 'It is sufficient that he restricted his lawful freedom of action within certain limits upon the faith of his uncle's agreement.' "[14]

The controlling aspect of consideration is, then, that of a "bargain." It is a *quid pro quo*. The benefit-detriment notion is what gives consideration its legal import.

---

[12] See Simpson, Law of Contracts 86 (1954).

[13] Cassinelli v. Stacy, 238 Ky. 827, 38 S.W.2d 980, 983 (1931).

[14] Miller v. Bank of Holly Springs, 131 Miss. 55, 95 So. 129, 130 (1923). See also McDevitt v. Stokes, 174 Ky. 515, 192 S.W. 681, 682 (1917).

2. *Dissatisfaction with consideration.* The opposition to the doctrine of consideration in contracts is well known. Dissatisfaction with it, even among common law men, has often been expressed. The insistence on a *quid pro quo* has been recognized as fostering, too often, injustice and frustration of honest claims. "The many cases of hardship and near dishonesty arising from the insistence on consideration as the exclusive test of enforceability of a simple contract are too well known to be again retailed. In many instances 'the doctrine of consideration is a mere technicality which is irreconcilable either with business expediency or common sense' and 'it frequently affords a man a loop hole for escape from a promise.' " [15]

The doctrine of consideration has been charged with bringing about "the most cynical disregard of promises solemnly undertaken . . . and many of us would like to see the doctrine abolished root and branch." [16] There are not a few who share the opinion that "the theory of consideration ought to find no place in our system of contract law." [17] What was merely evidential (proof of intention to bind legally) was mistakenly incorporated into contracts as something essential.

3. *Substitutes for consideration.* The dissatisfaction with consideration is confirmed in the growing use and acceptance of substitutes for consideration. These are in reality attempts to circumvent injustices caused by insistence on consideration.

a. *Moral obligation.* A man may have been cared for by a family of friends. Because of their beneficence he feels morally indebted to them and promises to pay them well for their kindnesses. This moral obligation to pay them is a sufficient consideration in some jurisdictions to support his promise. "Moreover, in this state we have adopted what is said to be the liberal rule as to moral consideration and have held that a receipt by the promisor of an actual benefit will support an executory promise and that a moral consideration may be sufficient to support an executory promise 'where the promisor originally received from the promisee something of value sufficient to arouse a moral, as distinguished from a legal, obligation.' " [18]

The substitution of moral obligation for bargain and exchange

[15] Stone, The Province and Function of Law 539, 545 (1950).
[16] Law Revision Committee's Sixth Interim Report, 1 Mod. L. Rev. 95, 100, 101 (1937).
[17] Lord Wright, Ought the Doctrine of Consideration Be Abolished From the Common Law? 49 Harv. L. Rev. 1225, 1252 (1936).
[18] In re Hatten's Estate, 233 Wis. 199, 288 N.W. 278, 287 (1940). See also Taylor v. Hotchkiss, 81 App. Div. 470, 80 N.Y. Supp. 1042, 1047 (1903).

consideration has not received wide acceptance chiefly because of the indefiniteness of moral duty. Besides, it has been opposed, quite enigmatically, because "the doctrine would annihilate the necessity for any consideration at all, inasmuch as the mere fact of giving a promise creates a moral obligation to perform it." [19]

b. *Promissory estoppel.* Another substitute for consideration is promissory estoppel. A common example regards charitable subscriptions. Parishioners subscribe to a fund to improve a church property. The church authorities act on these promises and contract for the improvements. The subscribers, who induce a substantial change of legal position by the church authorities in reliance on their promises, are estopped from denying their enforceability as lacking consideration.[20]

Although accepted to some extent, the doctrine of promissory estoppel is opposed in some jurisdictions on the grounds that a promise is unenforceable without sufficient reason, even though there be detrimental reliance on it.

c. *Uniform Written Obligations Act.* Of all the so-called "substitutes for consideration" the Uniform Written Obligations Act comes the closest to rejecting consideration completely. It does this by recognizing that a promise obliges regardless of consideration and that all that is necessary for a promise to be enforceable is that there be written *evidence* of the signer's intention that the contract be enforceable legally.

A letter stating that the writer assumed the indebtedness of his father was construed as such a writing. "A copy of the writing is made part of the pleadings and an examination thereof discloses that . . . defendant . . . wrote a letter to a legal firm in New York City about the indebtedness of his father . . . to plaintiff. In this letter he assumes full responsibility for his father's indebtedness. Upon this letter plaintiff bases his liability in this suit. No consideration for this promise to pay another person's indebtedness is pleaded. At the time of this promise, the goods had long since been delivered and the indebtedness long overdue. . . . It would appear, therefore, that this amounts to a bare promise and the position of defendant would be tenable were it not for the Uniform Written Obligations Act. . . . This act provides that a written promise 'shall not be invalid or unenforceable for lack of consideration, if the writing also contains an

[19] Eastwood v. Kenyon, 11 Ad. & El. 438, 450, 113 Eng. Rep. 482, 486 (1840).
[20] See Cottage Street Methodist Episcopal Church v. Kendall, 121 Mass. 528, 531 (1887).

additional express statement, in any form of language, that signer intends to be legally bound.' The act has been held constitutional. . . . It appears to the court that in the writing pleaded defendant . . . said that he intended to be legally bound. The purpose of the act . . . was to make the law 'substantially the same as it was when seals were in force, so far as the doctrine of consideration is concerned, except that in lieu of the formality of a seal, the formality of this statement is substituted.' " [21]

The constitutionality of the Act has already been passed on. "As a further reason for sustaining the judgment for the plaintiff, the opinion of the learned judge of the court below refers to the provisions of the Uniform Written Obligations Act. . . . Appellant asserts the act does not embrace negotiable instruments and is unconstitutional for indefiniteness of title. There is no substance in this argument and it need not be discussed." [22]

The Act has not been widely accepted. A glance at the reasons given why it has not been adopted furnishes a revealing topographical view of contemporary legal thinking about contracts. "Legislative refusal to adopt this Act is based fundamentally upon approval of consideration as the test of an enforceable promise, a reluctance to extend the field of substitutes therefore, and disagreement with the assumption that a gift promise where made deliberately and with intent to be bound should be legally enforceable." [23]

It is understandable how a lawman, if he thinks consideration is essential to a contract, would not be inclined to see the value of written evidence as a substitute for consideration. For, there can be no substitute for what is essential, since this is what essential means. But to be against it because of reluctance to extend the field of substitutes, would seem to indicate an abandonment of consideration as essential and a willingness to accept some substitutes at least. If consideration is not essential to contracts, however, it can be dropped and no substitutes are needed. Then written evidence of intent to bind legally appears for what it is: not the essence or substitute for the essence of a contract but simply evidence of intent that the contract bind legally. The essence of a contract is something else, as will appear presently. Further, if there is evidence that a promisor of a gift intends to bind himself legally, why should not the first attitude toward such a promise be that it is

[21] Galvanoni & Nevy Bros. v. Acquadro, 46 D. & C. 358, 44 Lack. J. 111 (Pa. 1942).
[22] Balliet v. Fetter, 314 Pa. 284, 171 Atl. 466, 468 (1934).
[23] Simpson, Law of Contracts 151 (1954).

legally enforceable? This is what the promisor intended. Attenuating circumstances may appear later which the court should take into account. But they do not change this prime point.

4. *Obligation from quid pro quo?* The dissatisfaction with bargain and exchange consideration and attempts to find substitutes for it, bespeak a deep-seated conviction that promises bind, not because of something added to them, but because of what they are in themselves.

Men make agreements every day and feel they can trust one another without a *quid pro quo.* There must be sound reason back of such confidence. As the old French proverb has it, "You bind an ox by his horns and a man by his words." Something intrinsic to a promise, and not something extrinsic, seems to be the ground for this trust. What this is, will be considered shortly.

Consideration, then, is not essential to a promise or contract. "The common law doctrine of consideration is one which other legal systems successfully dispense with. . . . [T]he doctrine is no natural or essential part of a theory of contractual liability." [24]

The substitutes for consideration, moral obligation and promissory estoppel, are open to the same criticism as consideration itself. In moral obligation cases, the promise is enforced, not because it is a promise, but on account of the reason back of the promise — the moral obligation to make the promise because of a benefit previously received. In promissory estoppel, the promise is enforced, again not because it is a promise, but on account of a substantial economic detriment suffered in reliance on the promise. These reasons are equivalently those of consideration. In written obligations the emphasis on written evidence is, as we shall see, correctly placed.

B.   *Cause*

The reason why contracts are said to be legally enforceable in the law of most continental European countries is their *cause.* The theory that cause is essential in the creation of contractual obligation prevails in France, Holland, Italy, Belgium, Spain and other countries of continental Europe, as well as in those countries that derive their law therefrom, such as the nations of

[24] Lord Wright, Ought the Doctrine of Consideration Be Abolished From the Common Law?, 49 Harv. L. Rev. 1225, 1252 (1936). At common law the seal was also regarded as a substitute for consideration or as raising a conclusive presumption of consideration. See Candor and Henderson's Appeal, 27 Pa. 119, 120 (1856).

Central and South America, Puerto Rico, the Canal Zone, the Philippine Islands, Ceylon and Scotland.

1. *Cause: Immediate end intended.* The cause of a contract is taken to be its immediate purpose. "The cause of an obligation is the immediate end . . . which the party has in view." [25] Thus, if I contract to convey property, my intention to exchange jural relations of title, claim and duty regarding it is my immediate end. This immediate end, however, carries the implication of benefit intended to another party. "If I make a gift to A, my desire to benefit A is the immediate cause." [26]

2. *Background of cause.* The function of cause in European contract law cannot be understood unless it be seen as an application of a more general idea of cause that has been current since Aristotle.[27]

a. *In making.* According to this analysis, actions and things may have a quadruple causal aspect about them. In the example, let us say, of the potter making the jar, what is the cause of the jar? An accurate answer to this question must be multiple, since there is multiple causality involved.

The potter who makes the jar is its efficient cause. The clay from which it is made is its material cause. The form it now has which constitutes it a jar is its formal cause (the idea of it in the potter's own mind which is the link with property, is the exemplar cause as we saw). The purpose which motivated the potter in making the jar is its final cause.

b. *In contracting.* Similarly, the cause of a contract is multifold. The consent, agreement or promise of the parties is its efficient cause. The terms of the contract are its material cause. The uniting of the parties by the promise is its formal cause. The end intended by the parties is its final cause. The immediate end intended is the exchange of jural relations, although more remote ends such as obtaining money or moving to a new location may also be implied.

In the doctrine of cause, then, it is the immediate end intended — the exchange of jural relations for another's benefit — that is the mark of a contract's being legally binding. Nothing besides evidence of this intention is required. Once had, it is sufficient cause to support a contract.

[25] Beaudry, Lancantinierie et Barde, Obligation, nn. 298-299; quoted by Glaser, Doctrine of Consideration and The Civil Law Principle of Cause, 46 Dick. L. Rev. 12, 15 (1941).

[26] Capetant, De la Cause des Obligations 23, 87 (2d ed. 1924); quoted by Glaser, *supra* at 15-16.

[27] Aristotle, 2 Physics 3, 194b20 (Hardie and Gaye trans. 1941).

3. Obligation from intention to benefit? The doctrine of cause has been adopted by a great part of the legal world. In locating the cause of contractual obligation in the immediate end intended, it comes closer to finding an intrinsic reason for obligation than does the doctrine of consideration. Nevertheless, inasmuch as the ground for obligation is still something extrinsic to the promise itself, this doctrine is open to the same criticism as consideration.

For, if cause be taken in the manner just explained, as the intention to benefit another and the contract be made binding for this reason, it is not the promise to exchange jural relations itself that is the source of the obligation. It is something outside the promise, namely the intention to benefit another, that causes the promise to be binding.

4. Cause as consideration. Cause in this sense is not too much different from consideration. For this reason, cause has sometimes been taken as synonymous with consideration and vice versa. ". . . [T]he doctrine of consideration in the form received by English law, is unknown elsewhere, it is — from the analytical if not also from the historical point of view — simply a modification of a doctrine known to the civil law and to several modern systems, more especially to that of France. . . . The *cause* or *causa* is a near synonym for consideration, and we find the terms used interchangeably in the earlier English authorities. There is, however, an essential difference between the English and the Continental principle. Unlike the former, the latter never rejects any cause or consideration as insufficient. Whatever motive or inducement is enough to satisfy the contracting parties is enough to satisfy the law, even though it is nothing more than the *causa liberalitatis* of a voluntary gift." [28] "Cause is consideration or motive. By the cause of the contract . . . is meant the consideration or motive for making it; and a contract is said to be without a cause, whenever the party was in error, supposing that which was his inducement for contracting to exist, when in fact it had never existed or had ceased to exist before the contract was made." [29]

Faced with this similarity, some jurisdictions have rejected both consideration and *causa*. In a case in South Africa, wherein the defendant was sued for cancelling a written option he had given on his farm, the court in deciding for the plaintiff pointed out

[28] Salmond, Jurisprudence 374 (8th ed. 1930).
[29] Louisiana Civil Code, art. 1896 (1890); see also Quebec Civil Code, art. 984.

that lawmen had made the grave mistake of taking what was required only as evidence of serious intent to bind legally and turning it into an essential of a contract. "The way the matter is looked at from the modern point of view is this. Donation itself within the restrictions imposed by law is a *justa causa, justum negotium*, a contract or transaction approved by law. And the same may be said of every lawful contract — if two or more persons, of sound mind and capable of contracting, enter into a lawful agreement, a valid contract arises between them enforceable by action. The agreement may be for the benefit of one of them or of both — the promise must have been made with the intention that it should be accepted — the agreement must have been entered into *serio ac deliberato animo*. And this is what is meant by saying that the only element that our law requires for a valid contract is *consensus*, naturally within proper limits. It was a serious mistake in English law when what was merely required as proof of a serious mind was converted into an essential of every contract. It would be equally a mistake with us to introduce for a valid contract the necessity for a causa, whether in the shape of a valuable consideration or any other ground of obligation." [30]

Commenting on the necessity of getting back to consent or promise as the substance of a contract, the same court said: "It is satisfactory to note that the German Code . . . has returned to the pristine simplicity of the law as it obtained among the foremost nations of the continent of Europe until the Code Napoleon . . . led them astray." [31]

C.   *Promissory Agreement*

What with the doctrines of consideration and cause being subject to the criticisms noted, it is necessary to locate more precisely the ground on which contractual obligation rests.

1. *Nature of contractual promise.*   What makes a contract what it is, is not what is exchanged or the reason why the exchange is made; it is the promise itself, the consent to effect an exchange of jural relations. ". . . [N]either consideration nor *causa* nor writing is to be regarded as the substance of the promise: all such

[30] Conradie v. Russouw, [1919] So. African L. Rep. App. Div. 279, 321. "Neither consideration nor causa is mentioned as essential to the validity of a contract in the Civil Code of Japan, in the German Code, in the Swiss Code of Obligations of 1911, in the Portuguese Code of 1867, in Brazil, or formerly, in Austria. In these countries all that is required is capacity, intention to contract, an object that is physically possible and legally permissible, and some special forms in certain cases." Glaser, id. at 17.

[31] Conradie v. Russouw, [1919] So. African L. Rep. App. Div. 279, 321.

matters are extrinsic and evidentiary, matters which go to establish and corroborate contractual intention. The substance is the promise itself." [32] It is in this promissory agreement that the ultimate reason why a contract obliges must be found.

Contractual promise or consent creates a reordering of jural relations of title, duty and claim. Because of these implications in justice, men rightly expect performance of promises and accordingly place reliance upon them. "A promise is an express undertaking or agreement to carry the purpose into effect; a declaration which binds the person who makes it, either in honor, conscience, or law, to do or forbear a certain specific act. It is a declaration which gives to the person to whom made a right to expect or claim the performance of some particular thing." [33]

The justice involved in contracts pertains directly to the private good of the individual contractors but it also concerns indirectly the public good of all the members of the community. Hence contractual promises relate to both commutative and contributive justice.

a. *Contractual commutative justice.* Performance of a contractual promise is necessary for the private good of the individual contractors. Jural relations have been reordered and non-performance is a violation of the new relations thereby created. Not to fulfill the promised terms of a contract disrupts this order and can be as much of a usurpation of property claims as conversion is in torts. Injurious reliance on the promise only increases the degree of this wrong. Since commutative justice is concerned with the private good of individuals, failure to perform a contractual promise is against commutative justice.

b. *Contractual contributive justice.* The fulfillment of contractual promises, however, pertains also to the public good of the community. It does this first somewhat in the manner that torts do. For, just as a tort is an act directly against the private good of an individual citizen and thereby indirectly against the public good, so also unfulfilled contractual promises are violations of claims that directly affect the individual citizen as individual but also indirectly affect the members of the community as a whole.

[32] Lord Wright, Ought the Doctrine of Consideration Be Abolished from the Common Law?, 49 Harv. L. Rev. 1225, 1252 (1936).
[33] Hoskins v. Black, 190 Ky. 98, 226 S.W. 384, 385 (1920). See also E. I. Du Pont de Nemours & Co. v. Claiborne-Reno Co., 64 F.2d 224, 227, 89 A.L.R. 238 (8th Cir. 1933); Beck v. Wilkins-Ricks Co., 186 N.C. 210, 119 S.E. 235, 236 (1923).

There is another very particular manner, however, in which unperformed contractual promises relate to the common welfare. This is in regard to a general condition necessary for all contracting: the *mutual confidence* that one man must have in another. Without this very actual prerequisite, promises would be meaningless. The moment complete distrust became the prevailing legal climate in a community, contracts as legal instruments would vanish.

Just as every performed contractual promise contributes somewhat to promoting this necessary trust, so also every failure to do so contributes to undermining it to some degree.[34] The man who breaks his word given in contractual promise injures, therefore, not only other parties to the contract, but also the other members of the community.

Citizens are obliged to contribute in justice what is necessary for the public good. Mutual confidence is such a necessity. It is a matter not only of commutative justice, therefore, but also of contributive justice that contractual promises be fulfilled.[35]

2. *Obligation of contractual promise.* The reason why contractual promises oblige, then, is that *keeping them is necessary for the public good.* For, obligation is founded on the necessity of means for an end.

A contractual promise does not bind, therefore, because it is supported by something extrinsic like sufficient consideration or a cause which is to be found in the intention to benefit another.

Nor does it oblige because injurious reliance has been placed on it.[36] Important though injurious reliance is in assessing the degree of injury following non-performance, it presupposes that a contract already obliges; otherwise why should any reliance be put on it?

Likewise a contractual promise does not oblige because non-performance breaks a mystical "union of wills" characterized by the intention of mutually obliging each other. Unless a lawman holds a "will-theory," obligation, like law, has to do with factual means-end situations and has its foundation therein.[37]

[34] Low credit ratings, because of failure to pay for goods received, could be cited as evidence of this.

[35] "Because man is a social animal, one man naturally owes another that without which human society could not be preserved. Men could not live together, however, unless they trusted each other as declaring truth one to the other." Aquinas, 2-2 Sum. Theol. 109, 3, 2.

[36] Pound, An Introduction to the Philosophy of Law 147-158 (1954).

[37] The relation of the basis of law and obligation to contracts and even to vow and prayer, has long ago been noted. Cf. Suárez, 6 De Statu Religionis, 1, 13; 1 De Legibus 4, 8, also id. at 5, 17-18 and 14, 13. See also Aquinas, 2-2 Sum. Theol. 83, 1 and 88, 1; Kant, 1 The Metaphysics of Ethics 3, 15.

The ground of contractual obligation is, then, this factual one: the relation between keeping promised agreements and the common good. Mutual confidence among men is necessary for peace and security.

Those who enter into contractual promises, therefore, have no more choice whether they bind or not than a lawmaker has whether a law will oblige or not. This is determined by the means-end relation of the facts involved. What contracting parties can determine, though, is whether they wish to make their agreement enforceable legally.

This distinction supposes that obligation and extrinsic sanction are different. In most of the citations mentioned above, however, to be "legally bound" is taken to mean the same as to be "legally enforceable." These two things are different and should not be confused. The ground on which contractual promises bind is one thing; the evidence of intent to make contractual promises legally enforceable is something entirely different.

3. *Evidence of intention to enforce legally.* With obligation and enforceability thus distinguishable, the search for a criterion of the legal enforceability of contract should center, not on consideration or cause, but on evidence of the intention to so enforce. Such evidence is chiefly witnesses, a writing and seal.

Because the seal has been abolished in some jurisdictions as now meaningless and witness testimony is cumbersome and unreliable, a writing seems the best evidence of the intention to make a contract legally enforceable.

Consistent with this emphasis on written evidence is the Uniform Written Obligations Act mentioned above. Its emphasis on a writing itself, and not on consideration, is a step in the right direction. For, "This act provides that a written promise 'shall not be invalid or unenforceable for lack of consideration, if the writing also contains an additional express statement, in any form of language, that the signer intends to be legally bound.' " [38]

Although the philosophy of contracts back of the act is not certain (for instance whether it assumes that "legally bound" is the same as "legally enforceable" as its title would seem to indicate), nonetheless its main inspiration is certainly correct.

D. *International Agreements*

The full import of a theory of contracts can be seen when it is applied to treaties and international agreements which are con-

[38] Galvanoni & Nevy Bros. v. Acquadro, 46 D. & C. 358, 44 Lack. J. 111 (Pa. 1942).

tracts. At stake are world conditions of peace or war — of survival.

1. *Treaties are contracts.* Treaties are essentially contractual promises and agreements. "A treaty is not only a law, but also a contract between two nations; and, under familiar rules, it must, if possible, be so construed as to give full force and effect to all its parts." [39] "A treaty is a written contract between sovereigns. Its terms are agreed upon, and it is signed by plenipotentiaries or commissioners, who are the authorized agents of the contracting powers. But after such agreement and signature it must be ratified by the governments, and the exchange of ratifications constitutes the delivery." [40]

Although the immediate ends intended by the signatory nations are their own particular benefits, the treaty contract takes its overall significance from its relation to the common welfare. "A treaty signifies 'a compact made between two or more independent nations, with a view to the public welfare.' " [41]

2. *Pacta sunt servanda.* Agreements ought to be kept. As this is a basic non-legal assumption in contracts between individual persons, so also is it in contracts between nations. But why should international agreements be kept?

a. *Not from consideration or cause.* Treaties between nations do not bind only when they are supported by sufficient consideration or cause. Even if there was a price paid for a promise in treaty contracts or an intention to benefit another which is highly questionable, there would be no court to assess their value and enforce the agreements.

b. *From necessity for common welfare.* The reason why nations are obliged to keep their treaty agreements is the same as why any person is bound to keep a contractual promise: non-performances is, as explained, not only a commutative injustice to individuals but also a contributive injustice to the common welfare because it destroys mutual trust.

Though nations are obliged for these reasons to keep their international agreements, their enforceability is another matter. Until there is a world political union with a world government and a world court, treaty contracts will have to be enforced on a different basis. "A treaty is primarily a compact between independent nations. It depends for the enforcement of its provisions on the interest and the honor of the governments which are

[39] United States v. Reid, 73 F.2d 153, 155 (9th Cir. 1934); see also Charlton v. Kelley, 229 U.S. 447, 474, 33 Sup. Ct. 945, 954 (1912).

[40] Ex parte Ortiz, 100 Fed. 955, 962 (C.C.D. Minn. 1900).

[41] Louis Wolf and Co. v. United States, 107 F.2d 819, 827 (C.C.P.A. 1939); see also United States v. Belmont, 301 U.S. 324, 57 Sup. Ct. 758, 761 (1937).

parties to it. If these fail, its infraction becomes the subject of international negotiations and reclamations, so far as the injured party chooses to seek redress, which may in the end be enforced by actual war." [42]

No better example of the necessary relation between performed promises and the common good of mutual trust can be found than that reflected in international relations. Where treaty agreements are repeatedly broken, there is distrust, fear, preparation for protection and perhaps war. Where they are kept, confidence and trust are engendered, friendly intercourse is enjoyed and there is peace.

E. *Comment*

The basic reason why legal contracts oblige, then, is the same as the ground of any obligation: fulfillment is a necessary means to an end — the common good. This situation is created by the contractual union brought about by promissory agreement. The union is the essence of the contract. Consideration and cause do not pertain to the essence. Evidence of intention to bind legally and thereby make the contract legally enforceable is necessary. Central in the cluster of evidences to bind legally is a writing. Witnesses and seal are less central. If consideration has any value at all it is, not as the essence of a contract or the source of contractual obligation, but as evidence, albeit peripheral, of intention to bind legally. Oral as well as written legal contracts have to be enforced. But it is in the written contract that the intention to bind legally, as distinguished from the obligation itself and its source, is best attested.

Contract law is undergoing changes. The substitutes for consideration are indications of this. What lines these developments will take in the future it would be hazardous even to guess. One thing, however, seems certain. The ensuing changes will be an expression of whatever underlying philosophy of law and contracts is most prevalent.

The field of contracts is undoubtedly one of the most important wherein the philosophy of law will have its impact. "Revived philosophical jurisprudence has its first and perhaps its greatest opportunity in the Anglo-American law of contracts. . . . Given an attractive philosophical theory of enforcement of promises, our courts in a new period of growth will begin to shape the law

[42] Edye v. Robertson, 112 U.S. 580, 598-599, 5 Sup. Ct. 247, 254 (1884); see also Charlton v. Kelley, 229 U.S. 447, 474, 33 Sup. Ct. 945, 954 (1912).

thereby and judicial empiricism and legal reason will bring about a workable system along new lines." [43]

III. Relations Created by Agreements

It was pointed out above how new relations of title created by occupancy or labor are the basis of new jural relations. Here we are concerned with the relations created by promissory agreements. These are especially important in the understanding of contracts that result in unions or associations.

A. *Agreements Regarding Exchanges*

Promissory agreements to do some particular thing are usually for the mutual good of the parties concerned. Such are the everyday bilateral contracts of exchange and the multi-lateral contracts of cooperative ventures.

1. *Relations of title.* In the ordinary contract of exchange, the act of consent or promissory agreement is the initiating cause of the exchange of relations of title. Depending upon stipulation, this exchange may take place immediately and coincidentally with the agreement, or it may occur later and dependent on the transfer of the things contracted for.

As a result of this consent the contracting parties do not stand to each other in the way they did before their agreement. They are related to each other in a new way. They are now united in their common purpose of exchange for mutual benefit. In other words, their act of promissory agreement to exchange relations of title has the effect of uniting them in a contractual union. This state of being so united lasts, of course, only from the initiation of the contract to the fulfilling of its terms.[44]

2. *Jural relations of commutative justice.* Upon exchange of titles, however, there arises in each of the contracting parties the duty to respect the new titles. The way the parties stand with reference to each other must now be one of non-interference with the titles of the other. In a word, they now have the duty in commutative justice of showing the owed respect, of establishing just regard, of maintaining right jural relations toward the other. This duty rests, as noted above, on the necessity of such relations for security and peaceful living conditions. In the event that

[43] Pound, An Introduction to the Philosophy of Law 158-159 (1954). By permission of the Yale University Press.

[44] For examples of this relation in cases where equitable title is recognized in a vendee although legal title has not yet passed, see Chapter 18.

such jural relations are not forthcoming if there is evidence of intention to bind legally, they can be enforced by law.

B.   *Agreements Regarding Cooperative Undertakings*

Other kinds of promissory agreements also create new jural and legal relations.   These are the agreements by which unions or associations are formed for the purpose of attaining some common end.   Such are the various types of corporations and the political union itself.

1. *Relations of union.*   Individual persons form a business association by agreeing to furnish effort or resources in the pursuit of a common goal, their mutual profit.   As a consequence of their individual acts of consent, they no longer stand in reference to each other in exactly the same way they did before their consent. As in any contract — business associations or corporations are contractual in origin[45] — their act of consent is a fact that causes them to be related now in an entirely different way.   They are now actually united in their pursuit of their common end.   They are a union of individual persons which has been created by their consent to work for a common goal.   This union endures as long as the persons consent to pursue this common end.

2. *Jural relations of contributive justice.*   Once the union or association is thus formed, each member has a duty to carry out his promissory agreement, as he would in any contract, to contribute to the promotion of the common goal.   His cooperation is owed to the others on the basis of his promissory agreement. His relations with the others should be one of cooperative effort. In a union or association, then, these are the jural relations that each member owes the others in contributive justice.   Again, if these are important enough to be embodied into law as is especially the case regarding political unions, these jural relations become legal relations that will be enforced.[46]

3. *"Artificial" and "legal" entities and persons.*   From the above explanation it would seem that the location of the entity or reality of unions or associations would not be a difficult matter. But in the meanderings of the law such has not been the case.

Associations have been said to be "artificial beings" that exist "only in contemplation of law," or beings that have "a distinct legal entity."   "A corporation is an artifical being, invisible, in-

[45] See note 53 infra.
[46] For further discussion of jural relations in the political union, see Chapter 20.

tangible, and existing only in contemplation of law." [47] "A corporation is, after all, but an association of individuals under an assumed name and with a distinct legal entity." [48]

Or corporations have been said to be artificial or legal persons as have the estates of a bankrupt or a deceased person. " 'While in its primary sense, it ('person') means a natural person only, the term is a broad one, and the sense in which it is used in any particular instance may often be ascertained from the context and intent with which it is employed.' Thus it has been held to include an 'agent . . . an estate.' . . . 'The estate of a decedent is a person in legal contemplation.' 'The word "person" . . . is a generic term, and includes artificial as well as natural persons.' . . . 'Persons are two kinds, natural and artificial. A natural person is a human being. Artificial persons include (1) a collection or succession of natural persons forming a corporation; (2) a collection of property to which the law attributes the capacity of having rights and duties. The latter class of artificial persons is recognized only to a limited extent in our law. Examples are the estate of a bankrupt or deceased person.' " [49]

Such legal persons have in turn been viewed in one of two ways. One way has been to see this person as a fiction, a symbol created by the state and with those rights which the state sees fit to give it and no more.[50] The other way, if it is a question of reacting to the omnipotence of the state, has been to go to the opposite extreme of exaggerated realism and reify the concept of "legal person." This has resulted in this person being looked upon as an organism with a body, mind and will of its own. It is as such an organism that corporations have been said to have relations with other corporations and the state.[51]

4. *Natural and legal elements of incorporated associations.* The lawman can easily avoid the extremes of fictionalizing or reifying associations by keeping hardheadedly in mind what the

[47] The Trustees of Dartmouth College v. Woodward, 4 Wheat. 518, 636, 4 L. Ed. 629, 657 (1819).

[48] Hale v. Henkel, 201 U.S. 43, 76, 26 Sup. Ct. 370, 379 (1906).

[49] Hogan v. Greenfield, 58 Wyo. 13, 122 P.2d 850, 853 (1942). See also Fox's Appeal, 112 Pa. 337, 4 Atl. 149, 152 (1886); Blair v. Worley, 1 Scam. 177, 179 (Ill. 1835).

[50] See Von Savigny, 2 System des Heutigen Romischen Rechts 236 (1840); Holland, Jurisprudence 336-337 (11th ed. 1910); Salmond, Jurisprudence 336-342 (8th ed. 1930).

[51] See Gierke, Das Wesen der Menschlichen Verbande (1902); and his Political Theories of the Middle Ages, vii-xiv (Maitland trans. 1922).

For a discussion of "legal personality," see Wolff, On the Nature of Legal Persons, 54 L. Q. Rev. 494-521 (1938); and Laski, The Personality of Associations, 29 Harv. L. Rev. 404-426 (1916).

factual elements of associations are. This will be his assurance of correctly assessing them.

a. *Natural elements.* The first element of associations are the natural persons, whether this be an association such as a corporation sole or a corporation aggregate. The second element is the act of consent of the various members to work for a common goal, which act causes them to stand in a relation of unity to the other members. These elements are presupposed before the act of incorporation and are implied in the petition for incorporation. " 'The statement that a corporation is an artificial person or entity, apart from its members is merely a description, in figurative language, of a corporation viewed as a collective body. A corporation is really an association of persons, and no judicial dictum or legislative enactment can alter this fact.' " [52]

b. *Legal elements.* This association of persons already united by their common purpose is privileged by the charter of incorporation to exist and function as a permanent organization. This franchise is a contract between the government and the incorporators. It is an agreement on the part of the government to recognize this association of persons as a permanently existing union, irrespective of changes in the membership that may occur as time goes on, and to allow them to carry on their corporate activity according to certain well-defined claims and duties; and it is an agreement by the members of this association to act accordingly. "The primary franchise of a corporation, the right and privilege to be a corporation, vests in the individuals who compose the corporation. This right granted by the state by general law upon certain conditions, express or implied, constitutes, when accepted, a contract between the corporation, or the corporators or members, and the state. 'The charter of a corporation, whether it is created by a special act or formed under a general corporation law, is a contract between the corporation, or the corporators or members, and the state. It is a contract between the state and the corporation, between the corporation and the stockholders, and between the stockholders and the state.' " [53]

The actual elements of an association are then: those presup-

[52] McIntosh v. Dakota Trust Co., 52 N.D. 752, 204 N.W. 818, 825 (1925). See also Dow v. Northern R.R. Co., 67 N.H. 1, 4, 36 Atl. 510, 511 (1887); State ex rel. Griffith v. Knights of Ku Klux Klan, 117 Kan. 564, 232 Pac. 254, 257 (1925).

[53] Bruun v. Cook, 280 Mich. 484, 273 N.W. 774, 777 (1937). See The Trustees of Dartmouth College v. Woodward, 4 Wheat. 518, 657, 4 L. Ed. 629, 664 (1819); Waterloo Water Co. v. Village of Waterloo, 200 App. Div. 718, 193 N.Y. Supp. 360, 362 (1922).

posed before incorporation, the natural persons and their contractual relations which unite them in their pursuit of a common end; and those elements consequent upon the act of incorporation, the added contractual relations between the members of the corporation and the persons in government.

c. *Consequences.* The determination of what an association actually is, is not merely a point of theoretical interest. Important consequences follow regarding the responsibility of shareholders. When a corporation is looked on as a legal person that somehow has a mind and will of its own and is separate from its members, the easy tendency is to locate this mind and will in the directors and managers, with the shareholders being relegated to vague economic and moral isolation. In this view, responsibility would rest with directors and managers and they alone would be liable for the crimes and torts of the corporation.

On the other hand, when a corporation is recognized as a union or association of natural persons, the mind and will of a corporation will be seen to be the minds and wills of the individual members which is sometimes expressed in a majority vote and implemented by managers and directors. Shareholders in this view cannot be conceived merely as peripheral sine qua non, but they will be numbered among those united for the common purpose. For, shareholders are the corporation. "The idea that the corporation is an entity distinct from the corporators who compose it, has been aptly characterized as 'a nebulous fiction of thought.' . . . When all has been said, it remains that a corporation is not *in reality* a person or a thing distinct from its constituent parts, and the constituent parts are the stockholders, as much so in essence and in reality as the several partners are the constituent parts of a partnership." [54]

The majority opinion of shareholders is represented by and in the prevailing management and its policies. It is on these grounds that stockholders actually share, however remotely, the responsibility of the directors who act on their behalf in managing the enterprise. This responsibility does not rule out civil and criminal liability.[55]

[54] Cincinnati Volksblatt Co. v. Hoffmeister, 62 Ohio St. 189, 200, 56 N.E. 1033, 1035 (1900). See also Hale v. Hardon, 95 Fed. 747, 752 (1st Cir. 1899).

[55] Diversey v. Smith, 103 Ill. 390, 42 Am. Rep. 14, 19 (1882). See also Conant v. Van Schaick, 24 Barb. 87, 88 (N.Y. 1857); United States v. Nearing, 252 Fed. 223, 231 (S.D.N.Y. 1918); United States v. MacAndrews and Forbes Co., 149 Fed. 823, 835 (C.C.S.D.N.Y. 1906); Telegram Newspaper Co. v. Commonwealth, 172 Mass. 294, 296, 52 N.E. 445, 446 (1899); Wilson v. United States, 221 U.S. 361, 384, 385, 31 Sup. Ct. 538 (1911).

CHAPTER 18

Equity

The question that concerns us in this Chapter is, how explain the phenomenon of equity in legal thinking and how justify law's adoption of its governing principle.

I. HUMANE INTERPRETATION

Equity is a datum that stands in the history of law as a constant witness to men's steadfast desire for equal justice in their dealings with one another. Equity is not an area of law, much less a "course" in law. It is rather a way of thinking about justice — the content of law — inasmuch as it cuts across all human activity that falls within the purview of law and the common good.

Equity has always had a place in the thinking of lawmen re- garding justice and law. The ancient Greeks called it "epieikeia" or "epikeia." [1] The Romans knew this epikeia as "aequitas." [2] The Middle Ages also recognized it as "aequitas." [3] Anglo- American lawyers call it "equity." ". . . [T]he primal meaning of the term 'equitas,' in the Roman law, was either the idea of equal proportionate distribution, or the idea of leveling, in the sense of removing inequalities. The term 'equity,' in English and American law is derived from the Roman 'equitas,' and in the long history of equity jurisprudence, from the Roman praetors to this day, its original meaning has never been obscured. The maxim, 'Equality is equity,' has long been familiar as a potent principle, and has lost none of its force." [4] "In common parlance, 'equity' and 'justice' have come to be if not synonymous, at least substantially equivalent terms." [5] "We have construed the words

---

[1] Aristotle, 5 Nicomachean Ethics 10, 1137a30 (Ross trans. 1941). Epikeia as emergency interpretation of legislation has already been noted in Chapter 4.

[2] Cicero, De Officiis, I, 10, 13; III, 16, 67.

[3] Aquinas, 2-2 Sum. Theol. 120, 1.

[4] Miller v. Kenniston, 86 Me. 550, 30 Atl. 114 (1894).

[5] In re Lessig's Estate, 168 Misc. 889, 6 N.Y.S.2d 720, 721 (1938).

'just and reasonable' to mean, or be equivalent to, an equitable division." [6]

The consistent core meaning of equity throughout the centuries has been the equality of justice beyond the letter of the law but according to its spirit. As mentioned above regarding the extent of legislation, statutes are framed to cover the general aspect of situations. They cannot include every possible detail that may arise under a particular head. There is a margin left for extraordinary cases. Consequently, there is a need for construing statutes according to the main intention of the lawmaker, which is the common good of the citizens. In emergency situations, as noted, this interpreting is done by individuals and is elemental epikeia. In other exceptional cases, this construing is done by courts of law or equity and is equity in the legal sense as will be seen presently.

Equity in its broadest meaning, then, has to do with a humane interpretation of law in general. Such an approach to law is essential to every rational system of justice.

II. DISCRETIONARY MODIFICATION

Equity, in the sense of the broad interpretative attitude of mind just described, when brought to bear by courts on exceptional cases results in a discretionary modification of law in these particular instances. It is characteristically benevolent rather than harsh. Its inspiration is the spirit of the law, that is, what the legislators would have done about the case under consideration.

Should the property of a testator pass to one who has murdered him by poisoning for the very purpose of obtaining his property? Although the statutes may not provide for such a case, it is only equitable to construe them according to what their framers would undoubtedly have intended: that the murderer would not acquire property by his crime and thereby be rewarded for its commission. "It is quite true that statutes regulating the making, proof and effect of wills and the devolution of property, if literally construed, and if their force and effect can in no way and under no circumstances be controlled or modified, give this property to the murderer . . . It is a familiar canon of construction that a thing which is within the intention of the makers of a statute is as much within the statute as if it were within the letter; and a thing which is within the letter of the statute is not within the

[6] Carter v. Carter, 181 Okla. 204, 73 P.2d 404, 405 (1937).

statute unless it be within the intention of the makers. The writers of laws do not always express their intention perfectly, but either exceed it or fall short of it, so that judges are to collect it from probable or rational conjecture only, and this is called 'rational interpretation.' " [7]

Equity demands, therefore, that in such a case the court look beyond the letter of the statute. "In some cases the letter of a legislative act is restrained by an equitable construction; in others, it is enlarged; in others, the construction is contrary to the letter . . . If the lawmakers could, as to this case, be consulted, would they say that they intended by their general language that the property of a testator or of an ancestor should pass to one who had taken his life for the express purpose of getting his property?" [8] The court held that the lawmakers would not so intend.

This looking beyond the letter of the law, according to its spirit, may also be needed sometimes regarding constitutions themselves when there is question of the constitutionality of a particular statute. Thus, an enactment giving the citizens of certain counties the right to decide by vote whether the sale of vinous and spiritous liquors should be continued within such counties, where the majority of votes had been against such sale, was held unconstitutional and void. The action of a legislature, the court said, ". . . may be invalid, though it contravene no express provision of the constitution, if it be in violation of the spirit of that instrument, and the genius of the public institutions designed to be created by it. Indeed, it is this species of insidious infraction that is more to be feared and guarded against than direct attacks upon any particular principle proclaimed as a part of the primordial law: for attempts of the latter description will, generally, be met by instant reprobation, while the stealthy and frequently seductive character of the former is apt to escape detection, until the innovation is made manifest by the infliction of some startling wrong." [9]

A.   Development

Equitable modification of law in particular cases has resulted, in Anglo-American law, in a supplementary jurisdiction. Law gave money judgments; equity was needed to give specific per-

[7] Riggs v. Palmer, 115 N.Y. 506, 22 N.E. 188, 189 (1889).
[8] Riggs v. Palmer at 189.
[9] Parker v. Commonwealth, 6 Barr. 507, 511 (Pa. 1847).

formance. Equity, originally in the hands of the Chancellor, became a technical system distinct from common law.

Chancery or equity courts grew alongside the courts of law. ". . . [W]e must inquire what is meant by chancery and common-law jurisdiction. Chancery jurisdiction may be defined to be a judicial power to hear and determine all cases wherein the law, for its universality, cannot afford relief. Early in the history of jurisprudence the administration of justice in the ordinary courts was found to be incomplete, and hence arose the necessity of separate courts of equity, which were organized about the reign of King Edward III [1327-1377] for the purpose of correcting that wherein the law was defective; and matters of fraud were among the objects to which the jurisdiction of chancery was originally confined. Soon after these courts were established in England a fierce struggle arose between the law and equity courts in relation to the jurisdiction and powers of each; but, as we trace the history of English jurisprudence, we find the prejudice which at first existed on the part of the common-law courts yielding to the necessity and utility of a distinctive equity jurisprudence." [10]

Eventually "chancery" and "equity" became synonymous. "The terms 'equity' and 'chancery' are commonly used in the United States in the same sense, as will appear from the books; this usage, no doubt, is due to the fact that jurisdiction exercised in equity by our courts is assimilated to the equity or extraordinary jurisdiction of the Court of Chancery in England. . . . A chancery case is one in which according to the usages and practices in courts of chancery prior to and at the time of the adoption of the Code of Civil Procedure, remedies were awarded in accordance with the principles of equity and not in accordance with rules of law. . . . The terms 'equity' and 'chancery' are interchangeable and are constantly used as synonymous in all of our states, as well as in England." [11]

Courts of equity or chancery and courts of law did not become two rival systems. Rather, there is a vital connection between the two and not a few doctrines of the common law are equitable in nature. Besides, just as in other legal systems the principles of law and equity can be comprised within one body of law and administered by the same courts, so also in England and America there has been a tendency in this direction.

What with equity not being limited to the remedies afforded by the common law, it seemed debatable for a while whether

[10] Kenyon v. Kenyon, 3 Utah 431, 24 Pac. 829, 830 (1861).
[11] Ireland v. Cheney, 129 Ohio St. 527, 196 N.E. 267, 270 (1935).

equity would not become arbitrary and capricious. It was said, in a much quoted passage that, "Equity is a roguish thing: for law we have a measure, know what to trust to; equity is according to the conscience of him that is Chancellor, and as that is larger, or narrower, so is equity. 'Tis all one, as if they should make his foot the standard for the measure we call a Chancellor's foot; what an uncertain measure would this be! One Chancellor has a long foot, another a short foot, a third an indifferent foot; 'tis the same thing in the Chancellor's conscience." [12]

As time went on, however, it became apparent that equity was destined to develop along consistent lines in England and the United States as it had in other countries and times. ". . . Nor is equity a chancellor's mere notions of what is equality; on the contrary, it is a system, both in England and this country, of well-established law. No rule of equity is better established in this state than that to set aside a written instrument the evidence must be 'clear, precise, and indubitable,' whether the allegation be fraud practiced by the beneficiary under it or incapacity on the part of him who executed it." [13] ". . . A court of equity is not entirely a free lance, which can be wielded independently of law or regulation. It is just as subservient to and dependent on the law, so far as its jurisdiction is concerned, as is a court of law. It is true that the rules governing the disposition of law and of enforcing and protecting rights under the law, as applied by courts of equity, are more pliable and adaptive than are the rules governing courts of law. The object of the establishment of courts of equity was to escape the rigidity of the rules governing cases of law, and to confer more discretionary powers upon the chancellor, thereby making the administration of the law more flexible and more effective for the elicitation of truth." [14]

B.   *Governing Principle*

The over-all norm of equity has been the objective "aequum et bonum" or, expressed subjectively, "conscience."

Mansfield's statement of this principle gave direction to legal thinking about equity. "If the defendant be under an obligation,

---

[12] Gee v. Pritchard, 2 Swans. 402, 414, 36 Eng. Rep. 670, 674 (1818).

[13] Laird v. Union Traction Co., 208 Pa. 574, 57 Atl. 987 (1904).

[14] Parmeter v. Bourne, 8 Wash. 45, 35 Pac. 586, 587 (1894). On the development of equity see Allen, Law In The Making 358-401 (5th ed. 1951); 1 Pollock and Maitland, The History Of The English Law 189-206 (1911); and 1 Holdsworth, A History of English Law 446-469 (1922).

from the ties of natural justice, to refund, the law implies a debt, and gives this action [indebitatus assumpsit] founded in the equity of the plaintiff's case, as it were upon a contract (*quasi ex contractus,* as the Roman law expresses it). . . .

"This kind of equitable action, to recover back money, which ought not in justice to be kept, is very beneficial, and therefore much to be encouraged. It lies only for money which, *ex aequo et bono,* the defendant ought to refund. It does not lie for money paid by the plaintiff, which is claimed of him as payable in point of honour and honesty, although it could not have been recovered from him by any course of law; as in payment of a debt barred by the Statute of Limitations, or contracted during his infancy, or to the extent of principal and legal interest upon an usurious contract, or for money fairly lost at play; because in all these cases the defendant may retain it with a safe conscience, though by positive law he was barred from recovering it. But it lies for money paid by mistake; or upon a consideration which happens to fail; or for money got through imposition (express or implied); or extortion; or oppression; or an undue advantage taken of the plaintiff's situation, contrary to laws made for the protection of persons under those circumstances.

"In one word, the gist of this kind of action is, that the defendant, upon the circumstances of the case, is obliged by the ties of natural justice and equity to refund the money." [15]

Though there was no little dissatisfaction with the vagueness of "natural justice" and "aequum et bonum" and "justice between man and man" was suggested in their place,[16] nevertheless it seems that criticisms of the principle ". . . may be regarded rather as pruning some of the exuberance . . . than as axes laid at the roots of it." [17]

This norm of equity was also expressed in terms of the judgments that men make regarding the rightness or wrongness of human actions — conscience.[18] Conscience, together with the concept of "aequum et bonum," attests the moral background of equity. "If we look for one general principle which more than any other influenced equity as it was developed by the Chancery, we find it in a philosophical and theological conception of con-

---

[15] Moses v. Macferlan, 2 Burr. 1005, 1008, 1012, 97 Eng. Rep. 676, 678, 680 (1760).
[16] Holt v. Markham, 1 K. B. 504, 513 (1923).
[17] Winfield, The Law of Quasi-Contracts 14 (1952).
[18] See Chapter 6 on "Conscience."

science . . . English equity begins to be systematized under the guidance of a governing moral principle." [19]

Conscience, as just noted, does not imply an arbitrary decision. It is a judgment reached according to principles. "The 'conscience' which is an element of the equitable jurisdiction is not the private opinion of an individual court, but is rather to be regarded 'as a metaphorical term, designating the common standard of civil right and expediency combined, based upon general principles and limited by established doctrines, to which the court appeals and by which it tests the conduct and rights of suitors — a judicial and not a personal conscience.' " [20]

1. *In law.* The principle of equity is evident both in courts of law as well as in courts of equity. A suit for restitution in quasi-contract to prevent unjust enrichment, though it may be an action at law, actually is equitable in character and is subject to the limitations of relief in equity.

Under the principle of quasi-contract ". . . a defendant has something of value at the plaintiff's expense under circumstances which impose legal duty of restitution." [21] Unjust enrichment of a person occurs ". . . when he has and retains money or benefits which in justice and equity belong to another." [22]

The ferment of equity is found at work in cases such as contracts unenforceable under the Statute of Frauds, contracts regarding sale of goods, and breach of valid contract.

a. *Statute of Frauds.* An appellee orally agreed to purchase from appellants a house and lot for a certain sum. The sellers agreed to accept as part of the purchase price a house and lot owned by the appellee at an agreed value. Part of the balance was to be paid in cash and the remainder in six months. On the day of the agreement the appellee paid appellants $850 in cash. Appellee later decided not to go through with the transaction, although appellants had not repudiated it and were ready and willing to perform it, and he sued to recover benefits conferred upon the appellants.

This oral contract was unenforceable because it did not meet the requirement of the Statute of Frauds. The court subscribed to the opinion, however, that it would be "wrongful" not to

[19] Allen, Law in the Making 381, 384 (5th ed. 1951). By permission of the Clarendon Press.

[20] National City Bank of New York v. Gelfert, 284 N.Y. 13, 29 N.E.2d 449, 452 (1940).

[21] Hermann v. Gleason, 126 F.2d 936, 940 (6th Cir. 1942).

[22] Hummel v. Hummel, 133 Ohio St. 520, 14 N.E.2d 923, 927 (1938).

complete the transaction.   In other words, until such time as appellee exercised his rights under the Statute of Frauds, the contract was enforceable — as is held in most jurisdictions.   Once he exercised his rights it was no longer enforceable in law, but it was still a morally valid agreement and therefore giving rise to a moral obligation to carry it out.   Hence, because of this moral obligation to fulfill his contractual undertaking, the appellee was not allowed to recover the benefits he had conferred upon the appellants.

The court said: "According to the great weight of authority the vendee, in a situation such as we have here, can not recover payments made on the purchase price.   If the vendee shows tender of compliance on his part and a refusal of compliance on the part of the vendor, a different result obtains, but that is not the situation here. . . .   'In nearly all jurisdictions of this country a vendee in default cannot, as a general rule, recover back the money he has paid on an executory contract.   So long as the vendor is not in default and is willing and able to perform, the purchaser cannot wrongfully refuse to complete the transaction and recover what he has paid toward the purchase money.   Moreover, according to the great weight of authority, this general rule applies even though the contract of sale is oral and for such reason cannot, on account of the statute of frauds, be enforced by action against the purchaser.' " [23]

The moral obligation of a contract is not to be overridden by the legal status of contract.   "The statute of frauds is intended to protect against fraud; it is not intended as an escape route for persons seeking to avoid obligations undertaken by or imposed upon them." [24]

b. *Sale of goods.*   In situations where the buyer uses goods delivered before he knows that the seller will not complete delivery, it is in terms of a "fair" or equitable value that the case is decided.   "Regarding delivery of wrong quantity: Where the seller delivers to the buyer a quantity of goods less than he contracted to sell, the buyer may reject them, but if the buyer accepts or retains the goods so delivered, knowing that the seller is not going to perform the contract in full, he must pay for them at contract rate.   If, however, the buyer has used or disposed of the goods delivered before he knows that the seller is not going to perform his contract in full, the buyer shall not be liable for

[23] Watkins v. Wells, 303 Ky. 728, 198 S.W.2d 662, 663, 664 (1946).
[24] Keirsey v. Hirsh, 58 N.M. 18, 265 P.2d 346, 351 (1954).

more than the fair value to him of the goods so received." [25]

c. *Breach of contract.* In some situations where there is a deliberate breach of contract, recovery for services rendered may be allowed on the basis of a "new case" which is implied on an equitable or moral basis. In a well known case P, who had agreed to work for D for a year, voluntarily abandoned his contract at the end of ten months. No evidence was adduced that P's failure to fulfill his contract caused damage to D. Although guilty of a deliberate default, P was allowed a quasi-contractual recovery for the services he had rendered. "The plaintiff was entitled to recover as much as the labor performed was reasonably worth. . . . This may be considered as making a new case, one not within the original agreement, and the party is entitled to 'recover on his new case, for the work done, not as agreed, but yet accepted by the defendant.' " [26]

Regarding this decision, it has been remarked: "That celebrated case has been criticized, doubted and denied to be sound. It is frequently said to be good equity, but bad law. Yet its principles have been gradually winning their way into professional and judicial favor. It is bottomed on justice, and is right upon principle, however it may be upon the technical and more illiberal rules of the common law, as found in the older cases." [27]

2. *In equity.* The drive for equity is well demonstrated in cases of specific performance (one of the main reasons for the origin and growth of courts of equity) and in cases of constructive trusts.

a. *Specific performance.* Contracts for sale of land may be enforced by specific performance because money may not be a "complete" remedy. "Courts of Equity decree the specific performance of contracts, not upon any distinction between realty and personalty, but because damages at law may not, in the particular case, afford a complete remedy. Thus a Court of Equity decrees performance of a contract of land, not because of the real nature of the land, but because damages at law, which must be calculated upon the general money value of land, may not be a complete remedy to the purchaser, to whom the land may have a peculiar and special value." [28]

Contracts involving speculative damages may also demand spe-

---

[25] New York Personal Property Law §125. Quoted in Guaranty Trust Co. v. Gerseta Corp., 212 App. Div. 76, 208 N.Y. Supp. 270, 272 (1925).

[26] Britton v. Turner, 6 N.H. 481, 495 (1834).

[27] McClay v. Hedge, 18 Iowa 66, 68 (1864).

[28] Adderly v. Dixon, 1 Sim. and St. 607, 610, 57 Eng. Rep. 239, 240 (1924). See also Kitchen v. Herring, 42 N.C. 191 (1851).

cific performance. P bought the entire stock of D's merchandise
for a lump sum which was paid. D delivered about two-thirds of
the goods but refused to deliver the remainder and concealed
them, so that P could not obtain possession by an action of
replevin. The court said that, " 'When an agreement for valuable
consideration between two parties has been partially performed,
the court ought to do its utmost to carry out that agreement by a
decree for specific performance.' In this particular case this rule
is especially emphasized, because, the sale being in lump, full payment having been made, and the chattels purchased partly delivered, the title to the remainder, both legally and in equity, has
rested in the complainant. Therefore the complainant is only
seeking to assert its title to chattels in the possession of the respondent to which it is legally entitled specifically, and which, the
same being secreted, it cannot obtain by any process at common
law. Of course, as we have already said in another connection,
this fact alone would not justify a chancellor in taking jurisdiction, but it emphasizes the propriety and justice of exercising in
this particular case the peculiar equitable jurisdiction of which
we have spoken. Therefore, on this ground, and on this ground
alone, although no precedent is produced, we deem it just and
proper, and within the limitations governing courts in equity, to
retain jurisdiction of this bill." [29]

Building contracts likewise represent another area where specific performance may be called for. P conveyed land to a railroad on condition that the railroad build a wharf for P's use. The
railroad did not fulfill its part of the agreement and the court
ordered specific performance. The lengths to which a court will
go to enforce specific performance and see justice done is shown
in this court's response to the objection brought forward that the
court would find it difficult to compel the building of the wharf.
The court said: "It would be monstrous if the company, having
got the whole benefit of the agreement, could turn round and
say, 'This is a sort of thing which the Court finds a difficulty in
doing, and will not do.' Rather than allow such a gross piece of
dishonesty go unredressed the Court would struggle with any
amount of difficulties in order to perform the agreement." [30]

b. *Constructive trusts.* Equity also finds expression in implied
or constructive trusts which are grounded on the concept of restitution. " 'Implied trusts arise by implication of law because
morality, justice, conscience, and fair dealing demand that the re-

[29] Raymond Syndicate v. Brown, 124 Fed. 80, 83 (D.N.H. 1903).
[30] Wilson and Furness Ry. Co., L.R. 9 Eq. Cas. 28, 33 (1869).

lation be established' . . . 'A constructive trust is the formula through which the conscience of equity finds expression. When property has been acquired in such circumstances that the holder of the legal title may not in good conscience retain the beneficial interest equity converts him into a trustee.' Courts act upon the same logic in implying a trust." [31]

III.   Rooted in Elementary Demands

How explain the fact that the concept of equity runs thus throughout legal thinking and how justify law's adoption of the governing principle of "aequum et bonum" or "conscience"?

A.   Drive for "Mine-Thine" Social Living

An explanation that is adequate must be related to the very nature of men; for, as we have seen, a rudimentary notion of justice is present even among primitives. It is only in the elementary demand expressed by men's nature that they live in community and in this living distinguish between "mine" and "thine" that the rationale of equity is ultimately found. Only if equity is seen in relation to this basic drive for elementary justice can its origin be conclusively located. The fact that men have always sought justness beyond the letter of man-made law — whether in the ancient, mediaeval or modern world and whether in terms of epikeia, aequitas, equity, natural justice, fairness or any other term — is evidence that all men judge without a reasoning process that elemental justice must be done.[32]

The force of this connatural judgment has been such that it causes men to gauge and measure justice, when necessary, by a norm other than a man-made one and to look for a corrective beyond enactment and precedent. The spirit of the law — fulfillment of the people's needs — is recognized as overriding the shortcomings of the letter of the law. It is true that equity as a system of remedial justice has developed a set of guiding maxims of its own.[33] Their significance, however, relates directly to their original purpose: the search for justness beyond legislation and adjudication.

[31] Reed v. Kellerman, 40 F. Supp. 46, 51 (E.D.Pa. 1941).

[32] It is more accurate to speak of a natural judgment regarding what is just or unjust than to use the phrase "sense of justice or injustice." For "sense" may too easily carry the connotation of "feeling" or "emotion." The basis of morality is not feeling or emotion but intellectual judgment.

[33] Isabelle Properties v. Edelman, 164 Misc. 192, 297 N.Y. Supp. 572, 574 (1937).

The presence of equity in the history of law is exactly what is to be expected, if every man has the basic drives outlined above. It would be inexplicable only if a different interpretation of man were adopted. If, for instance, men were mere economic units of matter, it would be difficult to account for the constant and consistent search for justice in equity, because in this supposition the idea itself of equity would change with varying economic conditions.

Law, then, is not only justified in taking account of the principle of equity but it is obliged to do so if its main concern is justice for the people.[34] Law directs individual persons to what is good for them. But the nature itself of these persons expresses an indication that justice is the basic jural good.

B. *Equity More Ethical than Law*

Because equity calls on norms of justice that are more fundamental than those expressed in the letter of man-made law, it is closer to the source of ethics and morality. In this sense, it is "more ethical than law." For equity uses the demands of man-discovered law, and it reasons therefrom. If the conclusions go beyond those of existing law, so be it — that is equity. "When according to the principles of natural justice and equity (*ex aequo et bono*) the defendant ought to pay, the law imposes a duty on him to pay." [35]

1. *Emphasis on duty.* Equity looks to the duty of the defendant rather than to the claim of the plaintiff as law usually does. ". . . The difference between the judgment at law and the decree in equity goes to the root of the whole matter. The law regards chiefly the right of the plaintiff, and gives judgment that he recover the land, debt, or damages. Because they are his. Equity lays the stress upon the duty of the defendant, and decrees that he do or refrain from doing a certain thing because he ought to act or forbear. It is because of this emphasis upon the defendant's duty that equity is so much more ethical than law." [36] In line with the "my title-your duty-my claim" analysis of right made

[34] The quest for equity or equal justice is manifested not only in civil but also in criminal law. The extension in early common law of clerical privilege or "benefit of clergy" to lay criminals in order to mitigate the severity of laws decreeing the death penalty for minor crimes, is a most interesting example of this. See 4 Blackstone, Commentaries 365-374; also 2 Burdick, Law of Crime 89-90 (1946). For the relation of this legal phenomenon to present day practices see Hall, Theft, Law and Society 68-121 (1935).

[35] Moses v. Macferlan, 2 Burr. 1005, 1012, 97 Eng. Rep. 676, 680 (1760).

[36] Ames, Law and Morals, 22 Harv. L. Rev. 97, 106 (1908).

above, equity stands one step closer to title with its emphasis on defendant's duty toward plaintiff's title than does law with its accent on plaintiff's claim on defendant's duty.

2. *Bridge between philosophical and legal thinking.* Equity can be a link between philosophical and legal thinking. The significance of equity is not only that it is a source of remedy against injustice. Equity is standing confirmation that man-discovered law is a prior and more fundamental law than man-made law. "The 'natural sense of justice' — or what has been called *vulgaris aequitas* — is not a meaningless term. All law must postulate some kind of common denominator of just instinct in the community. There is no meaning in any legal system unless this foundation exists. Incalculable though the variations of subjective opinion may be, it needs no subtle dialectic to demonstrate that there is in man at least an elementary perception of justice, as a form of the right and good, which no law dare flagrantly transgress." [37]

Equity, being a mode of applying elementary demands of justness to concrete situations, is, then, a way of thinking about the content of law. For this reason, it can be a bridge in a lawman's thinking between the philosophy of man and the philosophy of law.

[37] Allen, Law in the Making 362. By permission of the Clarendon Press.

PART IV

Background of Law

CHAPTER 19

Law — Instrument of Government

It is impossible to understand law in its full implications unless it is seen in its proper setting — that is, as an instrument of government. For, the immediate background of law is government. Government's purpose is to direct people in those areas that pertain to their common good. Law is the instrument by which government effects this direction. "In its last analysis, government, regardless of the form it takes, is nothing more than an instrument to preserve an ordered society. Laws are nothing more than rules promulgated by government as a means to an ordered society." [1]

Government itself takes its significance from the union or society of which it is the governing agency. Hence, political government can be understood only in relation to political union. Political union is not intelligible unless it is seen as a means of realizing goods that are common to all its members. Finally, the common good derives its meaning from the needs of men who, following a drive of their nature, must live in community.

The background of law, then, includes government, political union and the common good of men in community. It is in relation to this backdrop that a lawman must view law if he is to see it in its true perspective.

[1] Miami Laundry v. Florida Dry Cleaning and Laundry Board, 134 Fla. 1, 183 So. 759, 764 (1938). "The philosophical analysis and definition of law belongs, in our judgment, neither to the historical nor to the dogmatic science of law, but to the theoretical part of politics." Pollock and Maitland, 1 The History of English Law xxiii (2d ed. 1899).

I. Government in General

Men have various needs that must be fulfilled. They have goals to be reached. Direction in pursuing these ends is government. Government in general has to do with direction to an end. It bears immediately on the means conducive to this end.

A. *The Aim of Government*

The purpose of government comes from the meaning of direction. A man directs himself by choosing to do those things that will lead to a certain goal. If he wishes to be a lawyer, he will choose a law school and study law. Insofar as he continues this endeavor, he is governing himself regarding this goal.

A father of a family directs the members to do those things that will contribute to their common welfare. If he desires to take his family on a vacation, he must decide where, when and how it is to be spent. The success of the vacation will depend on his ability to direct himself and the members in such a way that a happy vacation is enjoyed by all. Thus would he govern well in this particular regard. The aim of government, then, is to achieve ends by directing the means that will lead to them.

B. *Kinds of Government*

The end to which government directs the means may be a man's proper good or it may be his common good. On this basis there are three kinds of government: individual, domestic and political.

1. *Individual.* Individual government concerns itself with the proper goods of the individual person. These are the goods that contribute directly to his own personal perfection. A man directs himself, as instanced, in acquiring his own education.

2. *Domestic.* Domestic government looks to the common good of the family, as well as to the proper good of the individuals during the period when they are not able to govern themselves. The father directs the activities of the family to the common welfare of all, so that within this condition their proper good may develop.

3. *Political.* Political government regards the common good of the body politic. The necessity of government comes from the nature of men. "The social right and power of government is es-

sentially inherent and inalienable because man is naturally social, and there can be no society without government." [2]   The purpose of political government is the common good.   "All free governments are established by the people for their benefit, and the powers delegated are to be exercised for their common good." [3]

The three types of government, individual, domestic and political, may be exercised by one and the same man.   A President of the United States, for instance, who had a family, would be engaged in governing himself, his family, and the people of the United States.

C.   *Unity of Directive Judgment in Government*

In individual government there is no problem of unity of directive judgment.   The judgment of the individual himself, according to which his decisions should be made, is the only one involved.   Consequently, there is no question of unity.   In domestic and political government, however, there is a problem of how to obtain unity of judgment so that direction may be assured.

1. *Unanimous agreement.*   One way unity of judgment may be obtained is by unanimous agreement.   A husband and wife may reach unanimous agreement on where to send their children to college.   The hundred citizens of a New England town could attain unanimous agreement on how stealing should be curbed — say, not by banishment, public flogging, or fines, but imprisonment.

Unanimous agreement, however, is not easy to obtain.   Men sometimes see the same things differently.   A steady and reliable principle of direction is needed if the procurement of the common good is not to be random and haphazard.

2. *Minority subjection to majority.*   An obvious way of achieving constancy is by one person *giving* to another authority over himself and thereby subjecting himself to the direction of the other.   If the husband and wife cannot agree on where to send their children to college, one will have to submit to the judgment of the other — if the children are to receive any directive help from their parents about their education.   If the hundred citizens of the New England town could not reach unanimous agreement on how to curb stealing, unity of judgment could only be had if one part of them subjected itself to the judgment of the other. And according to the only natural objective norm of division, the

[2] Mott v. Pennsylvania R.R. Co., 30 Pa. 9, 27, 35 (1858).
[3] Ibid.

minority would have to subject itself to the judgment of the majority. By this action the majority would be given authority over the minority. For, "authority over" is correlatively based on "subjection to," which implies that ultimately government is exercised by the consent of all the governed. However, majorities must recognize the basic natural claims of minorities, if they are not to become tyrannies.

Most commonly, unity of judgment is sought through governors elected on a majority-minority basis. This same majority-minority principle may also be the deciding factor in decisions of the governors themselves, for instance, in legislatures or courts of appeal.

3. *Permanent and temporal need of direction by others.* The need of arriving at unity of directive judgment on a minority-majority basis in government is permanent. The rarity of unanimous agreement makes it a practical constant.[4] Some giving of authority to others and some correlative subjection to them is inevitable.

There are some situations, however, in which there is need of direction by others but only as a temporary condition. Such is the subjection of a child to the directive judgments of his parents because of his own immaturity. This subjection is demanded by the natural condition of parent-child relationship. Primitive and colonial peoples may be subject to governments politically more experienced. This is not a subjection that is natural in the sense of a parent-child relationship. It is natural only in the sense that colonialism may be a natural, historical development.

Both of these types of direction by others — of immature children and peoples — are temporary. Their main concern is not only the common good of these individuals but also their proper good. Their ultimate purpose is to prepare these persons

---

[4] This would be true even if everyone were perfectly intelligent and perfectly goodwilled, which they are not. For even then the problem would still remain of determining which of many means would be necessary for the common good. See Aquinas, 1 Sum. Theol. 96, 4.

Unanimity or subjection would still be required even though there were only one means and therefore no question of a choice of means. There would still be need of determining whether or not this one means was actually necessary for the common welfare. Only if men were in the ideal state of perfect intelligence and good will would this not be true. In such a state their judgment would be unanimous because of the uniformity of their understanding and desires. It seems that the closest that men come to unity of judgment regarding a unique means is when their common good is directly threatened, say by invasion of an enemy, and war is obviously the only means of saving the nation. See Simon, Philosophy of Democratic Government 25, 29, 101 (1951).

for the day when they will be mature enough to govern themselves and enjoy autonomy.

D. *Government Is Prudence — Not Science*

Government directs means to an end by three principal acts: deliberation, evaluation, and decision.

A judge desires to go from his home to the Civil Courts Building. He considers or deliberates on the various means at his disposal to get there. He can drive his car. He can ride a bus. Or he can walk. He will evaluate these means in the light of circumstances. If he is in a hurry, perhaps driving his own car is the means to be employed. Or, if he finds driving too nerve-wracking, riding a bus may be better. Or, seeing it is such a beautiful morning, a brisk walk may be best of all. He decides to walk and directs himself accordingly.

1. *The habit of rightly directing means to end.* The habit of mind by which a man deliberates, evaluates and decides what means are actually to be used in best attaining an end and directs his actions accordingly, is the habit of *prudence.* For prudence means "sagacious in adapting means to ends; circumspect in action, or in determining any line of conduct." [5]

Prudence, through its deliberation, evaluation and decision, determines the content of the directives that are given to self, to the family, or the citizens. Hence prudence — like government — is individual, domestic or political. In governors the habit of prudence results in right directives to the governed regarding what is necessary for their common good. This habit may be said to be also in the governed inasmuch as it results in the governed directing themselves to obey the directives of their governors. [6]

2. *Government is not a science.* If government is prudence, it is not a science. And if government is not a science, neither is its

[5] Tureen v. Peoples Motorbus Co. of St. Louis, 97 S.W.2d 847, 848 (Mo. 1936).

[6] Sometimes prudence in governors is termed "regnative prudence" and prudence in the governed is called "political prudence" (Aquinas, 2-2 Sum. Theol. 50, 1 and 2). However, since both are concerned with the common good, it seems justified to locate them under "political" prudence. "Political" in this book refers to whatever pertains to the common good of a community of men.

When men govern themselves, their prudence has both a ruling and an obeying aspect inasmuch as they direct themselves and follow their own directives. When, however, men are governed by others, the prudence of the governors is ruling and primary insofar as it directs others, and that of the others is obeying and secondary inasmuch as by it they direct themselves to obey the directives of their governors.

instrument — law — a science. The attempt to make government and law a science has been the preoccupation of many lawmen during the last few years.

Science is a habit of the mind according to which a man judges correctly about the truth of things. It is concerned with knowing things as they are. The nature of uranium must be known, to some extent at least, before a prediction about its fission can be made. But the nature of a thing is what the thing necessarily is. Science is concerned with these necessary facts and must consider all possible pertinent factors before its conclusions can even approach certainty. If this inquiry and research requires much time, such is the demand of science.

3. *Government is prudence.* Prudence, however, is the habit of the mind of judging rightly what is to be done immediately, here and now. Its object is the means that will lead to an end. Many of its innumerable factors are variable and unknowable. They are not a datum like the nature of uranium. They are not necessary; they are contingent. "The knowledge of contingent things cannot have the certitude of truth which eliminates error . . . but [this] knowledge is useful inasmuch as it is directive of human activity which is concerned with contingent things." [7]

A father wishing to take his family on a vacation decides to take them by train rather than by automobile or plane. He judges a train is safer. There is a cracked journal on one of the cars. The train is wrecked and all members of his family are killed. Was his decision to take a train imprudent?

Certainly his conclusion was not a scientific one. A scientific conclusion in this instance would have been impossible. There is no particular necessary nature to be known here. Nor could any man known the exact condition of the material in every piece of equipment on the railroad which he would have to know if his conclusion were to be scientific.

His decision, however, was not imprudent. It was, in fact, prudent. Prudent decision does not require a completely scientific knowledge of every related factor. What it does require in many cases (law for instance) is as scientific a basis as possible. But this is not what characterizes prudence as such. After due caution and circumspection regarding scientific knowledge, it is the good intention of the one judging that ultimately makes the decisive judgment of prudence good or bad. The father, motivated by the good intention of taking his family on a vacation and exercis-

[7] Aquinas, 6 In Ethicorum Aristotelis 3.

ing due caution based on a knowledge of safety conditions accessible to him, decided prudently to take his family on a train. From the standpoint of prudence, it was a good decision.

4. *Government's instrument, law, is prudence.* The importance of stressing the fact that government is prudence and not science is that it throws a revealing light on the nature of government's instrument — law. Law, in determining what is just, is prudence and not science as already noted. One of the major mistakes in legal thinking of the past century has been to assume that law, like physics, chemistry, biology or mathematics, must be a science. Anything to be worthwhile must, seemingly, be science. Attempts have ensued to make law a science at all costs. But men necessarily lead the greater part of their lives in another area, that of prudence.

Law can never be a science because its very fabric is the innumerable and variable contingent facts of everyday life. Legislators, desiring to enact a statute controlling the pollution of streams by smelting plants, will want the expert testimony of science on the effect of iron oxide on the water, fish, vegetation, and the like. Their final draft of the bill to be enacted will already embody their prudent evaluation of contradictory testimony and their prudent rejection or acceptance of some of these scientific facts as immaterial or material. Their final directive judgment as embodied in the statute, will be prudential and not scientific.

A judge likewise may call in expert scientific testimony. There may be conflicting opinions. Which facts will be admitted as material or immaterial again will be determined by his prudence. His final decision and directive will, therefore, be in the realm of prudence and not of science.

A clear and firm distinction has to be made between the directive judgment that is law which pertains to prudence, and the more or less scientific judgments on which this directive may and should be based, if possible, which is a matter of science. Law may depend on science but it itself is not science.

5. *"Pure science" of law.* Law has its feet in the everchanging conditions of the market place. Attempts to make law a "pure science" divorced from the lives of the men trampling the dust of facts and needs is to cut law off from the one thing that gives it meaning — the contingent problems of men. There will never be pat scientific formulas that will relieve lawmen of the hard work of exercising prudent judgment in endeavoring to decide what is just. Much is gained "when it is realized that law is not a

pure science, that a law loses its vital meaning if it is not cor-
related to the organic society in which it lives." [8]

E. *Desiring the Common Good*

To govern is to exercise the habit of prudence and this is to
choose rightly means for an end. That the end be desired is
presupposed and from this intention comes the impetus for seeking and deciding on the means. It is the desire of reaching the
Civil Courts Building, to revert to the example mentioned above,
that motivates the judge's decision to use the means necessary to
get there.

1. *Main inspiration of government.* So also is the desire of
the common good the main inspiration in the government of
others. Those who govern must intend the general welfare in all
its phases and not merely as a vague ideal. Police protection at
the cost of taxed property, safe driving conditions at the price of
curbed speed and slower travel, the survival of a nation at the cost
of many lives in war, these and the like must be the common ends
spurring government on. This subordination of intermediate
proper goods to the common good which touches the nerve of political living, should be desired by all. But most especially should
it be desired by the government — whether this be by the majority of citizens directly governing themselves or by their elected

---

[8] Warring v. Colpoys, 122 F.2d 642 (D.C. Cir. 1941).

A further explanation may be in order with reference to the relation of
law to prudence and science. The habits of the intellect that we form concern what we know and what we do. Regarding what we *know,* these habits
may be about truth itself. These are the habits of first principles of truth,
of wisdom, and of the science or knowledge of subjects such as physics,
mathematics, philosophy, anthropology, economics and the like. (See Chapter 3, note 65.) Our intellectual habits regarding what we know are not only
about truth in itself but also about truth with a view to action. These are
the habits of the first principles of action and of science or knowledge of the
norms that guide our actions such as ethics or morals. Regarding what we
do, are the habits of prudence by which we govern ourselves rightly, and of
art by which we make things rightly. (See Klubertanz, Philosophy of Nature
283).

Hence, law in its making is an act of the habit of prudence as we have seen.
Law as received by us — whether creator-made or man-made — pertains to
the habit of science or knowledge of the norms that guide our actions. In
other words, although law in the making is an act of political prudence in
the one who authoritatively makes it, in others (and in the lawmaker himself, in fact, inasmuch as he is also governed by it) it becomes part of the
science or knowledge we have of the principles according to which we are
governed. In the case of man-made law, it is the certainty that the prudential judgment of the lawmakers is the best possible judgment at the time,
that gives it the aspect of a quasi-scientific directive for the citizens.

representatives by whom they allow themselves to be governed.

The necessity of the government's steadily desiring the common good is seen more pointedly in some situations than others. The punishment of criminals is a good and should be desired by all. This intention motivates the judge when he sentences the criminal to death. The wife of the condemned man, however, while desiring the common good in general, may not be able to bring herself to desire this particular means of accomplishing it which now so intimately affects her. The death of her husband and the father of her children is for her an evil opposed to her own proper good. To see and actually desire his death as a good is not to be expected of her.

Such instances multiplied indicate the need of those in government to intend steadfastly the whole of the means necessary for the common welfare. Upon this motivation depends the value of their directives as law.

2. *Furthered by punishment.* The desire of government to further the common good may be, and usually is, effectuated by the punishment imposed by laws. The purpose of punishment is to bring about right conduct. Its aim is to make men do what is right even though doing so be contrary to what they would otherwise desire.

3. *Fostered by instruction.* There is another way, however, the desire of government to procure the common good may be furthered. This is by instruction of the citizens. Instruction attempts to arouse a desire of obeying laws because of their reasonableness, that is, because of the relation between their provisions and the common good. Its purpose is to foster a change in motive within the subject, to cause him to desire to do what is right.[9]

F. *Authority in Government*

Government is often defined in terms of authority. "The meaning of the term 'government' is so commonly understood that to define the same does not appear to be necessary, yet the

---

[9] Such instruction could be called propaganda if by "propaganda" is meant what originally was signified by the word: the spreading of truth. But "propaganda" is a word, like "politics" and many others, that has taken on a sinister connotation implying the mass diffusion of falsehood for the purpose of promoting some selfish interest. On instruction and propaganda, see Simon, Philosophy of Democratic Government 108-127 (1951); Odegard and Helms, American Politics 546-550 (1947); Key, Politics, Parties, and Pressure Groups 423-429 (1947).

In other words, instruction has for its purpose the bringing about of formal virtue, while punishment and its threat may promote only material virtue.

term . . . may be defined as: 'The exercise of authority in the administration of the affairs of a state, community, or society; the authoritative direction and restraint, exercised over the actions of men in communities, societies or states.' " [10]

Authority in turn is described as a right or power. "Power is synonymous with authority or right." [11] "The word 'authority' . . . means the power delegated by a principal to an agent." [12] "The primary meaning of the word 'authorize' is to empower, to give a right to act." [13] In view of the ambiguous meaning of right and power, however, as already seen, the more exact nature of authority must be located.

1. *Source in individual men.* Authority concerns the directing of human actions. This is done first and foremost by individual men regarding their own actions. Every man is structured in such a way that his being dynamically demands that he strive to attain his highest development. Since he is a knowing and deciding person, this striving necessarily entails his freely directed actions. Hence, he is obliged so to direct his actions.

This self-direction is impossible unless he is allowed to do so by others. He therefore has a claim on others to be allowed to do what is demanded of him by his very nature, that is, to direct his own activities. This claim to direct means to end in his own life, or the right to do so, is the source of what is delegated as political authority. To follow the line of authority one step further, the source of this demand for self-direction, the Creator, is the ultimate source of all authority.

2. *Essence of authority.* When individual men become citizens of a political union and elect representatives to govern them in things pertaining to their common welfare, they delegate to them that part of their natural claim that relates to the attainment of their common good. This act of delegation of their claim subjects them to the direction of the elected governors, and the governors have authority over them. Authority of government in turn, based on the title of delegation, is a claim on those subject to them to follow their directives.

Authority, then, is a *claim to direct.* If it refers to self, it is a

[10] Chicago, B. & Q.R. Co. v. School District No. 1 in Yuma County, 63 Colo. 159, 165 Pac. 260, 263 (1917).

[11] State v. District Court of Eighth Jud. District for Natrona County, 33 Wyo. 281, 238 Pac. 545, 548 (1925).

[12] Clark v. Griffin, 95 N.J.L. 508, 113 Atl. 234, 235 (1921).

[13] Rucks-Brandt Construction Co. v. Price, 165 Okla. 178, 23 P.2d 690, 692 (1933). See also Doherty v. Kansas City Star Co., 143 Kan. 802, 57 P.2d 43, 45 (1936); Board of Commissioners of Sedgwick County v. Toland, 121 Kan. 109, 245 Pac. 1019, 1021 (1926).

claim to direct self to an end. It is the claim that the individual person has on others to be allowed to direct his own actions in such a way that he will progress toward his highest development. Others are obliged to respect this claim, lest the elementary demand for free direction be contravened and animal existence be the lot of all. If authority concerns others, it is a claim to direct others to an end. It is the claim that governors have on others to obey their directives.

Political authority in government, then, is the claim to direct citizens regarding those things that pertain to their common good.

II. Government of the Political Union

As has already been observed and as will be considered in the next chapter, men naturally form political unions. Just as inevitably, these political societies must be governed.

A. *Government by the Citizens Themselves*

The authority that the citizens have to direct themselves politically may be exercised by all of them acting together. The early New England town meeting, the Swiss canton and even the plebiscite are examples of this. "It is true that the existence of towns, and action by the inhabitants at town meetings, are contemplated by the Constitution . . . and that the form of government of a town has been described as pure democracy as distinguished from representative government." [14]

There seems to be no reason why citizens may not govern themselves politically, as well as individually and domestically, if their number is small enough. Unity of directive judgment could be reached, as noted, by unanimous agreement or by submission of the minority to the judgment of the majority.

B. *Government by Elected Governors*

The political societies are few indeed whose number of citizens is sufficiently small to enable them to govern themselves. Most of them have millions of citizens. Hence, government by the citizens themselves is a practical impossibility. It would be as cumbersome as a plebiscite.

[14] Commonwealth v. Town of Hudson, 315 Mass. 335, 52 N.E.2d 566, 572 (1943).

Nor would the average citizen have the time or the ability to participate directly in government. His time is well consumed by the process of making a living, and he has had no training or experience in the art of government.

Political government as a matter of practical necessity, then, must be carried on by a select group of men to whose directives the citizens have consented to subject themselves.[15]

C. Consent: Source of Delegated Political Authority

The immediate source of the political authority delegated to a governor is the people's consent to be subject to his directives. The claim that each citizen has to direct his actions in a manner contributive to the common good is in part entrusted to those he elects to direct him.[16]

1. *Explicit and implicit consent.* The consent to be governed by others politically, like the consent to be a member of a political union, is given explicitly or implicitly. Consent is given by a citizen explicitly when the man he voted for is elected by the majority. If he voted for White in a presidential election, he explicitly consented to be governed by White who now is President due to the action of the majority.

Consent is given implicitly when, after an election in which White for whom he voted is defeated, he remains in the political union thereby giving consent implicitly to be governed by Black. The fact of his remaining is evidence of this implicit consent. He could refuse such consent and give evidence of it by leaving the

[15] Britton v. Board of Election Commissioners, 129 Cal. 337, 344, 61 Pac. 1115, 1117 (1900).

[16] On the delegation of authority from the people to chosen governors, see Bellarmine, Controversiarum de membris ecclesiae, III (1581); Suárez, Defensio fidei, III (1613); Simon, Philosophy of Democratic Government 158-176 (1951). Noteworthy in this regard is the statement of Pius XII that political society is brought about "from below upwards": "The foundation of the church as a society has been brought about, contrary to the origin of the state, not from below upwards but from above downwards." Reported in Osservatore Romano, October 3, 1945 (my trans.).

There can be little doubt that the theory which held that political power was delegated to the ruler "immediately by God," was a consequence of the accepted doctrine of the Middle Ages that, when the pope anointed the emperor, political authority was thereby delegated to him. See Gilson, La Philosophie au Moyen Age 255, 575 (1947).

On authority delegated through elections see Gardina v. Board of Registrars of Jefferson County, 160 Ala. 155, 48 So. 788 (1909). See also Smith v. McQueen, 232 Ala. 90, 166 So. 788, 791 (1936); State v. Board of Canvassers, 788 S.C. 461, 59 S.E. 145, 147 (1907).

country and living under some other government. But to remain is to give evidence of subjection to Black's authority.[17]

Such implicit consent is the origin of delegated authority in political societies where no explicit elections are held. The members of primitive tribes, having the elementary claim to govern themselves, implicitly consent (whether they advert to it or not) to be subject to the directives of the chief or headman. Because of his abilities or fear of him or whatever reason, he is judged best qualified to govern them.

In past and present monarchies where succession is determined by heredity, implicit consent is also the origin of delegated political authority. The subjects of such a kingdom implicitly consent to be governed by the king.

In speaking of implicit consent, freedom (both legal and physical) to leave the political union is supposed. If it were illegal for a citizen to leave or if a citizen were held by physical force, his consequent remaining in the political union could not be interpreted as implied consent. Such positive obstacles to freedom, however, should not be confused with what are only deterrents. A man might say that he is not free to leave on account of his economic status, his health, his domestic and social responsibilities. These, however, are not obstructions to freedom in the sense that illegality or physical detention are. They are only factors which at times make the exercise of this freedom heroic.

Striking and tragic examples of this fact are the numberless exiles and refugees of all ages who, having refused implicit consent to a tyrannical government by remaining under it, have risked their all — even life itself — by leaving it and becoming citizens of a political union of their choice. In many cases their action has been all the more heroic, risked as it was in the face of both unjust statutes forbidding men and women to leave the country and the threat of severe punishment if they were apprehended doing so.

2. *Refusal of consent — real and apparent.* Refusal to give consent may be real or only apparent. Real refusal is manifested by such acts as leaving the country as mentioned, or by the extreme measure of revolt. Only apparent refusal is present in such instances as criticism of the government, refusal to obey cer-

[17] Locke maintained that an alien who lived under another government, even for a short time, had by that very fact given tacit consent to obey the directives of that government. Two Treatises on Government II, c. 8, 119 (1714). It has been held that an alien resident in this country owes a certain allegiance to the United States and may be tried for treason. See Carlisle v. United States, 16 Wall. 147, 154, 21 L. Ed. 426, 429 (1873).

tain laws because of religious convictions, passive resistance to specific governmental regulations.[18]   In none of these is there a real refusal to be subject to the government in general.   There is only a dissatisfaction with certain aspects of governmental conduct, or a refusal to obey a certain few of its specific directives.

D.   *Extent of Political Authority*

The extent of political authority is limited by the purpose of the political union, the common good.   Political authority extends to whatever pertains to the public good.   It does not extend to proper goods.   Citizens should give to their political governors only that part of their claim to direct themselves that is necessary for the fulfillment of common needs.   As already noted, precise determination of these needs may be difficult, but the principle of the common good remains the measure of the extent of political authority.   It is the bulwark that restrains the incursion of public authority into the domain of private goods.

The manner in which the people maintain a hand in the determination of what will contribute to the common good varies in a non-democratic and in a democratic regime.   For this reason a clear idea of what a democratic regime is should be kept in mind.   A democratic regime is one in which the *citizens control the governing personnel* through *periodic elections.*

1. *Non-democratic regime.*   In a non-democratic regime as in tribes and some monarchies, the citizens, by their implicit consent to be governed by the incumbent, delegate to him authority over all things he judges necessary for the common good.   The only authority they retain is the basic claim to act in their own self-protection if their common good is endangered by the governor's becoming a tyrannical dictator.

2. *Democratic regime.*   In a democratic regime, the citizens by their explicit or implicit consent to be governed by the one elected, also delegate authority to him over all areas which he shall consider as pertaining to the common good.   There is, however, this important difference.   In a democratic regime the citizens have a voice to some degree in determining what shall be considered as necessary for the common good.   Thus, if one of the planks of the platform on which a candidate runs for office declares he stands for governmental seizure and permanent operation of the steel mills and a citizen votes for him, in so voting the citizen is also helping to decide whether or not public ownership

[18] See Gandhi, Autobiography 575-576 (1948).

and operation of the steel mills is necessary for the common good for the people.

In a democratic regime, as well as in a non-democratic regime, the citizens retain the elemental claim to defend themselves against any action of a governor who is working against their common good. "The people's power is not parted with by the institution of government, but only delegated, and this delegation being essentially revocable, cannot possibly authorize an act that will prevent its complete revocation." [19]

Citizens should remember that the government, as long as it operates within its designated limits, has the free exercise of its authority. Hence, for the citizens to view their elected governors as "coach-drivers," who still must consult the citizens as to what means must be employed in the pursuit of the common good, can defeat the purpose of elected government. One of the principle reasons why men are chosen to govern is their supposed ability to judge better what is necessary for the common welfare.[20]

III. GOVERNMENT AND THE STATE

The manner in which the word "state" has been used, has given rise to serious confusion. It is sometimes used as synonymous with government. If state is used in this sense, a concise idea of what government actually is should be kept in mind, lest the word "state" be allowed to take on a disastrous and harmful meaning.

A. Directives by Men with Authority

To govern is to direct to an end. To govern politically is to direct to the public good. To possess authority and to govern politically is to have a claim, held conditionally from the citizens, to direct them in those activities that are related to their common good.

The basic supposition here is that government is carried on by men, by human beings, by individual persons. Whether it be

[19] Mott v. Pennsylvania R.R. Co., 30 Pa. 9, 27, 35 (1858).
[20] "Write your representative" is a phrase that may have a good connotation if its content is merely informative and advisory. If it is an attempt at direction, which it many times is, the purpose of representative government can well be in jeopardy, since those in government were elected precisely because of their superior ability to judge what means are necessary for the common good. On this subject see the excellent treatment by Lippmann, The Public Philosophy 16-27 (1955).

direction of oneself, or of a family, or of the body politic, it implies the decisions of natural — and not "artificial" — persons.[21] The whole concept of government, as an intelligent directing of means to end, has at its center the natural, human person.

B.   *The State*

The state, on the other hand, has been given a meaning by some which makes it an entity different from the natural persons who govern.   Some theorists attempt to make the state a mystical entity or a supreme being by defining it as "the Divine Idea as it exists on Earth."   As a consequence, "all the worth which the human being possesses — all spiritual reality, he possesses only through the State." [22]

Others have made the state a person over and above the human persons that compose it, somewhat as has been done regarding corporations.   It has been called a "moral person," that "has its affairs and interests" and "deliberates and takes resolutions." [23] Or the state has been considered to be even a new and separate physical person that has its own life.   It is born, matures, reproduces (its sexual activity is its relations with foreign countries!) and dies.[24]

Dictators have found in this "super-person" concept of the state a ready basis for their own "Realpolitik" and the complete submersion of the individual in the whole of the omnipotent state. "Fascism conceives of the State as an absolute, in comparison with which all individuals or groups are relative, only to be conceived of in relation to the State . . . the State is itself conscious, and has itself a will and a personality. . . .   The State, as conceived of and as created by Fascism, is a spiritual and moral fact in itself, since its political, juridical, and economic organization of the nation is a concrete thing." [25]

C.   *Government Is Not the State*

It is true that words may be used in any sense that people want to use them.   Such is the word "state."   It is not a word that has

[21] Stokes v. United States, 264 Fed. 18, 22 (8th Cir. 1920).

[22] Hegel, Philosophy of History 39 (Sibree trans. 1900).

[23] United States v. Kusche, 56 F. Supp. 201, 208 (S.D. Cal. 1944), quoting DeVattel.

[24] Bluntschli, The Theory of the State 15-24 (Ritchie trans. 1885).   See Chapter 20 for a discussion of person.

[25] Mussolini, Political and Social Doctrine of Fascism, 306 International Conciliation 13-14 (1935).

always been used in analysis of political society and its govern-ment. *Polis* or *civitas* (the city) and *principatus* or *potestas* (rul-ing authority) were expressions used by Aristotle and Aquinas to denote the political union and government.[26] It was only later, when will-theories of political society, government and law devel-oped in the seventeenth and eighteenth centuries, that the word "state" became prominent. After that the connotations of the word proliferated to such an extent that it lost all clear and con-cise meaning.

Certainly the use of "state" to denote some kind of a being or person separate and above the people actually constituting the political union or the government is to be vigorously rejected. Such an entity is purely fictional and its very concept implies disastrous consequences for the people's innate freedom.

The use of "state" to designate the government is, of course, valid if one so chooses to employ it.[27] However, there does seem to be a danger lurking behind such a use. The men in govern-ment already have the people subject to their directives. To set these men further apart as the state can easily lead to their being conceived as separate and above the people. Once this occurs, government ceases to be an agency whose authority is admittedly from the people and whose purpose is for the people.

It seems better, therefore, to say that government is not the state. Much safer is it to call the government simply what it is, "government."

1. *State of being united.* The word "state," if it is to be re-tained at all, would seem to be employed better in its limited pristine meaning of "state of political union." In this sense it is synonymous with political union, political society, and body poli-tic. "When we speak of the state we mean the organization of which government is the administrative organ. . . . [T]he po-litical structure itself, with its usages and traditions, with its framework of institutional relationships between the ruler and the ruled, should not be identified with its organ of govern-

[26] Aristotle, 1 Politics 2, 1252a-1253b (Jowett trans. 1941); Aquinas, 1 In Politicorum Aristotelis 1. The translation of the Greek word "polis" by the English word "state" is misleading. By "polis" Aristotle did not have in mind the meaning some people do today when they use the word "state": a supreme entity separate from the people and above them.

[27] "The State is only that part of the body politic especially concerned with the maintenance of law, the promotion of the common welfare and public order, and the administration of public affairs. The State is a part which specializes in the interests of the whole." ". . . [T]he body politic must control the State, which however contains the functions of government within its own fabric." Maritain, Man and the State 12, 24 (1951).

ment." [28] "A state is an association which, acting through law as promulgated by a government endowed to this end with coercive power, maintains within a community territorially demarcated the universal external conditions of social order." [29]

2. *"All rights come from the state."* The confusion attending the use of the word "state" is well brought out in the way the origin of rights is spoken of. If it is said that, "All rights come from the state," what does "state" mean? Does it refer to the people politically united? If so, then all rights derive from the people — which is obvious — regardless of executive decree, statutes or precedent. Or does state mean those in government? If it does, all rights come from the government and the government does not get its authority from the people and is not therefore representative of them. Government in this case would be some kind of mystical entity above and separate from the people, since it would be the sole source of the people's rights.

Or take the opposite statement, "All rights do not come from the state." What does the word "state" mean here? If it refers to the people, all basis of claims and obligation as deriving from the people is wiped out. If state means government, the statement has a meaning taken for granted by Americans today. No one holds that fundamental claims and obligations are parceled out by the government according to its whim — unless it be someone with ambitions for dictatorship.[30]

[28] MacIver, The Web of Government 31-32 (1947). By permission of the Macmillan Company.

[29] MacIver, The Modern State 22 (1926).

[30] Of course, to recall, all rights come ultimately from the peoples' Creator as explained above in this Chapter. This follows as a logical conclusion from Chapter 9.

On the interesting shift in Soviet ideology from state as government to state as society see Asparturian, The Contemporary Doctrine of the Soviet State and its Philosophical Foundations, 48 Am. Pol. Sci. Rev. 1031-1057 (1954).

Political Union and the Common Good

Law is the instrument of government. But it is the political union that gives import to government which is its agency. And it is the common good, in turn, that gives to the political union its purpose for existing and functioning.

I. Political Union to Obtain Common Good

The end and purpose of political union, then, is simply and solely the common good of its members. It is to bring about conditions of peace and security. These are the conditions necessary for the development of its members.

A. *Purposeful Union*

The political common good of the people, as observed above,[1] is characterized not only by its communicability to all, but also in great part by the fact that the cooperation of all is required if it is to be completely realized. Common goods are enjoyed in proportion to the combined efforts of all the members of the political union in producing them.

These efforts, however, are sporadic and disorganized unless the members are united in their intention to work for their common good. This formal uniting gives organization and direction to their endeavors. This is the political union or political society. It may be defined as the *union by free decision of the individual persons in a determined territory for the purpose of pursuing their common good.* "The very idea of a political community such as a nation is, implies an association of persons for the promotion of their general welfare. Each one of the persons associated becomes a member of the nation formed by the association."[2] " 'Association' and 'society' are convertible terms."[3]

[1] Chapter 2.
[2] Minor v. Happersett, 21 Wall. 162, 165, 22 L. Ed. 627 (1875).
[3] New York County Medical Association v. City of New York, 32 Misc. 116, 65 N.Y. Supp. 531 (1900). See also Josey v. Union Loan and Trust Co., 106 Ga. 608, 32 S.E. 628, 629 (1899).

1. *Society and community.* Although "community" and "society" are commonly used interchangeably, they are essentially different. The community is a grouping of persons who have been brought together by some already existing fact. A society, on the other hand, is a union of persons entered into knowingly and with free decision for the express purpose of bringing about conditions that do not yet exist.

Any union, then, formed by individuals for the purpose of obtaining a good that is common to them is a society. Such are marital, labor, business, professional, fraternal or political unions. The political union, however, is the matrix within which all other types of union function and on which they depend. The common good of the marital union, for instance, the loving procreation and rearing of children, can have little hope of accomplishment if the country is overrun and destroyed by enemies. The common good of a labor union — higher wages and better working conditions — cannot be obtained if its claims are not adopted and supported by law.

2. *Body politic.* The political union or society is also known as the "body politic." "The body politic is formed by a voluntary association of individuals: it is a social compact, by which the whole people covenants with each citizen, and each citizen with the whole people, that all shall be governed by certain laws for the common good." [4]   ". . . [T]he term 'body politic' is an old term for a corporation or an association of individuals, and usually applied to the state or other public associations." [5]

3. *State.* The word "state," as noted in the preceding chapter, is also commonly used to denote the political union. "A state has been defined to be 'a people permanently occupying a fixed territory, bound together by common laws, habits, and customs (or by a constitution) into one body politic, exercising, through the medium of an organized government, independent sovereignty and control over all persons and things within its boundaries, capable of making war and peace, and of entering into international relations with other communities." [6]

4. *Nation.* Nation also may refer to the political union. "Nations or states are bodies politic, societies of men united together

---

[4] In re Opinion of the Justices, 226 Mass. 607, 115 N.E. 921 (1917).

[5] Utah State Bldg. Com. v. Great American Ind. Co., 105 Utah 11, 140 P.2d 763, 766 (1943).

[6] Roche v. Washington, 19 Ind. 53, 81 Am. Dec. 376, 379 (1862). See also United States v. Kusche, 56 F. Supp. 201, 207, 208 (S.D. Cal. 1944); McLaughlin v. Poucher, 127 Conn. 441, 17 A. 2d 767 (1941).

to procure their mutual safety and advantage by means of their union." [7]

5. *Country.*   Country ordinarily, when referring to a political union, has a strong territorial connotation.   At times it may admit of an extended meaning.   ". . . [A]man's 'country' is more than the territory in which its people live.   The term is used generally to indicate the state, the organization of social life which exercises sovereign power in behalf of the people. . . .   Ordinarily the state exercises sovereignty only within the territory occupied by its people; but a different situation is presented when the territory is overrun by its enemies and its government is in exile in the territory of a friendly nation exercising power in international matters on behalf of its nationals.   In such case, the government in exile has taken over the only exercise of sovereign power left to the people of the country and is the only agency representing the country with which a foreign government can deal." [8]

6. *People.*   The word "people" may or may not have the same meaning as the political union or body politic.   "The word 'people' may have somewhat varying significations dependent upon the connection in which it is used.   In some connections in the constitution it is confined to citizens and means the same as citizens.   It excludes aliens.   It includes men, women and children.   It comprehends not only the sane, competent, law-abiding and educated, but also those who are wholly or in part dependents and charges upon society by reason of immaturity, mental or moral deficiency or lack of the common essentials of education." [9]

In line with what was said in the preceding chapter regarding the use of the word "government" as the safest word to designate those who govern, the word "people" seems apt to denote the citizens united in political union.   Such a use is already evidenced in the manner in which some cases are referred to: "People v. Jones."

B.   *Natural Development From Community*

Experience shows that whenever men inevitably find themselves living in some kind of community, it is not long before they

---

[7] United States v. Kusche, 56 F. Supp. 201, 208 (S.D. Cal. 1944).

[8] Delaney v. Moraitis, 136 F.2d 129, 130, 131 (4th Cir. 1943).

[9] In re Opinion of the Justices, 226 Mass. 607, 115 N.E. 921, 922 (1917). Regarding the concepts of community, society, nation and the like, see Maritain, Man and the State 1-27 (1951).

feel the need of uniting politically. Primitive communities have never been found that did not have some kind of political organization.[10] It is according to the line of their natural development that men progress from living with their fellows in community to being formally united with them in political society.

1. *Pioneering situations.* During the early years of development of the western part of the United States, for instance, men often found themselves grouped together in communities on account of their pursuit of gold. As these communities took on permanence of greater or less degree, it was not long before their members felt the need of organizing into political union to assure themselves of obtaining certain goods common to them all — among them especially the protection of life and property.

2. *Present conditions.* The need and necessity of development from community to political society can best be seen today in the urgency that faces the nations of the world to unite in a world political union. The people of the world are members of the world community. They are also citizens of this or that national political union. They are not, however, citizens of a world political union since none as yet exists.

The world community exists because all men and nations are already grouped together on the one globe we designate as the "earth." Their mutual security is a common good to them all. Men have no choice about the fact that they are a world community. They do have a choice regarding the formation of a world political union whose end will be to fill the common need of security and peace based on a just order. And if intelligent beings are ever found living on other planets there would be need for a universal political union for the same reason.

C. *Citizens of a Political Union*

When an individual person enters into political union with others, he becomes a fellow citizen of theirs. "Citizens are members of a community inspired to a common goal, who, in their associated relations, submit themselves to rules of conduct for the promotion of the general welfare and conservation of individual as well as collective rights." [11]

Such a member under certain conditions is designated as a

[10] See Hoebel, Man in the Primitive World 376 (1949) and Lowie, Primitive Society 358-396 (1920).

[11] In re McIntosh, 12 F. Supp. 177 (W.D. Wash. 1935).

"subject." ". . . [T]he words 'subject,' 'inhabitant' and 'citizen' have been used, and the choice between them is sometimes made to depend upon the form of the government. Citizen is now more commonly employed, however, and as it has been considered better suited to the description of one living under a republican government, it was adopted by nearly all of the States upon their separation from Great Britain, and was afterwards adopted in the Articles of Confederation and in the Constitution of the United States. When used in this sense it is understood as conveying the idea of membership of a nation and nothing more." [12]

A resident is not necessarily a citizen. "Citizen and resident . . . are not synonymous, and in some cases the distinction is important. It might well be that a resident of any one state in point of fact may be a citizen of that or any other state." [13]

Even though the citizens of a political union may find themselves grouped together in communities within that union by race, nationality, language, ideology, customs, and the like, nevertheless they are first and foremost citizens of the political union of which they are members and to it they owe their prime allegiance.

1. *Becoming a member of a new political union.* A man becomes a citizen of a new political union by explicitly consenting with others to form this union and thereby become one of its members. Such new political associations are rarely formed today. The formation of the United States by the people of the original thirteen states was such an occasion.

Perhaps the unique instance of the formation of a new political union yet remaining to be accomplished is, as mentioned, that of the World Political Union. If this most important event ever occurs, it will come into existence by the explicit consent of the member nations freely consenting to become citizen nations of the World Political Union.

2. *Becoming a member of an already existing political union.* A man becomes a citizen of an already formed political union by giving his consent either explicitly or implicitly, similar to the manner in which he consents to be governed. His citizenship may admit of degrees.

a. *Explicit consent.* He gives consent explicitly when he becomes a "naturalized" citizen. "Section I of the Fourteenth Amendment of the Constitution, authorizing the basic Naturalization Act of June 29, 1906 (34 Stat. 596 as amended), provides: 'All

[12] Minor v. Happersett, 21 Wall. 162, 165, 22 L. Ed. 627 (1875).
[13] Jeffcott v. Donovan, 135 F.2d 213, 214 (9th Cir. 1943).

persons born or naturalized in the United States, and subject to the jurisdiction thereof, are citizens of the United States and of the State wherein they reside.' The word 'naturalized' describes a completed process in which an alien has become a citizen of the United States. In the act of 1906, the word 'naturalization' relates to the status of citizenship which has been acquired. Naturalization 'is the act of adopting a foreigner, and clothing him with the privileges of the native citizen. . . .' The grant of citizenship or the benefits thereof are to be construed in favor of the government and against the party claiming the grant." [14]

b. *Implicit consent.* Consent is given implicitly by those who are born within the territorial confines of the political union.[15] This is the way most men become "natural" citizens of the country in which they are born. They consent implicitly to become a member by remaining within the boundaries, say of the United States of America. The action of remaining is an objective sign of his implicit consent.

This implied consent may be accompanied either by a clear realization of what citizenship means or by only a vague realization that the man wishes to remain where he is and be governed by the present governors. Such a vague realization and consent is perhaps all that politically immature people ever have regardless of time and place. Nothing more than this would seem to be present in the implicit consent of primitive peoples, of those who lived in feudalism, and even of many in twentieth century political societies.

c. *Complete and incomplete citizenship.* A man may be a "complete" or "incomplete" citizen. He is an incomplete citizen inasmuch as he owes allegiance to this particular political union, is subject to its jurisdiction, and is entitled to its protection, but does not have the claim to take part in government. He has civil rights but not political rights. It is only when he has both civil rights and political rights that he is a complete citizen.

To be a citizen implies having a distinctive rank. "The term citizen has come to us derived from antiquity. It appears to have been used in the Roman government to designate a person who had the freedom of the city, and the right to exercise all political and civil privileges of the government. There was

---

[14] United States v. Harbanuk, 62 F.2d 759, 761 (2d Cir. 1933).

[15] Those born outside the United States and its outlying possessions of parents one or both of whom is a United States citizen may become citizens, subject to conditions determined by statute. See 66 Stat. 235 (1952), 8 U.S.C. §1401.

also, at Rome, a partial citizenship, including civil but not political rights. Complete citizenship embraced both." [16]

A citizen may have civil and political rights. "A civil right is a right accorded to every member of a district, community, or nation, while a political right is a right exercisable in the administration of government. . . . Political rights consist in the power to participate, directly or indirectly, in the establishment or management of the government. These political rights are fixed by the Constitution. Every citizen has the right of voting for public officers, and of being elected. These are the political rights which the humblest citizen possesses. Civil rights are those which have no relation to the establishment, support, or management of the government. They consist in the power of acquiring and enjoying property, or exercising the paternal or marital powers, and the like. It will be observed that everyone, unless deprived of them by sentence of death, is in the enjoyment of the civil rights, which is not the case with political rights, for an alien, for example, has no political rights, although in full enjoyment of the civil rights." [17]

d. *Double citizenship.* In a political union composed of a federation of smaller political unions, such as is the case in the United States of America, a man may be a citizen of both an individual State and of the United States. "There are, then under our republican form of government, two classes of citizens, one of the United States and one of the state. One class of citizenship may exist in a person, without the other, as in the case of a resident of the District of Columbia; but both classes usually exist in the same person. The Federal Constitution, by this amendment, has undertaken to say who shall be citizens both of the states and the United States. Prior to this amendment, the states could probably have determined, respectively, who were citizens of each, though naturalization has been exclusively a national subject, rather than a state, since the Federal Constitution was first adopted." [18]

e. *Dignity of being a citizen.* To be a citizen is to be a man to whom honor and respect are due. "The word 'citizen' has come to us from the Roman law. In Roman law it designated a person who had the freedom of the city of Rome and could exercise

[16] Thomasson v. State, 15 Ind. 449, 451 (1860); See also Salmond, Citizenship and Allegiance, 17 L.Q. Rev. 270 (1901).

[17] Winnett v. Adams, 71 Neb. 817, 99 N.W. 681, 684 (1904). See also State v. Powers, 51 N.J.L. 432, 433, 17 Atl. 969, 970 (1889).

[18] Gardina v. Board of Registrars of Jefferson County, 160 Ala. 155, 48 So. 788 (1909).

the political and civil privileges of the Roman government. . . .
It was both an honor and a sacred privilege to be a Roman
citizen. Paul, the great Apostle of the Gentiles, claimed and asserted the right of a Roman citizen when apprehended in Jeru-
salem. The chief captain answered him: 'With a great sum obtained I this freedom; but Paul said, 'I was free born.' Again
this great Apostle is heard to say: 'I am a man which am a Jew,
of Tarsus, a city in Cilicia, a citizen of no mean city.' Citizenship
has always been regarded as the most sacred right or privilege
that the sovereign can confer. [He is] 'a person, native or naturalized, who has the privilege of voting for public officers and
who is qualified to fill public offices in the gift of the people." [19]

It is possible that modern democracies are not making enough
of the status of citizenship. The meaning and dignity of being a
citizen and having civic responsibilities seem not to be sufficiently inculcated. In failing to give official recognition to the
fact that an adolescent has become a full citizen with all the
political rights and obligations that this includes, as was done in
older political societies, the democracies may be allowing the full
idea of "citizen" to fall into desuetude.

D. Essence of Political Union

The problem of the essence of the political union is: what is
there factual or real about the political union? Attempts to solve
this problem must inevitably bring into play a philosophy of
jural relations and persons.

One endeavor to solve this problem, as noted, looks upon the
union itself as a separate and different person. This person is
called an "artificial person," a "moral person" or a "legal person"
and is considered to be either a fictionalized symbol or an actual
being with an intellect and will of its own. "Such a society
[state or body politic] has its affairs and interests, it deliberates
and takes resolutions in common, and thus becomes a moral person, having an understanding and will peculiar to itself." [20] The
well-known confusion engendered by such descriptions of unions,
associations and societies calls for a closer look at what their
essence is.

Political society is a union of individual persons in a deter-

---

[19] Ibid.

[20] United States v. Kusche, 56 F. Supp. 201, 208 (S.D. Cal. 1944). See also
Hogan v. Greenfield, 58 Wyo. 13, 122 P.2d 850, 853 (1942); Blair v. Worley,
1 Scam. 178, 180 (Ill. 1835); Fox's Appeal, 112 Pa. 337, 4 Atl. 149, 152 (1886).

mined territory for the purpose of procuring their common good. What is factual or real about this union? If factual is to have any meaning at all, it must refer to what exists independently of whether I think about it or not, as distinguished from what is fictional which has existence only because I conceive it to be so. An automobile is real, a winged horse is not. The relation between the left and right side of a sphere is fictional. On the other hand, the relations are real that arise from the physical facts of space and time, or those originating in the acts of consent in the parties to a contract or the parties of a political union.

1. *Relations of union.* What is factual about the political union, like any other union, are the individual *persons* who have united themselves by their free decision and the *relations* created between them by this action.

Each person who enters a political union does so by consenting, explicitly or implicitly, to work for the common good. He consents to direct and order certain of his future actions to the promotion of this common end. The other members have done the same thing. As a consequence, they all actually stand to each other in a way in which they did not before their individual agreements. When each man agrees to direct his actions toward realizing the common goal, by that very fact he sets up a new relation between himself and the others which unites them in their pursuit of their common end.

The important notandum here is that this relation is something factual. It is not simply a figment of the mind. The way that one man stands in regards to another after their consent is actually different than it was before. There is now a new fact, a new jural relation, which, when recognized and made enforceable by law, is a new legal relation. The part played by jural relations is basic. ". . . [J]ural relations is a fundamental concept; it is the basic idea through which the whole system of legal advantages is realized." [21]

It is true that such relations, although a segment of existing things, are not easily grasped. But for a lawman to dismiss them on this account as subtleties too difficult for him to understand and therefore dispensable, would be to cut himself off from a vast segment of the factual. Existing things in many instances are not simple and self-adapted to human understanding — a condition to which the long and intensive scientific research in many fields will testify. As was discerningly remarked concerning the state-

[21] Kocourek, Jural Relations 46 (1927).

ment of a court on such subtleties, "Is it not in fact necessary to have some clear view of their nature if a true decision is to be reached?" [22]

At last resort, the only alternative to viewing the reality of the political union as some kind of a separate self-subsisting person, is to see it as the factual relations that unite the individual persons in the pursuit of a common end, which relations arise from their personal consent and exist therefore dependently upon them.

2. *Person.* This interpretation of society or union presupposes a concise idea of what a person is. It is derived from our knowledge of men and women we meet every day. We shake hands with them, converse with them, understand them. We consider them to be human beings. They are not animals, much less mere abstractions. We form this concept because of observable data indicating that they are capable of highly developed thinking and direction of themselves in a way in which animals show no evidence. The powers in men capable of producing such phenomena we designate as intellect and will. As far as our experimental data go, these powers are present only in individual persons. We conclude, therefore, that a person is a *knowing and deciding being that exists as an individual.* Such are the persons united in any political society.

To extend the use of the word "person" to anything besides individual human beings is to confuse thing with person, the irrational with the rational. It is to humanize the non-human.

3. *Political union not a person.* If the political union is in fact the persons united along with the relations that unite them, and a person is an individual knowing and deciding being, then the political union is not a person. The relations that form the union are not a separately existing intellectual being. In the factual world there are only individual men and women and the relations that exist between them.

The political union, as well as other unions, has been called a person because of vague and imprecise notions of what a union of men by agreement actually is and what a person is. Legal fictions may be useful and the phrases "moral person," "legal person," and "artificial person" may serve to express them. But the difference between the fictitious and the factual must ever be hardheadedly kept in view. Otherwise the fictitious will be reified and treated as if it had an existence of its own.

[22] Laski, The Personality of Associations, 29 Harv. L. Rev. 414 (1916).

II.   COMMON GOOD OF THE COMMUNITY

Law, government and political union all find their unifying rationale in one and the same end: the pursuit of the common good of the people. Political unions are formed to promote the common good of their members, government is the agency that directs to this end, and law is the instrument that government employs for this purpose.

The common good as the end of man-made law is peace and security brought about chiefly through the maintenance of order as we have seen. As the end of man-discovered law the common good is the peace and security of the whole human community; but also it is something beyond this: the supreme good which, permanently possessed, assures perfect happiness.

A.   *Community Living Needed for Proper Goods*

The need of the political common good springs from community living. Community living is needed to obtain the proper goods of the members of the community. It is this fact that gives significance to the drive to live in community.

1. *Bodily needs.* Men need the cooperative effort of others in accomplishing the political common good, but they also need this cooperation in attaining even their own proper goods. To dwell for the moment on simple examples, men's bodily needs — food, clothing, shelter — are such that they cannot be fulfilled without the aid of other men. As has always been pointed out, men are not equipped, as animals are, with the protection of a tough hide or a coat of fur or with the use of sharp claws or long tusks. Men are vulnerable and indigent.

So complete is this dependence, that it is almost impossible to conceive of a man who could lead his entire life without having and using some object that came from the productive hands of other men. Even if he had only a knife this would be so — unless we are to suppose that the particular man discovered his own iron ore, mined it, smelted it, poured it into a mold and made the knife. All of which would presuppose that he had the idea of a knife.

2. *Mental needs.* The mental needs of men — ideas — equally show the dependence of men one upon the other. Men are not born with the ideas they will need in order to lead a human life even at its lowest level. A few elementary and pattern ideas are acquired, connaturally and without reasoning, from the basic

drives. Others are got from our reasoning and experiences. But the greater part of our ideas are got through the aid of other men. Even so-called "creative ideas" when analyzed are found to have a background of dependence on others.

Undoubtedly this is as it should be. The progress of men would be poorly served if each man had to discover for himself, let us say, the principle of the wheel.[23] Civilization and culture would be limited permanently to a primitive state if the ideas behind tools, skills, and arts, which sharply differentiate men from animals, could not be taught to succeeding generations. Significant also in this matter of dependence is men's power of expression. It takes on full meaning when seen as necessary especially in the fulfillment of men's mental needs.

A man, then, is not like an animal who, as a wolf, either runs with the pack or goes it alone. He needs the community of other men. He needs them not because of varying circumstances in which he may find himself, but because of the way he himself is structured — imperfect and dependent.

B. *Needs Give Meaning to Drive*

Nothing shows better the significance of the basic drive to live in community than these rudimentary needs of all men. It is only in community that these needs can be fulfilled. "For every man needs . . . human assistance because man is naturally a social animal in view of the fact that he is not self-sufficient for living." [24] Through community help life is preserved, the race is continued and learning is carried on.

1. *Natural groupings.* This drive, constantly at work, results in natural groupings. Individuals are born into families and families have always shown the tendency to group together in some sort of community. These communities may be brought about by kinship, race, language, locality, or social class. This tendency shows itself in more simple stages in the sibling, the clan, or the tribe; in more complex developments in the nation.

2. *Communities caused by circumstances.* Less obvious perhaps but of importance is the fact that communities come about, not as the result of a free decision or previous determination on

[23] As Cicero put it, "Nescire quid antea quam natus sis acciderit, id est semper esse puerum," that is, not to know what has happened before you were born, is always to remain a child. Cicero, Orator 34.120 (B.C. 46) (trans. mine).

[24] Aquinas, 2-2 Sum. Theol. 129, 6, 1.

the part of their members to live together, but by dint of circumstances that more or less throw them together. As already mentioned, a community is a group of persons who have been brought together by some already existing fact. This is the mark that distinguishes it from formal society or union which results from free decision.

Men, then, are so structured that they have manifold needs. They depend on each other for a life of multifold communication and the fulfillment of these needs. Their living in community is but the necessary way this is accomplished.

C. From Community Living: Need for Peace and Security

From the fact that men live in community another kind of need shows itself. This is the need for the common good. It is because men live together that claims regarding "mine" and "thine" arise and may possibly be violated — men being what they are. The consequence of this is strife and anxiety, conditions which can cut deeply into the progress and development of all. Hence, a prime need is the common good of peace and security.

It is this practical need on a world-wide scale at the present time that calls for the political union of world dimensions noted earlier. The work of achieving world peace and security has taken only a few faltering steps. What has been accomplished has depended on tenuous agreements. Not until there are laws passed by the government of a true, world political union can there be hope of enforcing the sanctions of these laws which are necessary if men or nations refuse to follow such directives.

III. BACKGROUND IN PERSPECTIVE

The beginning and end of law is, then, the common good of the people. The philosophy of the common good and government, which we have examined as the background of law, is necessarily part of a broader philosophy of man and existence. Some acquaintance with this range of inquiry is presupposed, ideally at least, from studies made during the pre-legal years. But, whereas a survey of the main outlines of government seems justified here because of law's immediate dependence on them, a review of the more fundamental matters of the nature of man and the meaning of existence must be left to the interest and initiative of the individual law student.

Conclusion

Law gives direction to life. It is the difference between order and disorder. To be a reliable guide law itself must point "true north." It must be conscious, at least vaguely, of the general direction in which it should be aiming. Law can get its principles from shifting economic, social and political situation data. But if it does so, it will be devoid of the stature and power necessary to rise above and direct these activities. Instead, it will only wander aimlessly over the innumerable and orderless sands of fact.

The one observable constant from which law can derive its principles for guiding men is the elementary demands of the nature of men themselves. It is only in relation to this compass that the needs of men and what is good for them can be accurately reckoned and made part of the content of law.

To say this is to throw into clear relief the importance of law's non-legal presuppositions such as the principles and patterns outlined in this book. These are the points from which law must ever calculate its position and plot its course. Law necessarily depends on philosophy. Legal thinking must be laced with philosophical insight.

The law profession is one of the highest. To direct men authoritatively to what is good for them, to judge their refusal to follow such guidance and to remedy or punish accordingly, is to participate in a divine prerogative. Such is the dignity of the position of men who make law. But in order to appreciate this privilege and be equal to their office, lawmen must know what is in man and realize wherein lies his destiny.

Table of Cases

Cases that are quoted are indicated by italic page numbers; cases that are only cited are designated by roman page numbers.

Selected Bibliography

Allen, Law in the Making (1951).
———, Legal Duties (1931).
Aquinas, Selected Political Writings (D'Entrèves ed. 1948).
———, Summa Theologiae (Dominican trans., American ed. 1947).
———, The Political Ideas of St. Thomas Aquinas (Bigongiari ed. 1953).
Aristotle, Nichomachean Ethics (Ross trans. 1941).
———, Politics (Jowett trans. 1941).
Barker, Essays on Government (2d ed. 1951).
———, Principles of Social and Political Theory (1951).
Baty, Basis of Responsibility, 32 *Juridical Review* 159 (1920).
———, Vicarious Liability (1916).
Bentham, An Introduction to the Principles of Morals and Legislation (1789).
———, The Limits of Jurisprudence Defined (1782).
Bodenheimer, Analytical Positivism, Legal Realism, and the Future of Legal Method, 44 *Virginia Law Review* 365 (1958).
———, Jurisprudence (1940).
Bourke, Ethics (1951).
Brunner, Justice and the Social Order (Hottinger trans. 1945).
Cahn, The Sense of Injustice (1949).
Cairns, Theory of Legal Science (1941).
Cardozo, The Growth of the Law (1924).
Carrel, Reflections on Life (1953).
Cicero, De Legibus (Keyes trans. 1928).
———, De Officiis (Miller trans. 1938).
———, De Re Publica (Keyes trans. 1928).
Cleckley, Mask of Sanity (2d ed. 1950).
Cohen, Dialogue on Private Property, 9 *Rutgers Law Review* 357 (1954).
Coing, Grundzüge der Rechtsphilosophie (Berlin, 1950).
Corwin, The "Higher Law" Background of American Constitutional Law (1955).
Dabin, La Philosophie de l'Ordre Juridique Positif (1929). Trans. by Wilk in The Legal Philosophies of Lask, Radbruch and Dabin, in 4 Twentieth Century Legal Philosophy Series 227-470 (1950).
Davidson, Criminal Responsibility: The Quest for a Formula in Psychiatry and the Law (1955).

Davitt, St. Thomas and the Natural Law, in Origins of the Natural Law Tradition (1954).

———, The Nature of Law (1951).

Delos, La Société Internationale et les Principes du Droit Public (1929).

Del Vecchio, Justice (Guthrie trans. 1953).

———, Philosophy of Law (Martin trans. 1953).

D'Entrèves, Natural Law (1951).

Duguit, Traité de Droit Constitutionnel (3d ed. 1927-1930).

East, An Introduction to Forensic Psychiatry in the Criminal Courts (1927).

———, Society and the Criminal (1951).

Ehrlich, Fundamental Principles of the Sociology of Law (Moll trans. 1936).

Frank, Courts on Trial (1949).

———, Law and the Modern Mind (1949).

Fridman, The Rise and Fall of Rylands v. Fletcher, 34 Canadian Bar Review 810 (1956).

Friedmann, Legal Theory (3d ed. 1953).

Friedrich and others, Authority (1958).

Fuller, Positivism and Fidelity to Law, 71 Harvard Law Review 630 (1958).

———, The Law in Quest of Itself (1940).

Geny, Méthode d'Interpretation et Sources en Droit Privé Positif (2d ed. 1932).

———, Science et Technique en Droit Privé Positif (1921-1930).

Gierke, Natural Law and the Theory of Society (Barker trans. 1934).

Glaser, Doctrine of Consideration and the Civil Law Principle of Cause, 45 Dickinson Law Review 12 (1941).

Goodhart, The Ratio Decidendi of a Case, in Jurisprudence in Action 189 (New York Bar ed. 1953).

Grant, The Natural Law Background of Due Process, 31 Columbia Law Review 56 (1931).

Haines, The Law of Nature in State and Federal Judicial Decisions, 25 Yale Law Journal 617 (1916).

———, The Revival of Natural Law Concepts (1930).

Hall, Living Law of Democratic Society (1949).

———, Principles of Criminal Law (1947).

———, Psychiatry and Criminal Responsibility, 65 Yale Law Journal 761 (1956).

Hallowell, The Moral Foundation of Democracy (1955).

Hariou, La Théorie de l'Institution et de la Fondation, in La Cité Moderne et les Transformations du Droit (1925).

Hoebel, Authority in Primitive Societies, in Authority (Friedrich ed. 1958).

———, The Law of Primitive Man (1954).

Hooker, Laws of Ecclesiastical Polity (1594).

Ibranyi, Ethica secundum S. Thomam et Kant (1931).

Jhering, Law as Means to End (Husik trans. 1924).

Joad, A Critique of Logical Positivism (1950).

Klubertanz, The Philosophy of Human Nature (1953).

Kohler, Philosophy of Law (Albrecht trans. 1914).

Lachance, Le Concept de Droit selon Aristote et S. Thomas (1948).

Leclercq, La Philosophie Morale de Saint Thomas devant le Pensée Contemporaine (1955).

Levi, An Introduction to Legal Reasoning (1950).

Levitt, Extent and Function of the Doctrine of Mens Rea, 17 *Illinois Law Review* 578 (1923).

Lippmann, The Public Philosophy (1955).

Lottin, Morale Fondamentale (1954).

McIlwain, The Growth of Political Thought in the West (1932).

Maritain, Freedom in the Modern World (1936).

———, Man and the State (1951).

———, The Rights of Man and Natural Law (1943).

Niebuhr, The Nature and Destiny of Man (1943).

Northrop, Contemporary Jurisprudence and International Law, 61 *Yale Law Journal* 623 (1952).

———, Philosophical Issues in Contemporary Law, 2 *Natural Law Forum* 41 (1957).

Note, Natural Law for Today's Lawyer, 9 *Stanford Law Review* 455 (1957).

O'Sullivan, The Bond of Freedom, 6 *Modern Law Review* 177 (1943).

———, The Inheritance of the Common Law (1951).

Plato, Republic (Shorey trans. 1953).

Polanyi, The Logic of Liberty (1951).

Pound, An Introduction to the Philosophy of Law (rev. ed. 1954).

———, Justice According to Law (1951).

Prosser, Selected Topics on the Law of Torts (1953).

Radbruch, Der Innere Weg (1951).

———, Rechtsphilosophie (1950).

Radin, Natural Law and Natural Rights, 59 *Yale Law Journal* 214 (1950).

Renard, R., La Théorie de l'Institution (1930).

Rommen, The Natural Law (Hanley trans. 1947).

Ruiz-Gimenez, Derecho y Vida Humana (1957).

Sabine, A History of Political Theory (rev. ed. 1955).

St. Germain, Dialogue of Doctor and Student (Muchall ed. 1874).

Saleilles, The Individualization of Punishment (Jastrow trans. 1913).

Schlesinger, Soviet Legal Theory (2d ed. 1946).

Simon, Philosophy of Democratic Government (1951).

Sinnott, The Biology of the Spirit (1955).

Snee, Leviathan at the Bar of Justice, in Government Under Law (Sutherland ed. 1956).

Stammler, Theory of Justice (Husik trans. 1925).

Stone, The Province and Function of Law (1950).

Strauss, Natural Right and History (1953).

Suárez, De Legibus (1612). Selections are translated in Classics of International Law (Scott ed. 1944).

Symposium, Insanity and the Criminal Law — A Critique of Durham v. United States, 22 *University of Chicago Law Review* 317 (1955).

Thorndike, Man and His Works (1943).

Vivas, The Moral Life and the Ethical Life (1950).

Werthem, A Psychiatrist Looks at Psychiatry and the Law, 3 *Buffalo Law Review* 41 (1943).

———, Psychoauthoritarianism and the Law, 22 *University of Chicago Law Review* 336 (1955).

Wild, Introduction to a Realistic Philosophy (1948).

———, Plato's Modern Enemies and the Theory of Natural Law (1953).

Winfield, The Myth of Absolute Liability, 42 *Law Quarterly Review* 37 (1926).

Wolf, Revolution or Evolution in Gustav Radbruch's Legal Philosophy, 3 *Natural Law Forum* 1 (1958).

Wolff, On the Nature of Legal Persons, 54 *Law Quarterly Review* 494 (1938).

Wright, B., American Interpretations of Natural Law (1931).

Wright, Lord, Ought the Doctrine of Consideration Be Abolished from the Common Law? 49 *Harvard Law Review* 1225 (1936).

Yankwich, Changing Concepts of Crime and Punishment, 32 *Georgetown Law Journal* 1 (1943).

Index